Department
of the
Treasury

**Internal
Revenue
Service**

Your Federal
Income Tax
For Individuals

Contents

What's New		1
Reminders		2
Introduction		4
Part One. The Income Tax Return		5
1	Filing Information	5
2	Filing Status	20
3	Dependents	25
4	Tax Withholding and Estimated Tax	36
Part Two. Income and Adjustments to Income		44
5	Wages, Salaries, and Other Earnings	45
6	Interest Income	52
7	Social Security and Equivalent Railroad Retirement Benefits	60
8	Other Income	65
9	Individual Retirement Arrangements (IRAs)	75
Part Three. Standard Deduction, Itemized Deductions, and Other Deductions		89
10	Standard Deduction	89
11	Taxes	93
12	Other Itemized Deductions	97
Part Four. Figuring Your Taxes, and Refundable and Nonrefundable Credits		103
13	How To Figure Your Tax	103
14	Child Tax Credit and Credit for Other Dependents	105
2022 Tax Table		108
2022 Tax Computation Worksheet		120
2022 Tax Rate Schedules		120
Your Rights as a Taxpayer		122
How To Get Tax Help		123
Index		125
Where To File		136

The explanations and examples in this publication reflect the interpretation by the Internal Revenue Service (IRS) of:

- Tax laws enacted by Congress,
- Treasury regulations, and
- Court decisions.

However, the information given does not cover every situation and is not intended to replace the law or change its meaning.

This publication covers some subjects on which a court may have made a decision more favorable to taxpayers than the interpretation by the IRS. Until these differing interpretations are resolved by higher court decisions or in some other way, this publication will continue to present the interpretations by the IRS.

All taxpayers have important rights when working with the IRS. These rights are described in *Your Rights as a Taxpayer* in the back of this publication.

D1709480

What's New

This section summarizes important tax changes that took effect in 2022. Most of these changes are discussed in more detail throughout this publication.

Future developments. For the latest information about the tax law topics covered in this publication, such as legislation enacted after it was published, go to *IRS.gov/Pub17*.

Due date of return. File Form 1040 or 1040-SR by April 18, 2023. The due date is April 18, instead of April 15, because of the Emancipation Day holiday in the District of Columbia even if you don't live in the District of Columbia. See chapter 1, later.

Filing status name changed to qualifying surviving spouse. The filing status qualifying widow(er) is now called qualifying surviving spouse. The rules for the filing status have not changed. The same rules that applied for qualifying widow(er) apply to qualifying surviving spouse.

Who must file. Generally, the amount of income you can receive before you must file a return has been increased. For more information, see chapter 1, later.

Standard deduction amount increased. For 2022, the standard deduction amount has been increased for all filers. The amounts are:

- Single or Married filing separately—$12,950;
- Married filing jointly or Qualifying surviving spouse—$25,900; and
- Head of household—$19,400.

See chapter 10, later.

New lines 1a through 1z on Form 1040 and 1040-SR. This year, line 1 is expanded and there are new lines 1a through 1z. Some amounts that in prior years were reported on Form 1040, and some amounts reported on Form 1040-SR are now reported on Schedule 1.

- Scholarships and fellowship grants are now reported on Schedule 1, line 8r.
- Pension or annuity from a nonqualified deferred compensation plan or a nongovernmental section 457 plan are now reported on Schedule 1, line 8t.
- Wages earned while incarcerated are now reported on Schedule 1, line 8u.

New line 6c on Form 1040 and 1040-SR. A checkbox was added on line 6c. Taxpayers who elect to use the lump-sum election method for their benefits will check this box. See Instructions for Form 1040.

Credits for sick and family leave for certain self-employed individuals are not available. The credit for sick and family leave for certain self-employed individuals were not extended and you can no longer claim these credits.

Health coverage tax credit is not available. The health coverage tax credit was not extended. The credit is not available after 2021.

Credit for child and dependent care expenses. The changes to the credit for child and dependent care expenses implemented by the American Rescue Plan Act of 2021 (ARP) were not extended. For 2022, the credit for the child and dependent care expenses is nonrefundable. The dollar limit on qualifying expenses is $3,000 for one qualifying person and $6,000 for two or more qualifying persons. The maximum credit amount allowed is 35% of your employment-related expenses. For more information, see the Instructions for Form 2441 and Pub. 503.

Child tax credit and additional child tax credit. The many changes to the child tax credit (CTC) implemented by ARP were not extended. For 2022,

- The credit amount of the CTC is $2,000 for each qualifying child.
- The amount of CTC that can be claimed as a refundable credit is limited as it was in 2020, except the maximum additional child tax credit amount (ACTC) has increased to $1,500 for each qualifying child.
- A child must be under age 17 at the end of 2022 to be a qualifying child.
- Bona fide residents of Puerto Rico are no longer required to have three or more qualifying children to be eligible to claim the ACTC. Bona fide residents of Puerto Rico may be eligible to claim the ACTC if they have one or more qualifying children.

For more information, see the Instructions for Schedule 8812 (Form 1040).

Election to use 2019 earned income to figure 2020 additional child tax credit. Recent legislation provided an election to use your 2019 earned income to figure your 2020 additional child tax credit. For more information, see the Instructions for Form 8812.

Child tax credit enhancements have expired. Many changes to the CTC for 2021 implemented by the American Rescue Plan Act of 2021 have expired. For tax year 2022:

- The enhanced credit allowed for qualifying children under age 6 and children under age 18 has expired. For 2022, the initial amount of the CTC is $2,000 for each qualifying child. The credit amount begins to phase out where modified adjusted gross income exceeds $200,000 ($400,000 in the case of a joint return). The amount of the CTC that can be claimed as a refundable credit is limited as it was in 2020 except that the maximum ACTC amount for each qualifying child increased to $1,500.
- The increased age allowance for a qualifying child has expired. A child must be under age 17 at the end of 2022 to be a qualifying child.

ACTC and bona fide residents of Puerto Rico. Bona fide residents of Puerto Rico are no longer required to have three or more qualifying children to be eligible to claim the ACTC. Bona fide residents of Puerto Rico may be eligible to claim the ACTC if they have one or more qualifying children.

Advance child tax credit payments. Advance child tax credit payments have not been issued for 2022.

Delayed refund for returns claiming ACTC. The IRS cannot issue refunds before mid-February 2023 for returns that properly claim ACTC. This time frame applies to the entire refund, not just the portion associated with ACTC.

Changes to the earned income credit (EIC). The enhancements for taxpayers without a qualifying child implemented by ARP don't apply for 2022. This means, to claim the EIC without a qualifying child in 2022, you must be at least age 25 but under age 65 at the end of 2022. If you are married filing a joint return, either you or your spouse must be at least age 25 but under age 65 at the end of 2022. It doesn't matter which spouse meets the age requirement, as long as one of the spouses does.

Nontaxable Medicaid waiver payments on Schedule 1. In 2021, the nontaxable amount of Medicaid waiver payments were reported on Schedule 1, line 8z. In 2022, these amounts will be reported on Schedule 1, line 8s.

Nontaxable combat pay election. In 2021, the amount of your nontaxable combat pay was reported on Form 1040 or 1040-SR, line 27b. In 2022, these amounts will be reported on Form 1040 or 1040-SR, line 1i.

Standard mileage rate. The 2022 rate for business use of a vehicle is 58.5 cents a mile from January 1, 2022 to June 30, 2022, and 62.5 cents a mile from July 1, 2022 to December 31, 2022. The 2022 rate for use of your vehicle to do volunteer work for certain charitable organizations is 14 cents a mile from January 1, 2022 to December 31, 2022. The 2022 rate for operating expenses for a car when you use it for medical reasons are 18 cents a mile from January 1, 2022 to June 30, 2022, and 22 cents a mile from July 1, 2022 to December 31, 2022.

Modified AGI limit for traditional IRA contributions. For 2022, if you are covered by a retirement plan at work, your deduction for contributions to a traditional IRA is reduced (phased out) if your modified AGI is:

- More than $109,000 but less than $129,000 for a married couple filing a joint return or a qualifying surviving spouse,
- More than $68,000 but less than $78,000 for a single individual or head of household, or
- Less than $10,000 for a married individual filing a separate return.

If you either live with your spouse or file a joint return, and your spouse is covered by a retirement plan at work but you aren't, your deduction is phased out if your modified AGI is more than $204,000 but less than $214,000. If your modified AGI is $214,000 or more, you can't take a deduction for contributions to a traditional IRA. See *How Much Can You Deduct* in chapter 9, later.

Modified AGI limit for Roth IRA contributions. For 2022, your

Roth IRA contribution limit is reduced (phased out) in the following situations.

- Your filing status is married filing jointly or qualifying surviving spouse and your modified AGI is at least $204,000. You can't make a Roth IRA contribution if your modified AGI is $214,000 or more.

- Your filing status is single, head of household, or married filing separately and you didn't live with your spouse at any time in 2022 and your modified AGI is at least $129,000.

You can't make a Roth IRA contribution if your modified AGI is $144,000 or more.

- Your filing status is married filing separately, you lived with your spouse at any time during the year, and your modified AGI is more than zero. You can't make a Roth IRA contribution if your modified AGI is $10,000 or more. See *Can You Contribute to a Roth IRA* in chapter 9, later.

2023 modified AGI limits. You can find information about the 2023 contribution and AGI limits in Pub. 590-A.

Tax law changes for 2022. When you figure how much income tax you want withheld from your pay and when you figure your estimated tax, consider tax law changes effective in 2022. For more information, see Pub. 505, Tax Withholding and Estimated Tax.

Alternative minimum tax (AMT) exemption amount increased. The AMT exemption amount is increased to $75,900 ($118,100 if married filing jointly or qualifying surviving spouse; $59,050 if married filing separately). The income levels at which the AMT exemption

begins to phase out have increased to $539,900 ($1,079,800 if married filing jointly or qualifying surviving spouse).

Adoption credit. The adoption credit and the exclusion for employer-provided adoption benefits have both increased to $15,950 per eligible child in 2022. The amount begins to phase out if you have modified AGI in excess of $239,230 and is completely phased out if your modified AGI is $279,230 or more.

Reminders

Listed below are important reminders and other items that may help you file your 2022 tax return. Many of these items are explained in more detail later in this publication.

Publication 17 changes. We removed the following 2019 chapters from this publication: 6, 8, 9, 10, 13, 14, 15, 16, 18, 19, 20, 22, 24, 25, 26, 29, 30, 31, 33, 34, 35, and 36. You can find most of the information previously found in those chapters in the primary publication. Please see Publication 17 changes, later.

Special rules for eligible gains invested in Qualified Opportunity Funds. If you have an eligible gain, you can invest that gain into a Qualified Opportunity Fund (QOF) and elect to defer part or all of the gain that is otherwise includible in income. The gain is deferred until the date you sell or exchange the investment or December 31, 2026, whichever is earlier. You may also be able to permanently exclude gain from the sale or exchange of an investment in a QOF if the investment is held for at least 10 years. For information about what types of gains entitle you to elect these special rules, see the Instructions for Schedule D (Form 1040). For information on how to elect to use these special rules, see the Instructions for Form 8949.

Secure your tax records from identity theft. Identity theft occurs when someone uses your personal information, such as your name, SSN, or other identifying information, without your permission, to commit fraud or other crimes. An identity thief may use your SSN to get a job or may file a tax return using your SSN to receive a refund. For more information about identity theft and how to reduce your risk from it, see chapter 1, later.

Taxpayer identification numbers. You must provide the taxpayer identification number for each person for whom you claim certain tax benefits. This applies even if the person was born in 2022. Generally, this number is the person's SSN. See chapter 1, later.

Tuition and fees deduction not available. The tuition and fees deduction is not available after 2020. Instead, the income limitations for the lifetime learning credit have been increased. See Form 8863 and its instructions.

Identity verification. The IRS launched an improved identity verification and sign-in process that enables more people to securely access and use IRS online tools and applications. To provide verification services, the IRS is using ID.me, a trusted technology provider. The new process is one more step the IRS is taking to ensure that taxpayer information is provided only to the person who legally has a right to the data. Taxpayers using the new mobile-friendly verification procedure can gain entry to existing IRS online services such as the *Child Tax Credit Update Portal, On-line Account, Get Transcript Online, Get an Identity Protection PIN (IP PIN),* and *Online Payment Agreement.* Additional IRS applications will transition to the new method over the next year. Each online service will also provide information that will instruct taxpayers on the steps they need to follow for access to the service. You can also see IR-2021-228 for more information.

Form 1040-X continuous-use form and instructions. Form 1040-X, Amended U.S. Individual Income Tax Return, and its instructions have been converted from an annual revision to continuous use beginning in tax year 2021. Both the form and instructions will be

updated as required. For the most recent version, go to *IRS.gov/Form1040X.* Section discussions and charts that were updated annually have been removed, or replaced with references to relevant forms, schedules, instructions, and publications. See the forms, schedules, instructions, and publications for the year of the tax return you are amending for guidance on specific topics.

Business meals. Section 210 of the Taxpayer Certainty and Disaster Tax Relief Act of 2020 provides for the temporary allowance of a 100% business meal deduction for food or beverages provided by a restaurant and paid or incurred after December 31, 2020, and before January 1, 2023.

Foreign-source income. If you are a U.S. citizen with income from sources outside the United States (foreign income), you must report all such income on your tax return unless it is exempt by law or a tax treaty. This is true whether you live inside or outside the United States and whether or not you receive a Form W-2 or Form 1099 from the foreign payer. This applies to earned income (such as wages and tips) as well as unearned income (such as interest, dividends, capital gains, pensions, rents, and royalties).

If you live outside the United States, you may be able to exclude part or all of your foreign earned income. For details, see Pub. 54, Tax Guide for U.S. Citizens and Resident Aliens Abroad.

Foreign financial assets. If you had foreign financial assets in 2022, you may have to file Form 8938 with your return. See Form 8938 and its instructions or visit *IRS.gov/Form8938* for details.

Automatic 6-month extension to file tax return. You can get an automatic 6-month extension of

time to file your tax return. See chapter 1, later.

Payment of taxes. You can pay your taxes by making electronic payments online; from a mobile device using the IRS2Go app; or in cash, or by check or money order. Paying electronically is quick, easy, and faster than mailing in a check or money order. See chapter 1, later.

Faster ways to file your return. The IRS offers fast, accurate ways to file your tax return information without filing a paper tax return. You can use IRS *e-file* (electronic filing). See chapter 1, later.

Free electronic filing. You may be able to file your 2022 taxes online for free. See chapter 1, later.

Change of address. If you change your address, notify the IRS. See chapter 1, later.

Refund on a late-filed return. If you were due a refund but you did not file a return, you must generally file your return within 3 years from the date the return was due (including extensions) to get that refund. See chapter 1, later.

Frivolous tax returns. The IRS has published a list of positions that are identified as frivolous. The penalty for filing a frivolous tax return is $5,000. See chapter 1, later.

Filing erroneous claim for refund or credit. You may have to pay a penalty if you file an erroneous claim for refund or credit. See chapter 1, later.

Access your online account. You must authenticate your identity. To securely log into your federal tax account, go to *IRS.gov/Account.* View the amount you owe, review 24 months of payment history, access online payment options, and create or modify an online payment agreement. You can also access your tax records online.

Health care coverage. If you need health care coverage, go to *HealthCare.gov* to learn about health insurance options for you and your family, how to buy health insurance, and how you might qualify to get financial assistance to buy health insurance.

Disclosure, Privacy Act, and paperwork reduction information. The IRS Restructuring and Reform Act of 1998, the Privacy Act of 1974, and the Paperwork Reduction Act of 1980 require that when we ask you for information, we must first tell you what our legal right is to ask for the information, why we are asking for it, how it will be used, what could happen if we do not receive it, and whether your response is voluntary, required to obtain a benefit, or mandatory under the law. A complete statement on this subject can be found in your tax form instructions.

Preparer *e-file* mandate. Most paid preparers must *e-file* returns they prepare and file. Your preparer may make you aware of this requirement and the options available to you.

Treasury Inspector General for Tax Administration. If you want to confidentially report misconduct, waste, fraud, or abuse by an IRS employee, you can call 800-366-4484 (call 800-877-8339 if you are deaf, hard of hearing, or have a speech disability, and are using TTY/TDD equipment). You can remain anonymous.

Photographs of missing children. The IRS is a proud partner with the *National Center for Missing & Exploited Children® (NCMEC)*. Photographs of missing children selected by the Center may appear in this publication on pages that would otherwise be blank. You can help bring these children home by looking at the photographs and calling 1-800-THE-LOST (800-843-5678) if you recognize a child.

Publication 17 Changes

Note. This publication does not cover the topics listed in the following table. Please see the primary publication.		
Chapter Removed	**Title of Chapter**	**Primary Publication**
6	Tip Income	*Pub. 531, Reporting Tip Income*
8	Dividends and Other Distributions	*Pub. 550, Investment Income and Expenses*
9	Rental Income and Expenses	*Pub. 527, Residential Rental Property (Including Rental of Vacation Homes)*
10	Retirement Plans, Pensions, and Annuities	*Pub. 575, Pension and Annuity Income*
13	Basis of Property	*Pub. 551, Basis of Assets*
14	Sale of Property	*Pub. 550*
15	Selling Your Home	*Pub. 523, Selling Your Home*
16	Reporting Gains and Losses	*Pub. 550*
18	Alimony	*Pub. 504, Divorced or Separated Individuals*
19	Education-Related Adjustments	*Pub. 970, Tax Benefits for Education*
20	Other Adjustments to Income	*Pub. 463, Travel, Gift, and Car Expenses*
22	Medical and Dental Expenses	*Pub. 502, Medical and Dental Expenses*
24	Interest Expense	*Pub. 550* *Pub. 936, Home Mortgage Interest Deduction*
25	Charitable Contributions	*Pub. 561, Determining the Value of Donated Property* *Pub. 526, Charitable Contributions*
26	Nonbusiness Casualty and Theft Losses	*Pub. 547, Casualties, Disasters, and Thefts*
29	Tax on Unearned Income of Certain Minor Children	*Pub. 929, Tax Rules for Children and Dependents*
30	Child and Dependent Care Credit	*Pub. 503, Child and Dependent Care Expenses*
31	Credit for the Elderly or the Disabled	*Pub. 524, Credit for the Elderly or the Disabled*
33	Education Credits	*Pub. 970, Tax Benefits for Education*
34	Earned Income Credit (EIC)	*Pub. 596, Earned Income Credit (EIC)*
35	Premium Tax Credit	*Pub. 974, Premium Tax Credit (PTC)*
36	Other Credits	

Introduction

This publication covers the general rules for filing a federal income tax return. It supplements the information contained in your tax form instructions. It explains the tax law to make sure you pay only the tax you owe and no more.

How this publication is arranged. Pub. 17 closely follows Form 1040, U.S. Individual Income Tax Return, and Form 1040-SR, U.S. Tax Return for Seniors, and their three Schedules 1 through 3. Pub. 17 is divided into four parts. Each part is further divided into chapters, most of which generally discuss one line of the form or one line of one of the three schedules. The introduction at the beginning of each part lists the schedule(s) discussed in that part.

The table of contents inside the front cover, the introduction to each part, and the index in the back of the publication are useful tools to help you find the information you need.

What is in this publication. This publication begins with the rules for filing a tax return. It explains:

1. Who must file a return,
2. When the return is due,
3. How to *e-file* your return, and
4. Other general information.

It will help you identify which filing status you qualify for, whether you can claim any dependents, and whether the income you receive is taxable. The publication goes on to explain the standard deduction, the kinds of expenses you may be able to deduct, and the various kinds of credits you may be able to take to reduce your tax.

Throughout this publication are examples showing how the tax law applies in typical situations. Also throughout this publication are flowcharts and tables that present tax information in an easy-to-understand manner.

Many of the subjects discussed in this publication are discussed in greater detail in other IRS publications. References to those other publications are provided for your information.

Icons. Small graphic symbols, or icons, are used to draw your attention to special information. See Table 1 for an explanation of each icon used in this publication.

What is not covered in this publication. Some material that you may find helpful is not included in this publication but can be found in your tax form instructions booklet. This includes lists of:

- Where to report certain items shown on information documents, and
- Tax Topics you can read at *IRS.gov/TaxTopics*.

If you operate your own business or have other self-employment income, such as from babysitting or selling crafts, see the following publications for more information.

- Pub. 334, Tax Guide for Small Business.
- Pub. 535, Business Expenses.
- Pub. 587, Business Use of Your Home.

Help from the IRS. There are many ways you can get help from the IRS. These are explained under *How To Get Tax Help* at the end of this publication.

Comments and suggestions. We welcome your comments about this publication and suggestions for future editions.

You can send us comments through *IRS.gov/FormComments*. Or, you can write to the Internal Revenue Service, Tax Forms and Publications, 1111 Constitution Ave. NW, IR-6526, Washington, DC 20224.

Although we can't respond individually to each comment received, we do appreciate your feedback and will consider your comments and suggestions as we revise our tax forms, instructions, and publications. **Don't** send tax questions, tax returns, or payments to the above address.

Getting answers to your tax questions. If you have a tax question not answered by this publication or the *How To Get Tax Help* section at the end of this publication, go to the IRS Interactive Tax Assistant page at *IRS.gov/Help/ITA* where you can find topics by using the search feature or viewing the categories listed.

Getting tax forms, instructions, and publications. Go to *IRS.gov/Forms* to download current and prior-year forms, instructions, and publications.

Ordering tax forms, instructions, and publications. Go to *IRS.gov/OrderForms* to order current forms, instructions, and publications; call 800-829-3676 to order prior-year forms and instructions. The IRS will process your order for forms and publications as soon as possible. **Don't** resubmit requests you've already sent us. You can get forms and publications faster online.

IRS mission. Provide America's taxpayers top-quality service by helping them understand and meet their tax responsibilities and enforce the law with integrity and fairness to all.

Table 1. **Legend of Icons**

Icon	Explanation
CAUTION	Items that may cause you particular problems, or an alert about pending legislation that may be enacted after this publication goes to print.
	An Internet site or an email address.
	An address you may need.
RECORDS	Items you should keep in your personal records.
	Items you may need to figure or a worksheet you may need to complete and keep for your records.
	An important phone number.
TIP	Helpful information you may need.

Part One.

The Income Tax Return

The four chapters in this part provide basic information on the tax system. They take you through the first steps of filling out a tax return. They also provide information about dependents, and discuss recordkeeping requirements, IRS e-file (electronic filing), certain penalties, and the two methods used to pay tax during the year: withholding and estimated tax.

The Form 1040 and 1040-SR schedules that are discussed in these chapters are:

- *Schedule 1, Additional Income and Adjustments to Income; and*
- *Schedule 3 (Part II), Other Payments and Refundable Credits.*

1.

Filing Information

What's New

Due date of return. File Form 1040 or 1040-SR by April 18, 2023. The due date is April 18, instead of April 15, because of the Emancipation Day holiday in the District of Columbia—even if you don't live in the District of Columbia.

Filing status name changed to qualifying surviving spouse. The filing status qualifying widow(er) is now called qualifying surviving spouse. The rules for the filing status have not changed. The same rules that applied for qualifying widow(er) apply to qualifying surviving spouse. See chapter 2 for information on filing status.

New lines 1a through 1z on Form 1040 and 1040-SR. This year line 1 is expanded and there are new lines 1a through 1z.

New lines on Schedule 1. This year there are new lines 8r through 8u.

Who must file. Generally, the amount of income you can receive before you must file a return has been increased. See Table 1-1, Table 1-2, and Table 1-3 for the specific amounts.

Reminders

File online. Rather than filing a return on paper, you may be able to file electronically using IRS *e-file*. For more information, see *Why Should I File Electronically*, later.

Access your online account (individual taxpayers only). Go to *IRS.gov/Account* to securely access information about your federal tax account.

- View the amount you owe and a breakdown by tax year.

- See payment plan details or apply for a new payment plan.
- Make a payment, view 5 years of payment history and any pending or scheduled payments.
- Access your tax records, including key data from your most recent tax return, your economic impact payment amounts, and transcripts.
- View digital copies of select notices from the IRS.
- Approve or reject authorization requests from tax professionals.
- Update your address or manage your communication preferences.
- Go to *IRS.gov/SecureAccess* to view the required identity authentication process.

Change of address. If you change your address, you should notify the IRS. You can use Form 8822 to notify the IRS of the change. See *Change of Address*, later, under *What Happens After I File*.

Enter your social security number. You must enter your social security number (SSN) in the spaces provided on your tax return. If you file a joint return, enter the SSNs in the same order as the names.

Direct deposit of refund. Instead of getting a paper check, you may be able to have your refund deposited directly into your account at a bank or other financial institution. See *Direct Deposit* under *Refunds*, later. If you choose direct deposit of your refund, you may be able to split the refund among two or three accounts.

Pay online or by phone. If you owe additional tax, you may be able to pay online or by phone. See *How To Pay*, later.

Installment agreement. If you can't pay the full amount due with your return, you may ask to make monthly installment payments. See *Installment Agreement*, later, under *Amount You Owe*. You may be able to apply online for a payment agreement if you owe federal tax, interest, and penalties.

Automatic 6-month extension. You can get an automatic 6-month extension to file your tax return if, no later than the date your return is due, you file Form 4868. See *Automatic Extension*, later.

Service in combat zone. You are allowed extra time to take care of your tax matters if you are a member of the Armed Forces who served in a combat zone, or if you served in a combat zone in support of the Armed Forces. See *Individuals Serving in Combat Zone*, later, under *When Do I Have To File*.

Adoption taxpayer identification number. If a child has been placed in your home for purposes of legal adoption and you won't be able to get a social security number for the child in time to file your return, you may be able to get an adoption taxpayer identification number (ATIN). For more information, see *Social Security Number (SSN)*, later.

Taxpayer identification number for aliens. If you or your dependent is a nonresident or resident alien who doesn't have and isn't eligible to get a social security number, file Form W-7, Application for IRS Individual Taxpayer Identification Number, with the IRS. For more information, see *Social Security Number (SSN)*, later.

Individual taxpayer identification number (ITIN) renewal. Some ITINs must be renewed. If you haven't used your ITIN on a U.S. tax return at least once for tax years 2019, 2020, or 2021, it expired at the end of 2022 and must be renewed if you need to file a U.S. federal tax return in 2023. You don't need to renew your ITIN if you don't need to file a federal tax return. You can find more information at *IRS.gov/ITIN*.

 ITINs assigned before 2013 have expired and must be renewed if you need to file a tax return in 2023. If you previously submitted a renewal application and it was approved, you do not need to renew again unless you haven't used your ITIN on a federal tax return at least once for tax years 2019, 2020, or 2021.

Frivolous tax submissions. The IRS has published a list of positions that are identified as frivolous. The penalty for filing a frivolous tax return is $5,000. Also, the $5,000 penalty will apply to other specified frivolous submissions. For more information, see *Civil Penalties*, later.

Introduction

This chapter discusses the following topics.

- Whether you have to file a return.

- How to file electronically.
- How to file for free.
- When, how, and where to file your return.
- What happens if you pay too little or too much tax.
- What records you should keep and how long you should keep them.
- How you can change a return you have already filed.

Do I Have To File a Return?

You must file a federal income tax return if you are a citizen or resident of the United States or a resident of Puerto Rico and you meet the filing requirements for any of the following categories that apply to you.

1. Individuals in general. (There are special rules for individuals whose spouse has died, executors, administrators, legal representatives, U.S. citizens and residents living outside the United States, residents of Puerto Rico, and individuals with income from U.S. possessions.)

2. Dependents.

3. Certain children under age 19 or full-time students.

4. Self-employed persons.

5. Aliens.

The filing requirements for each category are explained in this chapter.

The filing requirements apply even if you don't owe tax.

 Even if you don't have to file a return, it may be to your advantage to do so. See Who Should File, later.

 File only one federal income tax return for the year regardless of how many jobs you had, how many Forms W-2 you received, or how many states you lived in during the year. Don't file more than one original return for the same year, even if you haven't received your refund or haven't heard from the IRS since you filed.

Individuals—In General

If you are a U.S. citizen or resident, whether you must file a return depends on three factors.

1. Your gross income.
2. Your filing status.
3. Your age.

To find out whether you must file, see Table 1-1, Table 1-2, and Table 1-3. Even if no table shows that you must file, you may need to file to get money back. See Who Should File, later.

Gross income. This includes all income you receive in the form of money, goods, property, and services that isn't exempt from tax. It also includes income from sources outside the United States or from the sale of your main home

Table 1-1. **2022 Filing Requirements for Most Taxpayers**

IF your filing status is...	AND at the end of 2022 you were...*	THEN file a return if your gross income was at least...**
Single	under 65	$12,950
	65 or older	$14,700
Married filing jointly***	under 65 (both spouses)	$25,900
	65 or older (one spouse)	$27,300
	65 or older (both spouses)	$28,700
Married filing separately	any age	$5
Head of household	under 65	$19,400
	65 or older	$21,150
Qualifying surviving spouse	under 65	$25,900
	65 or older	$27,300

* If you were born on January 1, 1958, you are considered to be age 65 at the end of 2022. (If your spouse died in 2022 or if you are preparing a return for someone who died in 2022, see Pub. 501.)

** Gross income means all income you received in the form of money, goods, property, and services that isn't exempt from tax, including any income from sources outside the United States or from the sale of your main home (even if you can exclude part or all of it). Don't include any social security benefits unless (a) you are married filing a separate return and you lived with your spouse at any time during 2022, or (b) one-half of your social security benefits plus your other gross income and any tax-exempt interest is more than $25,000 ($32,000 if married filing jointly). If (a) or (b) applies, see the Instructions for Form 1040 or Pub. 915 to figure the taxable part of social security benefits you must include in gross income. Gross income includes gains, but not losses, reported on Form 8949 or Schedule D. Gross income from a business means, for example, the amount on Schedule C, line 7, or Schedule F, line 9. But, in figuring gross income, don't reduce your income by any losses, including any loss on Schedule C, line 7, or Schedule F, line 9.

*** If you didn't live with your spouse at the end of 2022 (or on the date your spouse died) and your gross income was at least $5, you must file a return regardless of your age.

(even if you can exclude all or part of it). Include part of your social security benefits if:

1. You were married, filing a separate return, and you lived with your spouse at any time during 2022; or

2. Half of your social security benefits plus your other gross income and any tax-exempt interest is more than $25,000 ($32,000 if married filing jointly).

If either (1) or (2) applies, see the Instructions for Form 1040 or Pub. 915 to figure the social security benefits you must include in gross income.

Common types of income are discussed in Part Two of this publication.

Community property states. Community property states include Arizona, California, Idaho, Louisiana, Nevada, New Mexico, Texas, Washington, and Wisconsin. If you and your spouse lived in a community property state, you must usually follow state law to determine what is community property and what is separate income. For details, see Form 8958 and Pub. 555.

Nevada, Washington, and California domestic partners. A registered domestic partner in Nevada, Washington, or California must generally report half the combined community income of the individual and their domestic partner. See Pub. 555.

Self-employed individuals. If you are self-employed, your gross income includes the amount on line 7 of Schedule C (Form 1040),

Profit or Loss From Business; and line 9 of Schedule F (Form 1040), Profit or Loss From Farming. See Self-Employed Persons, later, for more information about your filing requirements.

 If you don't report all of your self-employment income, your social security benefits may be lower when you retire.

Filing status. Your filing status depends on whether you are single or married and on your family situation. Your filing status is determined on the last day of your tax year, which is December 31 for most taxpayers. See chapter 2 for an explanation of each filing status.

Age. If you are 65 or older at the end of the year, you can generally have a higher amount of gross income than other taxpayers before you must file. See Table 1-1. You are considered 65 on the day before your 65th birthday. For example, if your 65th birthday is on January 1, 2023, you are considered 65 for 2022.

Surviving Spouses, Executors, Administrators, and Legal Representatives

You must file a final return for a decedent (a person who died) if both of the following are true.

- Your spouse died in 2022 or you are the executor, administrator, or legal representative.

- The decedent met the filing requirements at the date of death.

For more information on rules for filing a decedent's final return, see Pub. 559.

U.S. Citizens and Resident Aliens Living Abroad

To determine whether you must file a return, include in your gross income any income you received abroad, including any income you can exclude under the foreign earned income exclusion. For information on special tax rules that may apply to you, see Pub. 54. It is available online and at most U.S. embassies and consulates. See *How To Get Tax Help* in the back of this publication.

Residents of Puerto Rico

If you are a U.S. citizen and also a bona fide resident of Puerto Rico, you must generally file a U.S. income tax return for any year in which you meet the income requirements. This is in addition to any legal requirement you may have to file an income tax return with Puerto Rico.

If you are a bona fide resident of Puerto Rico for the entire year, your U.S. gross income doesn't include income from sources within Puerto Rico. It does, however, include any income you received for your services as an employee of the United States or a U.S. agency. If you receive income from Puerto Rican sources that isn't subject to U.S. tax, you must reduce your standard deduction. As a result, the amount of income you must have before you are required to file a U.S. income tax return is lower than the applicable amount in Table 1-1 or Table 1-2. For more information, see Pub. 570.

Individuals With Income From U.S. Possessions

If you had income from Guam, the Commonwealth of the Northern Mariana Islands, American Samoa, or the U.S. Virgin Islands, special rules may apply when determining whether you must file a U.S. federal income tax return. In addition, you may have to file a return with the individual island government. See Pub. 570 for more information.

Dependents

If you are a dependent (one who meets the dependency tests in chapter 3), see Table 1-2 to find out whether you must file a return. You must also file if your situation is described in Table 1-3.

Responsibility of parent. Generally, a child is responsible for filing their own tax return and for paying any tax on the return. If a dependent child must file an income tax return but can't file due to age or any other reason, then a parent, guardian, or other legally responsible person must file it for the child. If the child can't sign the return, the parent or guardian must sign the child's name followed by the words "By (your signature), parent for minor child."

Child's earnings. Amounts a child earns by performing services are included in the child's gross income and not the gross income of the parent. This is true even if under local law the child's parent has the right to the earnings and

may actually have received them. But if the child doesn't pay the tax due on this income, the parent is liable for the tax.

Certain Children Under Age 19 or Full-Time Students

If a child's only income is interest and dividends (including capital gain distributions and Alaska Permanent Fund dividends), the child was under age 19 at the end of 2022 or was a full-time student under age 24 at the end of 2022, and certain other conditions are met, a parent can elect to include the child's income on the parent's return. If this election is made, the child doesn't have to file a return. See Instructions for Form 8814, Parents' Election To Report Child's Interest and Dividends.

Self-Employed Persons

You are self-employed if you:

- Carry on a trade or business as a sole proprietor,
- Are an independent contractor,
- Are a member of a partnership, or
- Are in business for yourself in any other way.

Self-employment can include work in addition to your regular full-time business activities, such as certain part-time work you do at home or in addition to your regular job.

You must file a return if your gross income is at least as much as the filing requirement amount for your filing status and age (shown in Table 1-1). Also, you must file Form 1040 or 1040-SR and Schedule SE (Form 1040), Self-Employment Tax, if:

1. Your net earnings from self-employment (excluding church employee income) were $400 or more, or

2. You had church employee income of $108.28 or more. (See Table 1-3.)

Use Schedule SE (Form 1040) to figure your self-employment tax. Self-employment tax is comparable to the social security and Medicare tax withheld from an employee's wages. For more information about this tax, see Pub. 334.

Employees of foreign governments or international organizations. If you are a U.S. citizen who works in the United States for an international organization, a foreign government, or a wholly owned instrumentality of a foreign government, and your employer isn't required to withhold social security and Medicare taxes from your wages, you must include your earnings from services performed in the United States when figuring your net earnings from self-employment.

Ministers. You must include income from services you performed as a minister when figuring your net earnings from self-employment, unless you have an exemption from self-employment tax. This also applies to Christian Science practitioners and members of a religious order who have not taken a vow of poverty. For more information, see Pub. 517.

Aliens

Your status as an alien (resident, nonresident, or dual-status) determines whether and how you must file an income tax return.

The rules used to determine your alien status are discussed in Pub. 519.

Resident alien. If you are a resident alien for the entire year, you must file a tax return following the same rules that apply to U.S. citizens. Use the forms discussed in this publication.

Nonresident alien. If you are a nonresident alien, the rules and tax forms that apply to you are different from those that apply to U.S. citizens and resident aliens. See Pub. 519 to find out if U.S. income tax laws apply to you and which forms you should file.

Dual-status taxpayer. If you are a resident alien for part of the tax year and a nonresident alien for the rest of the year, you are a dual-status taxpayer. Different rules apply for each part of the year. For information on dual-status taxpayers, see Pub. 519.

Who Should File

Even if you don't have to file, you should file a federal income tax return to get money back if any of the following conditions apply.

1. You had federal income tax withheld or made estimated tax payments.

2. You qualify for the earned income credit. See Pub. 596 for more information.

3. You qualify for the additional child tax credit. See chapter 14 for more information.

4. You qualify for the premium tax credit. See Pub. 974 for more information.

5. You qualify for the American opportunity credit. See Pub. 970 for more information.

6. You qualify for the credit for federal tax on fuels. See chapter 13 for more information.

Form 1040 or 1040-SR

Use Form 1040 or 1040-SR to file your return. (But also see *Why Should I File Electronically*, later.)

You can use Form 1040 or 1040-SR to report all types of income, deductions, and credits.

Why Should I File Electronically?

Electronic Filing

If your adjusted gross income (AGI) is less than a certain amount, you are eligible for *Free File*, a free tax software service offered by IRS partners, to prepare and *e-file* your return for free. If your income is over the amount, you are still eligible for Free File Fillable Forms, an electronic

Table 1-2. 2022 Filing Requirements for Dependents

See chapter 3 to find out if someone can claim you as a dependent.

If your parents (or someone else) can claim you as a dependent, use this table to see if you must file a return. (See Table 1-3 for other situations when you must file.)

In this table, unearned income includes taxable interest, ordinary dividends, and capital gain distributions. It also includes unemployment compensation, taxable social security benefits, pensions, annuities, and distributions of unearned income from a trust. Earned income includes salaries, wages, tips, professional fees, and taxable scholarship and fellowship grants. (See *Scholarships and fellowships* in chapter 8.) Gross income is the total of your earned and unearned income.

Single dependents—Were you **either** age 65 or older or blind?

☐ **No.** You must file a return if **any** of the following apply.
- Your unearned income was more than $1,150.
- Your earned income was more than $12,950.
- Your gross income was more than the **larger** of:
  - $1,150, or
  - Your earned income (up to $12,550) plus $400.

☐ **Yes.** You must file a return if **any** of the following apply.
- Your unearned income was more than $2,900 ($4,650 if 65 or older **and** blind).
- Your earned income was more than $14,700 ($16,450 if 65 or older **and** blind).
- Your gross income was more than the **larger** of:
  - $2,900 ($4,650 if 65 or older **and** blind), or
  - Your earned income (up to $12,550) plus $2,150 ($3,900 if 65 or older **and** blind).

Married dependents—Were you **either** age 65 or older or blind?

☐ **No.** You must file a return if **any** of the following apply.
- Your unearned income was more than $1,150.
- Your earned income was more than $12,950.
- Your gross income was at least $5 and your spouse files a separate return and itemizes deductions.
- Your gross income was more than the **larger** of:
  - $1,150, or
  - Your earned income (up to $12,550) plus $400.

☐ **Yes.** You must file a return if **any** of the following apply.
- Your unearned income was more than $2,550 ($3,950 if 65 or older **and** blind).
- Your earned income was more than $14,350 ($15,750 if 65 or older **and** blind).
- Your gross income was at least $5 and your spouse files a separate return and itemizes deductions.
- Your gross income was more than the **larger** of:
  - $2,550 ($3,950 if 65 or older **and** blind), or
  - Your earned income (up to $12,550) plus $1,800 ($3,200 if 65 or older **and** blind).

version of IRS paper forms. Table 1-4 lists the free ways to electronically file your return.

 IRS *e-file* uses automation to replace most of the manual steps needed to process paper returns. As a result, the processing of *e-file* returns is faster and more accurate than the processing of paper returns. However, as with a paper return, you are responsible for making sure your return contains accurate information and is filed on time.

If your return is filed with IRS *e-file*, you will receive an acknowledgment that your return was received and accepted. If you owe tax, you can *e-file* and pay electronically. The IRS has processed more than one billion *e-filed* returns safely and securely. Using *e-file* doesn't affect your chances of an IRS examination of your return.

Requirements for an electronic return signature. To file your return electronically, you must sign the return electronically using a personal identification number (PIN). If you are filing online, you must use a Self-Select PIN. For 2022, if we issued you an identity protection personal identification number (IP PIN) (as described in more detail below), all six digits of your IP PIN must appear in the IP PIN spaces provided next to the space for your occupation for your electronic signature to be complete. Failure to include an issued IP PIN on the electronic return will result in an invalid signature and a rejected return. If you are filing a joint return and both taxpayers were issued an IP PIN, enter both IP PINs in the spaces provided. If you are filing electronically using a tax practitioner, you can use a Self-Select PIN or a Practitioner PIN.

Self-Select PIN. The Self-Select PIN method allows you to create your own PIN. If you are married filing jointly, you and your spouse will each need to create a PIN and enter these PINs as your electronic signatures.

A PIN is any combination of five digits you choose except five zeros. If you use a PIN, there is nothing to sign and nothing to mail—not even your Forms W-2.

Your electronic return is considered a valid signed return only when it includes your PIN; last name; date of birth; IP PIN, if applicable; and AGI from your originally filed 2021 federal income tax return, if applicable. If you're filing jointly, your electronic return must also include your spouse's PIN; last name; date of birth; IP PIN, if applicable; and AGI, if applicable, in order to be considered validly signed. Don't use AGI from an amended return (Form 1040-X) or a math error correction made by the IRS. AGI is the amount shown on your 2021 Form 1040 or Form 1040-SR, line 11. If you don't have your 2021 income tax return, you can request a transcript by using our automated self-service tool. Go to IRS.gov/Transcript. (If you filed electronically last year, you, and your spouse if filing jointly, may use your prior year PIN to verify your identity instead of your prior year AGI. The prior year PIN is the five-digit PIN you used to electronically sign your 2021 return.) You will also be prompted to enter your date of birth.

 You can't use the Self-Select PIN method if you are a first-time filer under age 16 at the end of 2022.

Practitioner PIN. The Practitioner PIN method allows you to authorize your tax practitioner to enter or generate your PIN. Your electronic return is considered a validly signed return only when it includes your PIN; last name; date of birth; and IP PIN, if applicable. If you're filing jointly, your electronic return must also include your spouse's PIN; last name; date of birth; and IP PIN, if applicable, in order to be considered a validly signed return. The practitioner can provide you with details.

Form 8453. You must send in a paper Form 8453 if you have to attach certain forms or other documents that can't be electronically filed. For details, see Form 8453. For more details, visit IRS.gov/efile.

Identity Protection PIN. If the IRS gave you an identity protection personal identification number (IP PIN), enter it in the spaces provided on your tax form. If the IRS hasn't given you this type of number, leave these spaces blank. For more information, see the Instructions for Form 1040.

 All taxpayers are now eligible for an IP PIN. For more information, see Pub. 5477. To apply for an IP PIN, go to IRS.gov/IPPIN and use the Get an IP PIN tool.

Power of attorney. If an agent is signing your return for you, a power of attorney (POA) must be filed. Attach the POA to Form 8453 and file it using that form's instructions. See *Signatures*, later, for more information on POAs.

State returns. In most states, you can file an electronic state return simultaneously with your federal return. For more information, check with

Table 1-3. **Other Situations When You Must File a 2022 Return**

You must file a return if any of the following apply for 2022.

1. You owe any special taxes, including any of the following (see the instructions for Schedule 2 (Form 1040)).
   a. Alternative minimum tax.
   b. Additional tax on a qualified plan, including an individual retirement arrangement (IRA), or other tax-favored account.
   c. Household employment taxes.
   d. Social security and Medicare tax on tips you didn't report to your employer or on wages you received from an employer who didn't withhold these taxes.
   e. Uncollected social security and Medicare or RRTA tax on tips you reported to your employer or on group-term life insurance and additional taxes on health savings accounts.
   f. Recapture taxes.

2. You (or your spouse, if filing jointly) received health savings account, Archer MSA, or Medicare Advantage MSA distributions.
3. You had net earnings from self-employment of at least $400.
4. You had wages of $108.28 or more from a church or qualified church-controlled organization that is exempt from employer social security and Medicare taxes.
5. Advance payments of the premium tax credit were made for you, your spouse, or a dependent who enrolled in coverage through the Marketplace. You or whoever enrolled you should have received Form(s) 1095-A showing the amount of the advance payments.
6. You are required to include amounts in income under section 965 or you have a net tax liability under section 965 that you are paying in installments under section 965(h) or deferred by making an election under section 965(i).

your local IRS office, state tax agency, tax professional, or the IRS website at *IRS.gov/efile*.

Refunds. You can have a refund check mailed to you, or you can have your refund deposited directly to your checking or savings account or split among two or three accounts. With *e-file*, your refund will be issued faster than if you filed on paper.

As with a paper return, you may not get all of your refund if you owe certain past-due amounts, such as federal tax, state income tax, state unemployment compensation debts, child support, spousal support, or certain other federal nontax debts, such as student loans. See *Offset against debts* under *Refunds*, later.

Refund inquiries. Information about your return will generally be available within 24 hours after the IRS receives your *e-filed* return. See *Refund Information*, later.

Amount you owe. To avoid late-payment penalties and interest, pay your taxes in full by April 18, 2023 (for most people). See *How To Pay*, later, for information on how to pay the amount you owe.

Using Your Personal Computer

You can file your tax return in a fast, easy, and convenient way using your personal computer. A computer with Internet access and tax preparation software are all you need. Best of all, you can *e-file* from the comfort of your home 24 hours a day, 7 days a week.

IRS-approved tax preparation software is available for online use on the Internet, for download from the Internet, and in retail stores. For information, visit *IRS.gov/efile*.

Table 1-4. **Free Ways To *e-file***

Use Free File for free tax software and free *e-file*.
• IRS partners offer name-brand products for free.
• Many taxpayers are eligible for Free File software.
• Everyone is eligible for Free File Fillable Forms, an electronic version of IRS paper forms.
• Free File software and Free File Fillable Forms are available only at *IRS.gov/FreeFile*.
Use VITA/TCE for free tax help from volunteers and free *e-file*.
• Volunteers prepare your return and *e-file* it for free.
• Some sites also offer do-it-yourself software.
• You are eligible based either on your income or age.
• Sites are located nationwide. Find one near you by visiting *IRS.gov/VITA*.

Through Employers and Financial Institutions

Some businesses offer free *e-file* to their employees, members, or customers. Others offer it for a fee. Ask your employer or financial institution if they offer IRS *e-file* as an employee, member, or customer benefit.

Free Help With Your Return

The Volunteer Income Tax Assistance (VITA) program offers free tax help to people who generally make $60,000 or less, persons with disabilities, and limited-English-speaking taxpayers who need help preparing their own tax returns. The Tax Counseling for the Elderly (TCE) program offers free tax help for all taxpayers, particularly those who are 60 years of age and older. TCE volunteers specialize in answering questions about pensions and retirement-related issues unique to seniors.

You can go to IRS.gov to see your options for preparing and filing your return, which include the following.

- **Free File.** Go to *IRS.gov/FreeFile*. See if you qualify to use brand-name software to prepare and *e-file* your federal tax return for free.

- **VITA.** Go to *IRS.gov/VITA*, download the free IRS2Go app, or call 800-906-9887 to find the nearest VITA location for free tax return preparation.

- **TCE.** Go to *IRS.gov/TCE*, download the free IRS2Go app, or call 888-227-7669 to find the nearest TCE location for free tax return preparation.

Using a Tax Professional

Many tax professionals electronically file tax returns for their clients. You may personally enter your PIN or complete Form 8879, IRS *e-file* Signature Authorization, to authorize the tax professional to enter your PIN on your return.

Note. Tax professionals may charge a fee for IRS *e-file*. Fees can vary depending on the professional and the specific services rendered.

When Do I Have To File?

April 18, 2023, is the due date for filing your 2022 income tax return if you use the calendar year. The due date is April 18, instead of April 15, because of the Emancipation Day holiday in the District of Columbia—even if you don't live in the District of Columbia. For a quick view of due dates for filing a return with or without an extension of time to file (discussed later), see Table 1-5.

If you use a fiscal year (a year ending on the last day of any month except December, or a 52-53-week year), your income tax return is due by the 15th day of the 4th month after the close of your fiscal year.

When the due date for doing any act for tax purposes—filing a return, paying taxes, etc.—falls on a Saturday, Sunday, or legal holiday, the due date is delayed until the next business day.

Filing paper returns on time. Your paper return is filed on time if it is mailed in an envelope that is properly addressed, has enough postage, and is postmarked by the due date. If you send your return by registered mail, the date of the registration is the postmark date. The registration is evidence that the return was delivered. If you send a return by certified mail and have your receipt postmarked by a postal employee, the date on the receipt is the postmark date. The postmarked certified mail receipt is evidence that the return was delivered.

Private delivery services. If you choose to mail your return, you can use certain private delivery services designated by the IRS to meet the "timely mailing treated as timely filing/paying" rule for tax returns and payments. These private delivery services include only the following.

- DHL Express 9:00, DHL Express 10:30, DHL Express 12:00, DHL Express Worldwide, DHL Express Envelope, DHL Import Express 10:30, DHL Import Express 12:00, and DHL Import Express Worldwide.

- UPS Next Day Air Early A.M., UPS Next Day Air, UPS Next Day Air Saver, UPS 2nd Day Air, UPS 2nd Day Air A.M., UPS Worldwide Express Plus, and UPS Worldwide Express.

- FedEx First Overnight, FedEx Priority Overnight, FedEx Standard Overnight, FedEx 2 Day, FedEx International Next Flight Out, FedEx International Priority, FedEx International First, and FedEx International Economy.

To check for any updates to the list of designated private delivery services, go to *IRS.gov/PDS*. For the IRS mailing addresses to use if you're using a private delivery service, go to *IRS.gov/PDSStreetAddresses*.

The private delivery service can tell you how to get written proof of the mailing date.

Filing electronic returns on time. If you use IRS *e-file*, your return is considered filed on time if the authorized electronic return transmitter postmarks the transmission by the due date. An authorized electronic return transmitter is a participant in the IRS *e-file* program that transmits electronic tax return information directly to the IRS.

The electronic postmark is a record of when the authorized electronic return transmitter received the transmission of your electronically filed return on its host system. The date and time in your time zone controls whether your electronically filed return is timely.

Filing late. If you don't file your return by the due date, you may have to pay a failure-to-file penalty and interest. For more information, see *Penalties*, later. Also see *Interest* under *Amount You Owe*, later.

If you were due a refund but you didn't file a return, you must generally file within 3 years from the date the return was due (including extensions) to get that refund.

Nonresident alien. If you are a nonresident alien and earn wages subject to U.S. income tax withholding, your 2022 U.S. income tax return (Form 1040-NR) is due by:

- April 18, 2023, if you use a calendar year; or

- The 15th day of the 4th month after the end of your fiscal year, if you use a fiscal year.

If you don't earn wages subject to U.S. income tax withholding, your return is due by:

- June 15, 2023, if you use a calendar year; or

- The 15th day of the 6th month after the end of your fiscal year, if you use a fiscal year.

See Pub. 519 for more filing information.

Filing for a decedent. If you must file a final income tax return for a taxpayer who died during the year (a decedent), the return is due by the 15th day of the 4th month after the end of the decedent's normal tax year. See Pub. 559.

Extensions of Time To File

You may be able to get an extension of time to file your return. There are three types of situations where you may qualify for an extension.

- Automatic extensions.

- You are outside the United States.

- You are serving in a combat zone.

Table 1-5. When To File Your 2022 Return

For U.S. citizens and residents who file returns on a calendar year basis.

	For Most Taxpayers	For Certain Taxpayers Outside the United States
No extension requested	April 18, 2023	June 15, 2023
Automatic extension	October 16, 2023	October 16, 2023

Automatic Extension

If you can't file your 2022 return by the due date, you may be able to get an automatic 6-month extension of time to file.

Example. If your return is due on April 18, 2023, you will have until October 16, 2023, to file.

 If you don't pay the tax due by the regular due date (April 15 for most taxpayers), you will owe interest. You may also be charged penalties, discussed later.

How to get the automatic extension. You can get the automatic extension by:

1. Using IRS *e-file* (electronic filing), or

2. Filing a paper form.

E-file **options.** There are two ways you can use *e-file* to get an extension of time to file. Complete Form 4868 to use as a worksheet. If you think you may owe tax when you file your return, use *Part II* of the form to estimate your balance due. If you *e-file* Form 4868 to the IRS, don't send a paper Form 4868.

E-file using your personal computer or a tax professional. You can use a tax software package with your personal computer or a tax professional to file Form 4868 electronically. Free File and Free File Fillable Forms, both available at IRS.gov, allow you to prepare and *e-file* Form 4868 for free. You will need to provide certain information from your 2021 tax return. If you wish to make a payment by direct transfer from your bank account, see *Pay online* under *How To Pay*, later, in this chapter.

E-file and pay by credit or debit card or by direct transfer from your bank account. You can get an extension by paying part or all of your estimate of tax due by using a credit or debit card or by direct transfer from your bank account. You can do this by phone or over the Internet. You don't file Form 4868. See *Pay online* under *How To Pay*, later, in this chapter.

Filing a paper Form 4868. You can get an extension of time to file by filing a paper Form 4868. If you are a fiscal year taxpayer, you must file a paper Form 4868. Mail it to the address shown in the form instructions.

If you want to make a payment with the form, make your check or money order payable to "United States Treasury." Write your SSN, daytime phone number, and "2022 Form 4868" on your check or money order.

When to file. You must request the automatic extension by the due date for your return. You can file your return any time before the 6-month extension period ends.

When you file your return. Enter any payment you made related to the extension of time to file on Schedule 3 (Form 1040), line 10.

Individuals Outside the United States

You are allowed an automatic 2-month extension, without filing Form 4868 (until June 15, 2023, if you use the calendar year), to file your 2022 return and pay any federal income tax due if:

1. You are a U.S. citizen or resident; and

2. On the due date of your return:

   a. You are living outside the United States and Puerto Rico, and your main place of business or post of duty is outside the United States and Puerto Rico; or

   b. You are in military or naval service on duty outside the United States and Puerto Rico.

However, if you pay the tax due after the regular due date (April 15 for most taxpayers), interest will be charged from that date until the date the tax is paid.

If you served in a combat zone or qualified hazardous duty area, you may be eligible for a longer extension of time to file. See *Individuals Serving in Combat Zone*, later, for special rules that apply to you.

Married taxpayers. If you file a joint return, only one spouse has to qualify for this automatic extension. If you and your spouse file separate returns, the automatic extension applies only to the spouse who qualifies.

How to get the extension. To use this automatic extension, you must attach a statement to your return explaining what situation qualified you for the extension. (See the situations listed under (2), earlier.)

Extensions beyond 2 months. If you can't file your return within the automatic 2-month extension period, you may be able to get an additional 4-month extension, for a total of 6 months. File Form 4868 and check the box on line 8.

No further extension. An extension of more than 6 months will generally not be granted. However, if you are outside the United States and meet certain tests, you may be granted a longer extension. For more information, see *When To File and Pay* in Pub. 54.

Individuals Serving in Combat Zone

The deadline for filing your tax return, paying any tax you may owe, and filing a claim for refund is automatically extended if you serve in a combat zone. This applies to members of the Armed Forces, as well as merchant marines serving aboard vessels under the operational control of the Department of Defense, Red Cross personnel, accredited correspondents, and civilians under the direction of the Armed Forces in support of the Armed Forces.

Combat zone. A combat zone is any area the President of the United States designates by executive order as an area in which the U.S. Armed Forces are engaging or have engaged in combat. An area usually becomes a combat zone and ceases to be a combat zone on the dates the President designates by executive order. For purposes of the automatic extension, the term "combat zone" includes the following areas.

1. The Arabian peninsula area, effective January 17, 1991.

2. The Kosovo area, effective March 24, 1999.

3. The Afghanistan area, effective September 19, 2001.

See Pub. 3 for more detailed information on the locations comprising each combat zone. Pub. 3 also has information about other tax benefits available to military personnel serving in a combat zone.

Extension period. The deadline for filing your return, paying any tax due, filing a claim for refund, and taking other actions with the IRS is extended in two steps. First, your deadline is extended for 180 days after the later of:

1. The last day you are in a combat zone or the last day the area qualifies as a combat zone, or

2. The last day of any continuous qualified hospitalization (defined later) for injury from service in the combat zone.

Second, in addition to the 180 days, your deadline is also extended by the number of days you had left to take action with the IRS when you entered the combat zone. For example, you have 3½ months (January 1–April 15) to file your tax return. Any days left in this period when you entered the combat zone (or the entire 3½ months if you entered it before the beginning of the year) are added to the 180 days. See *Extension of Deadlines* in Pub. 3 for more information.

The rules on the extension for filing your return also apply when you are deployed outside the United States (away from your permanent duty station) while participating in a designated contingency operation.

Qualified hospitalization. The hospitalization must be the result of an injury received while serving in a combat zone or a contingency operation. Qualified hospitalization means:

- Any hospitalization outside the United States, and

- Up to 5 years of hospitalization in the United States.

See Pub. 3 for more information on qualified hospitalizations.

How Do I Prepare My Return?

This section explains how to get ready to fill in your tax return and when to report your income and expenses. It also explains how to complete certain sections of the form. You may find Table 1-6 helpful when you prepare your paper return.

Table 1-6. **Six Steps for Preparing Your Paper Return**

1 — Get your records together for income and expenses.
2 — Get the forms, schedules, and publications you need.
3 — Fill in your return.
4 — Check your return to make sure it is correct.
5 — Sign and date your return.
6 — Attach all required forms and schedules.

Electronic returns. For information you may find useful in preparing an electronic return, see *Why Should I File Electronically*, earlier.

Substitute tax forms. You can't use your own version of a tax form unless it meets the requirements explained in Pub. 1167.

Form W-2. If you were an employee, you should receive Form W-2 from your employer. You will need the information from this form to prepare your return. See *Form W-2* under *Credit for Withholding and Estimated Tax for 2022* in chapter 4.

Your employer is required to provide or send Form W-2 to you no later than January 31, 2023. If it is mailed, you should allow adequate time to receive it before contacting your employer. If you still don't get the form by early February, the IRS can help you by requesting the form from your employer. When you request IRS help, be prepared to provide the following information.

- Your name, address (including ZIP code), and phone number.

- Your SSN.

- Your dates of employment.

- Your employer's name, address (including ZIP code), and phone number.

Form 1099. If you received certain types of income, you may receive a Form 1099. For example, if you received taxable interest of $10 or more, the payer is required to provide or send Form 1099 to you no later than January 31, 2023 (or by February 15, 2023, if furnished by a broker). If it is mailed, you should allow adequate time to receive it before contacting the payer. If you still don't get the form by February 15 (or by March 1, 2023, if furnished by a broker), call the IRS for help.

When Do I Report My Income and Expenses?

You must figure your taxable income on the basis of a tax year. A "tax year" is an annual accounting period used for keeping records and reporting income and expenses. You must account for your income and expenses in a way that clearly shows your taxable income. The way you do this is called an accounting method.

This section explains which accounting periods and methods you can use.

Accounting Periods

Most individual tax returns cover a calendar year—the 12 months from January 1 through December 31. If you don't use a calendar year, your accounting period is a fiscal year. A regular fiscal year is a 12-month period that ends on the last day of any month except December. A 52-53-week fiscal year varies from 52 to 53 weeks and always ends on the same day of the week.

You choose your accounting period (tax year) when you file your first income tax return. It can't be longer than 12 months.

More information. For more information on accounting periods, including how to change your accounting period, see Pub. 538.

Accounting Methods

Your accounting method is the way you account for your income and expenses. Most taxpayers use either the cash method or an accrual method. You choose a method when you file your first income tax return. If you want to change your accounting method after that, you must generally get IRS approval. Use Form 3115 to request an accounting method change.

Cash method. If you use this method, report all items of income in the year in which you actually or constructively receive them. Generally, you deduct all expenses in the year you actually pay them. This is the method most individual taxpayers use.

Constructive receipt. Generally, you constructively receive income when it is credited to your account or set apart in any way that makes it available to you. You don't need to have physical possession of it. For example, interest credited to your bank account on December 31, 2022, is taxable income to you in 2022 if you could have withdrawn it in 2022 (even if the amount isn't entered in your records or withdrawn until 2023).

Garnished wages. If your employer uses your wages to pay your debts, or if your wages are attached or garnished, the full amount is constructively received by you. You must include these wages in income for the year you would have received them.

Debts paid for you. If another person cancels or pays your debts (but not as a gift or loan), you have constructively received the amount and must generally include it in your gross income for the year. See *Canceled Debts* in chapter 8 for more information.

Payment to third party. If a third party is paid income from property you own, you have constructively received the income. It is the same as if you had actually received the income and paid it to the third party.

Payment to an agent. Income an agent receives for you is income you constructively received in the year the agent receives it. If you indicate in a contract that your income is to be paid to another person, you must include the amount in your gross income when the other person receives it.

Check received or available. A valid check that was made available to you before the end of the tax year is constructively received by you in that year. A check that was "made available to you" includes a check you have already received, but not cashed or deposited. It also includes, for example, your last paycheck of the year that your employer made available for you to pick up at the office before the end of the year. It is constructively received by you in that year whether or not you pick it up before the end of the year or wait to receive it by mail after the end of the year.

No constructive receipt. There may be facts to show that you didn't constructively receive income.

Example. Taxpayer Z, a teacher, agreed to the school board's condition that, in Z's absence, Z would receive only the difference between Z's regular salary and the salary of a substitute teacher hired by the school board. Therefore, Z didn't constructively receive the amount by which Z's salary was reduced to pay the substitute teacher.

Accrual method. If you use an accrual method, you generally report income when you earn it, rather than when you receive it. You generally deduct your expenses when you incur them, rather than when you pay them.

Income paid in advance. An advance payment of income is generally included in gross income in the year you receive it. Your method of accounting doesn't matter as long as the income is available to you. An advance payment may include rent or interest you receive in advance and pay for services you will perform later.

A limited deferral until the next tax year may be allowed for certain advance payments. See Pub. 538 for specific information.

Additional information. For more information on accounting methods, including how to change your accounting method, see Pub. 538.

Social Security Number (SSN)

You must enter your SSN on your return. If you are married, enter the SSNs for both you and your spouse, whether you file jointly or separately.

If you are filing a joint return, include the SSNs in the same order as the names. Use this same order in submitting other forms and documents to the IRS.

 If you, or your spouse if filing jointly, don't have an SSN (or ITIN) issued on or before the due date of your 2022 return (including extensions), you can't claim certain tax benefits on your original or an amended 2022 return.

Once you are issued an SSN, use it to file your tax return. Use your SSN to file your tax return even if your SSN does not authorize employment or if you have been issued an SSN that authorizes employment and you lose your employment authorization. An ITIN will not be issued to you once you have been issued an SSN. If you received your SSN after previously

using an ITIN, stop using your ITIN. Use your SSN instead.

Check that both the name and SSN on your Form 1040 or 1040-SR, W-2, and 1099 agree with your social security card. If they don't, certain deductions and credits on your Form 1040 or 1040-SR may be reduced or disallowed and you may not receive credit for your social security earnings. If your Form W-2 shows an incorrect SSN or name, notify your employer or the form-issuing agent as soon as possible to make sure your earnings are credited to your social security record. If the name or SSN on your social security card is incorrect, call the Social Security Administration (SSA) at 800-772-1213.

Name change. If you changed your name because of marriage, divorce, etc., be sure to report the change to your local SSA office before filing your return. This prevents delays in processing your return and issuing refunds. It also safeguards your future social security benefits.

Dependent's SSN. You must provide the SSN of each dependent you claim, regardless of the dependent's age. This requirement applies to all dependents (not just your children) claimed on your tax return.

Your child must have an SSN valid for employment issued before the due date of your 2022 return (including extensions) to be considered a qualifying child for certain tax benefits on your original or amended 2022 return. See chapter 14.

Exception. If your child was born and died in 2022 and didn't have an SSN, enter "DIED" in column (2) of the *Dependents* section of Form 1040 or 1040-SR and include a copy of the child's birth certificate, death certificate, or hospital records. The document must show that the child was born alive.

No SSN. File Form SS-5, Application for a Social Security Card, with your local SSA office to get an SSN for yourself or your dependent. It usually takes about 2 weeks to get an SSN. If you or your dependent isn't eligible for an SSN, see *Individual taxpayer identification number (ITIN)*, later.

If you are a U.S. citizen or resident alien, you must show proof of age, identity, and citizenship or alien status with your Form SS-5. If you are 12 or older and have never been assigned an SSN, you must appear in person with this proof at an SSA office.

Form SS-5 is available at any SSA office, on the Internet at *SSA.gov/forms/ss-5.pdf*, or by calling 800-772-1213. If you have any questions about which documents you can use as proof of age, identity, or citizenship, contact your SSA office.

If your dependent doesn't have an SSN by the time your return is due, you may want to ask for an extension of time to file, as explained earlier under *When Do I Have To File*.

If you don't provide a required SSN or if you provide an incorrect SSN, your tax may be increased and any refund may be reduced.

Adoption taxpayer identification number (ATIN). If you are in the process of adopting a child who is a U.S. citizen or resident and can't get an SSN for the child until the adoption is final, you can apply for an ATIN to use instead of an SSN.

File Form W-7A, Application for Taxpayer Identification Number for Pending U.S. Adoptions, with the IRS to get an ATIN if all of the following are true.

- You have a child living with you who was placed in your home for legal adoption.

- You can't get the child's existing SSN even though you have made a reasonable attempt to get it from the birth parents, the placement agency, and other persons.

- You can't get an SSN for the child from the SSA because, for example, the adoption isn't final.

- You are eligible to claim the child as a dependent on your tax return.

After the adoption is final, you must apply for an SSN for the child. You can't continue using the ATIN.

See Form W-7A for more information.

Nonresident alien spouse. If your spouse is a nonresident alien, your spouse must have either an SSN or an ITIN if:

- You file a joint return, or

- Your spouse is filing a separate return.

If your spouse isn't eligible for an SSN, see the following discussion on ITINs.

Individual taxpayer identification number (ITIN). The IRS will issue you an ITIN if you are a nonresident or resident alien and you don't have and aren't eligible to get an SSN. This also applies to an alien spouse or dependent. To apply for an ITIN, file Form W-7 with the IRS. It usually takes about 7 weeks to get an ITIN. Enter the ITIN on your tax return wherever an SSN is requested.

Make sure your ITIN hasn't expired. See _Individual taxpayer identification number (ITIN) renewal_, earlier, for more information on expiration and renewal of ITINs. You can also find more information at _IRS.gov/ITIN_.

 If you are applying for an ITIN for yourself, your spouse, or a dependent in order to file your tax return, attach your completed tax return to your Form W-7. See the Form W-7 instructions for how and where to file.

 You can't e-file a return using an ITIN in the calendar year the ITIN is issued; however, you can e-file returns in the following years.

ITIN for tax use only. An ITIN is for federal tax use only. It doesn't entitle you to social security benefits or change your employment or immigration status under U.S. law.

Penalty for not providing social security number. If you don't include your SSN or the SSN of your spouse or dependent as required, you may have to pay a penalty. See the discussion on _Penalties_, later, for more information.

SSN on correspondence. If you write to the IRS about your tax account, be sure to include your SSN (and the name and SSN of your spouse, if you filed a joint return) in your correspondence. Because your SSN is used to identify your account, this helps the IRS respond to your correspondence promptly.

Presidential Election Campaign Fund

This fund helps pay for Presidential election campaigns. The fund also helps pay for pediatric medical research. If you want $3 to go to this fund, check the box. If you are filing a joint return, your spouse can also have $3 go to the fund. If you check the box, your tax or refund won't change.

Computations

The following information may be useful in making the return easier to complete.

Rounding off dollars. You can round off cents to whole dollars on your return and schedules. If you do round to whole dollars, you must round all amounts. To round, drop amounts under 50 cents and increase amounts from 50 to 99 cents to the next dollar. For example, $1.39 becomes $1 and $2.50 becomes $3.

If you have to add two or more amounts to figure the amount to enter on a line, include cents when adding the amounts and round off only the total.

If you are entering amounts that include cents, make sure to include the decimal point. There is no cents column on Form 1040 or 1040-SR.

Equal amounts. If you are asked to enter the smaller or larger of two equal amounts, enter that amount.

Negative amounts. If you file a paper return and you need to enter a negative amount, put the amount in parentheses rather than using a minus sign. To combine positive and negative amounts, add all the positive amounts together and then subtract the negative amounts.

Attachments

Depending on the form you file and the items reported on your return, you may have to complete additional schedules and forms and attach them to your paper return.

 You may be able to file a paperless return using IRS e-file. There's nothing to attach or mail, not even your Forms W-2. See Why Should I File Electronically, _earlier._

Form W-2. Form W-2 is a statement from your employer of wages and other compensation paid to you and taxes withheld from your pay. You should have a Form W-2 from each employer. If you file a paper return, be sure to attach a copy of Form W-2 in the place indicated on your return. For more information, see _Form W-2_ in chapter 4.

Form 1099-R. If you received a Form 1099-R showing federal income tax withheld, and you file a paper return, attach a copy of that form in the place indicated on your return.

Form 1040 or 1040-SR. If you file a paper return, attach any forms and schedules behind Form 1040 or 1040-SR in order of the "Attachment Sequence No." shown in the upper right corner of the form or schedule. Then, arrange all other statements or attachments in the same order as the forms and schedules they relate to and attach them last. Don't attach items unless required to do so.

Third Party Designee

If you want to allow your preparer, a friend, a family member, or any other person you choose to discuss your 2022 tax return with the IRS, check the "Yes" box in the "Third Party Designee" area of your return. Also, enter the designee's name, phone number, and any five digits the designee chooses as his or her personal identification number (PIN).

If you check the "Yes" box, you, and your spouse if filing a joint return, are authorizing the IRS to call the designee to answer any questions that arise during the processing of your return. You are also authorizing the designee to:

- Give information that is missing from your return to the IRS;

- Call the IRS for information about the processing of your return or the status of your refund or payments;

- Receive copies of notices or transcripts related to your return, upon request; and

- Respond to certain IRS notices about math errors, offsets (see _Refunds_, later), and return preparation.

You aren't authorizing the designee to receive any refund check, bind you to anything (including any additional tax liability), or otherwise represent you before the IRS. If you want to expand the designee's authorization, see Pub. 947.

The authorization will automatically end no later than the due date (without any extensions) for filing your 2023 tax return. This is April 15, 2024, for most people.

See your form instructions for more information.

Signatures

You must sign and date your return. If you file a joint return, both you and your spouse must sign the return, even if only one of you had income.

 If you file a joint return, both spouses are generally liable for the tax, and the entire tax liability may be assessed against either spouse. See chapter 2.

Your return isn't considered a valid return unless you sign it in accordance with the requirements in the instructions for your return.

You must handwrite your signature on your return if you file it on paper. Digital, electronic, or typed-font signatures are not valid signatures for Forms 1040 or 1040-SR filed on paper.

If you electronically file your return, you can use an electronic signature to sign your return in accordance with the requirements contained in the instructions for your return.

Failure to sign your return in accordance with these requirements may prevent you from obtaining a refund.

Enter your occupation. If you file a joint return, enter both your occupation and your spouse's occupation.

When someone can sign for you. You can appoint an agent to sign your return if you are:

1. Unable to sign the return because of disease or injury,

2. Absent from the United States for a continuous period of at least 60 days before the due date for filing your return, or

3. Given permission to do so by the IRS office in your area.

Power of attorney. A return signed by an agent in any of these cases must have a power of attorney (POA) attached that authorizes the agent to sign for you. You can use a POA that states that the agent is granted authority to sign the return, or you can use Form 2848. Part I of Form 2848 must state that the agent is granted authority to sign the return.

Court-appointed conservator, guardian, or other fiduciary. If you are a court-appointed conservator, guardian, or other fiduciary for a mentally or physically incompetent individual who has to file a tax return, sign your name for the individual. File Form 56.

Unable to sign. If the taxpayer is mentally competent but physically unable to sign the return or POA, a valid "signature" is defined under state law. It can be anything that clearly indicates the taxpayer's intent to sign. For example, the taxpayer's "X" with the signatures of two witnesses might be considered a valid signature under a state's law.

Spouse unable to sign. If your spouse is unable to sign for any reason, see *Signing a joint return* in chapter 2.

Child's return. If a child has to file a tax return but can't sign the return, the child's parent, guardian, or another legally responsible person must sign the child's name, followed by the words "By (your signature), parent for minor child."

Paid Preparer

Generally, anyone you pay to prepare, assist in preparing, or review your tax return must sign it and fill in the other blanks, including their Preparer Tax Identification Number (PTIN), in the paid preparer's area of your return.

Many preparers are required to *e-file* the tax returns they prepare. They sign these e-filed returns using their tax preparation software. However, you can choose to have your return completed on paper if you prefer. In that case, the paid preparer can sign the paper return manually or use a rubber stamp or mechanical device. The preparer is personally responsible for affixing their signature to the return.

If the preparer is self-employed (that is, not employed by any person or business to prepare the return), the preparer should check the self-employed box in the "Paid Preparer Use Only" space on the return.

The preparer must give you a copy of your return in addition to the copy filed with the IRS.

If you prepare your own return, leave this area blank. If another person prepares your return and doesn't charge you, that person shouldn't sign your return.

If you have questions about whether a preparer must sign your return, contact any IRS office.

Refunds

When you complete your return, you will determine if you paid more income tax than you owed. If so, you can get a refund of the amount you overpaid or you can choose to apply all or part of the overpayment to your next year's (2023) estimated tax.

 If you choose to have a 2022 overpayment applied to your 2023 estimated tax, you can't change your mind and have any of it refunded to you after the due date (without extensions) of your 2022 return.

Follow the Instructions for Form 1040 to complete the entries to claim your refund and/or to apply your overpayment to your 2023 estimated tax.

 If your refund for 2022 is large, you may want to decrease the amount of income tax withheld from your pay in 2023. See chapter 4 for more information.

DIRECT DEPOSIT *Simple. Safe. Secure.* Instead of getting a paper check, you may be able to have your refund deposited directly into your checking or savings account, including an individual retirement arrangement (IRA). Follow the Instructions for Form 1040 to request direct deposit. If the direct deposit can't be done, the IRS will send a check instead.

Don't request a deposit of any part of your refund to an account that isn't in your name. Don't allow your tax preparer to deposit any part of your refund into the preparer's account. The number of direct deposits to a single account or prepaid debit card is limited to three refunds a year. After this limit is exceeded, paper checks will be sent instead. Learn more at *IRS.gov/Individuals/Direct-Deposit-Limits.*

IRA. You can have your refund (or part of it) directly deposited to a traditional IRA, Roth IRA, or SEP-IRA, but not a SIMPLE IRA. You must establish the IRA at a bank or financial institution before you request direct deposit.

TreasuryDirect®. You can request a deposit of your refund to a TreasuryDirect® online account to buy U.S. Treasury marketable securities (if available) and savings bonds. For more information, go to *https://TreasuryDirect.gov.*

Split refunds. If you choose direct deposit, you may be able to split the refund and have it deposited among two or three accounts or buy up to $5,000 in paper or electronic series I savings bonds. Complete Form 8888 and attach it to your return.

Overpayment less than one dollar. If your overpayment is less than one dollar, you won't get a refund unless you ask for it in writing.

Cashing your refund check. Cash your tax refund check soon after you receive it. Checks expire the last business day of the 12th month of issue.

If your check has expired, you can apply to the IRS to have it reissued.

Refund more or less than expected. If you receive a check for a refund you aren't entitled to, or for an overpayment that should have been credited to estimated tax, don't cash the check. Call the IRS.

If you receive a check for more than the refund you claimed, don't cash the check until you receive a notice explaining the difference.

If your refund check is for less than you claimed, it should be accompanied by a notice explaining the difference. Cashing the check doesn't stop you from claiming an additional amount of refund.

If you didn't receive a notice and you have any questions about the amount of your refund, you should wait 2 weeks. If you still haven't received a notice, call the IRS.

Offset against debts. If you are due a refund but haven't paid certain amounts you owe, all or part of your refund may be used to pay all or part of the past-due amount. This includes past-due federal income tax, other federal debts (such as student loans), state income tax, child and spousal support payments, and state unemployment compensation debt. You will be notified if the refund you claimed has been offset against your debts.

Joint return and injured spouse. When a joint return is filed and only one spouse owes a past-due amount, the other spouse can be considered an injured spouse. An injured spouse should file Form 8379, Injured Spouse Allocation, if both of the following apply and the spouse wants a refund of their share of the overpayment shown on the joint return.

1. You aren't legally obligated to pay the past-due amount.

2. You made and reported tax payments (such as federal income tax withheld from your wages or estimated tax payments), or claimed a refundable tax credit (see the credits listed under *Who Should File*, earlier).

Note. If the injured spouse's residence was in a community property state at any time during the tax year, special rules may apply. See the Instructions for Form 8379.

If you haven't filed your joint return and you know that your joint refund will be offset, file Form 8379 with your return. You should receive your refund within 14 weeks from the date the paper return is filed or within 11 weeks from the date the return is filed electronically.

If you filed your joint return and your joint refund was offset, file Form 8379 by itself. When filed after offset, it can take up to 8 weeks to receive your refund. Don't attach the previously filed tax return, but do include copies of all Forms W-2 and W-2G for both spouses and any Forms 1099 that show income tax withheld. The processing of Form 8379 may be delayed if these forms aren't attached, or if the form is incomplete when filed.

A separate Form 8379 must be filed for each tax year to be considered.

 An injured spouse claim is different from an innocent spouse relief request. An injured spouse uses Form 8379 to request the division of the tax overpayment attributed to each spouse. An innocent spouse uses Form 8857, Request for Innocent Spouse Relief, to request relief from joint liability for tax, interest, and penalties on a joint return for items of the other spouse (or former spouse) that were incorrectly reported on the joint return. For information on innocent spouses, see Relief from joint responsibility under Filing a Joint Return in chapter 2.

Amount You Owe

When you complete your return, you will determine if you have paid the full amount of tax that you owe. If you owe additional tax, you should pay it with your return.

 You don't have to pay if the amount you owe is under $1.

If the IRS figures your tax for you, you will receive a bill for any tax that is due. You should pay this bill within 30 days (or by the due date of your return, if later). See *Tax Figured by IRS* in chapter 13.

 If you don't pay your tax when due, you may have to pay a failure-to-pay penalty. See Penalties, later. For more information about your balance due, see Pub. 594.

 If the amount you owe for 2022 is large, you may want to increase the amount of income tax withheld from your pay or make estimated tax payments for 2023. See chapter 4 for more information.

How To Pay

You can pay online, by phone, by mobile device, in cash, or by check or money order. Don't include any estimated tax payment for 2023 in this payment. Instead, make the estimated tax payment separately.

Bad check or payment. The penalty for writing a bad check to the IRS is $25 or 2% of the check, whichever is more. This penalty also applies to other forms of payment if the IRS doesn't receive the funds.

Pay online. Paying online is convenient and secure and helps make sure we get your payments on time.

You can pay online with a direct transfer from your bank account using IRS Direct Pay or the Electronic Federal Tax Payment System (EFTPS), or by debit or credit card.

To pay your taxes online or for more information, go to *IRS.gov/Payments*.

Pay by phone. Paying by phone is another safe and secure method of paying online. Use one of the following methods.

- EFTPS.
- Debit or credit card.

To get more information about EFTPS or to enroll in EFTPS, visit *EFTPS.gov* or call 800-555-4477. To contact EFTPS using Telecommunications Relay Services (TRS) for people who are deaf, hard of hearing, or have a speech disability, dial 711 and then provide the TRS assistant the 800-555-4477 number or 800-733-4829. Additional information about EFTPS is also available in Pub. 966.

To pay using a debit or credit card, you can call one of the following service providers. There is a convenience fee charged by these providers that varies by provider, card type, and payment amount.

> Link2Gov Corporation
> 888-PAY-1040™ (888-729-1040)
> *www.PAY1040.com*
>
> WorldPay US, Inc.
> 844-PAY-TAX-8™ (844-729-8298)
> *www.payUSAtax.com*
>
> ACI Payments, Inc.
> 888-UPAY-TAX™ (888-872-9829)
> *fed.acipayonline.com*

For the latest details on how to pay by phone, go to *IRS.gov/Payments*.

Pay by cash. Cash is an in-person payment option for individuals provided through retail partners with a maximum of $1,000 per day per transaction. To make a cash payment, you must first be registered online at *fed.acipayonline.com*. Don't send cash payments through the mail.

Pay by check or money order. Make your check or money order payable to "United States Treasury" for the full amount due. Don't send cash. Don't attach the payment to your return. Show your correct name, address, SSN, daytime phone number, and the tax year and form number on the front of your check or money order. If you are filing a joint return, enter the SSN shown first on your tax return.

Notice to taxpayers presenting checks. When you provide a check as payment, you authorize us either to use information from your check to make a one-time electronic fund transfer from your account or to process the payment as a check transaction. When we use information from your check to make an electronic fund transfer, funds may be withdrawn from your account as soon as the same day we receive your payment, and you will not receive your check back from your financial institution.

No checks of $100 million or more accepted. The IRS can't accept a single check (including a cashier's check) for amounts of $100,000,000 ($100 million) or more. If you are sending $100 million or more by check, you'll need to spread the payment over two or more checks with each check made out for an amount less than $100 million. This limit doesn't apply to other methods of payment (such as electronic payments). Please consider a method of payment other than check if the amount of the payment is over $100 million.

Estimated tax payments. Don't include any 2023 estimated tax payment in the payment for

your 2022 income tax return. See chapter 4 for information on how to pay estimated tax.

Interest

Interest is charged on tax you don't pay by the due date of your return. Interest is charged even if you get an extension of time for filing.

 If the IRS figures your tax for you, to avoid interest for late payment, you must pay the bill by the date specified on the bill or by the due date of your return, whichever is later. For information, see Tax Figured by IRS in chapter 13.

Interest on penalties. Interest is charged on the failure-to-file penalty, the accuracy-related penalty, and the fraud penalty from the due date of the return (including extensions) to the date of payment. Interest on other penalties starts on the date of notice and demand, but isn't charged on penalties paid within 21 calendar days from the date of the notice (or within 10 business days if the notice is for $100,000 or more).

Interest due to IRS error or delay. All or part of any interest you were charged can be forgiven if the interest is due to an unreasonable error or delay by an officer or employee of the IRS in performing a ministerial or managerial act.

A ministerial act is a procedural or mechanical act that occurs during the processing of your case. A managerial act includes personnel transfers and extended personnel training. A decision concerning the proper application of federal tax law isn't a ministerial or managerial act.

The interest can be forgiven only if you aren't responsible in any important way for the error or delay and the IRS has notified you in writing of the deficiency or payment. For more information, see Pub. 556.

Interest and certain penalties may also be suspended for a limited period if you filed your return by the due date (including extensions) and the IRS doesn't provide you with a notice specifically stating your liability and the basis for it before the close of the 36-month period beginning on the later of:

- The date the return is filed, or
- The due date of the return without regard to extensions.

For more information, see Pub. 556.

Installment Agreement

If you can't pay the full amount due with your return, you can ask to make monthly installment payments for the full or a partial amount. However, you will be charged interest and may be charged a late payment penalty on the tax not paid by the date your return is due, even if your request to pay in installments is granted. If your request is granted, you must also pay a fee. To limit the interest and penalty charges, pay as much of the tax as possible with your return. But before requesting an installment agreement, you should consider other less costly alternatives, such as a bank loan or credit card payment.

To apply for an installment agreement online, go to *IRS.gov/OPA*. You can also use Form 9465.

In addition to paying by check or money order, you can use a credit or debit card or direct payment from your bank account to make installment agreement payments. See *How To Pay*, earlier.

Gift To Reduce Debt Held by the Public

 You can make a contribution (gift) to reduce debt held by the public. If you wish to do so, make a separate check payable to "Bureau of the Fiscal Service."

Send your check to:

Bureau of the Fiscal Service
ATTN: Department G
P.O. Box 2188
Parkersburg, WV 26106-2188

Or enclose your separate check in the envelope with your income tax return. Don't add this gift to any tax you owe.

For information on making this type of gift online, go to *TreasururyDirect.gov/Help-Center/ Public-Debt-FAQs/#DebtFinance* and see the information under "How do you make a contribution to reduce the debt?"

You may be able to deduct this gift as a charitable contribution on next year's tax return if you itemize your deductions on Schedule A (Form 1040).

Name and Address

After you have completed your return, fill in your name and address in the appropriate area of Form 1040 or 1040-SR.

 You must include your SSN in the correct place on your tax return.

P.O. box. If your post office doesn't deliver mail to your street address and you have a P.O. box, enter your P.O. box number on the line for your present home address instead of your street address.

Foreign address. If your address is outside the United States or its possessions or territories, enter the city name on the appropriate line of your Form 1040 or 1040-SR. Don't enter any other information on that line, but also complete the spaces below that line.

1. Foreign country name.
2. Foreign province/state/county.
3. Foreign postal code.

Don't abbreviate the country name. Follow the country's practice for entering the postal code and the name of the province, county, or state.

Where Do I File?

After you complete your return, you must send it to the IRS. You can mail it or you may be able to

file it electronically. See *Why Should I File Electronically*, earlier.

Mailing your paper return. Mail your paper return to the address shown in the Instructions for Form 1040.

What Happens After I File?

After you send your return to the IRS, you may have some questions. This section discusses concerns you may have about recordkeeping, your refund, and what to do if you move.

What Records Should I Keep?

This part discusses why you should keep records, what kinds of records you should keep, and how long you should keep them.

 You must keep records so that you can prepare a complete and accurate income tax return. The law doesn't require any special form of records. However, you should keep all receipts, canceled checks or other proof of payment, and any other records to support any deductions or credits you claim.

If you file a claim for refund, you must be able to prove by your records that you have overpaid your tax.

This part doesn't discuss the records you should keep when operating a business. For information on business records, see Pub. 583.

Why Keep Records?

Good records help you:

- **Identify sources of income.** Your records can identify the sources of your income to help you separate business from nonbusiness income and taxable from nontaxable income.
- **Keep track of expenses.** You can use your records to identify expenses for which you can claim a deduction. This helps you determine if you can itemize deductions on your tax return.
- **Keep track of the basis of property.** You need to keep records that show the basis of your property. This includes the original cost or other basis of the property and any improvements you made.
- **Prepare tax returns.** You need records to prepare your tax return.
- **Support items reported on tax returns.** The IRS may question an item on your return. Your records will help you explain any item and arrive at the correct tax. If you can't produce the correct documents, you may have to pay additional tax and be subject to penalties.

Kinds of Records To Keep

The IRS doesn't require you to keep your records in a particular way. Keep them in a manner that allows you and the IRS to determine your correct tax.

You can use your checkbook to keep a record of your income and expenses. You also need to keep documents, such as receipts and sales slips, that can help prove a deduction.

In this section, you will find guidance about basic records that everyone should keep. The section also provides guidance about specific records you should keep for certain items.

Electronic records. All requirements that apply to hard copy books and records also apply to electronic storage systems that maintain tax books and records. When you replace hard copy books and records, you must maintain the electronic storage systems for as long as they are material to the administration of tax law.

For details on electronic storage system requirements, see Revenue Procedure 97-22, which is on page 9 of Internal Revenue Bulletin 1997-13 at *IRS.gov/pub/irs-irbs/irb97-13.pdf*.

Copies of tax returns. You should keep copies of your tax returns as part of your tax records. They can help you prepare future tax returns, and you will need them if you file an amended return or are audited. Copies of your returns and other records can be helpful to your survivor or the executor or administrator of your estate.

If necessary, you can request a copy of a return and all attachments (including Form W-2) from the IRS by using Form 4506. There is a charge for a copy of a return. For information on the cost and where to file, see the Instructions for Form 4506.

If you just need information from your return, you can order a transcript in one of the following ways.

- Go to *IRS.gov/Transcript*.
- Call 800-908-9946.
- Use Form 4506-T or Form 4506T-EZ.

There is no fee for a transcript. For more information, see Form 4506-T.

Basic Records

Basic records are documents that everybody should keep. These are the records that prove your income and expenses. If you own a home or investments, your basic records should contain documents related to those items.

Income. Your basic records prove the amounts you report as income on your tax return. Your income may include wages, dividends, interest, and partnership or S corporation distributions. Your records can also prove that certain amounts aren't taxable, such as tax-exempt interest.

Note. If you receive a Form W-2, keep Copy C until you begin receiving social security benefits. This will help protect your benefits in case there is a question about your work record or earnings in a particular year.

Expenses. Your basic records prove the expenses for which you claim a deduction (or credit) on your tax return. Your deductions may include alimony, charitable contributions, mortgage interest, and real estate taxes. You may also have childcare expenses for which you can claim a credit.

Home. Your basic records should enable you to determine the basis or adjusted basis of your home. You need this information to determine if you have a gain or loss when you sell your home or to figure depreciation if you use part of your home for business purposes or for rent. Your records should show the purchase price, settlement or closing costs, and the cost of any improvements. They may also show any casualty losses deducted and insurance reimbursements for casualty losses.

For detailed information on basis, including which settlement or closing costs are included in the basis of your home, see Pub. 551.

When you sell your home, your records should show the sales price and any selling expenses, such as commissions. For information on selling your home, see Pub. 523.

Investments. Your basic records should enable you to determine your basis in an investment and whether you have a gain or loss when you sell it. Investments include stocks, bonds, and mutual funds. Your records should show the purchase price, sales price, and commissions. They may also show any reinvested dividends, stock splits and dividends, load charges, and original issue discount (OID).

For information on stocks, bonds, and mutual funds, see Pub. 550 and Pub. 551.

Proof of Payment

One of your basic records is proof of payment. You should keep these records to support certain amounts shown on your tax return. Proof of payment alone isn't proof that the item claimed on your return is allowable. You should also keep other documents that will help prove that the item is allowable.

Generally, you prove payment with a cash receipt, financial account statement, credit card statement, canceled check, or substitute check. If you make payments in cash, you should get a dated and signed receipt showing the amount and the reason for the payment.

If you make payments using your bank account, you may be able to prove payment with an account statement.

Account statements. You may be able to prove payment with a legible financial account statement prepared by your bank or other financial institution.

Pay statements. You may have deductible expenses withheld from your paycheck, such as medical insurance premiums. You should keep your year-end or final pay statements as proof of payment of these expenses.

How Long To Keep Records

You must keep your records as long as they may be needed for the administration of any provision of the Internal Revenue Code. Generally, this means you must keep records that support items shown on your return until the period of limitations for that return runs out. The period of limitations is the period of time in which you can amend your return to claim a credit or refund or the IRS can assess additional tax. Table 1-7 contains the periods of limitations that apply to income tax returns. Unless otherwise stated, the years refer to the period beginning after the return was filed. Returns filed before the due date are treated as being filed on the due date.

Table 1-7. **Period of Limitations**

IF you...	THEN the period is...
1 File a return and (2), (3), and (4) don't apply to you,	3 years.
2 Don't report income that you should and it is more than 25% of the gross income shown on your return,	6 years.
3 File a fraudulent return,	No limit.
4 Don't file a return,	No limit.
5 File a claim for credit or refund after you filed your return,	The later of 3 years or 2 years after tax was paid.
6 File a claim for a loss from worthless securities or bad debt deduction,	7 years.

Property. Keep records relating to property until the period of limitations expires for the year in which you dispose of the property in a taxable disposition. You must keep these records to figure your basis for computing gain or loss when you sell or otherwise dispose of the property.

Generally, if you received property in a nontaxable exchange, your basis in that property is the same as the basis of the property you gave up. You must keep the records on the old property, as well as the new property, until the period of limitations expires for the year in which you dispose of the new property in a taxable disposition.

Refund Information

You can go online to check the status of your 2022 refund 24 hours after the IRS receives your e-filed return, or 4 weeks after you mail a paper return. If you filed Form 8379 with your return, allow 14 weeks (11 weeks if you filed electronically) before checking your refund status. Be sure to have a copy of your 2022 tax return handy because you will need to know the filing status, the first SSN shown on the return, and the exact whole-dollar amount of the refund. To check on your refund, do one of the following.

- Go to IRS.gov/Refunds.

- Download the free IRS2Go app to your smart phone and use it to check your refund status.

- Call the automated refund hotline at 800-829-1954.

Interest on Refunds

If you are due a refund, you may get interest on it. The interest rates are adjusted quarterly.

If the refund is made within 45 days after the due date of your return, no interest will be paid. If you file your return after the due date (including extensions), no interest will be paid if the refund is made within 45 days after the date you filed. If the refund isn't made within this 45-day period, interest will be paid from the due date of the return or from the date you filed, whichever is later.

Accepting a refund check doesn't change your right to claim an additional refund and interest. File your claim within the period of time that applies. See _Amended Returns and Claims for Refund_, later. If you don't accept a refund check, no more interest will be paid on the overpayment included in the check.

Interest on erroneous refund. All or part of any interest you were charged on an erroneous refund will generally be forgiven. Any interest charged for the period before demand for repayment was made will be forgiven unless:

1. You, or a person related to you, caused the erroneous refund in any way; or

2. The refund is more than $50,000.

For example, if you claimed a refund of $100 on your return, but the IRS made an error and sent you $1,000, you wouldn't be charged interest for the time you held the $900 difference. You must, however, repay the $900 when the IRS asks.

Change of Address

If you have moved, file your return using your new address.

If you move after you filed your return, you should give the IRS clear and concise notification of your change of address. The notification may be written, electronic, or oral. Send written notification to the Internal Revenue Service Center serving your old address. You can use Form 8822, Change of Address. If you are expecting a refund, also notify the post office serving your old address. This will help in forwarding your check to your new address (unless you chose direct deposit of your refund). For more information, see Revenue Procedure 2010-16, 2010-19 I.R.B. 664, available at _IRS.gov/irb/2010-19_IRB/ar07.html_.

Be sure to include your SSN (and the name and SSN of your spouse if you filed a joint return) in any correspondence with the IRS.

What if I Made a Mistake?

Errors may delay your refund or result in notices being sent to you. If you discover an error, you can file an amended return or claim for refund.

Amended Returns and Claims for Refund

You should correct your return if, after you have filed it, you find that:

1. You didn't report some income,

2. You claimed deductions or credits you shouldn't have claimed,

3. You didn't claim deductions or credits you could have claimed, or

4. You should have claimed a different filing status. (Once you file a joint return, you can't choose to file separate returns for that year after the due date of the return. However, an executor may be able to make this change for a deceased spouse.)

If you need a copy of your return, see *Copies of tax returns* under *Kinds of Records To Keep*, earlier, in this chapter.

Form 1040-X. Use Form 1040-X to correct a return you have already filed.

Completing Form 1040-X. On Form 1040-X, enter your income, deductions, and credits as you originally reported them on your return; the changes you are making; and the corrected amounts. Then, figure the tax on the corrected amount of taxable income and the amount you owe or your refund.

If you owe tax, the IRS offers several payment options. See *How To Pay*, earlier. The tax owed won't be subtracted from any amount you had credited to your estimated tax.

If you can't pay the full amount due with your return, you can ask to make monthly installment payments. See *Installment Agreement*, earlier.

If you overpaid tax, you can have all or part of the overpayment refunded to you, or you can apply all or part of it to your estimated tax. If you choose to get a refund, it will be sent separately from any refund shown on your original return.

Filing Form 1040-X. When completing Form 1040-X, don't forget to show the year of your original return and explain all changes you made. Be sure to attach any forms or schedules needed to explain your changes. Mail your Form 1040-X to the Internal Revenue Service Center serving the area where you now live (as shown in the Instructions for Form 1040-X). However, if you are filing Form 1040-X in response to a notice you received from the IRS, mail it to the address shown on the notice.

File a separate form for each tax year involved.

You can file Form 1040-X electronically to amend 2019 or later Forms 1040 and 1040-SR. For more information, see Instructions for Form 1040-X.

Time for filing a claim for refund. Generally, you must file your claim for a credit or refund within 3 years after the date you filed your original return or within 2 years after the date you paid the tax, whichever is later. Returns filed before the due date (without regard to extensions) are considered filed on the due date (even if the due date was a Saturday, Sunday, or legal holiday). These time periods are suspended while you are financially disabled, discussed later.

If the last day for claiming a credit or refund is a Saturday, Sunday, or legal holiday, you can file the claim on the next business day.

If you don't file a claim within this period, you may not be entitled to a credit or a refund.

Federally declared disaster. If you were affected by a federally declared disaster, you may have additional time to file your amended return. See Pub. 556 for details.

Protective claim for refund. Generally, a protective claim is a formal claim or amended return for credit or refund normally based on current litigation or expected changes in tax law or other legislation. You file a protective claim when your right to a refund is contingent on future events and may not be determinable until after the statute of limitations expires. A valid protective claim doesn't have to list a particular dollar amount or demand an immediate refund. However, a valid protective claim must:

- Be in writing and signed;

- Include your name, address, SSN or ITIN, and other contact information;

- Identify and describe the contingencies affecting the claim;

- Clearly alert the IRS to the essential nature of the claim; and

- Identify the specific year(s) for which a refund is sought.

Mail your protective claim for refund to the address listed in the Instructions for Form 1040-X under *Where To File*.

Generally, the IRS will delay action on the protective claim until the contingency is resolved.

Limit on amount of refund. If you file your claim within 3 years after the date you filed your return, the credit or refund can't be more than the part of the tax paid within the 3-year period (plus any extension of time for filing your return) immediately before you filed the claim. This time period is suspended while you are financially disabled, discussed later.

Tax paid. Payments, including estimated tax payments, made before the due date (without regard to extensions) of the original return are considered paid on the due date. For example, income tax withheld during the year is considered paid on the due date of the return, which is April 15 for most taxpayers.

Example 1. You made estimated tax payments of $500 and got an automatic extension of time to October 15, 2019, to file your 2018 income tax return. When you filed your return on that date, you paid an additional $200 tax. On October 15, 2022, you filed an amended return and claimed a refund of $700. Because you filed your claim within 3 years after you filed your original return, you can get a refund of up to $700, the tax paid within the 3 years plus the 6-month extension period immediately before you filed the claim.

Example 2. The situation is the same as in *Example 1*, except you filed your return on October 30, 2019, 2 weeks after the extension period ended. You paid an additional $200 on that date. On October 31, 2022, you filed an amended return and claimed a refund of $700. Although you filed your claim within 3 years from the date you filed your original return, the refund was limited to $200, the tax paid within the 3 years plus the 6-month extension period immediately before you filed the claim. The estimated

tax of $500 paid before that period can't be refunded or credited.

If you file a claim more than 3 years after you file your return, the credit or refund can't be more than the tax you paid within the 2 years immediately before you file the claim.

Example. You filed your 2018 tax return on April 15, 2019. You paid taxes of $500. On November 5, 2020, after an examination of your 2018 return, you had to pay an additional tax of $200. On May 12, 2022, you file a claim for a refund of $300. However, because you filed your claim more than 3 years after you filed your return, your refund will be limited to the $200 you paid during the 2 years immediately before you filed your claim.

Financially disabled. The time periods for claiming a refund are suspended for the period in which you are financially disabled. For a joint income tax return, only one spouse has to be financially disabled for the time period to be suspended. You are financially disabled if you are unable to manage your financial affairs because of a medically determinable physical or mental impairment that can be expected to result in death or that has lasted or can be expected to last for a continuous period of not less than 12 months. However, you aren't treated as financially disabled during any period your spouse or any other person is authorized to act on your behalf in financial matters.

To claim that you are financially disabled, you must send in the following written statements with your claim for refund.

1. A statement from your qualified physician that includes:

    a. The name and a description of your physical or mental impairment;

    b. The physician's medical opinion that the impairment prevented you from managing your financial affairs;

    c. The physician's medical opinion that the impairment was or can be expected to result in death, or that its duration has lasted, or can be expected to last, at least 12 months;

    d. The specific time period (to the best of the physician's knowledge); and

    e. The following certification signed by the physician: "I hereby certify that, to the best of my knowledge and belief, the above representations are true, correct, and complete."

2. A statement made by the person signing the claim for credit or refund that no person, including your spouse, was authorized to act on your behalf in financial matters during the period of disability (or the exact dates that a person was authorized to act for you).

Exceptions for special types of refunds. If you file a claim for one of the items in the following list, the dates and limits discussed earlier may not apply. These items, and where to get more information, are as follows.

- Bad debt. See Pub. 550.

- Worthless security. See Pub. 550.
- Foreign tax paid or accrued. See Pub. 514.
- Net operating loss carryback. See Pub. 536.
- Carryback of certain business tax credits. See Form 3800.
- Claim based on an agreement with the IRS extending the period for assessment of tax

Processing claims for refund. Claims are usually processed 8–12 weeks after they are filed. Your claim may be accepted as filed, disallowed, or subject to examination. If a claim is examined, the procedures are the same as in the examination of a tax return.

If your claim is disallowed, you will receive an explanation of why it was disallowed.

Taking your claim to court. You can sue for a refund in court, but you must first file a timely claim with the IRS. If the IRS disallows your claim or doesn't act on your claim within 6 months after you file it, you can then take your claim to court. For information on the burden of proof in a court proceeding, see Pub. 556.

The IRS provides a direct method to move your claim to court if:

- You are filing a claim for a credit or refund based solely on contested income tax or on estate tax or gift tax issues considered in your previously examined returns, and
- You want to take your case to court instead of appealing it within the IRS.

When you file your claim with the IRS, you get the direct method by requesting in writing that your claim be immediately rejected. A notice of claim disallowance will be sent to you.

You have 2 years from the date of mailing of the notice of claim disallowance to file a refund suit in the U.S. District Court having jurisdiction or in the U.S. Court of Federal Claims.

Interest on refund. If you receive a refund because of your amended return, interest will be paid on it from the due date of your original return or the date you filed your original return, whichever is later, to the date you filed the amended return. However, if the refund isn't made within 45 days after you file the amended return, interest will be paid up to the date the refund is paid.

Reduced refund. Your refund may be reduced by an additional tax liability that has been assessed against you.

Also, your refund may be reduced by amounts you owe for past-due federal tax, state income tax, state unemployment compensation debts, child support, spousal support, or certain other federal nontax debts, such as student loans. If your spouse owes these debts, see *Offset against debts* under *Refunds*, earlier, for the correct refund procedures to follow.

Effect on state tax liability. If your return is changed for any reason, it may affect your state income tax liability. This includes changes made as a result of an examination of your return by the IRS. Contact your state tax agency for more information.

Penalties

The law provides penalties for failure to file returns or pay taxes as required.

Civil Penalties

If you don't file your return and pay your tax by the due date, you may have to pay a penalty. You may also have to pay a penalty if you substantially understate your tax, understate a reportable transaction, file an erroneous claim for refund or credit, file a frivolous tax submission, or fail to supply your SSN or ITIN. If you provide fraudulent information on your return, you may have to pay a civil fraud penalty.

Filing late. If you don't file your return by the due date (including extensions), you may have to pay a failure-to-file penalty. The penalty is usually 5% for each month or part of a month that a return is late, but not more than 25%. The penalty is based on the tax not paid by the due date (without regard to extensions).

Fraud. If your failure to file is due to fraud, the penalty is 15% for each month or part of a month that your return is late, up to a maximum of 75%.

Return over 60 days late. If you file your return more than 60 days after the due date, or extended due date, the minimum penalty is the smaller of $450 or 100% of the unpaid tax.

Exception. You won't have to pay the penalty if you show that you failed to file on time because of reasonable cause and not because of willful neglect.

Paying tax late. You will have to pay a failure-to-pay penalty of 1/2 of 1% (0.50%) of your unpaid taxes for each month, or part of a month, after the due date that the tax isn't paid. This penalty doesn't apply during the automatic 6-month extension of time to file period if you paid at least 90% of your actual tax liability on or before the due date of your return and pay the balance when you file the return.

The monthly rate of the failure-to-pay penalty is half the usual rate (0.25% instead of 0.50%) if an installment agreement is in effect for that month. You must have filed your return by the due date (including extensions) to qualify for this reduced penalty.

If a notice of intent to levy is issued, the rate will increase to 1% at the start of the first month beginning at least 10 days after the day that the notice is issued. If a notice and demand for immediate payment is issued, the rate will increase to 1% at the start of the first month beginning after the day that the notice and demand is issued.

This penalty can't be more than 25% of your unpaid tax. You won't have to pay the penalty if you can show that you had a good reason for not paying your tax on time.

Combined penalties. If both the failure-to-file penalty and the failure-to-pay penalty (discussed earlier) apply in any month, the 5% (or 15%) failure-to-file penalty is reduced by the failure-to-pay penalty. However, if you file your return more than 60 days after the due date or extended due date, the minimum penalty is the smaller of $450 or 100% of the unpaid tax.

Accuracy-related penalty. You may have to pay an accuracy-related penalty if you underpay your tax because:

1. You show negligence or disregard of the rules or regulations,
2. You substantially understate your income tax,
3. You claim tax benefits for a transaction that lacks economic substance, or
4. You fail to disclose a foreign financial asset.

The penalty is equal to 20% of the underpayment. The penalty is 40% of any portion of the underpayment that is attributable to an undisclosed noneconomic substance transaction or an undisclosed foreign financial asset transaction. The penalty won't be figured on any part of an underpayment on which the fraud penalty (discussed later) is charged.

Negligence or disregard. The term "negligence" includes a failure to make a reasonable attempt to comply with the tax law or to exercise ordinary and reasonable care in preparing a return. Negligence also includes failure to keep adequate books and records. You won't have to pay a negligence penalty if you have a reasonable basis for a position you took.

The term "disregard" includes any careless, reckless, or intentional disregard.

Adequate disclosure. You can avoid the penalty for disregard of rules or regulations if you adequately disclose on your return a position that has at least a reasonable basis. See *Disclosure statement*, later.

This exception won't apply to an item that is attributable to a tax shelter. In addition, it won't apply if you fail to keep adequate books and records, or substantiate items properly.

Substantial understatement of income tax. You understate your tax if the tax shown on your return is less than the correct tax. The understatement is substantial if it is more than the larger of 10% of the correct tax or $5,000. However, the amount of the understatement may be reduced to the extent the understatement is due to:

1. Substantial authority, or
2. Adequate disclosure and a reasonable basis.

If an item on your return is attributable to a tax shelter, there is no reduction for an adequate disclosure. However, there is a reduction for a position with substantial authority, but only if you reasonably believed that your tax treatment was more likely than not the proper treatment.

Substantial authority. Whether there is or was substantial authority for the tax treatment of an item depends on the facts and circumstances. Some of the items that may be considered are court opinions, Treasury regulations, revenue rulings, revenue procedures, and notices and announcements issued by the IRS and published in the Internal Revenue Bulletin that involve the same or similar circumstances as yours.

Disclosure statement. To adequately disclose the relevant facts about your tax treatment of an item, use Form 8275. You must also have a reasonable basis for treating the item the way you did.

In cases of substantial understatement only, items that meet the requirements of Revenue Procedure 2021-52 (or later update) are considered adequately disclosed on your return without filing Form 8275.

Use Form 8275-R to disclose items or positions contrary to regulations.

Transaction lacking economic substance. For more information on economic substance, see section 7701(o).

Foreign financial asset. For more information on undisclosed foreign financial assets, see section 6662(j).

Reasonable cause. You won't have to pay a penalty if you have a good reason (reasonable cause) for the way you treated an item. You must also show that you acted in good faith. This doesn't apply to a transaction that lacks economic substance.

Filing erroneous claim for refund or credit. You may have to pay a penalty if you file an erroneous claim for refund or credit. The penalty is equal to 20% of the disallowed amount of the claim, unless you can show a reasonable basis for the way you treated an item. However, any disallowed amount due to a transaction that lacks economic substance won't be treated as having a reasonable basis. The penalty won't be figured on any part of the disallowed amount of the claim that relates to the earned income credit or on which the accuracy-related or fraud penalties are charged.

Frivolous tax submission. You may have to pay a penalty of $5,000 if you file a frivolous tax return or other frivolous submissions. A frivolous tax return is one that doesn't include enough information to figure the correct tax or that contains information clearly showing that the tax you reported is substantially incorrect. For more information on frivolous returns, frivolous submissions, and a list of positions that are identified as frivolous, see Notice 2010-33, 2010-17 I.R.B. 609, available at *IRS.gov/irb/2010-17_IRB/ar13.html*.

You will have to pay the penalty if you filed this kind of return or submission based on a frivolous position or a desire to delay or interfere with the administration of federal tax laws. This includes altering or striking out the preprinted language above the space provided for your signature.

This penalty is added to any other penalty provided by law.

Fraud. If there is any underpayment of tax on your return due to fraud, a penalty of 75% of the underpayment due to fraud will be added to your tax.

Joint return. The fraud penalty on a joint return doesn't apply to a spouse unless some part of the underpayment is due to the fraud of that spouse.

Failure to supply SSN. If you don't include your SSN or the SSN of another person where required on a return, statement, or other document, you will be subject to a penalty of $50 for each failure. You will also be subject to a penalty of $50 if you don't give your SSN to another person when it is required on a return, statement, or other document.

For example, if you have a bank account that earns interest, you must give your SSN to the bank. The number must be shown on the Form 1099-INT or other statement the bank sends you. If you don't give the bank your SSN, you will be subject to the $50 penalty. (You may also be subject to "backup" withholding of income tax. See chapter 4.)

You won't have to pay the penalty if you are able to show that the failure was due to reasonable cause and not willful neglect.

Criminal Penalties

You may be subject to criminal prosecution (brought to trial) for actions such as:

1. Tax evasion;

2. Willful failure to file a return, supply information, or pay any tax due;

3. Fraud and false statements;

4. Preparing and filing a fraudulent return; or

5. Identity theft.

Identity Theft

Identity theft occurs when someone uses your personal information such as your name, SSN, or other identifying information, without your permission, to commit fraud or other crimes. An identity thief may use your SSN to get a job or may file a tax return using your SSN to receive a refund.

To reduce your risk:

• Protect your SSN,

• Ensure your employer is protecting your SSN, and

• Be careful when choosing a tax preparer.

If your tax records are affected by identity theft and you receive a notice from the IRS, respond right away to the name and phone number printed on the IRS notice or letter.

If your SSN has been lost or stolen or you suspect you are a victim of tax-related identity theft, visit *IRS.gov/IdentityTheft* to learn what steps you should take.

For more information, see Pub. 5027.

 All taxpayers are now eligible for an Identity Protection Personal Identification Number (IP PIN). For more information, see Pub. 5477. To apply for an IP PIN, go to IRS.gov/IPPIN and use the Get an IP PIN tool.

Victims of identity theft who are experiencing economic harm or a systemic problem, or are seeking help in resolving tax problems that have not been resolved through normal channels, may be eligible for Taxpayer Advocate Service (TAS) assistance. You can reach TAS by calling the National Taxpayer Advocate helpline at 877-777-4778 or 800-829-4059 (TTY/TDD). Deaf or hard-of-hearing individuals can also contact the IRS through the Telecommunications Relay Services (TRS) at *FCC.gov/TRS*.

Protect yourself from suspicious emails or phishing schemes. Phishing is the creation and use of email and websites designed to mimic legitimate business emails and websites. The most common form is the act of sending an email to a user falsely claiming to be an established legitimate enterprise in an attempt to scam the user into surrendering private information that will be used for identity theft.

The IRS doesn't initiate contacts with taxpayers via emails. Also, the IRS doesn't request detailed personal information through email or ask taxpayers for the PIN numbers, passwords, or similar secret access information for their credit card, bank, or other financial accounts.

If you receive an unsolicited email claiming to be from the IRS, forward the message to *phishing@irs.gov*. You may also report misuse of the IRS name, logo, forms, or other IRS property to the Treasury Inspector General for Tax Administration toll free at 800-366-4484. You can forward suspicious emails to the Federal Trade Commission (FTC) at *spam@uce.gov* or report them at *ftc.gov/complaint*. You can contact them at *ftc.gov/idtheft* or 877-IDTHEFT (877-438-4338). If you have been a victim of identity theft, see *IdentityTheft.gov* or Pub. 5027. People who are deaf, hard of hearing, or have a speech disability and who have access to TTY/TDD equipment can call 866-653-4261.

Go to *IRS.gov/IDProtection* to learn more about identity theft and how to reduce your risk.

2.

Filing Status

Introduction

This chapter helps you determine which filing status to use. There are five filing statuses.

• Single.

• Married Filing Jointly.

• Married Filing Separately.

• Head of Household.

• Qualifying Surviving Spouse.

 If more than one filing status applies to you, choose the one that will give you the lowest tax.

You must determine your filing status before you can determine whether you must file a tax return (chapter 1), your standard deduction (chapter 10), and your tax (chapter 11). You also use your filing status to determine whether you are eligible to claim certain deductions and credits.

Useful Items

You may want to see:

Publication

❑ **501** Dependents, Standard Deduction, and Filing Information

❑ **503** Child and Dependent Care Expenses

❑ **519** U.S. Tax Guide for Aliens

❑ **555** Community Property

❑ **559** Survivors, Executors, and Administrators

❑ **596** Earned Income Credit (EIC)

❑ **925** Passive Activity and At-Risk Rules

For these and other useful items, go to *IRS.gov/Forms*.

Marital Status

In general, your filing status depends on whether you are considered unmarried or married.

Unmarried persons. You are considered unmarried for the whole year if, on the last day of your tax year, you are either:

- Unmarried, or
- Legally separated from your spouse under a divorce or separate maintenance decree.

State law governs whether you are married or legally separated under a divorce or separate maintenance decree.

Divorced persons. If you are divorced under a final decree by the last day of the year, you are considered unmarried for the whole year.

Divorce and remarriage. If you obtain a divorce for the sole purpose of filing tax returns as unmarried individuals, and at the time of divorce you intend to and do, in fact, remarry each other in the next tax year, you and your spouse must file as married individuals in both years.

Annulled marriages. If you obtain a court decree of annulment, which holds that no valid marriage ever existed, you are considered unmarried even if you filed joint returns for earlier years. File Form 1040-X, Amended U.S. Individual Income Tax Return, claiming single or head of household status for all tax years that are affected by the annulment and not closed by the statute of limitations for filing a tax return. Generally, for a credit or refund, you must file Form 1040-X within 3 years (including extensions) after the date you filed your original return or within 2 years after the date you paid the tax, whichever is later. If you filed your original return early (for example, March 1), your return is considered filed on the due date (generally April 15). However, if you had an extension to file (for example, until October 15) but you filed earlier and we received it on July 1, your return is considered filed on July 1.

Head of household or qualifying surviving spouse. If you are considered unmarried, you may be able to file as head of household or as qualifying surviving spouse. See *Head of Household* and *Qualifying Surviving Spouse*, later, to see if you qualify.

Married persons. If you are considered married, you and your spouse can file a joint return or separate returns.

Considered married. You are considered married for the whole year if, on the last day of your tax year, you and your spouse meet any one of the following tests.

1. You are married and living together.

2. You are living together in a common law marriage recognized in the state where you now live or in the state where the common law marriage began.

3. You are married and living apart, but not legally separated under a decree of divorce or separate maintenance.

4. You are separated under an interlocutory (not final) decree of divorce.

Spouse died during the year. If your spouse died during the year, you are considered married for the whole year for filing status purposes.

If you didn't remarry before the end of the tax year, you can file a joint return for yourself and your deceased spouse. For the next 2 years, you may be entitled to the special benefits described later under *Qualifying Surviving Spouse*.

If you remarried before the end of the tax year, you can file a joint return with your new spouse. Your deceased spouse's filing status is married filing separately for that year.

Married persons living apart. If you live apart from your spouse and meet certain tests, you may be able to file as head of household even if you aren't divorced or legally separated. If you qualify to file as head of household instead of married filing separately, your standard deduction will be higher. Also, your tax may be lower, and you may be able to claim the earned income credit. See *Head of Household*, later.

Single

Your filing status is single if you are considered unmarried and you don't qualify for another filing status. To determine your marital status, see *Marital Status*, earlier.

Spouse died before January 1, 2022. Your filing status may be single if your spouse died before January 1, 2022, and you didn't remarry before the end of 2022. You may, however, be able to use another filing status that will give you a lower tax. See *Head of Household* and *Qualifying Surviving Spouse*, later, to see if you qualify.

How to file. On Form 1040 or 1040-SR, show your filing status as single by checking the "Single" box on the *Filing Status* line at the top of the form. Use the *Single* column of the Tax Table, or Section A of the Tax Computation Worksheet, to figure your tax.

Married Filing Jointly

You can choose married filing jointly as your filing status if you are considered married and both you and your spouse agree to file a joint return. On a joint return, you and your spouse report your combined income and deduct your combined allowable expenses. You can file a joint return even if one of you had no income or deductions.

If you and your spouse decide to file a joint return, your tax may be lower than your combined tax for the other filing statuses. Also, your standard deduction (if you don't itemize deductions) may be higher, and you may qualify for tax benefits that don't apply to other filing statuses.

How to file. On Form 1040 or 1040-SR, show your filing status as married filing jointly by checking the "Married filing jointly" box on the *Filing Status* line at the top of the form. Use the *Married filing jointly* column of the Tax Table, or Section B of the Tax Computation Worksheet, to figure your tax.

 If you and your spouse each have income, you may want to figure your tax both on a joint return and on separate returns (using the filing status of married filing separately). You can choose the method that gives the two of you the lower combined tax unless you are required to file separately.

Spouse died. If your spouse died during the year, you are considered married for the whole year and can choose married filing jointly as your filing status. See *Spouse died during the year*, under *Married persons*, earlier, for more information.

If your spouse died in 2023 before filing a 2022 return, you can choose married filing jointly as your filing status on your 2022 return.

Divorced persons. If you are divorced under a final decree by the last day of the year, you are considered unmarried for the whole year and you can't choose married filing jointly as your filing status.

Filing a Joint Return

Both you and your spouse must include all of your income and deductions on your joint return.

Accounting period. Both of you must use the same accounting period, but you can use different accounting methods. See *Accounting Periods* and *Accounting Methods* in chapter 1.

Joint responsibility. Both of you may be held responsible, jointly and individually, for the tax and any interest or penalty due on your joint return. This means that if one spouse doesn't pay the tax due, the other may have to. Or, if one spouse doesn't report the correct tax, both spouses may be responsible for any additional taxes assessed by the IRS. One spouse may be held responsible for all the tax due even if all the income was earned by the other spouse.

You may want to file separately if:

- You believe your spouse isn't reporting all of their income, or
- You don't want to be responsible for any taxes due if your spouse doesn't have enough tax withheld or doesn't pay enough estimated tax.

Divorced taxpayer. You may be held jointly and individually responsible for any tax, interest, and penalties due on a joint return filed before your divorce. This responsibility may apply even if your divorce decree states that your former spouse will be responsible for any amounts due on previously filed joint returns.

Relief from joint responsibility. In some cases, one spouse may be relieved of joint responsibility for tax, interest, and penalties on a joint return for items of the other spouse that were incorrectly reported on the joint return. You can ask for relief no matter how small the liability.

There are three types of relief available.

1. Innocent spouse relief.

2. Separation of liability (available only to joint filers whose spouse has died, or who are divorced, legally separated, or haven't lived together for the 12 months ending on the date the election for this relief is filed).

3. Equitable relief.

You must file Form 8857, Request for Innocent Spouse Relief, to request relief from joint responsibility. Pub. 971, Innocent Spouse Relief, explains these kinds of relief and who may qualify for them.

Signing a joint return. For a return to be considered a joint return, both spouses must generally sign the return.

Spouse died before signing. If your spouse died before signing the return, the executor or administrator must sign the return for your spouse. If neither you nor anyone else has yet been appointed as executor or administrator, you can sign the return for your spouse and enter "Filing as surviving spouse" in the area where you sign the return.

Spouse away from home. If your spouse is away from home, you should prepare the return, sign it, and send it to your spouse to sign so that it can be filed on time.

Injury or disease prevents signing. If your spouse can't sign because of disease or injury and tells you to sign for them, you can sign your spouse's name in the proper space on the return followed by the words "By (your name), Spouse." Be sure to sign in the space provided for your signature. Attach a dated statement, signed by you, to the return. The statement should include the form number of the return you are filing, the tax year, and the reason your spouse can't sign; it should also state that your spouse has agreed to your signing for them.

Signing as guardian of spouse. If you are the guardian of your spouse who is mentally incompetent, you can sign the return for your spouse as guardian.

Spouse in combat zone. You can sign a joint return for your spouse if your spouse can't sign because they are serving in a combat zone (such as the Persian Gulf Area, Serbia, Montenegro, Albania, or Afghanistan), even if you don't have a power of attorney or other statement. Attach a signed statement to your return explaining that your spouse is serving in a combat zone. For more information on special tax rules for persons who are serving in a combat zone, or who are in missing status as a result of serving in a combat zone, see Pub. 3, Armed Forces' Tax Guide.

Power of attorney. In order for you to sign a return for your spouse in any of these cases, you must attach to the return a power of attorney (POA) that authorizes you to sign for your spouse. You can use a POA that states that you have been granted authority to sign the return, or you can use Form 2848. Part I of Form 2848 must state that you are granted authority to sign the return.

Nonresident alien or dual-status alien. Generally, a married couple can't file a joint return if either one is a nonresident alien at any time during the tax year. However, if one spouse was a nonresident alien or dual-status alien who was married to a U.S. citizen or resident alien at the end of the year, the spouses can choose to file a joint return. If you do file a joint return, you and your spouse are both treated as U.S. residents for the entire tax year. See chapter 1 of Pub. 519, U.S. Tax Guide for Aliens.

Married Filing Separately

You can choose married filing separately as your filing status if you are married. This filing status may benefit you if you want to be responsible only for your own tax or if it results in less tax than filing a joint return.

If you and your spouse don't agree to file a joint return, you must use this filing status unless you qualify for head of household status, discussed later.

You may be able to choose head of household filing status if you are considered unmarried because you live apart from your spouse and meet certain tests (explained under *Head of Household*, later). This can apply to you even if you aren't divorced or legally separated. If you qualify to file as head of household, instead of as married filing separately, your tax may be lower, you may be able to claim the earned income credit and certain other benefits, and your standard deduction will be higher. The head of household filing status allows you to choose the standard deduction even if your spouse chooses to itemize deductions. See *Head of Household*, later, for more information.

 You will generally pay more combined tax on separate returns than you would on a joint return for the reasons listed under Special Rules, later. However, unless you are required to file separately, you should figure your tax both ways (on a joint return and on separate returns). This way, you can make sure you are using the filing status that results in the lowest combined tax. When figuring the combined tax of a married couple, you may want to consider state taxes as well as federal taxes.

How to file. If you file a separate return, you generally report only your own income, credits, and deductions.

Select this filing status by checking the "Married filing separately" box on the *Filing Status* line at the top of Form 1040 or 1040-SR. Enter your spouse's full name and SSN or ITIN in the entry space at the bottom of the *Filing Status* section. If your spouse doesn't have and isn't required to have an SSN or ITIN, enter "NRA" in the space for your spouse's SSN. Use the *Married filing separately* column of the Tax Table, or Section C of the Tax Computation Worksheet, to figure your tax.

Special Rules

If you choose married filing separately as your filing status, the following special rules apply. Because of these special rules, you usually pay more tax on a separate return than if you use another filing status you qualify for.

1. Your tax rate is generally higher than on a joint return.

2. Your exemption amount for figuring the alternative minimum tax is half that allowed on a joint return.

3. You can't take the credit for child and dependent care expenses in most cases, and the amount you can exclude from income under an employer's dependent care assistance program is limited to $2,500 (instead of $5,000 on a joint return). However, if you are legally separated or living apart from your spouse, you may be able to file a separate return and still take the credit. For more information about these expenses, the credit, and the exclusion, see *What's Your Filing Status?* in Pub. 503, Child and Dependent Care Expenses.

4. You can't take the earned income credit, unless you were separated from your spouse at the end of 2022 and meet certain requirements. For more information about these requirements, see *Rule 3—If Your Filing Status is Married Filing Separately, You Must Meet Certain Rules* in Pub. 596, Earned Income Credit (EIC).

5. You can't take the exclusion or credit for adoption expenses in most cases.

6. You can't take the education credits (the American opportunity credit and lifetime learning credit), or the deduction for student loan interest.

7. You can't exclude any interest income from qualified U.S. savings bonds you used for higher education expenses.

8. If you lived with your spouse at any time during the tax year:

    a. You can't claim the credit for the elderly or the disabled, and

    b. You must include in income a greater percentage (up to 85%) of any social security or equivalent railroad retirement benefits you received.

9. The following credits and deductions are reduced at income levels half of those for a joint return:

    a. The child tax credit and the credit for other dependents, and

    b. The retirement savings contributions credit.

10. Your capital loss deduction limit is $1,500 (instead of $3,000 on a joint return).

11. If your spouse itemizes deductions, you can't claim the standard deduction. If you can claim the standard deduction, your basic standard deduction is half of the amount allowed on a joint return.

Adjusted gross income (AGI) limits. If your AGI on a separate return is lower than it would have been on a joint return, you may be able to deduct a larger amount for certain deductions that are limited by AGI, such as medical expenses.

Individual retirement arrangements (IRAs). You may not be able to deduct all or part of your contributions to a traditional IRA if you or your spouse were covered by an employee retirement plan at work during the year. Your deduction is reduced or eliminated if your income is more than a certain amount. This amount is much lower for married individuals who file separately and lived together at any time during the year. For more information, see *How Much Can You Deduct* in chapter 9.

Rental activity losses. If you actively participated in a passive rental real estate activity that produced a loss, you can generally deduct the loss from your nonpassive income, up to $25,000. This is called a "special allowance." However, married persons filing separate returns who lived together at any time during the year can't claim this special allowance. Married persons filing separate returns who lived apart at all times during the year are each allowed a $12,500 maximum special allowance for losses from passive real estate activities. See *Rental Activities* in Pub. 925, Passive Activity and At-Risk Rules, for more information.

Community property states. If you live in a community property state and file separately, your income may be considered separate income or community income for income tax purposes. Community property states include Arizona, California, Idaho, Louisiana, Nevada, New Mexico, Texas, Washington, and Wisconsin. See Pub. 555, Community Property, for more information.

Joint Return After Separate Returns

You can change your filing status from a separate return to a joint return by filing an amended return using Form 1040-X.

You can generally change to a joint return any time within 3 years from the due date of the separate return or returns. This doesn't include any extensions. A separate return includes a return filed by you or your spouse claiming married filing separately, single, or head of household filing status.

Separate Returns After Joint Return

Once you file a joint return, you can't choose to file separate returns for that year after the due date of the return.

Exception. A personal representative for a decedent can change from a joint return elected by the surviving spouse to a separate return for the decedent. The personal representative has 1 year from the due date (including extensions) of the return to make the change. See Pub. 559, Survivors, Executors, and Administrators, for more information on filing a return for a decedent.

Head of Household

You may be able to file as head of household if you meet all of the following requirements.

1. You are unmarried or considered unmarried on the last day of the year. See *Marital Status*, earlier, and *Considered Unmarried*, later.

2. You paid more than half of the cost of keeping up a home for the year.

3. A qualifying person lived with you in the home for more than half the year (except for temporary absences, such as school). However, if the qualifying person is your dependent parent, your dependent parent doesn't have to live with you. See *Special rule for parent*, later, under *Qualifying Person*.

TIP *If you qualify to file as head of household, your tax rate will usually be lower than the rates for single or married filing separately. You will also receive a higher standard deduction than if you file as single or married filing separately.*

How to file. Indicate your choice of this filing status by checking the "Head of household" box on the *Filing Status* line at the top of Form 1040 or 1040-SR. If the child who qualifies you for this filing status isn't claimed as your dependent in the *Dependents* section of Form 1040 or 1040-SR, enter the child's name in the entry space at the bottom of the *Filing Status* section. Use the *Head of a household* column of the Tax Table, or Section D of the Tax Computation Worksheet, to figure your tax.

Considered Unmarried

To qualify for head of household status, you must be either unmarried or considered unmarried on the last day of the year. You are considered unmarried on the last day of the tax year if you meet all of the following tests.

1. You file a separate return. A separate return includes a return claiming married filing separately, single, or head of household filing status.

2. You paid more than half of the cost of keeping up your home for the tax year.

3. Your spouse didn't live in your home during the last 6 months of the tax year. Your spouse is considered to live in your home even if your spouse is temporarily absent due to special circumstances. See *Temporary absences* under *Qualifying Person*, later.

4. Your home was the main home of your child, stepchild, or foster child for more than half the year. (See *Home of qualifying person* under *Qualifying Person*, later, for rules applying to a child's birth, death, or temporary absence during the year.)

5. You must be able to claim the child as a dependent. However, you meet this test if you can't claim the child as a dependent only because the noncustodial parent can claim the child using the rules described in

Children of divorced or separated parents (or parents who live apart) under *Qualifying Child* in chapter 3, or referred to in *Support Test for Children of Divorced or Separated Parents (or Parents Who Live Apart)* under *Qualifying Relative* in chapter 3. The general rules for claiming a child as a dependent are explained in chapter 3.

 If you were considered married for part of the year and lived in a community property state (listed earlier under Married Filing Separately), special rules may apply in determining your income and expenses. See Pub. 555 for more information.

Nonresident alien spouse. You are considered unmarried for head of household purposes if your spouse was a nonresident alien at any time during the year and you don't choose to treat your nonresident spouse as a resident alien. However, your spouse isn't a qualifying person for head of household purposes. You must have another qualifying person and meet the other tests to be eligible to file as head of household.

Choice to treat spouse as resident. You are considered married if you choose to treat your spouse as a resident alien. See chapter 1 of Pub. 519.

Keeping Up a Home

To qualify for head of household status, you must pay more than half of the cost of keeping up a home for the year. You can determine whether you paid more than half of the cost of keeping up a home by using Worksheet 2-1.

Costs you include. Include in the cost of keeping up a home expenses, such as rent, mortgage interest, real estate taxes, insurance on the home, repairs, utilities, and food eaten in the home.

Costs you don't include. Don't include the costs of clothing, education, medical treatment, vacations, life insurance, or transportation. Also don't include the value of your services or those of a member of your household.

Qualifying Person

See Table 2-1 to see who is a qualifying person. Any person not described in Table 2-1 isn't a qualifying person.

Example 1—Child. Your unmarried child lived with you all year and was 18 years old at the end of the year. Your child didn't provide more than half of their own support and doesn't meet the tests to be a qualifying child of anyone else. As a result, this child is your qualifying child (see *Qualifying Child* in chapter 3) and, because this child is single, your qualifying person for head of household purposes.

Example 2—Child who isn't qualifying person. The facts are the same as in *Example 1*, except your child was 25 years old at the end of the year and your child's gross income was $5,000. Because your child doesn't meet the age test (explained under *Qualifying Child*

Worksheet 2-1. Cost of Keeping Up a Home

Keep for Your Records

	Amount You Paid	Total Cost
Property taxes	$	$
Mortgage interest expense		
Rent		
Utility charges		
Repairs/Maintenance		
Property insurance		
Food eaten in the home		
Other household expenses		
Totals	$	$
Minus total **amount you paid**		( )
Amount others paid		$

If the total amount you paid is more than the amount others paid, you meet the requirement of paying more than half of the cost of keeping up the home.

in chapter 3), your child isn't your qualifying child. Because the child doesn't meet the gross income test (explained under *Qualifying Relative* in chapter 3), the child isn't your qualifying relative. As a result, this child isn't your qualifying person for head of household purposes.

Example 3—Friend. Your friend lived with you all year. Even though your friend may be your qualifying relative if the gross income and support tests (explained in chapter 3) are met, your friend isn't your qualifying person for head of household purposes because your friend isn't related to you in one of the ways listed under *Relatives who don't have to live with you* in chapter 3. See Table 2-1.

Example 4—Friend's child. The facts are the same as in *Example 3*, except your friend's 10-year-old child also lived with you all year. Your friend's child isn't your qualifying child and, because the child is your friend's qualifying child, your friend's child isn't your qualifying relative (see *Not a Qualifying Child Test* in chapter 3). As a result, your friend's child isn't your qualifying person for head of household purposes.

Home of qualifying person. Generally, the qualifying person must live with you for more than half the year.

Special rule for parent. If your qualifying person is your parent, you may be eligible to file as head of household even if your parent doesn't live with you. However, you must be able to claim your parent as a dependent. Also, you must pay more than half of the cost of keeping up a home that was the main home for the entire year for your parent.

If you pay more than half of the cost of keeping your parent in a rest home or home for the elderly, that counts as paying more than half of the cost of keeping up your parent's main home.

Death or birth. You may be eligible to file as head of household even if the individual who qualifies you for this filing status is born or dies

during the year. If the individual is your qualifying child, the child must have lived with you for more than half the part of the year the child was alive. If the individual is anyone else, see Pub. 501 for more information.

Temporary absences. You and your qualifying person are considered to live together even if one or both of you are temporarily absent from your home due to special circumstances, such as illness, education, business, vacation, military service, or detention in a juvenile facility. It must be reasonable to assume the absent person will return to the home after the temporary absence. You must continue to keep up the home during the absence.

Kidnapped child. You may be eligible to file as head of household even if the child who is your qualifying person has been kidnapped. For more information, see Pub. 501.

Qualifying Surviving Spouse

If your spouse died in 2022, you can use married filing jointly as your filing status for 2022 if you otherwise qualify to use that status. The year of death is the last year for which you can file jointly with your deceased spouse. See *Married Filing Jointly*, earlier.

You may be eligible to use qualifying surviving spouse as your filing status for 2 years following the year your spouse died. For example, if your spouse died in 2021, and you haven't remarried, you may be able to use this filing status for 2022 and 2023.

This filing status entitles you to use joint return tax rates and the highest standard deduction amount (if you don't itemize deductions). It doesn't entitle you to file a joint return.

How to file. Indicate your choice of this filing status by checking the "Qualifying surviving spouse" box on the *Filing Status* line at the top of Form 1040 or 1040-SR. If the child who qualifies you for this filing status isn't claimed as your

dependent in the *Dependents* section of Form 1040 or 1040-SR, enter the child's name in the entry space at the bottom of the *Filing Status* section. Use the *Married filing jointly* column of the Tax Table, or Section B of the Tax Computation Worksheet, to figure your tax.

Eligibility rules. You are eligible to file your 2022 return as a qualifying surviving spouse if you meet all of the following tests.

- You were entitled to file a joint return with your spouse for the year your spouse died. It doesn't matter whether you actually filed a joint return.

- Your spouse died in 2020 or 2021 and you didn't remarry before the end of 2022.

- You have a child or stepchild (not a foster child) whom you can claim as a dependent or could claim as a dependent except that, for 2022:

   a. The child had gross income of $4,400 or more,

   b. The child filed a joint return, or

   c. You could be claimed as a dependent on someone else's return.

   If the child isn't claimed as your dependent in the *Dependents* section on Form 1040 or 1040-SR, enter the child's name in the entry space at the bottom of the *Filing Status* section. If you don't enter the name, it will take us longer to process your return.

- This child lived in your home all year, except for temporary absences. See *Temporary absences*, earlier, under *Head of Household*. There are also exceptions, described later, for a child who was born or died during the year and for a kidnapped child.

- You paid more than half of the cost of keeping up a home for the year. See *Keeping Up a Home*, earlier, under *Head of Household*.

Example. A's spouse died in 2020. A hasn't remarried. During 2021 and 2022, A continued to keep up a home for A and A's child, who lives with A and whom A can claim as a dependent. For 2020, A was entitled to file a joint return for A and A's deceased spouse. For 2021 and 2022, A can file as qualifying surviving spouse. After 2022, A can file as head of household if A qualifies.

Death or birth. You may be eligible to file as a qualifying surviving spouse if the child who qualifies you for this filing status is born or dies during the year. You must have provided more than half of the cost of keeping up a home that was the child's main home during the entire part of the year the child was alive.

Kidnapped child. You may be eligible to file as a qualifying surviving spouse even if the child who qualifies you for this filing status has been kidnapped. See Pub. 501 for more information.

As mentioned earlier, this filing status is available for only 2 years following the year your spouse died.

Table 2-1. Who Is a Qualifying Person Qualifying You To File as Head of Household?[1]

Caution. See the text of this chapter for the other requirements you must meet to claim head of household filing status.

IF the person is your . . .	AND . . .	THEN that person is . . .
qualifying child (such as a son, daughter, or grandchild who lived with you more than half the year and meets certain other tests)[2]	the child is single	a qualifying person, whether or not the child meets the *Citizen or Resident Test* in chapter 3.
	the child is married **and** you can claim the child as a dependent	a qualifying person.
	the child is married **and** you can't claim the child as a dependent	not a qualifying person.[3]
qualifying relative[4] who is your father or mother	you can claim your parent as a dependent[5]	a qualifying person.[6]
	you can't claim your parent as a dependent	not a qualifying person.
qualifying relative[4] other than your father or mother (such as a grandparent, brother, or sister who meets certain tests)	your relative lived with you more than half the year, **and** your relative is related to you in one of the ways listed under *Relatives who don't have to live with you* in chapter 3 **and** you can claim your relative as a dependent[5]	a qualifying person.
	your relative didn't live with you more than half the year	not a qualifying person.
	your relative isn't related to you in one of the ways listed under *Relatives who don't have to live with you* in chapter 3 **and** is your qualifying relative only because your relative lived with you all year as a member of your household	not a qualifying person.
	you can't claim your relative as a dependent	not a qualifying person.

[1] A person can't qualify more than one taxpayer to use the head of household filing status for the year.

[2] The term qualifying child is defined in chapter 3. **Note.** If you are a noncustodial parent, the term "qualifying child" for head of household filing status doesn't include a child who is your qualifying child only because of the rules described under *Children of divorced or separated parents (or parents who live apart)* under *Qualifying Child* in chapter 3. If you are the custodial parent and those rules apply, the child is generally your qualifying child for head of household filing status even though the child isn't a qualifying child you can claim as a dependent.

[3] This person is a qualifying person if the only reason you can't claim the person as a dependent is that you, or your spouse if filing jointly, can be claimed as a dependent on another taxpayer's return.

[4] The term qualifying relative is defined in chapter 3.

[5] If you can claim a person as a dependent only because of a multiple support agreement, that person isn't a qualifying person. See *Multiple Support Agreement* in chapter 3.

[6] See *Special rule for parent* under *Qualifying Person*, earlier.

3.

Dependents

Introduction

This chapter discusses the following topics.

- Dependents—You can generally claim your qualifying child or qualifying relative as a dependent.
- Social security number (SSN) requirement for dependents—You must list the SSN of any person you claim as a dependent.

How to claim dependents. On page 1 of your Form 1040 or 1040-SR, enter the names of your dependents in the *Dependents* section.

Useful Items

You may want to see:

Publication

❏ **501** Dependents, Standard Deduction, and Filing Information

❏ **503** Child and Dependent Care Expenses

❏ **526** Charitable Contributions

Form (and Instructions)

❏ **2120** Multiple Support Declaration

❏ **8332** Release/Revocation of Release of Claim to Exemption for Child by Custodial Parent

Dependents

The term "dependent" means:

- A qualifying child, or
- A qualifying relative.

The terms "qualifying child" and "qualifying relative" are defined later.

All the requirements for claiming a dependent are summarized in Table 3-1.

Housekeepers, maids, or servants. If these people work for you, you can't claim them as dependents.

Child tax credit. You may be entitled to a child tax credit for each qualifying child who was under age 17 at the end of the year if you claimed that child as a dependent. For more information, see chapter 14.

Table 3-1. Overview of the Rules for Claiming a Dependent

Caution. This table is only an overview of the rules. For details, see the rest of this chapter.

- You can't claim any dependents if you (or your spouse, if filing jointly) could be claimed as a dependent by another taxpayer.

- You can't claim a married person who files a joint return as a dependent unless that joint return is filed only to claim a refund of withheld income tax or estimated tax paid.

- You can't claim a person as a dependent unless that person is a U.S. citizen, U.S. resident alien, U.S. national, or a resident of Canada or Mexico.[1]

- You can't claim a person as a dependent unless that person is your **qualifying child** or **qualifying relative.**

Tests To Be a Qualifying Child	Tests To Be a Qualifying Relative
1. The child must be your son, daughter, stepchild, foster child, brother, sister, half brother, half sister, stepbrother, stepsister, or a descendant of any of them.	1. The person can't be your qualifying child or the qualifying child of any other taxpayer.
2. The child must be (a) under age 19 at the end of the year and younger than you (or your spouse, if filing jointly); (b) under age 24 at the end of the year, a student, and younger than you (or your spouse, if filing jointly); or (c) any age if permanently and totally disabled.	2. The person either (a) must be related to you in one of the ways listed under *Relatives who don't have to live with you*, or (b) must live with you all year as a member of your household[2] (and your relationship must not violate local law).
3. The child must have lived with you for more than half of the year.[2]	3. The person's gross income for the year must be less than $4,400.[3]
4. The child must not have provided more than half of the child's own support for the year.	4. You must provide more than half of the person's total support for the year.[4]
5. The child must not be filing a joint return for the year (unless that return is filed only to get a refund of income tax withheld or estimated tax paid).	
If the child meets the rules to be a qualifying child of more than one person, generally only one person can actually treat the child as a qualifying child. See *Qualifying Child of More Than One Person*, later, to find out which person is the person entitled to claim the child as a qualifying child.	

[1] There is an exception for certain adopted children.

[2] There are exceptions for temporary absences, children who were born or died during the year, children of divorced or separated parents (or parents who live apart), and kidnapped children.

[3] There is an exception if the person is disabled and has income from a sheltered workshop.

[4] There are exceptions for multiple support agreements, children of divorced or separated parents (or parents who live apart), and kidnapped children.

Credit for other dependents. You may be entitled to a credit for other dependents for each qualifying child who does not qualify you for the child tax credit and for each qualifying relative. For more information, see chapter 14.

Exceptions

Even if you have a qualifying child or qualifying relative, you can claim that person as a dependent only if these three tests are met.

1. Dependent taxpayer test.

2. Joint return test.

3. Citizen or resident test.

These three tests are explained in detail here.

Dependent Taxpayer Test

If you can be claimed as a dependent by another taxpayer, you can't claim anyone else as a dependent. Even if you have a qualifying child or qualifying relative, you can't claim that person as a dependent.

If you are filing a joint return and your spouse can be claimed as a dependent by another taxpayer, you and your spouse can't claim any dependents on your joint return.

Joint Return Test

You generally can't claim a married person as a dependent if that person files a joint return.

Exception. You can claim a person as a dependent who files a joint return if that person and that person's spouse file the joint return only to claim a refund of income tax withheld or estimated tax paid.

Example 1—Child files joint return. You supported your 18-year-old child who lived with you all year while your child's spouse was in the Armed Forces. Your child's spouse earned $35,000 for the year. The couple files a joint return. You can't claim your child as a dependent.

Example 2—Child files joint return only as claim for refund of withheld tax. Your 18-year-old child and your child's 17-year-old spouse had $800 of wages from part-time jobs and no other income. They lived with you all year. Neither is required to file a tax return. They don't have a child. Taxes were taken out of their pay, so they filed a joint return only to get a refund of the withheld taxes. The exception to the joint return test applies, so you aren't disqualified from claiming each of them as a dependent just because they file a joint return. You can claim each of them as a dependent if all the other tests to do so are met.

Example 3—Child files joint return to claim American opportunity credit. The facts are the same as in *Example 2*, except no taxes were taken out of your child's pay or your child's spouse's pay. However, they file a joint return to claim an American opportunity credit of $124 and get a refund of that amount. Because claiming the American opportunity credit is their reason for filing the return, they aren't filing it only to get a refund of income tax withheld or estimated tax paid. The exception to the joint return test doesn't apply, so you can't claim either of them as a dependent.

Citizen or Resident Test

You generally can't claim a person as a dependent unless that person is a U.S. citizen, U.S. resident alien, U.S. national, or a resident of Canada or Mexico. However, there is an exception for certain adopted children, as explained next.

Exception for adopted child. If you are a U.S. citizen or U.S. national who has legally adopted a child who isn't a U.S. citizen, U.S. resident alien, or U.S. national, this test is met if the child lived with you as a member of your household all year. This exception also applies if the child was lawfully placed with you for legal adoption and the child lived with you for the rest of the year after placement.

Child's place of residence. Children are usually citizens or residents of the country of their parents.

If you were a U.S. citizen when your child was born, the child may be a U.S. citizen and meet this test even if the other parent was a nonresident alien and the child was born in a foreign country.

Foreign students' place of residence. Foreign students brought to this country under a qualified international education exchange program and placed in American homes for a temporary period generally aren't U.S. residents and don't meet this test. You can't claim them as dependents. However, if you provided a home for a foreign student, you may be able to take a charitable contribution deduction. See *Expenses Paid for Student Living With You* in Pub. 526, Charitable Contributions.

U.S. national. A U.S. national is an individual who, although not a U.S. citizen, owes his or her allegiance to the United States. U.S. nationals include American Samoans and Northern Mariana Islanders who chose to become U.S. nationals instead of U.S. citizens.

Qualifying Child

Five tests must be met for a child to be your qualifying child. The five tests are:

1. Relationship,
2. Age,
3. Residency,
4. Support, and
5. Joint return.

These tests are explained next.

 If a child meets the five tests to be the qualifying child of more than one person, there are rules you must use to determine which person can actually treat the child as a qualifying child. See Qualifying Child of More Than One Person, *later.*

Relationship Test

To meet this test, a child must be:

- Your son, daughter, stepchild, or foster child, or a descendant (for example, your grandchild) of any of them; or
- Your brother, sister, half brother, half sister, stepbrother, or stepsister, or a descendant (for example, your niece or nephew) of any of them.

Adopted child. An adopted child is always treated as your own child. The term "adopted child" includes a child who was lawfully placed with you for legal adoption.

Foster child. A foster child is an individual who is placed with you by an authorized placement agency or by judgment, decree, or other order of any court of competent jurisdiction.

Age Test

To meet this test, a child must be:

- Under age 19 at the end of the year and younger than you (or your spouse if filing jointly);
- A student under age 24 at the end of the year and younger than you (or your spouse if filing jointly); or
- Permanently and totally disabled at any time during the year, regardless of age.

Example. Your child turned 19 on December 10. Unless this child was permanently and totally disabled or a student, this child doesn't meet the age test because, at the end of the year, this child wasn't **under** age 19.

Child must be younger than you or spouse. To be your qualifying child, a child who isn't permanently and totally disabled must be younger than you. However, if you are married filing jointly, the child must be younger than you or your spouse but doesn't have to be younger than both of you.

Example 1—Child not younger than you or spouse. Your 23-year-old sibling, who is a student and unmarried, lives with you and your spouse, who provide more than half of your sibling's support. Your sibling isn't disabled. Both you and your spouse are 21 years old, and you

file a joint return. Your sibling isn't your qualifying child because your sibling isn't younger than you or your spouse.

Example 2—Child younger than your spouse but not younger than you. The facts are the same as in *Example 1*, except your spouse is 25 years old. Because your sibling is younger than your spouse, and you and your spouse are filing a joint return, your sibling is your qualifying child, even though your sibling isn't younger than you.

Student defined. To qualify as a student, your child must be, during some part of each of any 5 calendar months of the year:

1. A full-time student at a school that has a regular teaching staff and course of study, and a regularly enrolled student body at the school; or
2. A student taking a full-time, on-farm training course given by a school described in (1), or by a state, county, or local government agency.

The 5 calendar months don't have to be consecutive.

Full-time student. A full-time student is a student who is enrolled for the number of hours or courses the school considers to be full-time attendance.

School defined. A school can be an elementary school; a junior or senior high school; a college; a university; or a technical, trade, or mechanical school. However, an on-the-job training course, correspondence school, or school offering courses only through the Internet doesn't count as a school.

Vocational high school students. Students who work on "co-op" jobs in private industry as a part of a school's regular course of classroom and practical training are considered full-time students.

Permanently and totally disabled. Your child is permanently and totally disabled if both of the following apply.

- Your child can't engage in any substantial gainful activity because of a physical or mental condition.
- A doctor determines the condition has lasted or can be expected to last continuously for at least a year or can lead to death.

Residency Test

To meet this test, your child must have lived with you for more than half the year. There are exceptions for temporary absences, children who were born or died during the year, kidnapped children, and children of divorced or separated parents.

Temporary absences. Your child is considered to have lived with you during periods of time when one of you, or both, is temporarily absent due to special circumstances such as:

- Illness,
- Education,
- Business,
- Vacation,

- Military service, or
- Detention in a juvenile facility.

Death or birth of child. A child who was born or died during the year is treated as having lived with you more than half of the year if your home was the child's home more than half of the time the child was alive during the year. The same is true if the child lived with you more than half the year except for any required hospital stay following birth.

Child born alive. You may be able to claim as a dependent a child born alive during the year, even if the child lived only for a moment. State or local law must treat the child as having been born alive. There must be proof of a live birth shown by an official document, such as a birth certificate. The child must be your qualifying child or qualifying relative, and all the other tests to claim the child as a dependent must be met.

Stillborn child. You can't claim a stillborn child as a dependent.

Kidnapped child. You may be able to treat your child as meeting the residency test even if the child has been kidnapped. See Pub. 501 for details.

Children of divorced or separated parents (or parents who live apart). In most cases, because of the residency test, a child of divorced or separated parents is the qualifying child of the custodial parent. However, the child will be treated as the qualifying child of the noncustodial parent if all four of the following statements are true.

1. The parents:
    a. Are divorced or legally separated under a decree of divorce or separate maintenance;
    b. Are separated under a written separation agreement; or
    c. Lived apart at all times during the last 6 months of the year, whether or not they are or were married.

2. The child received over half of the child's support for the year from the parents.

3. The child is in the custody of one or both parents for more than half of the year.

4. Either of the following statements is true.
    a. The custodial parent signs a written declaration, discussed later, that they won't claim the child as a dependent for the year, and the noncustodial parent attaches this written declaration to their return. (If the decree or agreement went into effect after 1984 and before 2009, see *Post-1984 and pre-2009 divorce decree or separation agreement*, later. If the decree or agreement went into effect after 2008, see *Post-2008 divorce decree or separation agreement*, later.)
    b. A pre-1985 decree of divorce or separate maintenance or written separation agreement that applies to 2022 states that the noncustodial parent can claim the child as a dependent, the decree or agreement wasn't

changed after 1984 to say the non-custodial parent can't claim the child as a dependent, and the noncustodial parent provides at least $600 for the child's support during the year.

If statements (1) through (4) are all true, only the noncustodial parent can:

- Claim the child as a dependent; and
- Claim the child as a qualifying child for the child tax credit or credit for other dependents.

However, this doesn't allow the noncustodial parent to claim head of household filing status, the credit for child and dependent care expenses, the exclusion for dependent care benefits, or the earned income credit. See *Applying the tiebreaker rules to divorced or separated parents (or parents who live apart)*, later.

Example—Earned income credit. Even if statements (1) through (4) are all true and the custodial parent signs Form 8332 or a substantially similar statement that the custodial parent won't claim the child as a dependent for 2022, this doesn't allow the noncustodial parent to claim the child as a qualifying child for the earned income credit. The custodial parent or another taxpayer, if eligible, can claim the child for the earned income credit.

Custodial parent and noncustodial parent. The custodial parent is the parent with whom the child lived for the greater number of nights during the year. The other parent is the noncustodial parent.

If the parents divorced or separated during the year and the child lived with both parents before the separation, the custodial parent is the one with whom the child lived for the greater number of nights during the rest of the year.

A child is treated as living with a parent for a night if the child sleeps:

- At that parent's home, whether or not the parent is present; or
- In the company of the parent, when the child doesn't sleep at a parent's home (for example, the parent and child are on vacation together).

Equal number of nights. If the child lived with each parent for an equal number of nights during the year, the custodial parent is the parent with the higher AGI.

December 31. The night of December 31 is treated as part of the year in which it begins. For example, the night of December 31, 2022, is treated as part of 2022.

Emancipated child. If a child is emancipated under state law, the child is treated as not living with either parent. See *Examples 5* and *6*.

Absences. If a child wasn't with either parent on a particular night (because, for example, the child was staying at a friend's house), the child is treated as living with the parent with whom the child normally would have lived for that night, except for the absence. But if it can't be determined with which parent the child normally would have lived or if the child wouldn't have lived with either parent that night, the child is treated as not living with either parent that night.

Parent works at night. If, due to a parent's nighttime work schedule, a child lives for a greater number of days, but not nights, with the parent who works at night, that parent is treated as the custodial parent. On a school day, the child is treated as living at the primary residence registered with the school.

Example 1—Child lived with one parent for a greater number of nights. You and your child's other parent are divorced. In 2022, your child lived with you 210 nights and with the other parent 155 nights. You are the custodial parent.

Example 2—Child is away at camp. In 2022, your child lives with each parent for alternate weeks. In the summer, your child spends 6 weeks at summer camp. During those 6 weeks, your child is treated as living with you for 3 weeks and with your child's other parent, your ex-spouse, for 3 weeks because this is how long the child would have lived with each parent if the child had not attended summer camp.

Example 3—Child lived same number of nights with each parent. Your child lived with you 180 nights during the year and lived the same number of nights with the child's other parent, your ex-spouse. Your AGI is $40,000. Your ex-spouse's AGI is $25,000. You are treated as your child's custodial parent because you have the higher AGI.

Example 4—Child is at parent's home but with other parent. Your child normally lives with you during the week and with the child's other parent, your ex-spouse, every other weekend. You become ill and are hospitalized. The other parent lives in your home with your child for 10 consecutive days while you are in the hospital. Your child is treated as living with you during this 10-day period because your child was living in your home.

Example 5—Child emancipated in May. Your child turned 18 in May 2022 and became emancipated under the law of the state where your child lives. As a result, your child isn't considered in the custody of either parent for more than half of the year. The special rule for children of divorced or separated parents doesn't apply.

Example 6—Child emancipated in August. Your child lives with you from January 1, 2022, until May 31, 2022, and lives with the child's other parent, your ex-spouse, from June 1, 2022, through the end of the year. Your child turns 18 and is emancipated under state law on August 1, 2022. Because your child is treated as not living with either parent beginning on August 1, your child is treated as living with you the greater number of nights in 2022. You are the custodial parent.

Written declaration. The custodial parent must use either Form 8332 or a similar statement (containing the same information required by the form) to make the written declaration to release a claim to an exemption for a child to the noncustodial parent. Although the exemption amount is zero for tax year 2022, this release allows the noncustodial parent to claim the child tax credit, additional child tax credit, and credit for other dependents, if applicable, for the child. The noncustodial parent must attach a copy of the form or statement to their tax return.

The release can be for 1 year, for a number of specified years (for example, alternate years), or for all future years, as specified in the declaration.

Post-1984 and pre-2009 divorce decree or separation agreement. If the divorce decree or separation agreement went into effect after 1984 and before 2009, the noncustodial parent may be able to attach certain pages from the decree or agreement instead of Form 8332. The decree or agreement must state all three of the following.

1. The noncustodial parent can claim the child as a dependent without regard to any condition, such as payment of support.

2. The custodial parent won't claim the child as a dependent for the year.

3. The years for which the noncustodial parent, rather than the custodial parent, can claim the child as a dependent.

The noncustodial parent must attach all of the following pages of the decree or agreement to their tax return.

- The cover page (write the other parent's SSN on this page).

- The pages that include all of the information identified in items (1) through (3) above.

- The signature page with the other parent's signature and the date of the agreement.

Post-2008 divorce decree or separation agreement. The noncustodial parent can't attach pages from the decree or agreement instead of Form 8332 if the decree or agreement went into effect after 2008. The custodial parent must sign either Form 8332 or a similar statement whose only purpose is to release the custodial parent's claim to an exemption for a child, and the noncustodial parent must attach a copy to their return. The form or statement must release the custodial parent's claim to the child without any conditions. For example, the release must not depend on the noncustodial parent paying support.

 The noncustodial parent must attach the required information even if it was filed with a return in an earlier year.

Revocation of release of claim to an exemption. The custodial parent can revoke a release of claim to an exemption. For the revocation to be effective for 2022, the custodial parent must have given (or made reasonable efforts to give) written notice of the revocation to the noncustodial parent in 2021 or earlier. The custodial parent can use Part III of Form 8332 for this purpose and must attach a copy of the revocation to their return for each tax year the custodial parent claims the child as a dependent as a result of the revocation.

Remarried parent. If you remarry, the support provided by your new spouse is treated as provided by you.

Parents who never married. This special rule for divorced or separated parents also applies to parents who never married and who lived apart at all times during the last 6 months of the year.

Support Test (To Be a Qualifying Child)

To meet this test, the child can't have provided more than half of the child's own support for the year.

This test is different from the support test to be a qualifying relative, which is described later. However, to see what is or isn't support, see *Support Test (To Be a Qualifying Relative)*, later. If you aren't sure whether a child provided more than half of their own support, you may find Worksheet 3-1 helpful.

Example. You provided $4,000 toward your 16-year-old child's support for the year and the child provided $6,000. Your child provided more than half their own support. The child isn't your qualifying child.

Foster care payments and expenses. Payments you receive for the support of a foster child from a child placement agency are considered support provided by the agency. Similarly, payments you receive for the support of a foster child from a state or county are considered support provided by the state or county.

If you aren't in the trade or business of providing foster care and your unreimbursed out-of-pocket expenses in caring for a foster child were mainly to benefit an organization qualified to receive deductible charitable contributions, the expenses are deductible as charitable contributions but aren't considered support you provided. For more information about the deduction for charitable contributions, see Pub. 526. If your unreimbursed expenses aren't deductible as charitable contributions, they may qualify as support you provided.

If you are in the trade or business of providing foster care, your unreimbursed expenses aren't considered support provided by you.

Example 1. L, a foster child, lived with married couple, A and B Smith for the last 3 months of the year. The Smiths cared for L because they wanted to adopt L (although L hadn't been placed with them for adoption). They didn't care for L as a trade or business or to benefit the agency that placed L in their home. The Smiths' unreimbursed expenses aren't deductible as charitable contributions but are considered support they provided for L.

Example 2. You provided $3,000 toward your 10-year-old foster child's support for the year. The state government provided $4,000, which is considered support provided by the state, not by the child. See *Support provided by the state (welfare, food stamps, housing, etc.)*, later. Your foster child didn't provide more than half of their own support for the year.

Scholarships. A scholarship received by a child who is a student isn't taken into account in determining whether the child provided more than half of their own support.

Joint Return Test (To Be a Qualifying Child)

To meet this test, the child can't file a joint return for the year.

Exception. An exception to the joint return test applies if your child and the child's spouse file a joint return only to claim a refund of income tax withheld or estimated tax paid.

Example 1—Child files joint return. You supported your 18-year-old child who lived with you all year while your child's spouse was in the Armed Forces. Your child's spouse earned $35,000 for the year. The couple files a joint return so this child isn't your qualifying child.

Example 2—Child files joint return only as a claim for refund of withheld tax. Your 18-year-old child and your child's 17-year-old spouse had $800 of wages from part-time jobs and no other income. They lived with you all year. Neither is required to file a tax return. They don't have a child. Taxes were taken out of their pay so they filed a joint return only to get a refund of the withheld taxes. The exception to the joint return test applies, so this child may be your qualifying child if all the other tests are met.

Example 3—Child files joint return to claim American opportunity credit. The facts are the same as in *Example 2*, except no taxes were taken out of either spouse's pay. However, they file a joint return to claim an American opportunity credit of $124 and get a refund of that amount. Because claiming the American opportunity credit is their reason for filing the return, they aren't filing it only to get a refund of income tax withheld or estimated tax paid. The exception to the joint return test doesn't apply, so this child isn't your qualifying child.

Qualifying Child of More Than One Person

 If your qualifying child isn't a qualifying child of anyone else, this topic doesn't apply to you and you don't need to read about it. This is also true if your qualifying child isn't a qualifying child of anyone else except your spouse with whom you plan to file a joint return.

 If a child is treated as the qualifying child of the noncustodial parent under the rules for children of divorced or separated parents (or parents who live apart) described earlier, see Applying the tiebreaker rules to divorced or separated parents (or parents who live apart), later.

Sometimes, a child meets the relationship, age, residency, support, and joint return tests to be a qualifying child of more than one person. Although the child is a qualifying child of each of these persons, generally only one person can actually treat the child as a qualifying child to take all of the following tax benefits (provided the person is eligible for each benefit).

1. The child tax credit, credit for other dependents, or additional child tax credit.

Funds Belonging to the Person You Supported

1. Enter the total funds belonging to the person you supported, including income received (taxable and nontaxable) and amounts borrowed during the year, plus the amount in savings and other accounts at the beginning of the year. Don't include funds provided by the state; include those amounts on line 23 instead .... **1.** _____

2. Enter the amount on line 1 that was used for the person's support .... **2.** _____

3. Enter the amount on line 1 that was used for other purposes .... **3.** _____

4. Enter the total amount in the person's savings and other accounts at the end of the year ...... **4.** _____

5. Add lines 2 through 4. (This amount should equal line 1.) .... **5.** _____

Expenses for Entire Household (where the person you supported lived)

6. Lodging (complete line 6a or 6b):
   a. Enter the total rent paid .... **6a.** _____
   b. Enter the fair rental value of the home. If the person you supported owned the home, also include this amount in line 21 .... **6b.** _____

7. Enter the total food expenses .... **7.** _____

8. Enter the total amount of utilities (heat, light, water, etc., not included in line 6a or 6b) .... **8.** _____

9. Enter the total amount of repairs (not included in line 6a or 6b) .... **9.** _____

10. Enter the total of other expenses. Don't include expenses of maintaining the home, such as mortgage interest, real estate taxes, and insurance .... **10.** _____

11. Add lines 6a through 10. These are the total household expenses .... **11.** _____

12. Enter total number of persons who lived in the household .... **12.** _____

Expenses for the Person You Supported

13. Divide line 11 by line 12. This is the person's share of the household expenses .... **13.** _____

14. Enter the person's total clothing expenses .... **14.** _____

15. Enter the person's total education expenses .... **15.** _____

16. Enter the person's total medical and dental expenses not paid for or reimbursed by insurance .... **16.** _____

17. Enter the person's total travel and recreation expenses .... **17.** _____

18. Enter the total of the person's other expenses .... **18.** _____

19. Add lines 13 through 18. This is the total cost of the person's support for the year .... **19.** _____

Did the Person Provide More Than Half of the Person's Own Support?

20. Multiply line 19 by 50% (0.50) .... **20.** _____

21. Enter the amount from line 2, plus the amount from line 6b if the person you supported owned the home. This is the amount the person provided for their own support .... **21.** _____

22. Is line 21 more than line 20?

   ☐ **No.** You meet the support test for this person to be your qualifying child. If this person also meets the other tests to be a qualifying child, stop here; don't complete lines 23–26. Otherwise, go to line 23 and fill out the rest of the worksheet to determine if this person is your qualifying relative.

   ☐ **Yes.** You don't meet the support test for this person to be either your qualifying child or your qualifying relative. **Stop here.**

Did You Provide More Than Half?

23. Enter the amount others provided for the person's support. Include amounts provided by state, local, and other welfare societies or agencies. Don't include any amounts included on line 1 .... **23.** _____

24. Add lines 21 and 23 .... **24.** _____

25. Subtract line 24 from line 19. This is the amount you provided for the person's support .... **25.** _____

26. Is line 25 more than line 20?

   ☐ **Yes.** You meet the support test for this person to be your qualifying relative.

   ☐ **No.** You don't meet the support test for this person to be your qualifying relative. You can't claim this person as a dependent unless you can do so under a multiple support agreement, the support test for children of divorced or separated parents, or the special rule for kidnapped children. See *Multiple Support Agreement* or *Support Test for Children of Divorced or Separated Parents (or Parents Who Live Apart)*, or *Kidnapped child* under *Qualifying Relative*.

2. Head of household filing status.

3. The credit for child and dependent care expenses.

4. The exclusion from income for dependent care benefits.

5. The earned income credit.

The other person can't take any of these benefits based on this qualifying child. In other words, you and the other person can't agree to divide these benefits between you.

Tiebreaker rules. To determine which person can treat the child as a qualifying child to claim these five tax benefits, the following tiebreaker rules apply.

- If only one of the persons is the child's parent, the child is treated as the qualifying child of the parent.

- If the parents file a joint return together and can claim the child as a qualifying child, the child is treated as the qualifying child of the parents.

- If the parents don't file a joint return together but both parents claim the child as a qualifying child, the IRS will treat the child as the qualifying child of the parent with whom the child lived for the longer period of time during the year. If the child lived with each parent for the same amount of time, the IRS will treat the child as the qualifying child of the parent who had the higher AGI for the year.

- If no parent can claim the child as a qualifying child, the child is treated as the qualifying child of the person who had the highest AGI for the year.

- If a parent can claim the child as a qualifying child but no parent does so claim the child, the child is treated as the qualifying child of the person who had the highest AGI for the year, but only if that person's AGI is higher than the highest AGI of any of the child's parents who can claim the child.

Subject to these tiebreaker rules, you and the other person may be able to choose which of you claims the child as a qualifying child.

 You may be able to qualify for the earned income credit under the rules for taxpayers without a qualifying child if you have a qualifying child for the earned income credit who is claimed as a qualifying child by another taxpayer. For more information, see Pub. 596.

Example 1—Child lived with parent and grandparent. You and your 3-year-old child J lived with your parent all year. You are 25 years old and unmarried, and your AGI is $9,000. Your parent's AGI is $15,000. Your child's other parent didn't live with you or your child. You haven't signed Form 8332 (or a similar statement).

J is a qualifying child of both you and your parent because J meets the relationship, age, residency, support, and joint return tests for both you and your parent. However, only one of you can claim J. J isn't a qualifying child of anyone else, including J's other parent. You agree to let your parent claim J. This means your parent can claim J as a qualifying child for all of the five tax benefits listed earlier, if your parent qualifies for each of those benefits (and if you don't claim J as a qualifying child for any of those tax benefits).

Example 2—Parent has higher AGI than grandparent. The facts are the same as in *Example 1*, except your AGI is $18,000. Because your parent's AGI isn't higher than yours, your parent can't claim J. Only you can claim J.

Example 3—Two persons claim same child. The facts are the same as in *Example 1*, except you and your parent both claim J as a qualifying child. In this case, you, as the child's parent, will be the only one allowed to claim J as a qualifying child. The IRS will disallow your parent's claim to the five tax benefits listed earlier based on J. However, your parent may qualify for the earned income credit as a taxpayer without a qualifying child.

Example 4—Qualifying children split between two persons. The facts are the same as in *Example 1*, except you also have two other young children who are qualifying children of both you and your parent. Only one of you can claim each child. However, if your parent's AGI is higher than yours, you can allow your parent to claim one or more of the children. For example, if you claim one child, your parent can claim the other two.

Example 5—Taxpayer who is a qualifying child. The facts are the same as in *Example 1*, except you are only 18 years old and didn't provide more than half of your own support for the year. This means you are your parent's qualifying child. If your parent can claim you as a dependent, then you can't claim your child as a dependent because of the *Dependent Taxpayer Test*, explained earlier.

Example 6—Separated parents. You, your spouse, and your 10-year-old child lived together until August 1, 2022, when your spouse moved out of the household. In August and September, your child lived with you. For the rest of the year, your child lived with your spouse, the child's parent. Your child is a qualifying child of both you and your spouse because your child lived with each of you for more than half the year and because your child met the relationship, age, support, and joint return tests for both of you. At the end of the year, you and your spouse still weren't divorced, legally separated, or separated under a written separation agreement, so the rule for children of divorced or separated parents (or parents who live apart) doesn't apply.

You and your spouse will file separate returns. Your spouse agrees to let you treat your child as a qualifying child. This means, if your spouse doesn't claim your child as a qualifying child, you can claim this child as a qualifying child for the child tax credit and exclusion for dependent care benefits (if you qualify for each of those tax benefits). However, you can't claim head of household filing status because you and your spouse didn't live apart for the last 6 months of the year. As a result, your filing status is married filing separately, so you can't claim the earned income credit because you and your spouse didn't live apart for the last 6 months of 2022, and you aren't legally separated under a written separation agreement or decree of separate maintenance. Therefore, you don't meet the requirements to take the earned income credit as married filing separately. You also can't take the credit for child and dependent care expenses because your filing status is married filing separately and you and your spouse didn't live apart for the last 6 months of 2022.

Example 7—Separated parents claim same child. The facts are the same as in *Example 6*, except you and your spouse both claim your child as a qualifying child. In this case, only your spouse will be allowed to treat your child as a qualifying child. This is because, during 2022, the child lived with your spouse longer than with you. If you claimed the child tax credit for your child, the IRS will disallow your claim to the child tax credit. If you don't have another qualifying child or dependent, the IRS will also disallow your claim to the exclusion for dependent care benefits. In addition, because you and your spouse didn't live apart for the last 6 months of the year, your spouse can't claim head of household filing status. As a result, your spouse's filing status is married filing separately, so your spouse can't claim the earned income credit because you and your spouse didn't live apart for the last 6 months of 2022, and you aren't legally separated under a written separation agreement or decree of separate maintenance. Therefore, your spouse doesn't meet the requirements to take the earned income credit as married filing separately. Your spouse also can't take the credit for child and dependent care expenses because your spouse's filing status is married filing separately and you and your spouse didn't live apart for the last 6 months of 2022.

Example 8—Unmarried parents. You, your 5-year-old child, L, and L's other parent lived together all year. You and L's other parent aren't married. L is a qualifying child of both you and L's other parent because L meets the relationship, age, residency, support, and joint return tests for both you and L's other parent. Your AGI is $12,000 and L's other parent's AGI is $14,000. L's other parent agrees to let you claim the child as a qualifying child. This means you can claim L as a qualifying child for the child tax credit, head of household filing status, the credit for child and dependent care expenses, the exclusion for dependent care benefits, and the earned income credit, if you qualify for each of those tax benefits (and if L's other parent doesn't claim L as a qualifying child for any of those tax benefits).

Example 9—Unmarried parents claim same child. The facts are the same as in *Example 8*, except you and L's other parent both claim L as a qualifying child. In this case, only L's other parent will be allowed to treat L as a qualifying child. This is because L's other parent's AGI, $14,000, is more than your AGI, $12,000. If you claimed the child tax credit for L, the IRS will disallow your claim to this credit. If you don't have another qualifying child or dependent, the IRS will also disallow your claim to head of household filing status, the credit for child and dependent care expenses, and the exclusion for dependent care benefits. However, you may be able to claim the earned income credit as a taxpayer without a qualifying child.

Example 10—Child didn't live with a parent. You and your sibling's child, M, lived with your parent all year. You are 25 years old, and your AGI is $9,300. Your parent's AGI is $15,000. M's parents file jointly, have an AGI of less than $9,000, and don't live with you or M. M is a qualifying child of both you and your parent because M meets the relationship, age, residency, support, and joint return tests for both you and your parent. However, only your parent can treat M as a qualifying child. This is because your parent's AGI, $15,000, is more than your AGI, $9,300.

Applying the tiebreaker rules to divorced or separated parents (or parents who live apart). If a child is treated as the qualifying child of the noncustodial parent under the rules described earlier for children of divorced or separated parents (or parents who live apart), only the noncustodial parent can claim the child as a dependent and claim the child tax credit or credit for other dependents for the child. However, only the custodial parent can claim the credit for child and dependent care expenses or the exclusion for dependent care benefits for the child. Also, generally, the noncustodial parent can't claim the child as a qualifying child for head of household filing status or the earned income credit. Instead, generally, the custodial parent, if eligible, or other eligible person can claim the child as a qualifying child for those two benefits. If the child is the qualifying child of more than one person for these benefits, then the tiebreaker rules just explained determine whether the custodial parent or another eligible person can treat the child as a qualifying child.

Example 1. You and your 5-year-old child, E, lived all year with your parent, who paid the entire cost of keeping up the home. Your AGI is $10,000. Your parent's AGI is $25,000. E's other parent didn't live with you or E.

Under the rules explained earlier for children of divorced or separated parents (or parents who live apart), E is treated as the qualifying child of E's other parent, who can claim the child tax credit for E. Because of this, you can't claim the child tax credit for E. However, those rules don't allow E's other parent to claim E as a qualifying child for head of household filing status, the credit for child and dependent care expenses, the exclusion for dependent care benefits, or the earned income credit.

You and your parent didn't have any child care expenses or dependent care benefits, so neither of you can claim the credit for child and dependent care expenses or the exclusion for dependent care benefits. But E is a qualifying child of both you and your parent for head of household filing status and the earned income credit because E meets the relationship, age, residency, support, and joint return tests for both you and your parent. (The support test doesn't apply for the earned income credit.) However, you agree to let your parent claim E. This means your parent can claim E for head of household filing status and the earned income credit if your parent qualifies for each and if you

don't claim E as a qualifying child for the earned income credit. (You can't claim head of household filing status because your parent paid the entire cost of keeping up the home.) You may be able to claim the earned income credit as a taxpayer without a qualifying child.

Example 2. The facts are the same as in Example 1, except your AGI is $25,000 and your parent's AGI is $21,000. Your parent can't claim E as a qualifying child for any purpose because your parent's AGI isn't higher than yours.

Example 3. The facts are the same as in Example 1, except you and your parent both claim E as a qualifying child for the earned income credit. Your parent also claims E as a qualifying child for head of household filing status. You, as the child's parent, will be the only one allowed to claim E as a qualifying child for the earned income credit. The IRS will disallow your parent's claim to head of household filing status unless your parent has another qualifying child or dependent. Your parent can't claim the earned income credit as a taxpayer without a qualifying child because your parent's AGI is more than $16,480.

Qualifying Relative

Four tests must be met for a person to be your qualifying relative. The four tests are:

1. Not a qualifying child test,

2. Member of household or relationship test,

3. Gross income test, and

4. Support test.

Age. Unlike a qualifying child, a qualifying relative can be any age. There is no age test for a qualifying relative.

Kidnapped child. You may be able to treat a child as your qualifying relative even if the child has been kidnapped. See Pub. 501 for details.

Not a Qualifying Child Test

A child isn't your qualifying relative if the child is your qualifying child or the qualifying child of any other taxpayer.

Example 1. Your 22-year-old child, who is a student, lives with you and meets all the tests to be your qualifying child. This child isn't your qualifying relative.

Example 2. Your 2-year-old child lives with your parents and meets all the tests to be their qualifying child. This child isn't your qualifying relative.

Example 3. Your 30-year old child lives with you. This child isn't a qualifying child because the age test isn't met. This child may be your qualifying relative if the gross income test and the support test are met.

Example 4. Your 13-year-old grandchild only lived with you for 5 months during the year. Your grandchild isn't your qualifying child because the residency test isn't met. Your grandchild may be your qualifying relative if the gross income test and the support test are met.

Child of person not required to file a return. A child isn't the qualifying child of any other taxpayer and so may qualify as your qualifying relative if the child's parent (or other person for whom the child is defined as a qualifying child) isn't required to file an income tax return and either:

- Doesn't file an income tax return, or

- Files a return only to get a refund of income tax withheld or estimated tax paid.

Example 1—Return not required. You support an unrelated friend and your friend's 3-year-old child, who lived with you all year in your home. Your friend has no gross income, isn't required to file a 2022 tax return, and doesn't file a 2022 tax return. Both your friend and your friend's child are your qualifying relatives if the support test is met.

Example 2—Return filed to claim refund. The facts are the same as in Example 1, except your friend had wages of $1,500 during the year and had income tax withheld from your friend's wages. Your friend files a return only to get a refund of the income tax withheld and doesn't claim the earned income credit or any other tax credits or deductions. Both your friend and your friend's child are your qualifying relatives if the support test is met.

Example 3—Earned income credit claimed. The facts are the same as in Example 2, except your friend had wages of $8,000 during the year and claimed the earned income credit. Your friend's child is the qualifying child of another taxpayer (your friend), so you can't claim your friend's child as your qualifying relative. Also, you can't claim your friend as your qualifying relative because of the gross income test explained later.

Child in Canada or Mexico. You may be able to claim your child as a dependent even if the child lives in Canada or Mexico. If the child doesn't live with you, the child doesn't meet the residency test to be your qualifying child. However, the child may still be your qualifying relative. If the persons the child does live with aren't U.S. citizens and have no U.S. gross income, those persons aren't "taxpayers," so the child isn't the qualifying child of any other taxpayer. If the child isn't the qualifying child of any other taxpayer, the child is your qualifying relative as long as the gross income test and the support test are met.

You can't claim as a dependent a child who lives in a foreign country other than Canada or Mexico, unless the child is a U.S. citizen, U.S. resident alien, or U.S. national. There is an exception for certain adopted children who lived with you all year. See Citizen or Resident Test, earlier.

Example. You provide all the support of your children, ages 6, 8, and 12, who live in Mexico with your parent and have no income. You are single and live in the United States. Your parent isn't a U.S. citizen and has no U.S. income, so your parent isn't a "taxpayer." Your children aren't your qualifying children because they don't meet the residency test. But since they aren't the qualifying children of any other taxpayer, they may be your qualifying relatives and you may be permitted to claim them as dependents. You may also be able to claim your parent as a dependent if the gross income and support tests are met.

Member of Household or Relationship Test

To meet this test, a person must either:

1. Live with you all year as a member of your household, or

2. Be related to you in one of the ways listed under *Relatives who don't have to live with you* below.

If at any time during the year the person was your spouse, that person can't be your qualifying relative.

Relatives who don't have to live with you. A person related to you in any of the following ways doesn't have to live with you all year as a member of your household to meet this test.

- Your child, stepchild, or foster child, or a descendant of any of them (for example, your grandchild). (A legally adopted child is considered your child.)

- Your brother, sister, half brother, half sister, stepbrother, or stepsister.

- Your father, mother, grandparent, or other direct ancestor, but not foster parent.

- Your stepfather or stepmother.

- A son or daughter of your brother or sister.

- A son or daughter of your half brother or half sister.

- A brother or sister of your father or mother.

- Your son-in-law, daughter-in-law, father-in-law, mother-in-law, brother-in-law, or sister-in-law.

Any of these relationships that were established by marriage aren't ended by death or divorce.

Example. In 2016, you and your spouse began supporting your spouse's unmarried parent, G. Your spouse died in 2021. Despite your spouse's death, G continues to meet this test, even if G doesn't live with you. You can claim G as a dependent if all other tests are met, including the gross income and support tests.

Foster child. A foster child is an individual who is placed with you by an authorized placement agency or by judgment, decree, or other order of any court of competent jurisdiction.

Joint return. If you file a joint return, the person can be related to either you or your spouse. Also, the person doesn't need to be related to the spouse who provides support.

For example, you provide more than half the support for your spouse's stepparent. Your spouse's stepparent may be your qualifying relative even if the stepparent doesn't live with you. However, if you and your spouse file separate returns, your spouse's stepparent can be your qualifying relative only if the stepparent lives with you all year as a member of your household.

Temporary absences. A person is considered to live with you as a member of your household during periods of time when one of you, or both,

is temporarily absent due to special circumstances such as:

- Illness,

- Education,

- Business,

- Vacation,

- Military service, or

- Detention in a juvenile facility.

If the person is placed in a nursing home for an indefinite period of time to receive constant medical care, the absence may be considered temporary.

Death or birth. A person who died during the year, but lived with you as a member of your household until death, will meet this test. The same is true for a child who was born during the year and lived with you as a member of your household for the rest of the year. The test is also met if a child lived with you as a member of your household except for any required hospital stay following birth.

If your dependent died during the year and you otherwise qualify to claim that person as a dependent, you can still claim that person as a dependent.

Example. Your parent, who met the tests to be your qualifying relative, died on January 15. You can claim your parent as a dependent on your return.

Local law violated. A person doesn't meet this test if at any time during the year the relationship between you and that person violates local law.

Example. Your significant other, T, lived with you as a member of your household all year. However, your relationship with T violated the laws of the state where you live because T was married to someone else. Therefore, T doesn't meet this test and you can't claim T as a dependent.

Adopted child. An adopted child is always treated as your own child. The term "adopted child" includes a child who was lawfully placed with you for legal adoption.

Cousin. Your cousin must live with you all year as a member of your household to meet this test. A cousin is a descendant of a brother or sister of your father or mother.

Gross Income Test

To meet this test, a person's gross income for the year must be less than $4,400.

Gross income defined. Gross income is all income in the form of money, property, and services that isn't exempt from tax.

In a manufacturing, merchandising, or mining business, gross income is the total net sales minus the cost of goods sold, plus any miscellaneous income from the business.

Gross receipts from rental property are gross income. Don't deduct taxes, repairs, or other expenses to determine the gross income from rental property.

Gross income includes a partner's share of the gross (not a share of the net) partnership income.

Gross income also includes all taxable unemployment compensation, taxable social security benefits, and certain amounts received as scholarship and fellowship grants. Scholarships received by degree candidates and used for tuition, fees, supplies, books, and equipment required for particular courses generally aren't included in gross income. For more information about scholarships, see chapter 8.

Disabled dependent working at sheltered workshop. For purposes of the gross income test, the gross income of an individual who is permanently and totally disabled at any time during the year doesn't include income for services the individual performs at a sheltered workshop. The availability of medical care at the workshop must be the main reason for the individual's presence there. Also, the income must come solely from activities at the workshop that are incident to this medical care.

A "sheltered workshop" is a school that:

- Provides special instruction or training designed to alleviate the disability of the individual; and

- Is operated by certain tax-exempt organizations, or by a state, a U.S. possession, a political subdivision of a state or possession, the United States, or the District of Columbia.

Permanently and totally disabled has the same meaning here as under *Qualifying Child*, earlier.

Support Test (To Be a Qualifying Relative)

To meet this test, you must generally provide more than half of a person's total support during the calendar year.

However, if two or more persons provide support, but no one person provides more than half of a person's total support, see *Multiple Support Agreement*, later.

How to determine if support test is met. You figure whether you have provided more than half of a person's total support by comparing the amount you contributed to that person's support with the entire amount of support that person received from all sources. This includes support the person provided from the person's own funds.

You may find Worksheet 3-1 helpful in figuring whether you provided more than half of a person's support.

Person's own funds not used for support. A person's own funds aren't support unless they are actually spent for support.

Example. Your parent received $2,400 in social security benefits and $300 in interest, paid $2,000 for lodging and $400 for recreation, and put $300 in a savings account.

Even though your parent received a total of $2,700 ($2,400 + $300), your parent spent only $2,400 ($2,000 + $400) for your parent's own support. If you spent more than $2,400 for your parent's support and no other support was received, you have provided more than half of your parent's support.

Child's wages used for own support. You can't include in your contribution to your child's support any support paid for by the child with the child's own wages, even if you paid the wages.

Year support is provided. The year you provide the support is the year you pay for it, even if you do so with borrowed money that you repay in a later year.

If you use a fiscal year to report your income, you must provide more than half of the dependent's support for the calendar year in which your fiscal year begins.

Armed Forces dependency allotments. The part of the allotment contributed by the government and the part taken out of your military pay are both considered provided by you in figuring whether you provide more than half of the support. If your allotment is used to support persons other than those you name, you can claim them as dependents if they otherwise qualify.

Example. You are in the Armed Forces. You authorize an allotment for your surviving parent that your surviving parent uses to support themselves and their sibling. If the allotment provides more than half of each person's support, you can claim each of them as a dependent, if they otherwise qualify, even though you authorize the allotment only for your surviving parent.

Tax-exempt military quarters allowances. These allowances are treated the same way as dependency allotments in figuring support. The allotment of pay and the tax-exempt basic allowance for quarters are both considered as provided by you for support.

Tax-exempt income. In figuring a person's total support, include tax-exempt income, savings, and borrowed amounts used to support that person. Tax-exempt income includes certain social security benefits, welfare benefits, nontaxable life insurance proceeds, Armed Forces family allotments, nontaxable pensions, and tax-exempt interest.

Example 1. You provide $4,000 towards your parent's support during the year. Your parent has earned income of $600, nontaxable social security benefits of $4,800, and tax-exempt interest of $200, all of which your parent uses for self-support. You can't claim your parent as a dependent because the $4,000 you provide isn't more than half of your parent's total support of $9,600 ($4,000 + $600 + $4,800 + $200).

Example 2. K, your sibling's child, takes out a student loan of $2,500 and uses it to pay college tuition. K is personally responsible for the loan. You provide $2,000 toward K's total support. You can't claim K as a dependent because you provide less than half of K's support.

Social security benefits. If a married couple receives benefits that are paid by one check made out to both of them, half of the total paid is considered to be for the support of each spouse, unless they can show otherwise.

If a child receives social security benefits and uses them toward their own support, the benefits are considered as provided by the child.

Support provided by the state (welfare, food stamps, housing, etc.). Benefits provided by the state to a needy person are generally considered support provided by the state. However, payments based on the needs of the recipient won't be considered as used entirely for that person's support if it is shown that part of the payments weren't used for that purpose.

Foster care. Payments you receive for the support of a foster child from a child placement agency are considered support provided by the agency. See *Foster care payments and expenses,* earlier.

Home for the aged. If you make a lump-sum advance payment to a home for the aged to take care of your relative for life and the payment is based on that person's life expectancy, the amount of support you provide each year is the lump-sum payment divided by the relative's life expectancy. The amount of support you provide also includes any other amounts you provided during the year.

Total Support

To figure if you provided more than half of a person's support, you must first determine the total support provided for that person. Total support includes amounts spent to provide food, lodging, clothing, education, medical and dental care, recreation, transportation, and similar necessities.

Generally, the amount of an item of support is the amount of the expense incurred in providing that item. For lodging, the amount of support is the fair rental value of the lodging.

Expenses not directly related to any one member of a household, such as the cost of food for the household, must be divided among the members of the household.

Example 1. G Brown, parent of M Miller, lives with F and M Miller and their two children. G gets social security benefits of $2,400, which G spends for clothing, transportation, and recreation. G has no other income. F and M's total food expense for the household is $5,200. They pay G's medical and drug expenses of $1,200. The fair rental value of the lodging provided for G is $1,800 a year, based on the cost of similar rooming facilities. Figure G's total support as follows.

Fair rental value of lodging	$1,800
Clothing, transportation, and recreation	2,400
Medical expenses	1,200
Share of food (1/5 of $5,200)	1,040
Total support	$6,440

The support F and M provide, $4,040 ($1,800 lodging + $1,200 medical expenses + $1,040 food), is more than half of G's $6,440 total support.

Example 2. Your parents, A and B, live with you, your spouse, and your two children in a house you own. The fair rental value of your parents' share of the lodging is $2,000 a year ($1,000 each), which includes furnishings and utilities. A receives a nontaxable pension of $4,200, which A spends equally between A and B for items of support such as clothing, transportation, and recreation. Your total food expense for the household is $6,000. Your heat and utility bills amount to $1,200. B has hospital and medical expenses of $600, which you pay during the year. Figure your parents' total support as follows.

Support provided	A	B
Fair rental value of lodging . . .	$1,000	$1,000
Pension spent for their support	2,100	2,100
Share of food (1/6 of $6,000)	1,000	1,000
Medical expenses for B		600
Parents' total support	$4,100	$4,700

You must apply the support test separately to each parent. You provide $2,000 ($1,000 lodging + $1,000 food) of A's total support of $4,100—less than half. You provide $2,600 to B ($1,000 lodging + $1,000 food + $600 medical)—more than half of B's total support of $4,700. You meet the support test for B, but not A. Heat and utility costs are included in the fair rental value of the lodging, so these aren't considered separately.

Lodging. If you provide a person with lodging, you are considered to provide support equal to the fair rental value of the room, apartment, house, or other shelter in which the person lives. Fair rental value includes a reasonable allowance for the use of furniture and appliances, and for heat and other utilities that are provided.

Fair rental value defined. Fair rental value is the amount you could reasonably expect to receive from a stranger for the same kind of lodging. It is used instead of actual expenses such as taxes, interest, depreciation, paint, insurance, utilities, and the cost of furniture and appliances. In some cases, fair rental value may be equal to the rent paid.

If you provide the total lodging, the amount of support you provide is the fair rental value of the room the person uses, or a share of the fair rental value of the entire dwelling if the person has use of your entire home. If you don't provide the total lodging, the total fair rental value must be divided depending on how much of the total lodging you provide. If you provide only a part and the person supplies the rest, the fair rental value must be divided between both of you according to the amount each provides.

Example. Your parents live rent free in a house you own. It has a fair rental value of $5,400 a year furnished, which includes a fair rental value of $3,600 for the house and $1,800 for the furniture. This doesn't include heat and utilities. The house is completely furnished with furniture belonging to your parents. You pay $600 for their utility bills. Utilities usually aren't included in rent for houses in the area where your parents live. Therefore, you consider the total fair rental value of the lodging to be $6,000 ($3,600 fair rental value of the unfurnished house + $1,800 allowance for the furnishings provided by your parents + $600 cost of utilities) of which you are considered to provide $4,200 ($3,600 + $600).

Person living in their own home. The total fair rental value of a person's home that the person owns is considered support contributed by that person.

Living with someone rent free. If you live with a person rent free in that person's home, you must reduce the amount you provide for support of that person by the fair rental value of lodging the person provides you.

Property. Property provided as support is measured by its fair market value. Fair market value is the price that property would sell for on the open market. It is the price that would be agreed upon between a willing buyer and a willing seller, with neither being required to act, and both having reasonable knowledge of the relevant facts.

Capital expenses. Capital items, such as furniture, appliances, and cars, bought for a person during the year can be included in total support under certain circumstances.

The following examples show when a capital item is or isn't support.

Example 1. You buy a $200 power lawn mower for your 13-year-old child. The child is given the duty of keeping the lawn trimmed. Because the lawn mower benefits all members of the household, don't include the cost of the lawn mower in the support of your child.

Example 2. You buy a $150 television set as a birthday present for your 12-year-old child. The television set is placed in your child's bedroom. You can include the cost of the television set in the support of your child.

Example 3. You pay $5,000 for a car and register it in your name. You and your 17-year-old child use the car equally. Because you own the car and don't give it to your child but merely let your child use it, don't include the cost of the car in your child's total support. However, you can include in your child's support your out-of-pocket expenses of operating the car for your child's benefit.

Example 4. Your 17-year-old child, using personal funds, buys a car for $4,500. You provide the rest of your child's support, $4,000. Because the car is bought and owned by your child, the car's fair market value ($4,500) must be included in your child's support. Your child has provided more than half of their own total support of $8,500 ($4,500 + $4,000), so this child isn't your qualifying child. You didn't provide more than half of this child's total support, so this child isn't your qualifying relative. You can't claim this child as a dependent.

Medical insurance premiums. Medical insurance premiums you pay, including premiums for supplementary Medicare coverage, are included in the support you provide.

Medical insurance benefits. Medical insurance benefits, including basic and supplementary Medicare benefits, aren't part of support.

Tuition payments and allowances under the GI Bill. Amounts veterans receive under the GI Bill for tuition payments and allowances while they attend school are included in total support.

Example. During the year, your child receives $2,200 from the government under the GI Bill. Your child uses this amount for your child's education. You provide the rest of his support, $2,000. Because GI benefits are included in total support, your child's total support is $4,200 ($2,200 + $2,000). You haven't provided more than half of your child's support.

Childcare expenses. If you pay someone to provide child or dependent care, you can include these payments in the amount you provided for the support of your child or disabled dependent, even if you claim a credit for the payments. For information on the credit, see Pub. 503, Child and Dependent Care Expenses.

Other support items. Other items may be considered as support depending on the facts in each case.

Don't Include in Total Support

The following items aren't included in total support.

1. Federal, state, and local income taxes paid by persons from their own income.

2. Social security and Medicare taxes paid by persons from their own income.

3. Life insurance premiums.

4. Funeral expenses.

5. Scholarships received by your child if your child is a student.

6. Survivors' and Dependents' Educational Assistance payments used for the support of the child who receives them.

Multiple Support Agreement

Sometimes no one provides more than half of the support of a person. Instead, two or more persons, each of whom would be able to claim the person as a dependent but for the support test, together provide more than half of the person's support.

When this happens, you can agree that any one of you who individually provides more than 10% of the person's support, but only one, can claim the person as a dependent. Each of the others must sign a statement agreeing not to claim the person as a dependent for that year. The person who claims the person as a dependent must keep these signed statements for their own records. A multiple support declaration identifying each of the others who agreed not to claim the person as a dependent must be attached to the return of the person claiming the person as a dependent. Form 2120 can be used for this purpose.

You can claim someone as a dependent under a multiple support agreement for someone related to you or for someone who lived with you all year as a member of your household.

Example 1. You, and your siblings, S, B, and D, provide the entire support of your parent for the year. You provide 45%, S provides 35%, and B and D each provide 10%. Either you or S can claim your parent as a dependent; the one who doesn't must sign a statement agreeing not to claim your parent as a dependent. The one who claims your parent as a dependent must

attach Form 2120, or a similar declaration, to their return and must keep the statement signed by the other for their records. Because neither B nor D provides more than 10% of the support, neither can claim your parent as a dependent and neither has to sign a statement.

Example 2. You and your sibling each provide 20% of your parent's support for the year. The remaining 60% of your parent's support is provided equally by two persons who are unrelated. Your parent doesn't live with them. Because more than half of your parent's support is provided by persons who can't claim your parent as a dependent, no one can claim your parent as a dependent.

Support Test for Children of Divorced or Separated Parents (or Parents Who Live Apart)

In most cases, a child of divorced or separated parents (or parents who live apart) will be a qualifying child of one of the parents. See *Children of divorced or separated parents (or parents who live apart)* under *Qualifying Child*, earlier. However, if the child doesn't meet the requirements to be a qualifying child of either parent, the child may be a qualifying relative of one of the parents. If you think this might apply to you, see Pub. 501.

Social Security Numbers (SSNs) for Dependents

You must show the SSN of any dependent you list in the *Dependents* section of your Form 1040 or 1040-SR.

 If you don't show the dependent's SSN when required, or if you show an incorrect SSN, certain tax benefits may be disallowed.

No SSN. If a person whom you expect to claim as a dependent on your return doesn't have an SSN, either you or that person should apply for an SSN as soon as possible by filing Form SS-5, Application for a Social Security Card, with the Social Security Administration (SSA). You can get Form SS-5 online at *SSA.gov/forms/ss-5.pdf* or at your local SSA office.

It usually takes about 2 weeks to get an SSN once the SSA has all the information it needs. If you don't have a required SSN by the filing due date, you can file Form 4868 for an extension of time to file.

Born and died in 2022. If your child was born and died in 2022, and you don't have an SSN for the child, you may attach a copy of the child's birth certificate, death certificate, or hospital records instead. The document must show the child was born alive. If you do this, enter "DIED" in column (2) of the *Dependents* section of your Form 1040 or 1040-SR.

Alien or adoptee with no SSN. If your dependent doesn't have and can't get an SSN, you must show the ITIN or adoption taxpayer identification number (ATIN) instead of an SSN.

Taxpayer identification numbers for aliens. If your dependent is a resident or nonresident alien who doesn't have and isn't eligible to get an SSN, your dependent must apply for an ITIN. For details on how to apply, see Form W-7, Application for IRS Individual Taxpayer Identification Number.

Taxpayer identification numbers for adoptees. If you have a child who was placed with you by an authorized placement agency, you may be able to claim the child as a dependent. However, if you can't get an SSN or an ITIN for the child, you must get an adoption taxpayer identification number (ATIN) for the child from the IRS. See Form W-7A, Application for Taxpayer Identification Number for Pending U.S. Adoptions, for details.

4.

Tax Withholding and Estimated Tax

What's New for 2023

Tax law changes for 2023. When you figure how much income tax you want withheld from your pay and when you figure your estimated tax, consider tax law changes effective in 2023. For more information, see Pub. 505, Tax Withholding and Estimated Tax.

Reminders

Estimated tax safe harbor for higher income taxpayers. If your 2022 adjusted gross income was more than $150,000 ($75,000 if you are married filing a separate return), you must pay the smaller of 90% of your expected tax for 2023 or 110% of the tax shown on your 2022 return to avoid an estimated tax penalty.

Introduction

This chapter discusses how to pay your tax as you earn or receive income during the year. In general, the federal income tax is a pay-as-you-go tax. There are two ways to pay as you go.

- **Withholding.** If you are an employee, your employer probably withholds income tax from your pay. Tax may also be withheld from certain other income, such as pensions, bonuses, commissions, and gambling winnings. The amount withheld is paid to the IRS in your name.

- **Estimated tax.** If you don't pay your tax through withholding, or don't pay enough

tax that way, you may have to pay estimated tax. People who are in business for themselves will generally have to pay their tax this way. Also, you may have to pay estimated tax if you receive income such as dividends, interest, capital gains, rent, and royalties. Estimated tax is used to pay not only income tax, but self-employment tax and alternative minimum tax as well.

This chapter explains these methods. In addition, it also explains the following.

- **Credit for withholding and estimated tax.** When you file your 2022 income tax return, take credit for all the income tax withheld from your salary, wages, pensions, etc., and for the estimated tax you paid for 2022. Also take credit for any excess social security or railroad retirement tax withheld. See Pub. 505.

- **Underpayment penalty.** If you didn't pay enough tax during the year, either through withholding or by making estimated tax payments, you may have to pay a penalty. In most cases, the IRS can figure this penalty for you. See *Underpayment Penalty for 2022* at the end of this chapter.

Useful Items

You may want to see:

Publication

❏ **505** Tax Withholding and Estimated Tax

Form (and Instructions)

❏ **W-4** Employee's Withholding Certificate

❏ **W-4P** Withholding Certificate for Periodic Pension or Annuity Payments

❏ **W-4S** Request for Federal Income Tax Withholding From Sick Pay

❏ **W-4V** Voluntary Withholding Request

❏ **1040-ES** Estimated Tax for Individuals

❏ **2210** Underpayment of Estimated Tax by Individuals, Estates, and Trusts

❏ **2210-F** Underpayment of Estimated Tax by Farmers and Fishermen

Tax Withholding for 2023

This section discusses income tax withholding on:

- Salaries and wages,
- Tips,
- Taxable fringe benefits,
- Sick pay,
- Pensions and annuities,
- Gambling winnings,
- Unemployment compensation, and
- Certain federal payments.

This section explains the rules for withholding tax from each of these types of income.

This section also covers backup withholding on interest, dividends, and other payments.

Salaries and Wages

Income tax is withheld from the pay of most employees. Your pay includes your regular pay, bonuses, commissions, and vacation allowances. It also includes reimbursements and other expense allowances paid under a nonaccountable plan. See *Supplemental Wages*, later, for more information about reimbursements and allowances paid under a nonaccountable plan.

If your income is low enough that you won't have to pay income tax for the year, you may be exempt from withholding. This is explained under *Exemption From Withholding*, later.

You can ask your employer to withhold income tax from noncash wages and other wages not subject to withholding. If your employer doesn't agree to withhold tax, or if not enough is withheld, you may have to pay estimated tax, as discussed later under *Estimated Tax for 2023*.

Military retirees. Military retirement pay is treated in the same manner as regular pay for income tax withholding purposes, even though it is treated as a pension or annuity for other tax purposes.

Household workers. If you are a household worker, you can ask your employer to withhold income tax from your pay. A household worker is an employee who performs household work in a private home, local college club, or local fraternity or sorority chapter.

Tax is withheld only if you want it withheld and your employer agrees to withhold it. If you don't have enough income tax withheld, you may have to pay estimated tax, as discussed later under *Estimated Tax for 2023*.

Farmworkers. Generally, income tax is withheld from your cash wages for work on a farm unless your employer does both of these:

- Pays you cash wages of less than $150 during the year, and

- Has expenditures for agricultural labor totaling less than $2,500 during the year.

Differential wage payments. When employees are on leave from employment for military duty, some employers make up the difference between the military pay and civilian pay. Payments to an employee who is on active duty for a period of more than 30 days will be subject to income tax withholding, but not subject to social security, Medicare, or federal unemployment (FUTA) tax withholding. The wages and withholding will be reported on Form W-2, Wage and Tax Statement.

Determining Amount of Tax Withheld Using Form W-4

The amount of income tax your employer withholds from your regular pay depends on two things.

- The amount you earn in each payroll period.

- The information you give your employer on Form W-4.

Form W-4 includes steps to help you figure your withholding. Complete Steps 2 through 4 only if they apply to you.

- **Step 1.** Enter your personal information including your filing status.
- **Step 2.** Complete this step if you have more than one job at the same time or are married filing jointly and you and your spouse both work.
- **Step 3.** Complete this step if you claim dependents and other credits.
- **Step 4.** Complete this optional step to make other adjustments.
  *Other income
  *Deductions
  *Extra withholding

New Job

When you start a new job, you must fill out Form W-4 and give it to your employer. Your employer should have copies of the form. If you need to change the information later, you must fill out a new form.

If you work only part of the year (for example, you start working after the beginning of the year), too much tax may be withheld. You may be able to avoid overwithholding if your employer agrees to use the part-year method. See *Part-Year Method* in chapter 1 of Pub. 505 for more information.

Employee also receiving pension income. If you receive pension or annuity income and begin a new job, you will need to file Form W-4 with your new employer. However, you can choose to split your withholding between your pension and job in any manner.

Changing Your Withholding

During the year, changes may occur to your marital status, adjustments, deductions, or credits you expect to claim on your tax return. When this happens, you may need to give your employer a new Form W-4 to change your withholding status.

If a change in personal circumstances reduces the amount of withholding you are entitled to claim, you are required to give your employer a new Form W-4 within 10 days after the change occurs.

Changing your withholding for 2024. If events in 2023 will change the amount of withholding you should claim for 2024, you must give your employer a new Form W-4 by December 1, 2023. If the event occurs in December 2023, submit a new Form W-4 within 10 days.

Checking Your Withholding

After you have given your employer a Form W-4, you can check to see whether the amount of tax withheld from your pay is too little or too much. If too much or too little tax is being withheld, you should give your employer a new Form W-4 to change your withholding. You should try to have your withholding match your actual tax liability. If not enough tax is withheld, you will owe tax at the end of the year and may have to pay interest and a penalty. If too much tax is withheld, you will lose the use of that money until you get your refund. Always check

your withholding if there are personal or financial changes in your life or changes in the law that might change your tax liability.

Note. You can't give your employer a payment to cover withholding on salaries and wages for past pay periods or a payment for estimated tax.

Completing Form W-4 and Worksheets

Form W-4 has worksheets to help you figure the correct amount of withholding you can claim. The worksheets are for your own records. Don't give them to your employer.

Multiple Jobs Worksheet. If you have income from more than one job at the same time, or are married filing jointly and you and your spouse both work, complete the Multiple Jobs Worksheet on the Form W-4.

If you and your spouse expect to file separate returns, figure your withholding using separate worksheets based on your own individual income, adjustments, deductions, and credits.

Deductions Worksheet. Use the Deductions Worksheet on Form W-4 if you plan to itemize deductions or claim certain adjustments to income and you want to reduce your withholding. Also complete this worksheet when you have changes to these items to see if you need to change your withholding.

Getting the Right Amount of Tax Withheld

In most situations, the tax withheld from your pay will be close to the tax you figure on your return if you follow these two rules.

- You accurately complete all the Form W-4 worksheets that apply to you.
- You give your employer a new Form W-4 when changes occur.

But because the worksheets and withholding methods don't account for all possible situations, you may not be getting the right amount withheld. This is most likely to happen in the following situations.

- You are married and both you and your spouse work.
- You have more than one job at a time.
- You have nonwage income, such as interest, dividends, alimony, unemployment compensation, or self-employment income.
- You will owe additional amounts with your return, such as self-employment tax.
- Your withholding is based on obsolete Form W-4 information for a substantial part of the year.
- You work only part of the year.
- You change the amount of your withholding during the year.
- You are subject to Additional Medicare Tax or Net Investment Income Tax (NIIT). If you anticipate liability for Additional Medicare Tax or NIIT, you may request that your employer withhold an additional amount of income tax withholding on Form W-4.

Cumulative wage method. If you change the amount of your withholding during the year, too much or too little tax may have been withheld for the period before you made the change. You may be able to compensate for this if your employer agrees to use the cumulative wage withholding method for the rest of the year. You must ask your employer in writing to use this method.

To be eligible, you must have been paid for the same kind of payroll period (weekly, biweekly, etc.) since the beginning of the year.

Publication 505

To make sure you are getting the right amount of tax withheld, get Pub. 505. It will help you compare the total tax to be withheld during the year with the tax you can expect to figure on your return. It will also help you determine how much, if any, additional withholding is needed each payday to avoid owing tax when you file your return. If you don't have enough tax withheld, you may have to pay estimated tax, as explained under *Estimated Tax for 2023*, later.

TIP *You can use the Tax Withholding Estimator at IRS.gov/W4App, instead of Pub. 505 or the worksheets included with Form W-4, to determine whether you need to have your withholding increased or decreased.*

Rules Your Employer Must Follow

It may be helpful for you to know some of the withholding rules your employer must follow. These rules can affect how to fill out your Form W-4 and how to handle problems that may arise.

New Form W-4. When you start a new job, your employer should have you complete a Form W-4. Beginning with your first payday, your employer will use the information you give on the form to figure your withholding.

If you later fill out a new Form W-4, your employer can put it into effect as soon as possible. The deadline for putting it into effect is the start of the first payroll period ending 30 or more days after you turn it in.

No Form W-4. If you don't give your employer a completed Form W-4, your employer must withhold at the highest rate, as if you were single.

Repaying withheld tax. If you find you are having too much tax withheld because you didn't claim the correct amount of withholding you are entitled to, you should give your employer a new Form W-4. Your employer can't repay any of the tax previously withheld. Instead, claim the full amount withheld when you file your tax return.

However, if your employer has withheld more than the correct amount of tax for the Form W-4 you have in effect, you don't have to fill out a new Form W-4 to have your withholding lowered to the correct amount. Your employer can repay the amount that was withheld incorrectly. If you aren't repaid, your Form W-2 will reflect the full amount actually withheld, which you would claim when you file your tax return.

Exemption From Withholding

If you claim exemption from withholding, your employer won't withhold federal income tax from your wages. The exemption applies only to income tax, not to social security, Medicare, or FUTA tax withholding.

You can claim exemption from withholding for 2023 only if both of the following situations apply.

- For 2022, you had a right to a refund of all federal income tax withheld because you had no tax liability.

- For 2023, you expect a refund of all federal income tax withheld because you expect to have no tax liability.

Students. If you are a student, you aren't automatically exempt. See chapter 1 to find out if you must file a return. If you work only part time or only during the summer, you may qualify for exemption from withholding.

Age 65 or older or blind. If you are 65 or older or blind, use Worksheet 1-1 or 1-2 in chapter 1 of Pub. 505 to help you decide if you qualify for exemption from withholding. Don't use either worksheet if you will itemize deductions or claim tax credits on your 2023 return. Instead, see *Itemizing deductions or claiming credits* in chapter 1 of Pub. 505.

Claiming exemption from withholding. To claim exemption, you must give your employer a Form W-4. Write "Exempt" on the form in the space below Step 4(c) and complete the applicable steps of the form.

If you claim exemption, but later your situation changes so that you will have to pay income tax after all, you must file a new Form W-4 within 10 days after the change. If you claim exemption in 2023, but you expect to owe income tax for 2024, you must file a new Form W-4 by December 1, 2023.

Your claim of exempt status may be reviewed by the IRS.

An exemption is good for only 1 year. You must give your employer a new Form W-4 by February 15 each year to continue your exemption.

Supplemental Wages

Supplemental wages include bonuses, commissions, overtime pay, vacation allowances, certain sick pay, and expense allowances under certain plans. The payer can figure withholding on supplemental wages using the same method used for your regular wages. However, if these payments are identified separately from your regular wages, your employer or other payer of supplemental wages can withhold income tax from these wages at a flat rate.

Expense allowances. Reimbursements or other expense allowances paid by your employer under a nonaccountable plan are treated as supplemental wages.

Reimbursements or other expense allowances paid under an accountable plan that are more than your proven expenses are treated as paid under a nonaccountable plan if you don't return the excess payments within a reasonable period of time.

For more information about accountable and nonaccountable expense allowance plans, see Pub. 505.

Penalties

You may have to pay a penalty of $500 if both of the following apply.

- You make statements or claim withholding on your Form W-4 that reduce the amount of tax withheld.

- You have no reasonable basis for those statements or withholding at the time you prepare your Form W-4.

There is also a criminal penalty for willfully supplying false or fraudulent information on your Form W-4 or for willfully failing to supply information that would increase the amount withheld. The penalty upon conviction can be either a fine of up to $1,000 or imprisonment for up to 1 year, or both.

These penalties will apply if you deliberately and knowingly falsify your Form W-4 in an attempt to reduce or eliminate the proper withholding of taxes. A simple error or an honest mistake won't result in one of these penalties.

Tips

The tips you receive while working on your job are considered part of your pay. You must include your tips on your tax return on the same line as your regular pay. However, tax isn't withheld directly from tip income, as it is from your regular pay. Nevertheless, your employer will take into account the tips you report when figuring how much to withhold from your regular pay.

For more information on reporting your tips to your employer and on the withholding rules for tip income, see Pub. 531, Reporting Tip Income.

How employer figures amount to withhold. The tips you report to your employer are counted as part of your income for the month you report them. Your employer can figure your withholding in either of two ways.

- By withholding at the regular rate on the sum of your pay plus your reported tips.

- By withholding at the regular rate on your pay plus a percentage of your reported tips.

Not enough pay to cover taxes. If your regular pay isn't enough for your employer to withhold all the tax (including income tax and social security and Medicare taxes (or the equivalent railroad retirement tax)) due on your pay plus your tips, you can give your employer money to cover the shortage. See Pub. 531 for more information.

Allocated tips. Your employer shouldn't withhold income tax, Medicare tax, social security tax, or railroad retirement tax on any allocated tips. Withholding is based only on your pay plus your reported tips. Your employer should refund to you any incorrectly withheld tax. See Pub. 531 for more information.

Taxable Fringe Benefits

The value of certain noncash fringe benefits you receive from your employer is considered part of your pay. Your employer must generally withhold income tax on these benefits from your regular pay.

For information on fringe benefits, see *Fringe Benefits* under *Employee Compensation* in chapter 5.

Although the value of your personal use of an employer-provided car, truck, or other highway motor vehicle is taxable, your employer can choose not to withhold income tax on that amount. Your employer must notify you if this choice is made.

For more information on withholding on taxable fringe benefits, see chapter 1 of Pub. 505.

Sick Pay

Sick pay is a payment to you to replace your regular wages while you are temporarily absent from work due to sickness or personal injury. To qualify as sick pay, it must be paid under a plan to which your employer is a party.

If you receive sick pay from your employer or an agent of your employer, income tax must be withheld. An agent who doesn't pay regular wages to you may choose to withhold income tax at a flat rate.

However, if you receive sick pay from a third party who isn't acting as an agent of your employer, income tax will be withheld only if you choose to have it withheld. See *Form W-4S*, later.

If you receive payments under a plan in which your employer doesn't participate (such as an accident or health plan where you paid all the premiums), the payments aren't sick pay and usually aren't taxable.

Union agreements. If you receive sick pay under a collective bargaining agreement between your union and your employer, the agreement may determine the amount of income tax withholding. See your union representative or your employer for more information.

Form W-4S. If you choose to have income tax withheld from sick pay paid by a third party, such as an insurance company, you must fill out Form W-4S. Its instructions contain a worksheet you can use to figure the amount you want withheld. They also explain restrictions that may apply.

Give the completed form to the payer of your sick pay. The payer must withhold according to your directions on the form.

Estimated tax. If you don't request withholding on Form W-4S, or if you don't have enough tax withheld, you may have to make estimated tax payments. If you don't pay enough tax, either through estimated tax or withholding, or a combination of both, you may have to pay a penalty. See *Underpayment Penalty for 2022* at the end of this chapter.

Pensions and Annuities

Income tax will usually be withheld from your pension or annuity distributions unless you choose not to have it withheld. This rule applies to distributions from:

- A traditional individual retirement arrangement (IRA);
- A life insurance company under an endowment, annuity, or life insurance contract;
- A pension, annuity, or profit-sharing plan;
- A stock bonus plan; and
- Any other plan that defers the time you receive compensation.

The amount withheld depends on whether you receive payments spread out over more than 1 year (periodic payments), within 1 year (nonperiodic payments), or as an eligible rollover distribution (ERD). Income tax withholding from an ERD is mandatory.

More information. For more information on withholding on pensions and annuities, including a discussion of Form W-4P, see *Pensions and Annuities* in chapter 1 of Pub. 505.

Gambling Winnings

Income tax is withheld at a flat 24% rate from certain kinds of gambling winnings.

Gambling winnings of more than $5,000 from the following sources are subject to income tax withholding.

- Any sweepstakes; wagering pool, including payments made to winners of poker tournaments; or lottery.
- Any other wager, if the proceeds are at least 300 times the amount of the bet.

It doesn't matter whether your winnings are paid in cash, in property, or as an annuity. Winnings not paid in cash are taken into account at their fair market value.

Exception. Gambling winnings from bingo, keno, and slot machines generally aren't subject to income tax withholding. However, you may need to provide the payer with a social security number to avoid withholding. See *Backup withholding on gambling winnings* in chapter 1 of Pub. 505. If you receive gambling winnings not subject to withholding, you may need to pay estimated tax. See *Estimated Tax for 2023*, later.

If you don't pay enough tax, either through withholding or estimated tax, or a combination of both, you may have to pay a penalty. See *Underpayment Penalty for 2022* at the end of this chapter.

Form W-2G. If a payer withholds income tax from your gambling winnings, you should receive a Form W-2G, Certain Gambling Winnings, showing the amount you won and the amount withheld. Report the tax withheld on Form 1040 or 1040-SR, line 25c.

Unemployment Compensation

You can choose to have income tax withheld from unemployment compensation. To make this choice, fill out Form W-4V (or a similar form provided by the payer) and give it to the payer.

All unemployment compensation is taxable. If you don't have income tax withheld, you may have to pay estimated tax. See *Estimated Tax for 2023*, later.

If you don't pay enough tax, either through withholding or estimated tax, or a combination of both, you may have to pay a penalty. See *Underpayment Penalty for 2022* at the end of this chapter.

Federal Payments

You can choose to have income tax withheld from certain federal payments you receive. These payments are the following.

1. Social security benefits.

2. Tier 1 railroad retirement benefits.

3. Commodity credit corporation loans you choose to include in your gross income.

4. Payments under the Agricultural Act of 1949 (7 U.S.C. 1421 et seq.), as amended, or title II of the Disaster Assistance Act of 1988, that are treated as insurance proceeds and that you receive because:

   a. Your crops were destroyed or damaged by drought, flood, or any other natural disaster; or

   b. You were unable to plant crops because of a natural disaster described in (a).

5. Any other payment under federal law as determined by the Secretary.

To make this choice, fill out Form W-4V (or a similar form provided by the payer) and give it to the payer.

If you don't choose to have income tax withheld, you may have to pay estimated tax. See *Estimated Tax for 2023*, later.

If you don't pay enough tax, either through withholding or estimated tax, or a combination of both, you may have to pay a penalty. See *Underpayment Penalty for 2022* at the end of this chapter.

More information. For more information about the tax treatment of social security and railroad retirement benefits, see chapter 7. Get Pub. 225, Farmer's Tax Guide, for information about the tax treatment of commodity credit corporation loans or crop disaster payments.

Backup Withholding

Banks or other businesses that pay you certain kinds of income must file an information return (Form 1099) with the IRS. The information return shows how much you were paid during the year. It also includes your name and taxpayer identification number (TIN). TINs are explained in chapter 1 under *Social Security Number (SSN)*.

These payments generally aren't subject to withholding. However, "backup" withholding is required in certain situations. Backup withholding can apply to most kinds of payments that are reported on Form 1099.

The payer must withhold at a flat 24% rate in the following situations.

- You don't give the payer your TIN in the required manner.

- The IRS notifies the payer that the TIN you gave is incorrect.

- You are required, but fail, to certify that you aren't subject to backup withholding.

- The IRS notifies the payer to start withholding on interest or dividends because you have underreported interest or dividends on your income tax return. The IRS will do this only after it has mailed you four notices.

Go to *IRS.gov/Businesses/Small-Businesses-Self-Employed/Backup-Withholding* for more information on kinds of payments subject to backup withholding.

Penalties. There are civil and criminal penalties for giving false information to avoid backup withholding. The civil penalty is $500. The criminal penalty, upon conviction, is a fine of up to $1,000 or imprisonment of up to 1 year, or both.

Estimated Tax for 2023

Estimated tax is the method used to pay tax on income that isn't subject to withholding. This includes income from self-employment, interest, dividends, alimony, rent, gains from the sale of assets, prizes, and awards. You may also have to pay estimated tax if the amount of income tax being withheld from your salary, pension, or other income isn't enough.

Estimated tax is used to pay both income tax and self-employment tax, as well as other taxes and amounts reported on your tax return. If you don't pay enough tax, either through withholding or estimated tax, or a combination of both, you may have to pay a penalty. If you don't pay enough by the due date of each payment period (see *When To Pay Estimated Tax*, later), you may be charged a penalty even if you are due a refund when you file your tax return. For information on when the penalty applies, see *Underpayment Penalty for 2022* at the end of this chapter.

Who Doesn't Have To Pay Estimated Tax

If you receive salaries or wages, you can avoid having to pay estimated tax by asking your employer to take more tax out of your earnings. To do this, give a new Form W-4 to your employer. See chapter 1 of Pub. 505.

Estimated tax not required. You don't have to pay estimated tax for 2023 if you meet all three of the following conditions.

- You had no tax liability for 2022.

- You were a U.S. citizen or resident alien for the whole year.

- Your 2022 tax year covered a 12-month period.

You had no tax liability for 2022 if your total tax was zero or you didn't have to file an income tax return. For the definition of "total tax" for 2022, see Pub. 505, chapter 2.

Figure 4-A. **Do You Have To Pay Estimated Tax?**

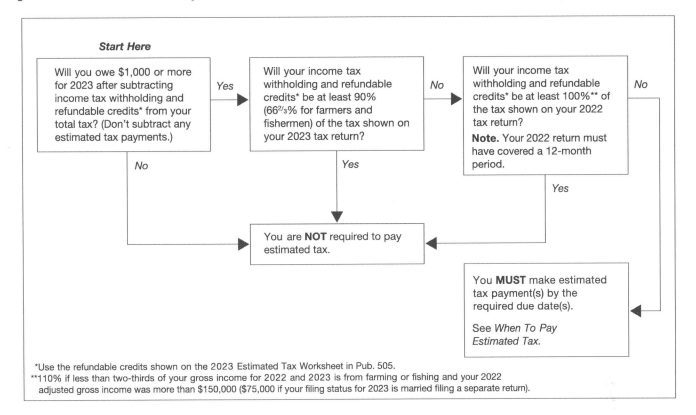

*Use the refundable credits shown on the 2023 Estimated Tax Worksheet in Pub. 505.
**110% if less than two-thirds of your gross income for 2022 and 2023 is from farming or fishing and your 2022
   adjusted gross income was more than $150,000 ($75,000 if your filing status for 2023 is married filing a separate return).

Who Must Pay Estimated Tax

If you owe additional tax for 2022, you may have to pay estimated tax for 2023.

You can use the following general rule as a guide during the year to see if you will have enough withholding, or if you should increase your withholding or make estimated tax payments.

General rule. In most cases, you must pay estimated tax for 2023 if both of the following apply.

1. You expect to owe at least $1,000 in tax for 2023, after subtracting your withholding and refundable credits.

2. You expect your withholding plus your refundable credits to be less than the smaller of:

   a. 90% of the tax to be shown on your 2023 tax return, or

   b. 100% of the tax shown on your 2022 tax return (but see *Special rules for farmers, fishermen, and higher income taxpayers*, later). Your 2022 tax return must cover all 12 months.

 If the result from using the general rule above suggests that you won't have enough withholding, complete the 2023 Estimated Tax Worksheet in Pub. 505 for a more accurate calculation.

Special rules for farmers, fishermen, and higher income taxpayers. If at least two-thirds of your gross income for tax year 2022 or 2023 is from farming or fishing,

substitute 66⅔% for 90% in (2a) under the *General rule*, earlier. If your AGI for 2022 was more than $150,000 ($75,000 if your filing status for 2023 is married filing a separate return), substitute 110% for 100% in (2b) under *General rule*, earlier. See *Figure 4-A* and Pub. 505, chapter 2, for more information.

Aliens. Resident and nonresident aliens may also have to pay estimated tax. Resident aliens should follow the rules in this chapter unless noted otherwise. Nonresident aliens should get Form 1040-ES (NR), U.S. Estimated Tax for Nonresident Alien Individuals.

You are an alien if you aren't a citizen or national of the United States. You are a resident alien if you either have a green card or meet the substantial presence test. For more information about the substantial presence test, see Pub. 519, U.S. Tax Guide for Aliens.

Married taxpayers. If you qualify to make joint estimated tax payments, apply the rules discussed here to your joint estimated income.

You and your spouse can make joint estimated tax payments even if you aren't living together.

However, you and your spouse can't make joint estimated tax payments if:

- You are legally separated under a decree of divorce or separate maintenance,

- You and your spouse have different tax years, or

- Either spouse is a nonresident alien (unless that spouse elected to be treated as a resident alien for tax purposes (see chapter 1 of Pub. 519)).

If you and your spouse can't make estimated tax payments, apply these rules to your separate estimated income. Making joint or separate estimated tax payments won't affect your choice of filing a joint tax return or separate returns for 2023.

2022 separate returns and 2023 joint return. If you plan to file a joint return with your spouse for 2023 but you filed separate returns for 2022, your 2022 tax is the total of the tax shown on your separate returns. You filed a separate return if you filed as single, head of household, or married filing separately.

2022 joint return and 2023 separate returns. If you plan to file a separate return for 2023 but you filed a joint return for 2022, your 2022 tax is your share of the tax on the joint return. You file a separate return if you file as single, head of household, or married filing separately.

To figure your share of the tax on the joint return, first figure the tax both you and your spouse would have paid had you filed separate returns for 2022 using the same filing status as for 2023. Then, multiply the tax on the joint return by the following fraction.

$$\frac{\text{The tax you would have paid had you filed a separate return}}{\text{The total tax you and your spouse would have paid had you filed separate returns}}$$

Example. Taxpayer A and Taxpayer B filed a joint return for 2022 showing taxable income of $48,500 and tax of $5,412. Of the $48,500 taxable income, $40,100 was Taxpayer A's and the rest was Taxpayer B's. For 2023, they plan to file married filing separately. Taxpayer A figures tax on the 2022 joint return as follows.

Tax on $40,100 based on a separate return	$4,610
Tax on $8,400 based on a separate return	843
Total	$5,453
Taxpayer A's percentage of total ($4,610 ÷ $5,453) . . .	85%
Taxpayer A's share of tax on joint return ($5,412 × 85%)	$4,600

How To Figure Estimated Tax

To figure your estimated tax, you must figure your expected adjusted gross income (AGI), taxable income, taxes, deductions, and credits for the year.

When figuring your 2023 estimated tax, it may be helpful to use your income, deductions, and credits for 2022 as a starting point. Use your 2022 federal tax return as a guide. You can use Form 1040-ES and Pub. 505 to figure your estimated tax. Nonresident aliens use Form 1040-ES (NR) and Pub. 505 to figure estimated tax (see chapter 8 of Pub. 519 for more information).

You must make adjustments both for changes in your own situation and for recent changes in the tax law. For a discussion of these changes, visit *IRS.gov*.

For more complete information on how to figure your estimated tax for 2023, see chapter 2 of Pub. 505.

When To Pay Estimated Tax

For estimated tax purposes, the tax year is divided into four payment periods. Each period has a specific payment due date. If you don't pay enough tax by the due date of each payment period, you may be charged a penalty even if you are due a refund when you file your income tax return. The payment periods and due dates for estimated tax payments are shown next.

For the period:	Due date:*
Jan. 1–March 31	April 18
April 1–May 31	June 15
June 1–August 31	Sept. 15
Sept. 1–Dec. 31	Jan. 16, next year

*See *Saturday, Sunday, holiday rule* and *January payment*.

Saturday, Sunday, holiday rule. If the due date for an estimated tax payment falls on a Saturday, Sunday, or legal holiday, the payment will be on time if you make it on the next day that isn't a Saturday, Sunday, or legal holiday.

January payment. If you file your 2023 Form 1040 or 1040-SR by January 31, 2024, and pay the rest of the tax you owe, you don't need to make the payment due on January 16, 2024.

Fiscal year taxpayers. If your tax year doesn't start on January 1, see the Form 1040-ES instructions for your payment due dates.

When To Start

You don't have to make estimated tax payments until you have income on which you will owe income tax. If you have income subject to estimated tax during the first payment period, you must make your first payment by the due date for the first payment period. You can pay all your estimated tax at that time, or you can pay it in installments. If you choose to pay in installments, make your first payment by the due date for the first payment period. Make your remaining installment payments by the due dates for the later periods.

No income subject to estimated tax during first period. If you don't have income subject to estimated tax until a later payment period, you must make your first payment by the due date for that period. You can pay your entire estimated tax by the due date for that period or you can pay it in installments by the due date for that period and the due dates for the remaining periods.

Table 4-1. **General Due Dates for Estimated Tax Installment Payments**

If you first have income on which you must pay estimated tax:	Make installments by:*	Make later installments by:*
Before April 1	April 15	June 15 Sept. 15 Jan. 15, next year
April 1–May 31	June 15	Sept. 15 Jan. 15, next year
June 1–Aug. 31	Sept. 15	Jan. 15, next year
After Aug. 31	Jan. 15, next year	(None)

*See *Saturday, Sunday, holiday rule* and *January payment*.

How much to pay to avoid a penalty. To determine how much you should pay by each payment due date, see *How To Figure Each Payment* next.

How To Figure Each Payment

You should pay enough estimated tax by the due date of each payment period to avoid a penalty for that period. You can figure your required payment for each period by using either the regular installment method or the annualized income installment method. These methods are described in chapter 2 of Pub. 505. If

you don't pay enough during each payment period, you may be charged a penalty even if you are due a refund when you file your tax return.

If the earlier discussion of *No income subject to estimated tax during first period* or the later discussion of *Change in estimated tax* applies to you, you may benefit from reading *Annualized Income Installment Method* in chapter 2 of Pub. 505 for information on how to avoid a penalty.

Underpayment penalty. Under the regular installment method, if your estimated tax payment for any period is less than one-fourth of your estimated tax, you may be charged a penalty for underpayment of estimated tax for that period when you file your tax return. Under the annualized income installment method, your estimated tax payments vary with your income, but the amount required must be paid each period. See *Instructions for Form 2210* for more information.

Change in estimated tax. After you make an estimated tax payment, changes in your income, adjustments, deductions, or credits may make it necessary for you to refigure your estimated tax. Pay the unpaid balance of your amended estimated tax by the next payment due date after the change or in installments by that date and the due dates for the remaining payment periods.

Estimated Tax Payments Not Required

You don't have to pay estimated tax if your withholding in each payment period is at least as much as:

- One-fourth of your required annual payment, or
- Your required annualized income installment for that period.

You also don't have to pay estimated tax if you will pay enough through withholding to keep the amount you owe with your return under $1,000.

How To Pay Estimated Tax

There are several ways to pay estimated tax.

- Credit an overpayment on your 2022 return to your 2023 estimated tax.
- Pay by direct transfer from your bank account, or pay by debit or credit card using a pay-by-phone system or the Internet.
- Send in your payment (check or money order) with a payment voucher from Form 1040-ES.

Credit an Overpayment

If you show an overpayment of tax after completing your Form 1040 or 1040-SR for 2022, you can apply part or all of it to your estimated tax for 2023. On line 36 of Form 1040 or 1040-SR, enter the amount you want credited to your estimated tax rather than refunded. Take the amount you have credited into account when figuring your estimated tax payments.

You can't have any of the amount you credited to your estimated tax refunded to you until you file your tax return for the following year.

You also can't use that overpayment in any other way.

Pay Online

The IRS offers an electronic payment option that is right for you. Paying online is convenient, secure, and helps make sure we get your payments on time. To pay your taxes online or for more information, go to *IRS.gov/Payments*. You can pay using any of the following methods.

- **IRS Direct Pay.** For online transfers directly from your checking or savings account at no cost to you, go to *IRS.gov/Payments*.

- **Pay by Card.** To pay by debit or credit card, go to *IRS.gov/Payments*. A convenience fee is charged by these service providers.

- **Electronic Funds Withdrawal (EFW).** This is an integrated *e-file/e-pay* option offered only when filing your federal taxes electronically using tax preparation software, through a tax professional, or the IRS at *IRS.gov/Payments*.

- **Online Payment Agreement.** If you can't pay in full by the due date of your tax return, you can apply for an online monthly installment agreement at *IRS.gov/Payments*. Once you complete the online process, you will receive immediate notification of whether your agreement has been approved. A user fee is charged.

- **IRS2GO.** This is the mobile application of the IRS. You can access Direct Pay or Pay By Card by downloading the application.

Pay by Phone

Paying by phone is another safe and secure method of paying electronically. Use one of the following methods: **(1)** call one of the debit or credit card providers, or **(2)** use the Electronic Federal Tax Payment System (EFTPS).

Debit or credit card. Call one of our service providers. Each charges a fee that varies by provider, card type, and payment amount.

> ACI Payments, Inc. (Formerly Official Payments)
> 888-272-9829
> *www.fed.acipayonline.com*
>
> Link2Gov Corporation
> 888-PAY-1040™ (888-729-1040)
> *www.PAY1040.com*
>
> WorldPay US, Inc.
> 844-PAY-TAX-8™ (844-729-8298)
> *www.payUSAtax.com*

EFTPS. To get more information about EFTPS or to enroll in EFTPS, visit *EFTPS.gov* or call 800-555-4477. To contact EFTPS using Telecommunications Relay Services (TRS) for people who are deaf, hard of hearing, or have a speech disability, dial 711 and then provide the TRS assistant the 800-555-4477 number above or 800-733-4829. Additional information about EFTPS is also available in Pub. 966.

Pay by Mobile Device

To pay through your mobile device, download the IRS2Go application.

Pay by Cash

Cash is an in-person payment option for individuals provided through retail partners with a maximum of $1,000 per day per transaction. To make a cash payment, you must first be registered online at *www.fed.acipayonline.com*, our Official Payment provider.

Pay by Check or Money Order Using the Estimated Tax Payment Voucher

Before submitting a payment through the mail using the estimated tax payment voucher, please consider alternative methods. One of our safe, quick, and easy electronic payment options might be right for you.

If you choose to mail in your payment, each payment of estimated tax by check or money order must be accompanied by a payment voucher from Form 1040-ES.

During 2022, if you:

- Made at least one estimated tax payment but not by electronic means,

- Didn't use software or a paid preparer to prepare or file your return,

then you should receive a copy of the 2023 Form 1040-ES with payment vouchers.

The enclosed payment vouchers will be preprinted with your name, address, and social security number. Using the preprinted vouchers will speed processing, reduce the chance of error, and help save processing costs.

Use the window envelopes that came with your Form 1040-ES package. If you use your own envelopes, make sure you mail your payment vouchers to the address shown in the Form 1040-ES instructions for the place where you live.

No checks of $100 million or more accepted. The IRS can't accept a single check (including a cashier's check) for amounts of $100,000,000 ($100 million) or more. If you are sending $100 million or more by check, you'll need to spread the payment over two or more checks with each check made out for an amount less than $100 million. This limit doesn't apply to other methods of payment (such as electronic payments). Please consider a method of payment other than check if the amount of the payment is over $100 million.

Note. These criteria can change without notice. If you don't receive a Form 1040-ES package and you are required to make an estimated tax payment, you should go to *IRS.gov/Form1040ES* and print a copy of Form 1040-ES that includes four blank payment vouchers. Complete one of these and make your payment timely to avoid penalties for paying late.

 Don't use the address shown in the Instructions for Form 1040 for your estimated tax payments.

If you didn't pay estimated tax last year, you can order Form 1040-ES from the IRS (see the inside back cover of this publication) or download it from IRS.gov. Follow the instructions to make sure you use the vouchers correctly.

Joint estimated tax payments. If you file a joint return and are making joint estimated tax payments, enter the names and social security numbers on the payment voucher in the same order as they will appear on the joint return.

Change of address. You must notify the IRS if you are making estimated tax payments and you changed your address during the year. Complete Form 8822, Change of Address, and mail it to the address shown in the instructions for that form.

Credit for Withholding and Estimated Tax for 2022

When you file your 2022 income tax return, take credit for all the income tax and excess social security or railroad retirement tax withheld from your salary, wages, pensions, etc. Also take credit for the estimated tax you paid for 2022. These credits are subtracted from your total tax. Because these credits are refundable, you should file a return and claim these credits, even if you don't owe tax.

Two or more employers. If you had two or more employers in 2022 and were paid wages of more than $147,000, too much social security or tier 1 railroad retirement tax may have been withheld from your pay. You may be able to claim the excess as a credit against your income tax when you file your return. See the Instructions for Form 1040 for more information.

Withholding

If you had income tax withheld during 2022, you should be sent a statement by January 31, 2023, showing your income and the tax withheld. Depending on the source of your income, you should receive:

- Form W-2, Wage and Tax Statement;

- Form W-2G, Certain Gambling Winnings; or

- A form in the 1099 series.

Forms W-2 and W-2G. If you file a paper return, always file Form W-2 with your income tax return. File Form W-2G with your return only if it shows any federal income tax withheld from your winnings.

You should get at least two copies of each form. If you file a paper return, attach one copy to the front of your federal income tax return. Keep one copy for your records. You should also receive copies to file with your state and local returns.

Form W-2

Your employer is required to provide or send Form W-2 to you no later than January 31, 2023. You should receive a separate Form W-2 from each employer you worked for.

If you stopped working before the end of 2022, your employer could have given you your

Form W-2 at any time after you stopped working. However, your employer must provide or send it to you by January 31, 2023.

If you ask for the form, your employer must send it to you within 30 days after receiving your written request or within 30 days after your final wage payment, whichever is later.

If you haven't received your Form W-2 by January 31, you should ask your employer for it. If you don't receive it by early February, call the IRS.

Form W-2 shows your total pay and other compensation and the income tax, social security tax, and Medicare tax that was withheld during the year. Include the federal income tax withheld (as shown in box 2 of Form W-2) on Form 1040 or 1040-SR, line 25a.

In addition, Form W-2 is used to report any taxable sick pay you received and any income tax withheld from your sick pay.

Form W-2G

If you had gambling winnings in 2022, the payer may have withheld income tax. If tax was withheld, the payer will give you a Form W-2G showing the amount you won and the amount of tax withheld.

Report the amounts you won on Schedule 1 (Form 1040). Take credit for the tax withheld on Form 1040 or 1040-SR, line 25c.

The 1099 Series

Most forms in the 1099 series aren't filed with your return. These forms should be furnished to you by January 31, 2023 (or, for Forms 1099-B, 1099-S, and certain Forms 1099-MISC, by February 15, 2023). Unless instructed to file any of these forms with your return, keep them for your records. There are several different forms in this series, which are not listed. See the instructions for the specific Form 1099 for more information.

Form 1099-R. Attach Form 1099-R to your paper return if box 4 shows federal income tax withheld. Include the amount withheld in the total on line 25b of Form 1040 or 1040-SR.

Backup withholding. If you were subject to backup withholding on income you received during 2022, include the amount withheld, as shown on your Form 1099, in the total on line 25b of Form 1040 or 1040-SR.

Form Not Correct

If you receive a form with incorrect information on it, you should ask the payer for a corrected form. Call the telephone number or write to the address given for the payer on the form. The corrected Form W-2G or Form 1099 you receive will have an "X" in the "CORRECTED" box at the top of the form. A special form, Form W-2c, Corrected Wage and Tax Statement, is used to correct a Form W-2.

In certain situations, you will receive two forms in place of the original incorrect form. This will happen when your taxpayer identification number is wrong or missing, your name and address are wrong, or you received the wrong type of form (for example, a Form 1099-DIV, Dividends and Distributions, instead of a Form 1099-INT, Interest Income). One new form you receive will be the same incorrect form or have the same incorrect information, but all money amounts will be zero. This form will have an "X" in the "CORRECTED" box at the top of the form. The second new form should have all the correct information, prepared as though it is the original (the "CORRECTED" box won't be checked).

Form Received After Filing

If you file your return and you later receive a form for income that you didn't include on your return, you should report the income and take credit for any income tax withheld by filing Form 1040-X, Amended U.S. Individual Income Tax Return.

Separate Returns

If you are married but file a separate return, you can take credit only for the tax withheld from your own income. Don't include any amount withheld from your spouse's income. However, different rules may apply if you live in a community property state.

Community property states are listed in chapter 2. For more information on these rules, and some exceptions, see Pub. 555, Community Property.

Estimated Tax

Take credit for all your estimated tax payments for 2022 on Form 1040 or 1040-SR, line 26. Include any overpayment from 2021 that you had credited to your 2022 estimated tax.

Name changed. If you changed your name, and you made estimated tax payments using your old name, attach a brief statement to the front of your paper tax return indicating:

- When you made the payments,
- The amount of each payment,
- Your name when you made the payments, and
- Your social security number.

The statement should cover payments you made jointly with your spouse as well as any you made separately.

Be sure to report the change to the Social Security Administration. This prevents delays in processing your return and issuing any refunds.

Separate Returns

If you and your spouse made separate estimated tax payments for 2022 and you file separate returns, you can take credit only for your own payments.

If you made joint estimated tax payments, you must decide how to divide the payments between your returns. One of you can claim all of the estimated tax paid and the other none, or you can divide it in any other way you agree on.

If you can't agree, you must divide the payments in proportion to each spouse's individual tax as shown on your separate returns for 2022.

Divorced Taxpayers

If you made joint estimated tax payments for 2022, and you were divorced during the year, either you or your former spouse can claim all of the joint payments, or you each can claim part of them. If you can't agree on how to divide the payments, you must divide them in proportion to each spouse's individual tax as shown on your separate returns for 2022.

If you claim any of the joint payments on your tax return, enter your former spouse's social security number (SSN) in the space provided on the front of Form 1040 or 1040-SR. If you divorced and remarried in 2022, enter your present spouse's SSN in the space provided on the front of Form 1040 or 1040-SR. Also, on the dotted line next to line 26, enter your former spouse's SSN, followed by "DIV."

Underpayment Penalty for 2022

If you didn't pay enough tax, either through withholding or by making timely estimated tax payments, you will have an underpayment of estimated tax and you may have to pay a penalty.

Generally, you won't have to pay a penalty for 2022 if any of the following apply.

- The total of your withholding and estimated tax payments was at least as much as your 2021 tax (or 110% of your 2021 tax if your AGI was more than $150,000, $75,000 if your 2022 filing status is married filing separately) and you paid all required estimated tax payments on time;

- The tax balance due on your 2022 return is no more than 10% of your total 2022 tax, and you paid all required estimated tax payments on time;

- Your total 2022 tax minus your withholding and refundable credits is less than $1,000;

- You didn't have a tax liability for 2021 and your 2021 tax year was 12 months; or

- You didn't have any withholding taxes and your current year tax less any household employment taxes is less than $1,000.

Farmers and fishermen. Special rules apply if you are a farmer or fisherman. See the *Instructions for Form 2210-F* for more information.

IRS can figure the penalty for you. If you think you owe the penalty but you don't want to figure it yourself when you file your tax return, you may not have to. Generally, the IRS will figure the penalty for you and send you a bill. However, if you think you are able to lower or eliminate your penalty, you must complete Form 2210 or Form 2210-F and attach it to your paper return. See *Instructions for Form 2210* for more information.

Part Two.

Income and Adjustments to Income

The five chapters in this part discuss many kinds of income and adjustments to income. They explain which income is and isn't taxed and discuss some of the adjustments to income that you can make in figuring your adjusted gross income.

The Form 1040 and 1040-SR schedules that are discussed in these chapters are:

- *Schedule 1, Additional Income and Adjustments to Income;*
- *Schedule 2 (Part II), Other Taxes; and*
- *Schedule 3 (Part II), Other Payments and Refundable Credits.*

Table V. **Other Adjustments to Income**

Use this table to find information about other adjustments to income not covered in this part of the publication.

IF you are looking for more information about the deduction for...	THEN see...
contributions to a health savings account	*Pub. 969, Health Savings Accounts and Other Tax-Favored Health Plans.*
moving expenses	*Pub. 3, Armed Forces' Tax Guide.*
part of your self-employment tax	*chapter 11.*
self-employed health insurance	*Pub. 502, Medical and Dental Expenses.*
payments to self-employed SEP, SIMPLE, and qualified plans	*Pub. 560, Retirement Plans for Small Business.*
penalty on the early withdrawal of savings	*chapter 6.*
contributions to an Archer MSA	*Pub. 969.*
reforestation amortization or expense	*chapters 7 and 8 of Pub. 535, Business Expenses.*
contributions to Internal Revenue Code section 501(c)(18)(D) pension plans	*Pub. 525, Taxable and Nontaxable Income.*
expenses from the rental of personal property	*chapter 8.*
certain required repayments of supplemental unemployment benefits (sub-pay)	*chapter 8.*
foreign housing costs	*chapter 4 of Pub. 54, Tax Guide for U.S. Citizens and Resident Aliens Abroad.*
jury duty pay given to your employer	*chapter 8.*
contributions by certain ministers or chaplains to Internal Revenue Code section 403(b) plans	*Pub. 517, Social Security and Other Information for Members of the Clergy and Religious Workers.*
attorney fees and certain costs for actions involving IRS awards to whistleblowers	*Pub. 525.*

5.

Wages, Salaries, and Other Earnings

Reminders

Deferred compensation contribution limit. If you participate in a 401(k) plan, 403(b) plan, or the federal government's Thrift Savings Plan, the total annual amount you can contribute is increased to $20,500 for 2022. This also applies to most 457 plans.

Introduction

This chapter discusses compensation received for services as an employee, such as wages, salaries, and fringe benefits. The following topics are included.

- Bonuses and awards.
- Special rules for certain employees.
- Sickness and injury benefits.

The chapter explains what income is included and isn't included in the employee's gross income and what's not included.

Useful Items

You may want to see:

Publication

- ❏ **463** Travel, Gift, and Car Expenses
- ❏ **502** Medical and Dental Expenses
- ❏ **524** Credit for the Elderly or the Disabled
- ❏ **525** Taxable and Nontaxable Income
- ❏ **526** Charitable Contributions
- ❏ **550** Investment Income and Expenses
- ❏ **554** Tax Guide for Seniors
- ❏ **575** Pension and Annuity Income
- ❏ **907** Tax Highlights for Persons With Disabilities
- ❏ **926** Household Employer's Tax Guide
- ❏ **3920** Tax Relief for Victims of Terrorist Attacks

For these and other useful items, go to *IRS.gov/Forms*.

Employee Compensation

This section discusses various types of employee compensation, including fringe benefits, retirement plan contributions, stock options, and restricted property.

Form W-2. If you're an employee, you should receive a Form W-2 from your employer showing the pay you received for your services. Include your pay on line 1 of Form 1040 or 1040-SR, even if you don't receive a Form W-2.

In some instances, your employer isn't required to give you a Form W-2. Your employer isn't required to give you a Form W-2 if you perform household work in your employer's home for less than $2,400 in cash wages during the calendar year and you have no federal income taxes withheld from your wages. Household work is work done in or around an employer's home. Some examples of workers who do household work are:

- Babysitters,
- Caretakers,
- House cleaning workers,
- Domestic workers,
- Drivers,
- Health aides,
- Housekeepers,
- Maids,
- Nannies,
- Private nurses, and
- Yard workers.

See Schedule H (Form 1040), Household Employment Taxes, and its instructions, and Pub. 926 for more information.

If you performed services, other than as an independent contractor, and your employer didn't withhold social security and Medicare taxes from your pay, you must file Form 8919, Uncollected Social Security and Medicare Tax on Wages, with your Form 1040 or 1040-SR. See Form 8919 and its instructions for more information on how to figure unreported wages and taxes and how to include them on your income tax return.

Childcare providers. If you provide childcare, either in the child's home or in your home or other place of business, the pay you receive must be included in your income. If you aren't an employee, you're probably self-employed and must include payments for your services on Schedule C (Form 1040), Profit or Loss From Business. You generally aren't an employee unless you're subject to the will and control of the person who employs you as to what you're to do and how you're to do it.

Babysitting. If you're paid to babysit, even for relatives or neighborhood children, whether on a regular basis or only periodically, the rules for childcare providers apply to you.

Employment tax. Whether you're an employee or self-employed person, your income could be subject to self-employment tax. See the instructions for Schedules C and SE (Form 1040) if you're self-employed. Also, see Pub. 926 for more information.

Miscellaneous Compensation

This section discusses different types of employee compensation.

Advance commissions and other earnings. If you receive advance commissions or other amounts for services to be performed in the future and you're a cash-method taxpayer, you must include these amounts in your income in the year you receive them.

If you repay unearned commissions or other amounts in the same year you receive them, reduce the amount included in your income by the repayment. If you repay them in a later tax year, you can deduct the repayment as an itemized deduction on your Schedule A (Form 1040), line 16, or you may be able to take a credit for that year. See *Repayments* in chapter 8.

Allowances and reimbursements. If you receive travel, transportation, or other business expense allowances or reimbursements from your employer, see Pub. 463, Travel, Gift, and Car Expenses. If you're reimbursed for moving expenses, see Pub. 521, Moving Expenses.

Back pay awards. If you receive an amount in payment of a settlement or judgment for back pay, you must include the amount of the payment in your income. This includes payments made to you for damages, unpaid life insurance premiums, and unpaid health insurance premiums. They should be reported to you by your employer on Form W-2.

Bonuses and awards. If you receive a bonus or award (cash, goods, services, etc.) from your employer, you must include its value in your income. However, if your employer merely promises to pay you a bonus or award at some future time, it isn't taxable until you receive it or it's made available to you.

Employee achievement award. If you receive tangible personal property (other than cash, a gift certificate, or an equivalent item) as an award for length of service or safety achievement, you can generally exclude its value from your income. The amount you can exclude is limited to your employer's cost and can't be more than $1,600 for qualified plan awards or $400 for nonqualified plan awards for all such awards you receive during the year. Your employer can tell you whether your award is a qualified plan award. Your employer must make the award as part of a meaningful presentation, under conditions and circumstances that don't create a significant likelihood of it being disguised pay.

However, the exclusion doesn't apply to the following awards.

- A length-of-service award if you received it for less than 5 years of service or if you received another length-of-service award during the year or the previous 4 years.

- A safety achievement award if you're a manager, administrator, clerical employee, or other professional employee or if more than 10% of eligible employees previously received safety achievement awards during the year.

Example. Ben Green received three employee achievement awards during the year: a nonqualified plan award of a watch valued at $250, two qualified plan awards of a stereo valued at $1,000, and a set of golf clubs valued at $500. Assuming that the requirements for qualified plan awards are otherwise satisfied, each award by itself would be excluded from income. However, because the $1,750 total value of the awards is more than $1,600, Ben must include $150 ($1,750 – $1,600) in his income.

Differential wage payments. This is any payment made to you by an employer for any period during which you are, for a period of more than 30 days, an active duty member of the uniformed services and represents all or a portion of the wages you would have received from the employer during that period. These payments are treated as wages and are subject to income tax withholding, but not FICA or FUTA taxes. The payments are reported as wages on Form W-2.

Government cost-of-living allowances. Most payments received by U.S. Government civilian employees for working abroad are taxable. However, certain cost-of-living allowances are tax free. Pub. 516, U.S. Government Civilian Employees Stationed Abroad, explains the tax treatment of allowances, differentials, and other special pay you receive for employment abroad.

Nonqualified deferred compensation plans. Your employer may report to you the total amount of deferrals for the year under a nonqualified deferred compensation plan on Form W-2, box 12, using code Y. This amount isn't included in your income.

However, if at any time during the tax year, the plan fails to meet certain requirements, or isn't operated under those requirements, all amounts deferred under the plan for the tax year and all preceding tax years to the extent vested and not previously included in income are included in your income for the current year. This amount is included in your wages shown on Form W-2, box 1. It's also shown on Form W-2, box 12, using code Z.

Note received for services. If your employer gives you a secured note as payment for your services, you must include the fair market value (usually the discount value) of the note in your income for the year you receive it. When you later receive payments on the note, a proportionate part of each payment is the recovery of the fair market value that you previously included in your income. Don't include that part again in your income. Include the rest of the payment in your income in the year of payment.

If your employer gives you a nonnegotiable unsecured note as payment for your services, payments on the note that are credited toward the principal amount of the note are compensation income when you receive them.

Severance pay. If you receive a severance payment when your employment with your employer ends or is terminated, you must include this amount in your income.

Accrued leave payment. If you're a federal employee and receive a lump-sum payment for accrued annual leave when you retire or resign, this amount will be included as wages on your Form W-2.

If you resign from one agency and are reemployed by another agency, you may have to repay part of your lump-sum annual leave payment to the second agency. You can reduce gross wages by the amount you repaid in the same tax year in which you received it. Attach to your tax return a copy of the receipt or statement given to you by the agency you repaid to explain the difference between the wages on the return and the wages on your Forms W-2.

Outplacement services. If you choose to accept a reduced amount of severance pay so that you can receive outplacement services (such as training in résumé writing and interview techniques), you must include the unreduced amount of the severance pay in income.

Sick pay. Pay you receive from your employer while you're sick or injured is part of your salary or wages. In addition, you must include in your income sick pay benefits received from any of the following payers.

- A welfare fund.
- A state sickness or disability fund.
- An association of employers or employees.
- An insurance company, if your employer paid for the plan.

However, if you paid the premiums on an accident or health insurance policy yourself, the benefits you receive under the policy aren't taxable. For more information, see Pub. 525, Taxable and Nontaxable Income.

Social security and Medicare taxes paid by employer. If you and your employer have an agreement that your employer pays your social security and Medicare taxes without deducting them from your gross wages, you must report the amount of tax paid for you as taxable wages on your tax return. The payment is also treated as wages for figuring your social security and Medicare taxes and your social security and Medicare benefits. However, these payments aren't treated as social security and Medicare wages if you're a household worker or a farm worker.

Stock appreciation rights. Don't include a stock appreciation right granted by your employer in income until you exercise (use) the right. When you use the right, you're entitled to a cash payment equal to the fair market value of the corporation's stock on the date of use minus the fair market value on the date the right was granted. You include the cash payment in your income in the year you use the right.

Fringe Benefits

Fringe benefits received in connection with the performance of your services are included in your income as compensation unless you pay fair market value for them or they're specifically excluded by law. Refraining from the performance of services (for example, under a covenant not to compete) is treated as the performance of services for purposes of these rules.

Accounting period. You must use the same accounting period your employer uses to report your taxable noncash fringe benefits. Your employer has the option to report taxable noncash fringe benefits by using either of the following rules.

- The general rule: benefits are reported for a full calendar year (January 1–December 31).

- The special accounting period rule: benefits provided during the last 2 months of the calendar year (or any shorter period) are treated as paid during the following calendar year. For example, each year your employer reports the value of benefits provided during the last 2 months of the prior year and the first 10 months of the current year.

Your employer doesn't have to use the same accounting period for each fringe benefit, but must use the same period for all employees who receive a particular benefit.

You must use the same accounting period that you use to report the benefit to claim an employee business deduction (for use of a car, for example).

Form W-2. Your employer must include all taxable fringe benefits in box 1 of Form W-2 as wages, tips, and other compensation and, if applicable, in boxes 3 and 5 as social security and Medicare wages. Although not required, your employer may include the total value of fringe benefits in box 14 (or on a separate statement). However, if your employer provided you with a vehicle and included 100% of its annual lease value in your income, the employer must separately report this value to you in box 14 (or on a separate statement).

Accident or Health Plan

In most cases, the value of accident or health plan coverage provided to you by your employer isn't included in your income. Benefits you receive from the plan may be taxable, as explained later under *Sickness and Injury Benefits*.

For information on the items covered in this section, other than long-term care coverage, see Pub. 969, Health Savings Accounts and Other Tax-Favored Health Plans.

Long-term care coverage. Contributions by your employer to provide coverage for long-term care services generally aren't included in your income. However, contributions made through a flexible spending or similar arrangement offered by your employer must be included in your income. This amount will be reported as wages in box 1 of your Form W-2.

Contributions you make to the plan are discussed in Pub. 502, Medical and Dental Expenses.

Archer MSA contributions. Contributions by your employer to your Archer MSA generally aren't included in your income. Their total will be reported in box 12 of Form W-2 with code R. You must report this amount on Form 8853, Archer MSAs and Long-Term Care Insurance Contracts. File the form with your return.

Health flexible spending arrangement (health FSA). If your employer provides a health FSA that qualifies as an accident or health plan, the amount of your salary reduction, and reimbursements of your medical care expenses, in most cases, aren't included in your income.

Note. Health FSAs are subject to a limit on salary reduction contributions for plan years beginning after 2012. For tax years beginning in

2022, the dollar limitation (as indexed for inflation) on voluntary employee salary reductions for contributions to health FSAs is $2,850.

Health reimbursement arrangement (HRA). If your employer provides an HRA that qualifies as an accident or health plan, coverage and reimbursements of your medical care expenses generally aren't included in your income.

Health savings account (HSA). If you're an eligible individual, you and any other person, including your employer or a family member, can make contributions to your HSA. Contributions, other than employer contributions, are deductible on your return whether or not you itemize deductions. Contributions made by your employer aren't included in your income. Distributions from your HSA that are used to pay qualified medical expenses aren't included in your income. Distributions not used for qualified medical expenses are included in your income. See Pub. 969 for the requirements of an HSA.

Contributions by a partnership to a bona fide partner's HSA aren't contributions by an employer. The contributions are treated as a distribution of money and aren't included in the partner's gross income. Contributions by a partnership to a partner's HSA for services rendered are treated as guaranteed payments that are includible in the partner's gross income. In both situations, the partner can deduct the contribution made to the partner's HSA.

Contributions by an S corporation to a 2% shareholder-employee's HSA for services rendered are treated as guaranteed payments and are includible in the shareholder-employee's gross income. The shareholder-employee can deduct the contribution made to the shareholder-employee's HSA.

Qualified HSA funding distribution. You can make a one-time distribution from your individual retirement account (IRA) to an HSA and you generally won't include any of the distribution in your income.

Adoption Assistance

You may be able to exclude from your income amounts paid or expenses incurred by your employer for qualified adoption expenses in connection with your adoption of an eligible child. See the Instructions for Form 8839, Qualified Adoption Expenses, for more information.

Adoption benefits are reported by your employer in box 12 of Form W-2 with code T. They are also included as social security and Medicare wages in boxes 3 and 5. However, they aren't included as wages in box 1. To determine the taxable and nontaxable amounts, you must complete Part III of Form 8839. File the form with your return.

De Minimis (Minimal) Benefits

If your employer provides you with a product or service and the cost of it is so small that it would be unreasonable for the employer to account for it, you generally don't include its value in your income. In most cases, don't include in your income the value of discounts at company cafeterias, cab fares home when working overtime, and company picnics.

Holiday gifts. If your employer gives you a turkey, ham, or other item of nominal value at Christmas or other holidays, don't include the value of the gift in your income. However, if your employer gives you cash or a cash equivalent, you must include it in your income.

Educational Assistance

You can exclude from your income up to $5,250 of qualified employer-provided educational assistance. For more information, see Pub. 970, Tax Benefits for Education.

Group-Term Life Insurance

In most cases, the cost of up to $50,000 of group-term life insurance coverage provided to you by your employer (or former employer) isn't included in your income. However, you must include in income the cost of employer-provided insurance that is more than the cost of $50,000 of coverage reduced by any amount you pay toward the purchase of the insurance.

For exceptions, see *Entire cost excluded* and *Entire cost taxed*, later.

If your employer provided more than $50,000 of coverage, the amount included in your income is reported as part of your wages in box 1 of your Form W-2. Also, it's shown separately in box 12 with code C.

Group-term life insurance. This insurance is term life insurance protection (insurance for a fixed period of time) that:

- Provides a general death benefit,

- Is provided to a group of employees,

- Is provided under a policy carried by the employer, and

- Provides an amount of insurance to each employee based on a formula that prevents individual selection.

Permanent benefits. If your group-term life insurance policy includes permanent benefits, such as a paid-up or cash surrender value, you must include in your income, as wages, the cost of the permanent benefits minus the amount you pay for them. Your employer should be able to tell you the amount to include in your income.

Accidental death benefits. Insurance that provides accidental or other death benefits but doesn't provide general death benefits (travel insurance, for example) isn't group-term life insurance.

Former employer. If your former employer provided more than $50,000 of group-term life insurance coverage during the year, the amount included in your income is reported as wages in box 1 of Form W-2. Also, it's shown separately in box 12 with code C. Box 12 will also show the amount of uncollected social security and Medicare taxes on the excess coverage, with codes M and N. You must pay these taxes with your income tax return. Include them on Schedule 2 (Form 1040), line 13.

Two or more employers. Your exclusion for employer-provided group-term life insurance coverage can't exceed the cost of $50,000 of coverage, whether the insurance is provided by a single employer or multiple employers. If two or more employers provide insurance coverage

that totals more than $50,000, the amounts reported as wages on your Forms W-2 won't be correct. You must figure how much to include in your income. Reduce the amount you figure by any amount reported with code C in box 12 of your Forms W-2, add the result to the wages reported in box 1, and report the total on your return.

Figuring the taxable cost. Use Worksheet 5-1 to figure the amount to include in your income.

Worksheet 5-1. Figuring the Cost of Group-Term Life Insurance To Include in Income
Keep for Your Records

1. Enter the total amount of your insurance coverage from your employer(s)	1. _____
2. Limit on exclusion for employer-provided group-term life insurance coverage	2. **50,000**
3. Subtract line 2 from line 1	3. _____
4. Divide line 3 by $1,000. Figure to the nearest tenth	4. _____
5. Go to Table 5-1. Using your age on the last day of the tax year, find your age group in the left column, and enter the cost from the column on the right for your age group	5. _____
6. Multiply line 4 by line 5	6. _____
7. Enter the number of full months of coverage at this cost	7. _____
8. Multiply line 6 by line 7	8. _____
9. Enter the premiums you paid per month . . . . . 9. _____	
10. Enter the number of months you paid the premiums . . . . . 10. _____	
11. Multiply line 9 by line 10	11. _____
12. Subtract line 11 from line 8. **Include this amount in your income as wages**	12. _____

Table 5-1. Cost of $1,000 of Group-Term Life Insurance for 1 Month

Age	Cost
Under 25	$ 0.05
25 through 29	0.06
30 through 34	0.08
35 through 39	0.09
40 through 44	0.10
45 through 49	0.15
50 through 54	0.23
55 through 59	0.43
60 through 64	0.66
65 through 69	1.27
70 and above	2.06

Example. You are 51 years old and work for employers A and B. Both employers provide group-term life insurance coverage for you for the entire year. Your coverage is $35,000 with employer A and $45,000 with employer B. You pay premiums of $4.15 a month under the employer B group plan. You figure the amount to include in your income as shown in Worksheet 5-1. Figuring the Cost of Group-Term Life Insurance To Include in Income—Illustrated next.

Worksheet 5-1. Figuring the Cost of Group-Term Life Insurance To Include in Income—Illustrated

Keep for Your Records

1.	Enter the total amount of your insurance coverage from your employer(s)	1. **80,000**
2.	Limit on exclusion for employer-provided group-term life insurance coverage	2. **50,000**
3.	Subtract line 2 from line 1	3. **30,000**
4.	Divide line 3 by $1,000. Figure to the nearest tenth	4. **30.0**
5.	Go to Table 5-1. Using your age on the last day of the tax year, find your age group in the left column, and enter the cost from the column on the right for your age group	5. **0.23**
6.	Multiply line 4 by line 5	6. **6.90**
7.	Enter the number of full months of coverage at this cost	7. **12**
8.	Multiply line 6 by line 7	8. **82.80**
9.	Enter the premiums you paid per month	9. **4.15**
10.	Enter the number of months you paid the premiums	10. **12**
11.	Multiply line 9 by line 10	11. **49.80**
12.	Subtract line 11 from line 8. **Include this amount in your income as wages**	12. **33.00**

Entire cost excluded. You aren't taxed on the cost of group-term life insurance if any of the following circumstances apply.

1. You're permanently and totally disabled and have ended your employment.

2. Your employer is the beneficiary of the policy for the entire period the insurance is in force during the tax year.

3. A charitable organization (defined in Pub. 526, Charitable Contributions) to which contributions are deductible is the only beneficiary of the policy for the entire period the insurance is in force during the tax year. (You aren't entitled to a deduction for a charitable contribution for naming a charitable organization as the beneficiary of your policy.)

4. The plan existed on January 1, 1984, and:

   a. You retired before January 2, 1984, and were covered by the plan when you retired, or

   b. You reached age 55 before January 2, 1984, and were employed by the employer or its predecessor in 1983.

Entire cost taxed. You're taxed on the entire cost of group-term life insurance if either of the following circumstances apply.

- The insurance is provided by your employer through a qualified employees' trust, such as a pension trust or a qualified annuity plan.

- You're a key employee and your employer's plan discriminates in favor of key employees.

Retirement Planning Services

Generally, don't include the value of qualified retirement planning services provided to you and your spouse by your employer's qualified retirement plan. Qualified services include retirement planning advice, information about your employer's retirement plan, and information about how the plan may fit into your overall individual retirement income plan. You can't exclude the value of any tax preparation, accounting, legal, or brokerage services provided by your employer.

Transportation

If your employer provides you with a qualified transportation fringe benefit, it can be excluded from your income, up to certain limits. A qualified transportation fringe benefit is:

- Transportation in a commuter highway vehicle (such as a van) between your home and work place,

- A transit pass, or

- Qualified parking.

Cash reimbursement by your employer for these expenses under a bona fide reimbursement arrangement is also excludable. However, cash reimbursement for a transit pass is excludable only if a voucher or similar item that can be exchanged only for a transit pass isn't readily available for direct distribution to you.

Exclusion limit. The exclusion for commuter vehicle transportation and transit pass fringe benefits can't be more than $280 a month.

The exclusion for the qualified parking fringe benefit can't be more than $280 a month.

If the benefits have a value that is more than these limits, the excess must be included in your income.

Commuter highway vehicle. This is a highway vehicle that seats at least six adults (not including the driver). At least 80% of the vehicle's mileage must reasonably be expected to be:

- For transporting employees between their homes and workplace, and

- On trips during which employees occupy at least half of the vehicle's adult seating capacity (not including the driver).

Transit pass. This is any pass, token, farecard, voucher, or similar item entitling a person to ride mass transit (whether public or private) free or at a reduced rate or to ride in a commuter highway vehicle operated by a person in the business of transporting persons for compensation.

Qualified parking. This is parking provided to an employee at or near the employer's place of business. It also includes parking provided on or near a location from which the employee commutes to work by mass transit, in a commuter highway vehicle, or by carpool. It doesn't include parking at or near the employee's home.

Retirement Plan Contributions

Your employer's contributions to a qualified retirement plan for you aren't included in income at the time contributed. (Your employer can tell you whether your retirement plan is qualified.) However, the cost of life insurance coverage included in the plan may have to be included. See *Group-Term Life Insurance*, earlier, under *Fringe Benefits*.

If your employer pays into a nonqualified plan for you, you must generally include the contributions in your income as wages for the tax year in which the contributions are made. However, if your interest in the plan isn't transferable or is subject to a substantial risk of forfeiture (you have a good chance of losing it) at the time of the contribution, you don't have to include the value of your interest in your income until it's transferable or is no longer subject to a substantial risk of forfeiture.

 For information on distributions from retirement plans, see Pub. 575, Pension and Annuity Income (or Pub. 721, Tax Guide to U.S. Civil Service Retirement Benefits, if you're a federal employee or retiree).

Elective deferrals. If you're covered by certain kinds of retirement plans, you can choose to have part of your compensation contributed by your employer to a retirement fund, rather than have it paid to you. The amount you set aside (called an "elective deferral") is treated as an employer contribution to a qualified plan. An elective deferral, other than a designated Roth contribution (discussed later), isn't included in wages subject to income tax at the time contributed. Rather, it's subject to income tax when distributed from the plan. However, it's included in wages subject to social security and Medicare taxes at the time contributed.

Elective deferrals include elective contributions to the following retirement plans.

1. Cash or deferred arrangements (section 401(k) plans).

2. The Thrift Savings Plan for federal employees.

3. Salary reduction simplified employee pension plans (SARSEP).

4. Savings incentive match plans for employees (SIMPLE plans).

5. Tax-sheltered annuity plans (section 403(b) plans).

6. Section 501(c)(18)(D) plans.

7. Section 457 plans.

Qualified automatic contribution arrangements. Under a qualified automatic contribution arrangement, your employer can treat you as having elected to have a part of your compensation contributed to a section 401(k) plan. You are to receive written notice of your rights and obligations under the qualified automatic contribution arrangement. The notice must explain:

• Your rights to elect not to have elective contributions made, or to have contributions made at a different percentage; and

• How contributions made will be invested in the absence of any investment decision by you.

You must be given a reasonable period of time after receipt of the notice and before the first elective contribution is made to make an election with respect to the contributions.

Overall limit on deferrals. For 2022, in most cases, you shouldn't have deferred more than a total of $20,500 of contributions to the plans listed in (1) through (3) and (5) above. The limit for SIMPLE plans is $14,000. The limit for section 501(c)(18)(D) plans is the lesser of $7,000 or 25% of your compensation. The limit for section 457 plans is the lesser of your includible compensation or $20,500. Amounts deferred under specific plan limits are part of the overall limit on deferrals.

Designated Roth contributions. Employers with section 401(k) and section 403(b) plans can create qualified Roth contribution programs so that you may elect to have part or all of your elective deferrals to the plan designated as after-tax Roth contributions. Designated Roth contributions are treated as elective deferrals, except that they're included in income at the time contributed.

Excess deferrals. Your employer or plan administrator should apply the proper annual limit when figuring your plan contributions. However, you're responsible for monitoring the total you defer to ensure that the deferrals aren't more than the overall limit.

If you set aside more than the limit, the excess must generally be included in your income

for that year, unless you have an excess deferral of a designated Roth contribution. See Pub. 525 for a discussion of the tax treatment of excess deferrals.

Catch-up contributions. You may be allowed catch-up contributions (additional elective deferral) if you're age 50 or older by the end of the tax year.

Stock Options

If you receive a nonstatutory option to buy or sell stock or other property as payment for your services, you will usually have income when you receive the option, when you exercise the option (use it to buy or sell the stock or other property), or when you sell or otherwise dispose of the option. However, if your option is a statutory stock option, you won't have any income until you sell or exchange your stock. Your employer can tell you which kind of option you hold. For more information, see Pub. 525.

Restricted Property

In most cases, if you receive property for your services, you must include its fair market value in your income in the year you receive the property. However, if you receive stock or other property that has certain restrictions that affect its value, you don't include the value of the property in your income until it has substantially vested. (Although you can elect to include the value of the property in your income in the year it's transferred to you.) For more information, see *Restricted Property* in Pub. 525.

Dividends received on restricted stock. Dividends you receive on restricted stock are treated as compensation and not as dividend income. Your employer should include these payments on your Form W-2.

Stock you elected to include in income. Dividends you receive on restricted stock you elected to include in your income in the year transferred are treated the same as any other dividends. Report them on your return as dividends. For a discussion of dividends, see Pub. 550, Investment Income and Expenses.

For information on how to treat dividends reported on both your Form W-2 and Form 1099-DIV, see *Dividends received on restricted stock* in Pub. 525.

Special Rules for Certain Employees

This section deals with special rules for people in certain types of employment: members of the clergy, members of religious orders, people working for foreign employers, military personnel, and volunteers.

Clergy

Generally, if you're a member of the clergy, you must include in your income offerings and fees you receive for marriages, baptisms, funerals, masses, etc., in addition to your salary. If the offering is made to the religious institution, it isn't taxable to you.

If you're a member of a religious organization and you give your outside earnings to the religious organization, you must still include the earnings in your income. However, you may be entitled to a charitable contribution deduction for the amount paid to the organization. See Pub. 526.

Pension. A pension or retirement pay for a member of the clergy is usually treated as any other pension or annuity. It must be reported on lines 5a and 5b of Form 1040 or 1040-SR.

Housing. Special rules for housing apply to members of the clergy. Under these rules, you don't include in your income the rental value of a home (including utilities) or a designated housing allowance provided to you as part of your pay. However, the exclusion can't be more than the reasonable pay for your services. If you pay for the utilities, you can exclude any allowance designated for utility cost, up to your actual cost. The home or allowance must be provided as compensation for your services as an ordained, licensed, or commissioned minister. However, you must include the rental value of the home or the housing allowance as earnings from self-employment on Schedule SE (Form 1040) if you're subject to the self-employment tax. For more information, see Pub. 517, Social Security and Other Information for Members of the Clergy and Religious Workers.

Members of Religious Orders

If you're a member of a religious order who has taken a vow of poverty, how you treat earnings that you renounce and turn over to the order depends on whether your services are performed for the order.

Services performed for the order. If you're performing the services as an agent of the order in the exercise of duties required by the order, don't include in your income the amounts turned over to the order.

If your order directs you to perform services for another agency of the supervising church or an associated institution, you're considered to be performing the services as an agent of the order. Any wages you earn as an agent of an order that you turn over to the order aren't included in your income.

Example. You're a member of a church order and have taken a vow of poverty. You renounce any claims to your earnings and turn over to the order any salaries or wages you earn. You're a registered nurse, so your order assigns you to work in a hospital that is an associated institution of the church. However, you remain under the general direction and control of the order. You're considered to be an agent of the order and any wages you earn at the hospital that you turn over to your order aren't included in your income.

Services performed outside the order. If you're directed to work outside the order, your services aren't an exercise of duties required by the order unless they meet both of the following requirements.

• They're the kind of services that are ordinarily the duties of members of the order.

- They're part of the duties that you must exercise for, or on behalf of, the religious order as its agent.

If you're an employee of a third party, the services you perform for the third party won't be considered directed or required of you by the order. Amounts you receive for these services are included in your income, even if you have taken a vow of poverty.

Example. Mark Brown is a member of a religious order and has taken a vow of poverty. He renounces all claims to his earnings and turns over his earnings to the order.

Mark is a schoolteacher. He was instructed by the superiors of the order to get a job with a private tax-exempt school. Mark became an employee of the school, and, at his request, the school made the salary payments directly to the order.

Because Mark is an employee of the school, he is performing services for the school rather than as an agent of the order. The wages Mark earns working for the school are included in his income.

Foreign Employer

Special rules apply if you work for a foreign employer.

U.S. citizen. If you're a U.S. citizen who works in the United States for a foreign government, an international organization, a foreign embassy, or any foreign employer, you must include your salary in your income.

Social security and Medicare taxes. You're exempt from social security and Medicare employee taxes if you're employed in the United States by an international organization or a foreign government. However, you must pay self-employment tax on your earnings from services performed in the United States, even though you aren't self-employed. This rule also applies if you're an employee of a qualifying wholly owned instrumentality of a foreign government.

Employees of international organizations or foreign governments. Your compensation for official services to an international organization is exempt from federal income tax if you aren't a citizen of the United States or you're a citizen of the Philippines (whether or not you're a citizen of the United States).

Your compensation for official services to a foreign government is exempt from federal income tax if all of the following are true.

- You aren't a citizen of the United States or you're a citizen of the Philippines (whether or not you're a citizen of the United States).

- Your work is like the work done by employees of the United States in foreign countries.

- The foreign government gives an equal exemption to employees of the United States in its country.

Waiver of alien status. If you're an alien who works for a foreign government or international organization and you file a waiver under section 247(b) of the Immigration and Nationality Act to keep your immigrant status, different

rules may apply. See *Foreign Employer* in Pub. 525.

Employment abroad. For information on the tax treatment of income earned abroad, see Pub. 54.

Military

Payments you receive as a member of a military service are generally taxed as wages except for retirement pay, which is taxed as a pension. Allowances generally aren't taxed. For more information on the tax treatment of military allowances and benefits, see Pub. 3, Armed Forces' Tax Guide.

Differential wage payments. Any payments made to you by an employer during the time you're performing service in the uniformed services are treated as compensation. These wages are subject to income tax withholding and are reported on a Form W-2. See the discussion under *Miscellaneous Compensation*, earlier.

Military retirement pay. If your retirement pay is based on age or length of service, it's taxable and must be included in your income as a pension on lines 5a and 5b of Form 1040 or 1040-SR. Don't include in your income the amount of any reduction in retirement or retainer pay to provide a survivor annuity for your spouse or children under the Retired Serviceman's Family Protection Plan or the Survivor Benefit Plan.

For more detailed discussion of survivor annuities, see Pub. 575, Pension and Annuity Income.

Disability. If you're retired on disability, see *Military and Government Disability Pensions* under *Sickness and Injury Benefits*, later.

Veterans' benefits. Don't include in your income any veterans' benefits paid under any law, regulation, or administrative practice administered by the Department of Veterans Affairs (VA). The following amounts paid to veterans or their families aren't taxable.

- Education, training, and subsistence allowances.

- Disability compensation and pension payments for disabilities paid either to veterans or their families.

- Grants for homes designed for wheelchair living.

- Grants for motor vehicles for veterans who lost their sight or the use of their limbs.

- Veterans' insurance proceeds and dividends paid either to veterans or their beneficiaries, including the proceeds of a veteran's endowment policy paid before death.

- Interest on insurance dividends you leave on deposit with the VA.

- Benefits under a dependent-care assistance program.

- The death gratuity paid to a survivor of a member of the Armed Forces who died after September 10, 2001.

- Payments made under the compensated work therapy program.

- Any bonus payment by a state or political subdivision because of service in a combat zone.

Volunteers

The tax treatment of amounts you receive as a volunteer worker for the Peace Corps or similar agency is covered in the following discussions.

Peace Corps. Living allowances you receive as a Peace Corps volunteer or volunteer leader for housing, utilities, household supplies, food, and clothing are generally exempt from tax.

Taxable allowances. The following allowances, however, must be included in your income and reported as wages.

- Allowances paid to your spouse and minor children while you're a volunteer leader training in the United States.

- Living allowances designated by the Director of the Peace Corps as basic compensation. These are allowances for personal items such as domestic help, laundry and clothing maintenance, entertainment and recreation, transportation, and other miscellaneous expenses.

- Leave allowances.

- Readjustment allowances or termination payments. These are considered received by you when credited to your account.

Example. Gary Carpenter, a Peace Corps volunteer, gets $175 a month as a readjustment allowance during his period of service, to be paid to him in a lump sum at the end of his tour of duty. Although the allowance isn't available to him until the end of his service, Gary must include it in his income on a monthly basis as it's credited to his account.

Volunteers in Service to America (VISTA). If you're a VISTA volunteer, you must include meal and lodging allowances paid to you in your income as wages.

National Senior Services Corps programs. Don't include in your income amounts you receive for supportive services or reimbursements for out-of-pocket expenses from the following programs.

- Retired Senior Volunteer Program (RSVP).

- Foster Grandparent Program.

- Senior Companion Program.

Service Corps of Retired Executives (SCORE). If you receive amounts for supportive services or reimbursements for out-of-pocket expenses from SCORE, don't include these amounts in gross income.

Volunteer tax counseling. Don't include in your income any reimbursements you receive for transportation, meals, and other expenses you have in training for, or actually providing, volunteer federal income tax counseling for the elderly (TCE).

You can deduct as a charitable contribution your unreimbursed out-of-pocket expenses in taking part in the volunteer income tax assistance (VITA) program. See Pub. 526.

Volunteer firefighters and emergency medical responders. If you are a volunteer firefighter or emergency medical responder, don't include in your income the following benefits you receive from a state or local government.

- Rebates or reductions of property or income taxes you receive because of services you performed as a volunteer firefighter or emergency medical responder.

- Payments you receive because of services you performed as a volunteer firefighter or emergency medical responder, up to $50 for each month you provided services.

The excluded income reduces any related tax or contribution deduction.

Sickness and Injury Benefits

This section discusses sickness and injury benefits, including disability pensions, long-term care insurance contracts, workers' compensation, and other benefits.

In most cases, you must report as income any amount you receive for personal injury or sickness through an accident or health plan that is paid for by your employer. If both you and your employer pay for the plan, only the amount you receive that is due to your employer's payments is reported as income. However, certain payments may not be taxable to you. For information on nontaxable payments, see _Military and Government Disability Pensions_ and _Other Sickness and Injury Benefits_, later in this discussion.

 Don't report as income any amounts paid to reimburse you for medical expenses you incurred after the plan was established.

Cost paid by you. If you pay the entire cost of a health or accident insurance plan, don't include any amounts you receive from the plan for personal injury or sickness as income on your tax return. If your plan reimbursed you for medical expenses you deducted in an earlier year, you may have to include some, or all, of the reimbursement in your income. See _What if You Receive Insurance Reimbursement in a Later Year?_ in Pub. 502, Medical and Dental Expenses.

Cafeteria plans. In most cases, if you're covered by an accident or health insurance plan through a cafeteria plan, and the amount of the insurance premiums wasn't included in your income, you aren't considered to have paid the premiums and you must include any benefits you receive in your income. If the amount of the premiums was included in your income, you're considered to have paid the premiums, and any benefits you receive aren't taxable.

Disability Pensions

If you retired on disability, you must include in income any disability pension you receive under a plan that is paid for by your employer. You must report your taxable disability payments as wages on line 1a of Form 1040 or 1040-SR until you reach minimum retirement age. Minimum

retirement age is generally the age at which you can first receive a pension or annuity if you're not disabled.

 You may be entitled to a tax credit if you were permanently and totally disabled when you retired. For information on this credit and the definition of permanent and total disability, see Pub. 524, Credit for the Elderly or the Disabled.

Beginning on the day after you reach minimum retirement age, payments you receive are taxable as a pension or annuity. Report the payments on lines 5a and 5b of Form 1040 or 1040-SR. The rules for reporting pensions are explained in Disability Pensions in Pub. 575.

For information on disability payments from a governmental program provided as a substitute for unemployment compensation, see _Unemployment Benefits_ in chapter 8.

Retirement and profit-sharing plans. If you receive payments from a retirement or profit-sharing plan that doesn't provide for disability retirement, don't treat the payments as a disability pension. The payments must be reported as a pension or annuity. For more information on pensions, see Pub. 575.

Accrued leave payment. If you retire on disability, any lump-sum payment you receive for accrued annual leave is a salary payment. The payment is not a disability payment. Include it in your income in the tax year you receive it.

Military and Government Disability Pensions

Certain military and government disability pensions aren't taxable.

Service-connected disability. You may be able to exclude from income amounts you receive as a pension, annuity, or similar allowance for personal injury or sickness resulting from active service in one of the following government services.

- The armed forces of any country.

- The National Oceanic and Atmospheric Administration.

- The Public Health Service.

- The Foreign Service.

Conditions for exclusion. Don't include the disability payments in your income if any of the following conditions apply.

1. You were entitled to receive a disability payment before September 25, 1975.

2. You were a member of a listed government service or its reserve component, or were under a binding written commitment to become a member, on September 24, 1975.

3. You receive the disability payments for a combat-related injury. This is a personal injury or sickness that:

   a. Results directly from armed conflict;

   b. Takes place while you're engaged in extra-hazardous service;

   c. Takes place under conditions simulating war, including training exercises such as maneuvers; or

   d. Is caused by an instrumentality of war.

4. You would be entitled to receive disability compensation from the Department of Veterans Affairs (VA) if you filed an application for it. Your exclusion under this condition is equal to the amount you would be entitled to receive from the VA.

Pension based on years of service. If you receive a disability pension based on years of service, in most cases you must include it in your income. However, if the pension qualifies for the exclusion for a service-connected disability (discussed earlier), don't include in income the part of your pension that you would have received if the pension had been based on a percentage of disability. You must include the rest of your pension in your income.

Retroactive VA determination. If you retire from the armed services based on years of service and are later given a retroactive service-connected disability rating by the VA, your retirement pay for the retroactive period is excluded from income up to the amount of VA disability benefits you would have been entitled to receive. You can claim a refund of any tax paid on the excludable amount (subject to the statute of limitations) by filing an amended return on Form 1040-X for each previous year during the retroactive period. You must include with each Form 1040-X a copy of the official VA Determination letter granting the retroactive benefit. The letter must show the amount withheld and the effective date of the benefit.

If you receive a lump-sum disability severance payment and are later awarded VA disability benefits, exclude 100% of the severance benefit from your income. However, you must include in your income any lump-sum readjustment or other nondisability severance payment you received on release from active duty, even if you're later given a retroactive disability rating by the VA.

Special period of limitation. In most cases, under the period of limitation, a claim for credit or refund must be filed within 3 years from the time a return was filed or 2 years from the time the tax was paid. However, if you receive a retroactive service-connected disability rating determination, the period of limitation is extended by a 1-year period beginning on the date of the determination. This 1-year extended period applies to claims for credit or refund filed after June 17, 2008, and doesn't apply to any tax year that began more than 5 years before the date of the determination.

Terrorist attack or military action. Don't include in your income disability payments you receive for injuries incurred as a direct result of a terrorist attack directed against the United States (or its allies), whether outside or within the United States or from military action. See Pub. 3920 and Pub. 907 for more information.

Long-Term Care Insurance Contracts

Long-term care insurance contracts in most cases are treated as accident and health insurance contracts. Amounts you receive from them (other than policyholder dividends or premium refunds) in most cases are excludable from income as amounts received for personal injury or sickness. To claim an exclusion for payments made on a per diem or other periodic basis under a long-term care insurance contract, you must file Form 8853 with your return.

A long-term care insurance contract is an insurance contract that only provides coverage for qualified long-term care services. The contract must:

- Be guaranteed renewable;

- Not provide for a cash surrender value or other money that can be paid, assigned, pledged, or borrowed;

- Provide that refunds, other than refunds on the death of the insured or complete surrender or cancellation of the contract, and dividends under the contract, may only be used to reduce future premiums or increase future benefits; and

- In most cases, not pay or reimburse expenses incurred for services or items that would be reimbursed under Medicare, except where Medicare is a secondary payer or the contract makes per diem or other periodic payments without regard to expenses.

Qualified long-term care services. Qualified long-term care services are:

- Necessary diagnostic, preventive, therapeutic, curing, treating, mitigating, and rehabilitative services, and maintenance and personal care services; and

- Required by a chronically ill individual and provided pursuant to a plan of care prescribed by a licensed health care practitioner.

Chronically ill individual. A chronically ill individual is one who has been certified by a licensed health care practitioner within the previous 12 months as one of the following.

- An individual who, for at least 90 days, is unable to perform at least two activities of daily living without substantial assistance due to loss of functional capacity. Activities of daily living are eating, toileting, transferring, bathing, dressing, and continence.

- An individual who requires substantial supervision to be protected from threats to health and safety due to severe cognitive impairment.

Limit on exclusion. You can generally exclude from gross income up to $390 a day for 2022. See *Limit on exclusion*, under *Long-Term Care Insurance Contracts*, under *Sickness and Injury Benefits* in Pub. 525 for more information.

Workers' Compensation

Amounts you receive as workers' compensation for an occupational sickness or injury are fully exempt from tax if they're paid under a workers' compensation act or a statute in the nature of a workers' compensation act. The exemption also applies to your survivors. The exemption, however, doesn't apply to retirement plan benefits you receive based on your age, length of service, or prior contributions to the plan, even if you retired because of an occupational sickness or injury.

 If part of your workers' compensation reduces your social security or equivalent railroad retirement benefits received, that part is considered social security (or equivalent railroad retirement) benefits and may be taxable. For more information, see Pub. 915, Social Security and Equivalent Railroad Retirement Benefits.

Return to work. If you return to work after qualifying for workers' compensation, salary payments you receive for performing light duties are taxable as wages.

Other Sickness and Injury Benefits

In addition to disability pensions and annuities, you may receive other payments for sickness or injury.

Railroad sick pay. Payments you receive as sick pay under the Railroad Unemployment Insurance Act are taxable and you must include them in your income. However, don't include them in your income if they're for an on-the-job injury.

If you received income because of a disability, see *Disability Pensions*, earlier.

Federal Employees' Compensation Act (FECA). Payments received under this Act for personal injury or sickness, including payments to beneficiaries in case of death, aren't taxable. However, you're taxed on amounts you receive under this Act as continuation of pay for up to 45 days while a claim is being decided. Report this income as wages. Also, pay for sick leave while a claim is being processed is taxable and must be included in your income as wages.

 If part of the payments you receive under FECA reduces your social security or equivalent railroad retirement benefits received, that part is considered social security (or equivalent railroad retirement) benefits and may be taxable. See Pub. 554 for more information.

Other compensation. Many other amounts you receive as compensation for sickness or injury aren't taxable. These include the following amounts.

- Compensatory damages you receive for physical injury or physical sickness, whether paid in a lump sum or in periodic payments.

- Benefits you receive under an accident or health insurance policy on which either you paid the premiums or your employer paid the premiums but you had to include them in your income.

- Disability benefits you receive for loss of income or earning capacity as a result of injuries under a no-fault car insurance policy.

- Compensation you receive for permanent loss or loss of use of a part or function of your body, or for your permanent disfigurement. This compensation must be based only on the injury and not on the period of your absence from work. These benefits aren't taxable even if your employer pays for the accident and health plan that provides these benefits.

Reimbursement for medical care. A reimbursement for medical care is generally not taxable. However, it may reduce your medical expense deduction. For more information, see Pub. 502.

6.

Interest Income

Reminders

Foreign-source income. If you are a U.S. citizen with interest income from sources outside the United States (foreign income), you must report that income on your tax return unless it is exempt by U.S. law. This is true whether you reside inside or outside the United States and whether or not you receive a Form 1099 from the foreign payer.

Automatic 6-month extension. If you receive your Form 1099 reporting your interest income late and you need more time to file your tax return, you can request a 6-month extension of time to file. See *Automatic Extension* in chapter 1.

Children who have unearned income. See Form 8615 and its instructions for the rules and rates that apply to certain children with unearned income.

Introduction

This chapter discusses the following topics.

- Different types of interest income.

- What interest is taxable and what interest is nontaxable.

- When to report interest income.

- How to report interest income on your tax return.

In general, any interest you receive or that is credited to your account and can be withdrawn is taxable income. Exceptions to this rule are discussed later in this chapter.

You may be able to deduct expenses you have in earning this income on Schedule A (Form 1040) if you itemize your deductions. See *Money borrowed to invest in certificate of deposit*, later, and chapter 12.

Useful Items

You may want to see:

Publication

❏ **537** Installment Sales

❏ **550** Investment Income and Expenses

□ **1212** Guide to Original Issue Discount (OID) Instruments

Form (and Instructions)

□ **Schedule A (Form 1040)** Itemized Deductions

□ **Schedule B (Form 1040)** Interest and Ordinary Dividends

□ **8615** Tax for Certain Children Who Have Unearned Income

□ **8814** Parents' Election To Report Child's Interest and Dividends

□ **8815** Exclusion of Interest From Series EE and I U.S. Savings Bonds Issued After 1989

□ **8818** Optional Form To Record Redemption of Series EE and I U.S. Savings Bonds Issued After 1989

For these and other useful items, go to *IRS.gov/ Forms*.

General Information

A few items of general interest are covered here.

 Recordkeeping. You should keep a list showing sources of interest income and interest amounts received during the year. Also, keep the forms you receive showing your interest income (Forms 1099-INT, for example) as an important part of your records.

Tax on unearned income of certain children. Part of a child's 2022 unearned income may be taxed at the parent's tax rate. If so, Form 8615 must be completed and attached to the child's tax return. If not, Form 8615 isn't required and the child's income is taxed at his or her own tax rate.

Some parents can choose to include the child's interest and dividends on the parent's return. If you can, use Form 8814 for this purpose.

For more information about the tax on unearned income of children and the parents' election, go to *Form 8615*.

Beneficiary of an estate or trust. Interest you receive as a beneficiary of an estate or trust is generally taxable income. You should receive a Schedule K-1 (Form 1041), Beneficiary's Share of Income, Deductions, Credits, etc., from the fiduciary. Your copy of Schedule K-1 (Form 1041) and its instructions will tell you where to report the income on your Form 1040 or 1040-SR.

Taxpayer identification number (TIN). You must give your name and TIN (either a social security number (SSN), an employer identification number (EIN), an adoption taxpayer identification number (ATIN), or an individual tax identification number (ITIN)) to any person required by federal tax law to make a return, statement, or other document that relates to you. This includes payers of interest. If you don't give your TIN to the payer of interest, the payer will generally be required to backup withhold on the interest payments at a rate of 24%, and you may also be subject to a penalty.

TIN for joint account. If the funds in a joint account belong to one person, list that person's name first on the account and give that person's TIN to the payer. (For information on who owns the funds in a joint account, see *Joint accounts*, later.) If the joint account contains combined funds, give the TIN of the person whose name is listed first on the account. This is because only one name and TIN can be shown on Form 1099.

These rules apply to both joint ownership by a married couple and to joint ownership by other individuals. For example, if you open a joint savings account with your child using funds belonging to the child, list the child's name first on the account and give the child's TIN.

Custodian account for your child. If your child is the actual owner of an account that is recorded in your name as custodian for the child, give the child's TIN to the payer. For example, you must give your child's SSN to the payer of interest on an account owned by your child, even though the interest is paid to you as custodian.

Penalty for failure to supply TIN. If you don't give your TIN to the payer of interest, you may have to pay a penalty. See *Failure to supply SSN* under *Penalties* in chapter 1. Backup withholding may also apply.

Backup withholding. Your interest income is generally not subject to regular withholding. However, it may be subject to backup withholding to ensure that income tax is collected on the income. Under backup withholding, the payer of interest must withhold, as income tax, on the amount you are paid, by applying the appropriate withholding rate. The current rate is 24%. Withholding is required only if there is a condition for backup withholding, such as failing to provide your TIN to the payer or failing to certify your TIN under penalties of perjury, if required.

Backup withholding may also be required if the IRS has determined that you underreported your interest or dividend income. For more information, see *Backup Withholding* in chapter 4.

Reporting backup withholding. If backup withholding is deducted from your interest income, the amount withheld will be reported on your Form 1099-INT. The Form 1099-INT will show any backup withholding as "Federal income tax withheld."

Joint accounts. If two or more persons hold property (such as a savings account or bond) as joint tenants, tenants by the entirety, or tenants in common, each person's share of any interest from the property is determined by local law.

Income from property given to a child. Property you give as a parent to your child under the Model Gifts of Securities to Minors Act, the Uniform Gifts to Minors Act, or any similar law becomes the child's property.

Income from the property is taxable to the child, except that any part used to satisfy a legal obligation to support the child is taxable to the parent or guardian having that legal obligation.

Savings account with parent as trustee. Interest income from a savings account opened for a minor child, but placed in the name and subject to the order of the parents as trustees, is taxable to the child if, under the law of the state in which the child resides, both of the following are true.

- The savings account legally belongs to the child.
- The parents aren't legally permitted to use any of the funds to support the child.

Form 1099-INT. Interest income is generally reported to you on Form 1099-INT, or a similar statement, by banks, savings and loans, and other payers of interest. This form shows you the interest income you received during the year. Keep this form for your records. You don't have to attach it to your tax return.

Report on your tax return the total interest income you receive for the tax year. See the Form 1099-INT Instructions for Recipient to see whether you need to adjust any of the amounts reported to you.

Interest not reported on Form 1099-INT. Even if you don't receive a Form 1099-INT, you must still report all of your interest income. For example, you may receive distributive shares of interest from partnerships or S corporations. This interest is reported to you on Schedule K-1 (Form 1065), Partner's Share of Income, Deduction, Credits, etc.; or Schedule K-1 (Form 1120-S), Shareholder's Share of Income, Deductions, Credits, etc.

Nominees. Generally, if someone receives interest as a nominee for you, that person must give you a Form 1099-INT showing the interest received on your behalf.

If you receive a Form 1099-INT that includes amounts belonging to another person, see the discussion on nominee distributions under *How To Report Interest Income* in chapter 1 of *IRS.gov/Pub550*, or the Schedule B (Form 1040) instructions.

Incorrect amount. If you receive a Form 1099-INT that shows an incorrect amount or other incorrect information, you should ask the issuer for a corrected form. The new Form 1099-INT you receive will have the "CORRECTED" box checked.

Form 1099-OID. Reportable interest income may also be shown on Form 1099-OID, Original Issue Discount. For more information about amounts shown on this form, see *Original Issue Discount (OID)*, later in this chapter.

 The box references discussed below are from the January 2022 revisions of Form 1099-INT and Form 1099-DIV. Later revisions may have different box references.

Exempt-interest dividends. Exempt-interest dividends you receive from a mutual fund or other regulated investment company (RIC) aren't included in your taxable income. (However, see *Information reporting requirement* next.) Exempt-interest dividends should be shown on Form 1099-DIV, box 12. You don't reduce your basis for distributions that are exempt-interest dividends.

Information reporting requirement. Although exempt-interest dividends aren't taxable, you must show them on your tax return if you have to file. This is an information reporting requirement and doesn't change the exempt-interest dividends into taxable income.

Note. Exempt-interest dividends paid by a mutual fund or other RIC on specified private activity bonds may be subject to the alternative minimum tax. This amount is generally reported in box 13 of Form 1099-DIV. See *Alternative Minimum Tax (AMT)* in chapter 13 for more information. Chapter 1 of *IRS.gov/Pub550* contains a discussion on private activity bonds under *State or Local Government Obligations*.

Interest on VA dividends. Interest on insurance dividends left on deposit with the Department of Veterans Affairs (VA) isn't taxable. This includes interest paid on dividends on converted United States Government Life Insurance and on National Service Life Insurance policies.

Individual retirement arrangements (IRAs). Interest on a Roth IRA generally isn't taxable. Interest on a traditional IRA is tax deferred. You generally don't include interest earned in an IRA in your income until you make withdrawals from the IRA. See chapter 9.

Taxable Interest

Taxable interest includes interest you receive from bank accounts, loans you make to others, and other sources. The following are some sources of taxable interest.

Dividends that are actually interest. Certain distributions commonly called dividends are actually interest. You must report as interest so-called dividends on deposits or on share accounts in:

- Cooperative banks,
- Credit unions,
- Domestic building and loan associations,
- Domestic savings and loan associations,
- Federal savings and loan associations, and
- Mutual savings banks.

The "dividends" will be shown as interest income on Form 1099-INT.

Money market funds. Money market funds pay dividends and are offered by nonbank financial institutions, such as mutual funds and stock brokerage houses. Generally, amounts you receive from money market funds should be reported as dividends, not as interest.

Certificates of deposit and other deferred interest accounts. If you open any of these accounts, interest may be paid at fixed intervals of 1 year or less during the term of the account. You must generally include this interest in your income when you actually receive it or are entitled to receive it without paying a substantial penalty. The same is true for accounts that mature in 1 year or less and pay interest in a single payment at maturity. If interest is deferred for more than 1 year, see *Original Issue Discount (OID)*, later.

Interest subject to penalty for early withdrawal. If you withdraw funds from a deferred interest account before maturity, you may have

to pay a penalty. You must report the total amount of interest paid or credited to your account during the year, without subtracting the penalty. See *Penalty on early withdrawal of savings* in chapter 1 of *IRS.gov/Pub550* for more information on how to report the interest and deduct the penalty.

Money borrowed to invest in certificate of deposit. The interest you pay on money borrowed from a bank or savings institution to meet the minimum deposit required for a certificate of deposit from the institution and the interest you earn on the certificate are two separate items. You must report the total interest income you earn on the certificate in your income. If you itemize deductions, you can deduct the interest you pay as investment interest, up to the amount of your net investment income. See *Interest Expenses* in chapter 3 of *IRS.gov/Pub550*.

Example. You deposited $5,000 with a bank and borrowed $5,000 from the bank to make up the $10,000 minimum deposit required to buy a 6-month certificate of deposit. The certificate earned $575 at maturity in 2022, but you received only $265, which represented the $575 you earned minus $310 interest charged on your $5,000 loan. The bank gives you a Form 1099-INT for 2022 showing the $575 interest you earned. The bank also gives you a statement showing that you paid $310 of interest for 2022. You must include the $575 in your income. If you itemize your deductions on Schedule A (Form 1040), you can deduct $310, subject to the net investment income limit.

Gift for opening account. If you receive noncash gifts or services for making deposits or for opening an account in a savings institution, you may have to report the value as interest.

For deposits of less than $5,000, gifts or services valued at more than $10 must be reported as interest. For deposits of $5,000 or more, gifts or services valued at more than $20 must be reported as interest. The value is determined by the cost to the financial institution.

Example. You open a savings account at your local bank and deposit $800. The account earns $20 interest. You also receive a $15 calculator. If no other interest is credited to your account during the year, the Form 1099-INT you receive will show $35 interest for the year. You must report $35 interest income on your tax return.

Interest on insurance dividends. Interest on insurance dividends left on deposit with an insurance company that can be withdrawn annually is taxable to you in the year it is credited to your account. However, if you can withdraw it only on the anniversary date of the policy (or other specified date), the interest is taxable in the year that date occurs.

Prepaid insurance premiums. Any increase in the value of prepaid insurance premiums, advance premiums, or premium deposit funds is interest if it is applied to the payment of premiums due on insurance policies or made available for you to withdraw.

U.S. obligations. Interest on U.S. obligations issued by any agency or instrumentality of the

United States, such as U.S. Treasury bills, notes, and bonds, is taxable for federal income tax purposes.

Interest on tax refunds. Interest you receive on tax refunds is taxable income.

Interest on condemnation award. If the condemning authority pays you interest to compensate you for a delay in payment of an award, the interest is taxable.

Installment sale payments. If a contract for the sale or exchange of property provides for deferred payments, it also usually provides for interest payable with the deferred payments. Generally, that interest is taxable when you receive it. If little or no interest is provided for in a deferred payment contract, part of each payment may be treated as interest. See *Unstated Interest and Original Issue Discount* in Pub. 537, Installment Sales.

Interest on annuity contract. Accumulated interest on an annuity contract you sell before its maturity date is taxable.

Usurious interest. Usurious interest is interest charged at an illegal rate. This is taxable as interest unless state law automatically changes it to a payment on the principal.

Interest income on frozen deposits. Exclude from your gross income interest on frozen deposits. A deposit is frozen if, at the end of the year, you can't withdraw any part of the deposit because:

- The financial institution is bankrupt or insolvent, or
- The state where the institution is located has placed limits on withdrawals because other financial institutions in the state are bankrupt or insolvent.

The amount of interest you must exclude is the interest that was credited on the frozen deposits minus the sum of:

- The net amount you withdrew from these deposits during the year, and
- The amount you could have withdrawn as of the end of the year (not reduced by any penalty for premature withdrawals of a time deposit).

If you receive a Form 1099-INT for interest income on deposits that were frozen at the end of 2022, see *Frozen deposits* under *How To Report Interest Income* in chapter 1 of *IRS.gov/Pub550* for information about reporting this interest income exclusion on your tax return.

The interest you exclude is treated as credited to your account in the following year. You must include it in income in the year you can withdraw it.

Example. $100 of interest was credited on your frozen deposit during the year. You withdrew $80 but couldn't withdraw any more as of the end of the year. You must include $80 in your income and exclude $20 from your income for the year. You must include the $20 in your income for the year you can withdraw it.

Bonds traded flat. If you buy a bond at a discount when interest has been defaulted or when the interest has accrued but hasn't been paid, the transaction is described as trading a bond flat. The defaulted or unpaid interest isn't income and isn't taxable as interest if paid later. When you receive a payment of that interest, it is a return of capital that reduces the remaining cost basis of your bond. Interest that accrues after the date of purchase, however, is taxable interest income for the year it is received or accrued. See *Bonds Sold Between Interest Dates*, later, for more information.

Below-market loans. In general, a below-market loan is a loan on which no interest is charged or on which interest is charged at a rate below the applicable federal rate. If you are the lender of a below-market loan, you may have additional interest income. See *Below-Market Loans* in chapter 1 of *IRS.gov/Pub550* for more information.

U.S. Savings Bonds

This section provides tax information on U.S. savings bonds. It explains how to report the interest income on these bonds and how to treat transfers of these bonds.

For other information on U.S. savings bonds, write to:

Treasury Retail Securities Services
P.O. Box 9150
Minneapolis, MN 55480-9150

Or, on the Internet, visit *TreasuryDirect.gov/savings-bonds/*.

Accrual method taxpayers. If you use an accrual method of accounting, you must report interest on U.S. savings bonds each year as it accrues. You can't postpone reporting interest until you receive it or until the bonds mature. Accrual methods of accounting are explained in chapter 1 under *Accounting Methods*.

Cash method taxpayers. If you use the cash method of accounting, as most individual taxpayers do, you generally report the interest on U.S. savings bonds when you receive it. The cash method of accounting is explained in chapter 1 under *Accounting Methods*. But see *Reporting options for cash method taxpayers*, later.

Series H and HH bonds. These bonds were issued at face value in exchange for other savings bonds. Series HH bonds were issued between 1980 and 2004. They mature 20 years after issue. Series HH bonds that have not matured pay interest twice a year (usually by direct deposit to your bank account). If you are a cash method taxpayer, you must report this interest as income in the year you receive it.

Most H/HH bonds have a deferred interest component. The reporting of this as income is addressed later in this chapter.

Series H bonds were issued before 1980. All Series H bonds have matured and are no longer earning interest.

Series EE and Series I bonds. Interest on these bonds is payable when you redeem the bonds. The difference between the purchase price and the redemption value is taxable interest.

Series E and EE bonds. Series E bonds were issued before July of 1980. All Series E bonds have matured and are no longer earning interest. Series EE bonds were first offered in January 1980 and have a maturity period of 30 years; they were offered in paper (definitive) form until 2012. Paper Series EE and Series E bonds were issued at a discount and increase in value as they earn interest. Electronic (book-entry) Series EE bonds were first offered in 2003; they are issued at face value and increase in value as they earn interest. For all Series E and Series EE bonds, the purchase price plus all accrued interest is payable to you at redemption.

Series I bonds. Series I bonds were first offered in 1998. These are inflation-indexed bonds issued at face value with a maturity period of 30 years. Series I bonds increase in value as they earn interest. The face value plus all accrued interest is payable to you at redemption.

Reporting options for cash method taxpayers. If you use the cash method of reporting income, you can report the interest on Series EE and Series I bonds in either of the following ways.

1. ***Method 1.*** Postpone reporting the interest until the earlier of the year you cash or dispose of the bonds or the year they mature. (However, see *Savings bonds traded*, later.)
   Note. Series EE bonds issued in 1992 matured in 2022. If you used method 1, you must generally report the interest on these bonds on your 2022 return.

2. ***Method 2.*** Choose to report the increase in redemption value as interest each year.

You must use the same method for all Series EE, Series E, and Series I bonds you own. If you don't choose method 2 by reporting the increase in redemption value as interest each year, you must use method 1.

 If you plan to cash your bonds in the same year you will pay for higher education expenses, you may want to use method 1 because you may be able to exclude the interest from your income. To learn how, see Education Savings Bond Program, *later.*

Change from method 1. If you want to change your method of reporting the interest from method 1 to method 2, you can do so without permission from the IRS. In the year of change, you must report all interest accrued to date and not previously reported for all your bonds.

Once you choose to report the interest each year, you must continue to do so for all Series EE and Series I bonds you own and for any you get later, unless you request permission to change, as explained next.

Change from method 2. To change from method 2 to method 1, you must request permission from the IRS. Permission for the change is automatically granted if you send the IRS a statement that meets all the following requirements.

1. You have typed or printed the following number at the top: "131."

2. It includes your name and social security number under "131."

3. It includes the year of change (both the beginning and ending dates).

4. It identifies the savings bonds for which you are requesting this change.

5. It includes your agreement to:

   a. Report all interest on any bonds acquired during or after the year of change when the interest is realized upon disposition, redemption, or final maturity, whichever is earliest; and

   b. Report all interest on the bonds acquired before the year of change when the interest is realized upon disposition, redemption, or final maturity, whichever is earliest, with the exception of the interest reported in prior tax years.

You must attach this statement to your tax return for the year of change, which you must file by the due date (including extensions).

You can have an automatic extension of 6 months from the due date of your return for the year of change (excluding extensions) to file the statement with an amended return. On the statement, type or print "Filed pursuant to section 301.9100-2." To get this extension, you must have filed your original return for the year of the change by the due date (including extensions).

Instead of filing this statement, you can request permission to change from method 2 to method 1 by filing Form 3115, Application for Change in Accounting Method. In that case, follow the form instructions for an automatic change. No user fee is required.

Co-owners. If a U.S. savings bond is issued in the names of co-owners, such as you and your child or you and your spouse, interest on the bond is generally taxable to the co-owner who bought the bond.

One co-owner's funds used. If you used your funds to buy the bond, you must pay the tax on the interest. This is true even if you let the other co-owner redeem the bond and keep all the proceeds. Under these circumstances, the co-owner who redeemed the bond will receive a Form 1099-INT at the time of redemption and must provide you with another Form 1099-INT showing the amount of interest from the bond taxable to you. The co-owner who redeemed the bond is a "nominee." See *Nominee distributions* under *How To Report Interest Income* in chapter 1 of *IRS.gov/Pub550* for more information about how a person who is a nominee reports interest income belonging to another person.

Both co-owners' funds used. If you and the other co-owner each contribute part of the bond's purchase price, the interest is generally taxable to each of you, in proportion to the amount each of you paid.

Community property. If you and your spouse live in a community property state and hold bonds as community property, one-half of the interest is considered received by each of you. If you file separate returns, each of you must generally report one-half of the bond

Table 6-1. Who Pays the Tax on U.S. Savings Bond Interest

IF...	THEN the interest must be reported by...
you buy a bond in your name and the name of another person as co-owners, using only your own funds	you.
you buy a bond in the name of another person, who is the sole owner of the bond	the person for whom you bought the bond.
you and another person buy a bond as co-owners, each contributing part of the purchase price	both you and the other co-owner, in proportion to the amount each paid for the bond.
you and your spouse, who live in a community property state, buy a bond that is community property	you and your spouse. If you file separate returns, both you and your spouse generally report one-half of the interest.

interest. For more information about community property, see Pub. 555.

Table 6-1. These rules are also shown in Table 6-1.

Ownership transferred. If you bought Series EE or Series I bonds entirely with your own funds and had them reissued in your co-owner's name or beneficiary's name alone, you must include in your gross income for the year of reissue all interest that you earned on these bonds and have not previously reported. But, if the bonds were reissued in your name alone, you don't have to report the interest accrued at that time.

This same rule applies when bonds (other than bonds held as community property) are transferred between spouses or incident to divorce.

Purchased jointly. If you and a co-owner each contributed funds to buy Series EE or Series I bonds jointly and later have the bonds reissued in the co-owner's name alone, you must include in your gross income for the year of reissue your share of all the interest earned on the bonds that you have not previously reported. The former co-owner doesn't have to include in gross income at the time of reissue his or her share of the interest earned that was not reported before the transfer. This interest, however, as well as all interest earned after the reissue, is income to the former co-owner.

This income-reporting rule also applies when a new co-owner purchases your share of the bond and the bonds are reissued in the name of your former co-owner and a new co-owner. But the new co-owner will report only his or her share of the interest earned after the transfer.

If bonds that you and a co-owner bought jointly are reissued to each of you separately in the same proportion as your contribution to the purchase price, neither you nor your co-owner has to report at that time the interest earned before the bonds were reissued.

Example 1. You and your spouse each spent an equal amount to buy a $1,000 Series EE savings bond. The bond was issued to you and your spouse as co-owners. You both postpone reporting interest on the bond. You later have the bond reissued as two $500 bonds, one in your name and one in your spouse's name. At that time, neither you nor your spouse has to report the interest earned to the date of reissue.

Example 2. You bought a $1,000 Series EE savings bond entirely with your own funds. The bond was issued to you and your spouse as co-owners. You both postpone reporting interest on the bond. You later have the bond

reissued as two $500 bonds, one in your name and one in your spouse's name. You must report half the interest earned to the date of reissue.

Transfer to a trust. If you own Series EE or Series I bonds and transfer them to a trust, giving up all rights of ownership, you must include in your income for that year the interest earned to the date of transfer if you have not already reported it. However, if you are considered the owner of the trust and if the increase in value both before and after the transfer continues to be taxable to you, you can continue to defer reporting the interest earned each year. You must include the total interest in your income in the year you cash or dispose of the bonds or the year the bonds finally mature, whichever is earlier.

The same rules apply to previously unreported interest on Series EE or Series E bonds if the transfer to a trust consisted of Series HH bonds you acquired in a trade for the Series EE or Series E bonds. See *Savings bonds traded*, later.

Decedents. The manner of reporting interest income on Series EE or Series I bonds, after the death of the owner (decedent), depends on the accounting and income-reporting methods previously used by the decedent. This is explained in chapter 1 of *IRS.gov/Pub550*.

Savings bonds traded. Prior to September 2004, you could trade (exchange) Series E or EE bonds for Series H or HH bonds. At the time of the trade, you had the choice to postpone (defer) reporting the interest earned on your Series E or EE bonds until the Series H or HH bonds received in the trade were redeemed or matured. Any cash you received in the transaction was income up to the amount of the interest that had accrued on the Series E or EE bonds. The amount of income that you chose to postpone reporting was recorded on the face of the Series H or HH bonds as "Deferred Interest"; this amount is also equal to the difference between the redemption value of the Series H or HH bonds and your cost. Your cost is the sum of the amount you paid for the exchanged Series E or EE bonds plus any amount you had to pay at the time of the transaction.

Example. You traded Series EE bonds (on which you postponed reporting the interest) for $2,500 in Series HH bonds and $223 in cash. You reported the $223 as taxable income on your tax return. At the time of the trade, the Series EE bonds had accrued interest of $523 and a redemption value of $2,723. You hold the Series HH bonds until maturity, when you receive $2,500. You must report $300 as interest income in the year of maturity. This is the difference between their redemption value, $2,500,

and your cost, $2,200 (the amount you paid for the Series EE bonds). It is also the difference between the accrued interest of $523 on the Series EE bonds and the $223 cash received on the trade.

Note. The $300 amount that is reportable upon redemption or maturity may be found recorded on the face of the Series HH bond as "Deferred Interest." If more than one Series HH bond is received in the exchange, the total amount of interest postponed/deferred in the transaction is divided proportionally among the Series HH bonds.

Choice to report interest in year of trade. You can choose to treat all of the previously unreported accrued interest on the Series E or EE bonds traded for Series H or HH bonds as income in the year of the trade. If you choose to report the interest, then the "Deferred Interest" notation on the face of the Series H or HH bonds received in the trade will be $0 or blank.

Form 1099-INT for U.S. savings bonds interest. When you cash a bond, the bank or other payer that redeems it must give you a Form 1099-INT if the interest part of the payment you receive is $10 or more. Box 3 of your Form 1099-INT should show the interest as the difference between the amount you received and the amount paid for the bond. However, your Form 1099-INT may show more interest than you have to include on your income tax return. For example, this may happen if any of the following are true.

- You chose to report the increase in the redemption value of the bond each year. The interest shown on your Form 1099-INT won't be reduced by amounts previously included in income.

- You received the bond from a decedent. The interest shown on your Form 1099-INT won't be reduced by any interest reported by the decedent before death, or on the decedent's final return, or by the estate on the estate's income tax return.

- Ownership of the bond was transferred. The interest shown on your Form 1099-INT won't be reduced by interest that accrued before the transfer.
  Note. This is true for paper bonds, but the Treasury reporting process for electronic bonds is more refined—if Treasury is aware that the transfer of an electronic savings bond is a reportable event, then the transferor will receive a Form 1099-INT for the year of the transfer for the interest accrued up to the time of the transfer; when the transferee later disposes of the bond (redemption, maturity, or further transfer), the transferee will receive a Form 1099-INT reduced by the amount reported to the transferor at the time of the original transfer.

- You were named as a co-owner, and the other co-owner contributed funds to buy the bond. The interest shown on your Form 1099-INT won't be reduced by the amount you received as nominee for the other co-owner. (See *Co-owners*, earlier in this chapter, for more information about the reporting requirements.)

- You received the bond in a taxable distribution from a retirement or profit-sharing plan. The interest shown on your Form 1099-INT won't be reduced by the interest portion of the amount taxable as a distribution from the plan and not taxable as interest. (This amount is generally shown on Form 1099-R, Distributions From Pensions, Annuities, Retirement or Profit-Sharing Plans, IRAs, Insurance Contracts, etc., for the year of distribution.)

For more information on including the correct amount of interest on your return, see *How To Report Interest Income*, later. Pub. 550 includes examples showing how to report these amounts.

 Interest on U.S. savings bonds is exempt from state and local taxes. The Form 1099-INT you receive will indicate the amount that is for U.S. savings bond interest in box 3.

Education Savings Bond Program

You may be able to exclude from income all or part of the interest you receive on the redemption of qualified U.S. savings bonds during the year if you pay qualified higher educational expenses during the same year. This exclusion is known as the Education Savings Bond Program.

You don't qualify for this exclusion if your filing status is married filing separately.

Form 8815. Use Form 8815 to figure your exclusion. Attach the form to your Form 1040 or 1040-SR.

Qualified U.S. savings bonds. A qualified U.S. savings bond is a Series EE bond issued after 1989 or a Series I bond. The bond must be issued either in your name (sole owner) or in your and your spouse's names (co-owners). You must be at least 24 years old before the bond's issue date. For example, a bond bought by a parent and issued in the name of his or her child under age 24 doesn't qualify for the exclusion by the parent or child.

 The issue date of a bond may be earlier than the date the bond is purchased because the issue date assigned to a bond is the first day of the month in which it is purchased.

Beneficiary. You can designate any individual (including a child) as a beneficiary of the bond.

Verification by IRS. If you claim the exclusion, the IRS will check it by using bond redemption information from the Department of the Treasury.

Qualified expenses. Qualified higher education expenses are tuition and fees required for you, your spouse, or your dependent (for whom you claim an exemption) to attend an eligible educational institution.

Qualified expenses include any contribution you make to a qualified tuition program or to a Coverdell education savings account (ESA).

Qualified expenses don't include expenses for room and board or for courses involving sports, games, or hobbies that aren't part of a degree- or certificate-granting program.

Eligible educational institutions. These institutions include most public, private, and nonprofit universities, colleges, and vocational schools that are accredited and eligible to participate in student aid programs run by the U.S. Department of Education.

Reduction for certain benefits. You must reduce your qualified higher education expenses by all of the following tax-free benefits.

1. Tax-free part of scholarships and fellowships (see *Scholarships and fellowships* in chapter 8).

2. Expenses used to figure the tax-free portion of distributions from a Coverdell ESA.

3. Expenses used to figure the tax-free portion of distributions from a qualified tuition program.

4. Any tax-free payments (other than gifts or inheritances) received for educational expenses, such as:

   a. Veterans' educational assistance benefits,

   b. Qualified tuition reductions, or

   c. Employer-provided educational assistance.

5. Any expense used in figuring the American opportunity and lifetime learning credits.

Amount excludable. If the total proceeds (interest and principal) from the qualified U.S. savings bonds you redeem during the year aren't more than your adjusted qualified higher education expenses for the year, you may be able to exclude all of the interest. If the proceeds are more than the expenses, you may be able to exclude only part of the interest.

To determine the excludable amount, multiply the interest part of the proceeds by a fraction. The numerator of the fraction is the qualified higher education expenses you paid during the year. The denominator of the fraction is the total proceeds you received during the year.

Example. In February 2022, Mark and Joan, a married couple, cashed qualified Series EE U.S. savings bonds with a total denomination of $10,000 that they bought in April 2006 for $5,000. They received proceeds of $8,264, representing principal of $5,000 and interest of $3,264. In 2022, they paid $4,000 of their daughter's college tuition. They aren't claiming an education credit for that amount, and their daughter doesn't have any tax-free educational assistance. They can exclude $1,580 ($3,264 × ($4,000 ÷ $8,264)) of interest in 2022. They must include the remaining $1,684 ($3,264 − $1,580) interest in gross income.

Modified adjusted gross income limit. The interest exclusion is limited if your modified adjusted gross income (modified AGI) is:

- $128,650 to $158,650 for married taxpayers filing jointly, and

- $85,800 to $100,800 for all other taxpayers.

You don't qualify for the interest exclusion if your modified AGI is equal to or more than the upper limit for your filing status.

Modified AGI, for purposes of this exclusion, is adjusted gross income (Form 1040 or 1040-SR, line 11) figured before the interest exclusion, and modified by adding back any:

1. Foreign earned income exclusion,

2. Foreign housing exclusion and deduction,

3. Exclusion of income for bona fide residents of American Samoa,

4. Exclusion for income from Puerto Rico,

5. Exclusion for adoption benefits received under an employer's adoption assistance program, and

6. Deduction for student loan interest.

Use the Line 9 Worksheet in the Form 8815 instructions to figure your modified AGI.

If you have investment interest expense incurred to earn royalties and other investment income, see *Education Savings Bond Program* in chapter 1 of *IRS.gov/Pub550*.

 Recordkeeping. If you claim the interest exclusion, you must keep a written record of the qualified U.S. savings bonds you redeem. Your record must include the serial number, issue date, face value, and total redemption proceeds (principal and interest) of each bond. You can use Form 8818 to record this information. You should also keep bills, receipts, canceled checks, or other documentation that shows you paid qualified higher education expenses during the year.

U.S. Treasury Bills, Notes, and Bonds

Treasury bills, notes, and bonds are direct debts (obligations) of the U.S. Government.

Taxation of interest. Interest income from Treasury bills, notes, and bonds is subject to federal income tax but is exempt from all state and local income taxes. You should receive a Form 1099-INT showing the interest paid to you for the year in box 3.

Treasury bills. These bills generally have a 4-week, 8-week, 13-week, 26-week, or 52-week maturity period. They are generally issued at a discount in the amount of $100 and multiples of $100. The difference between the discounted price you pay for the bills and the face value you receive at maturity is interest income. Generally, you report this interest income when the bill is paid at maturity. If you paid a premium for a bill (more than the face value), you generally report the premium as a section 171 deduction when the bill is paid at maturity.

Treasury notes and bonds. Treasury notes generally have maturity periods of more than 1 year, ranging up to 10 years. Maturity periods for Treasury bonds are generally longer than 10 years. Both are generally issued in denominations of $100 to $1,000,000 and generally pay interest every 6 months. Generally, you report this interest for the year paid. For more information, see *U.S. Treasury Bills, Notes, and Bonds* in chapter 1 of *IRS.gov/Pub550*.

For other information on paper Treasury notes or bonds, write to:

Treasury Retail Securities Services
P.O. Box 9150
Minneapolis, MN 55480-9150

Or, click on the link to the Treasury website at: *TreasuryDirect.gov/ marketable-securities/*.

For information on Series EE, Series I, and Series HH savings bonds, see *U.S. Savings Bonds*, earlier.

Treasury inflation-protected securities (TIPS). These securities pay interest twice a year at a fixed rate, based on a principal amount adjusted to take into account inflation and deflation. For the tax treatment of these securities, see *Inflation-Indexed Debt Instruments* under *Original Issue Discount (OID)* in *IRS.gov/ Pub550*.

Bonds Sold Between Interest Dates

If you sell a bond between interest payment dates, part of the sales price represents interest accrued to the date of sale. You must report that part of the sales price as interest income for the year of sale.

If you buy a bond between interest payment dates, part of the purchase price represents interest accrued before the date of purchase. When that interest is paid to you, treat it as a nontaxable return of your capital investment, rather than as interest income. See *Accrued interest on bonds* under *How To Report Interest Income* in chapter 1 of *IRS.gov/Pub550* for information on reporting the payment.

Insurance

Life insurance proceeds paid to you as beneficiary of the insured person are usually not taxable. But if you receive the proceeds in installments, you must usually report a part of each installment payment as interest income.

For more information about insurance proceeds received in installments, see Pub. 525, Taxable and Nontaxable Income.

Annuity. If you buy an annuity with life insurance proceeds, the annuity payments you receive are taxed as pension and annuity income from a nonqualified plan, not as interest income. See chapter 5 for information on pension and annuity income from nonqualified plans.

State or Local Government Obligations

Interest on a bond used to finance government operations generally isn't taxable if the bond is issued by a state, the District of Columbia, a possession of the United States, or any of their political subdivisions.

Bonds issued after 1982 by an Indian tribal government (including tribal economic development bonds issued after February 17, 2009) are treated as issued by a state. Interest on these bonds is generally tax exempt if the bonds are part of an issue of which substantially all proceeds are to be used in the exercise of any essential government function. However, the essential government function requirement does not apply to tribal economic development bonds issued after February 17, 2009. See section 7871(f).

For information on federally guaranteed bonds, mortgage revenue bonds, arbitrage bonds, private activity bonds, qualified tax credit bonds, and Build America bonds, including whether interest on some of these bonds is taxable, see *State or Local Government Obligations* in chapter 1 of *IRS.gov/Pub550*.

Information reporting requirement. If you file a tax return, you are required to show any tax-exempt interest you received on your return. Tax-exempt interest paid to you will be reported to you on Form 1099-INT, box 8. This is an information reporting requirement only. It doesn't change tax-exempt interest to taxable interest.

Original Issue Discount (OID)

Original issue discount (OID) is a form of interest. You generally include OID in your income as it accrues over the term of the debt instrument, whether or not you receive any payments from the issuer.

A debt instrument generally has OID when the instrument is issued for a price that is less than its stated redemption price at maturity. OID is the difference between the stated redemption price at maturity and the issue price.

All debt instruments that pay no interest before maturity are presumed to be issued at a discount. Zero coupon bonds are one example of these instruments.

The OID accrual rules generally don't apply to short-term obligations (those with a fixed maturity date of 1 year or less from date of issue). See *Discount on Short-Term Obligations* in chapter 1 of *IRS.gov/Pub550*.

De minimis OID. You can treat the discount as zero if it is less than one-fourth of 1% (0.0025) of the stated redemption price at maturity multiplied by the number of full years from the date of original issue to maturity. This small discount is known as de minimis OID.

Example 1. You bought a 10-year bond with a stated redemption price at maturity of $1,000, issued at $980 with OID of $20. One-fourth of 1% of $1,000 (stated redemption price) times 10 (the number of full years from the date of original issue to maturity) equals $25. Because the $20 discount is less than $25, the OID is treated as zero. (If you hold the bond at maturity, you will recognize $20 ($1,000 − $980) of capital gain.)

Example 2. The facts are the same as in *Example 1*, except that the bond was issued at $950. The OID is $50. Because the $50 discount is more than the $25 figured in *Example 1*, you must include the OID in income as it accrues over the term of the bond.

Debt instrument bought after original issue. If you buy a debt instrument with de minimis OID at a premium, the de minimis OID isn't includible in income. If you buy a debt instrument with de minimis OID at a discount, the discount is reported under the market discount rules. See *Market Discount Bonds* in chapter 1 of *IRS.gov/Pub550*.

Exceptions to reporting OID as current income. The OID rules discussed in this chapter don't apply to the following debt instruments.

1. Tax-exempt obligations. (However, see *Stripped tax-exempt obligations* under *Stripped Bonds and Coupons* in chapter 1 of *IRS.gov/Pub550*.)

2. U.S. savings bonds.

3. Short-term debt instruments (those with a fixed maturity date of not more than 1 year from the date of issue).

4. Loans between individuals if all the following are true.

   a. The loan is not made in the course of a trade or business of the lender.

   b. The amount of the loan, plus the amount of any outstanding prior loans between the same individuals, is $10,000 or less.

   c. Avoiding any federal tax isn't one of the principal purposes of the loan.

5. A debt instrument purchased at a premium.

Form 1099-OID. The issuer of the debt instrument (or your broker if you held the instrument through a broker) should give you Form 1099-OID, or a similar statement, if the total OID for the calendar year is $10 or more. Form 1099-OID will show, in box 1, the amount of OID for the part of the year that you held the bond. It will also show, in box 2, the stated interest you must include in your income. Box 8 shows OID on a U.S. Treasury obligation for the part of the year you owned it and isn't included in box 1. A copy of Form 1099-OID will be sent to the IRS. Don't file your copy with your return. Keep it for your records.

In most cases, you must report the entire amount in boxes 1, 2, and 8 of Form 1099-OID as interest income. But see *Refiguring OID shown on Form 1099-OID*, later in this discussion, for more information.

Form 1099-OID not received. If you had OID for the year but didn't receive a Form 1099-OID, you may have to figure the correct amount of OID to report on your return. See Pub. 1212 for details on how to figure the correct OID.

Nominee. If someone else is the holder of record (the registered owner) of an OID instrument belonging to you and receives a Form 1099-OID on your behalf, that person must give you a Form 1099-OID.

Refiguring OID shown on Form 1099-OID. You may need to refigure the OID shown in box 1 or box 8 of Form 1099-OID if either of the following applies.

- You bought the debt instrument after its original issue and paid a premium or an acquisition premium.

- The debt instrument is a stripped bond or a stripped coupon (including certain zero coupon instruments).

If you acquired your debt instrument before 2014, your payer is only required to report a gross amount of OID in box 1 or box 8 of Form 1099-OID.

For information about figuring the correct amount of OID to include in your income, see *Figuring OID on Long-Term Debt Instruments* in Pub. 1212 and the Form 1099-OID Instructions for Recipient.

If you acquired your debt instrument after 2013, unless you have informed your payer that you do not want to amortize bond premium, your payer must generally report either (1) a net amount of OID that reflects the offset of OID by the amount of bond premium or acquisition premium amortization for the year, or (2) a gross amount for both the OID and the bond premium or acquisition premium amortization for the year.

Refiguring periodic interest shown on Form 1099-OID. If you disposed of a debt instrument or acquired it from another holder during the year, see *Bonds Sold Between Interest Dates*, earlier, for information about the treatment of periodic interest that may be shown in box 2 of Form 1099-OID for that instrument.

Certificates of deposit (CDs). If you buy a CD with a maturity of more than 1 year, you must include in income each year a part of the total interest due and report it in the same manner as other OID.

This also applies to similar deposit arrangements with banks, building and loan associations, etc., including:

- Time deposits,
- Bonus plans,
- Savings certificates,
- Deferred income certificates,
- Bonus savings certificates, and
- Growth savings certificates.

Bearer CDs. CDs issued after 1982 must generally be in registered form. Bearer CDs are CDs not in registered form. They aren't issued in the depositor's name and are transferable from one individual to another.

Banks must provide the IRS and the person redeeming a bearer CD with a Form 1099-INT.

More information. See chapter 1 of *IRS.gov/Pub550* for more information about OID and related topics, such as market discount bonds.

When To Report Interest Income

When to report your interest income depends on whether you use the cash method or an accrual method to report income.

Cash method. Most individual taxpayers use the cash method. If you use this method, you generally report your interest income in the year in which you actually or constructively receive it. However, there are special rules for reporting the discount on certain debt instruments. See

U.S. Savings Bonds and *Original Issue Discount (OID)*, earlier.

Example. On September 1, 2020, you loaned another individual $2,000 at 4% interest, compounded annually. You aren't in the business of lending money. The note stated that principal and interest would be due on August 31, 2022. In 2022, you received $2,163.20 ($2,000 principal and $163.20 interest). If you use the cash method, you must include in income on your 2022 return the $163.20 interest you received in that year.

Constructive receipt. You constructively receive income when it is credited to your account or made available to you. You don't need to have physical possession of it. For example, you are considered to receive interest, dividends, or other earnings on any deposit or account in a bank, savings and loan, or similar financial institution, or interest on life insurance policy dividends left to accumulate, when they are credited to your account and subject to your withdrawal.

You constructively receive income on the deposit or account even if you must:

- Make withdrawals in multiples of even amounts;
- Give a notice to withdraw before making the withdrawal;
- Withdraw all or part of the account to withdraw the earnings; or
- Pay a penalty on early withdrawals, unless the interest you are to receive on an early withdrawal or redemption is substantially less than the interest payable at maturity.

Accrual method. If you use an accrual method, you report your interest income when you earn it, whether or not you have received it. Interest is earned over the term of the debt instrument.

Example. If, in the previous example, you use an accrual method, you must include the interest in your income as you earn it. You would report the interest as follows: 2020, $26.67; 2021, $81.06; and 2022, $55.47.

Coupon bonds. Interest on bearer bonds with detachable coupons is generally taxable in the year the coupon becomes due and payable. It doesn't matter when you mail the coupon for payment.

How To Report Interest Income

Generally, you report all your taxable interest income on Form 1040 or 1040-SR, line 2b.

Schedule B (Form 1040). You must also complete Schedule B (Form 1040), Part I, if you file Form 1040 or 1040-SR and any of the following apply.

1. Your taxable interest income is more than $1,500.

2. You are claiming the interest exclusion under the *Education Savings Bond Program* (discussed earlier).

3. You received interest from a seller-financed mortgage, and the buyer used the property as a home.

4. You received a Form 1099-INT for U.S. savings bond interest that includes amounts you reported in a previous tax year.

5. You received, as a nominee, interest that actually belongs to someone else.

6. You received a Form 1099-INT for interest on frozen deposits.

7. You received a Form 1099-INT for interest on a bond you bought between interest payment dates.

8. You are reporting OID in an amount less than the amount shown on Form 1099-OID.

9. You reduce interest income from bonds by amortizable bond premium.

In Part I, line 1, list each payer's name and the amount received from each. If you received a Form 1099-INT or Form 1099-OID from a brokerage firm, list the brokerage firm as the payer.

 The box references discussed below are from the January 2022 revisions of Form 1099-INT and Form 1099-DIV. Later revisions may have different box references.

Reporting tax-exempt interest. Total your tax-exempt interest (such as interest or accrued OID on certain state and municipal bonds, including zero coupon municipal bonds) reported on Form 1099-INT, box 8, Form 1099-OID, box 11, and exempt-interest dividends from a mutual fund or other regulated investment company reported on Form 1099-DIV, box 12. Add these amounts to any other tax-exempt interest you received. Report the total on line 2a of Form 1040 or 1040-SR.

Form 1099-INT, box 9, and Form 1099-DIV, box 13, show the tax-exempt interest subject to the alternative minimum tax on Form 6251. These amounts are already included in the amounts on Form 1099-INT, box 8, and Form 1099-DIV, box 12. Don't add the amounts in Form 1099-INT, box 9, and Form 1099-DIV, box 13, to, or subtract them from, the amounts on Form 1099-INT, box 8, and Form 1099-DIV, box 12.

 Don't report interest from an IRA as tax-exempt interest.

Form 1099-INT. Your taxable interest income, except for interest from U.S. savings bonds and Treasury obligations, is shown in box 1 of Form 1099-INT. Add this amount to any other taxable interest income you received. See the Form 1099-INT Instructions for Recipient if you have interest from a security acquired at a premium. You must report all of your taxable interest income even if you don't receive a Form 1099-INT. Contact your financial institution if you don't receive a Form 1099-INT by February 15. Your identifying number may be truncated on any Form 1099-INT you receive.

If you forfeited interest income because of the early withdrawal of a time deposit, the deductible amount will be shown on Form

1099-INT in box 2. See *Penalty on early withdrawal of savings* in chapter 1 of *IRS.gov/Pub550*.

Box 3 of Form 1099-INT shows the interest income you received from U.S. savings bonds, Treasury bills, Treasury notes, and Treasury bonds. Generally, add the amount shown in box 3 to any other taxable interest income you received. If part of the amount shown in box 3 was previously included in your interest income, see *U.S. savings bond interest previously reported*, later. If you acquired the security at a premium, see the Form 1099-INT Instructions for Recipient.

Box 4 of Form 1099-INT will contain an amount if you were subject to backup withholding. Include the amount from box 4 on Form 1040 or 1040-SR, line 25b (federal income tax withheld).

Box 5 of Form 1099-INT shows investment expenses. This amount is not deductible. See chapter 12 for more information about investment expenses.

Box 6 of Form 1099-INT shows foreign tax paid. You may be able to claim this tax as a deduction or a credit on your Form 1040 or 1040-SR. See your tax return instructions.

Box 7 of Form 1099-INT shows the country or U.S. possession to which the foreign tax was paid.

U.S. savings bond interest previously reported. If you received a Form 1099-INT for U.S. savings bond interest, the form may show interest you don't have to report. See *Form 1099-INT for U.S. savings bonds interest*, earlier.

On Schedule B (Form 1040), Part I, line 1, report all the interest shown on your Form 1099-INT. Then follow these steps.

1. Several rows above line 2, enter a subtotal of all interest listed on line 1.

2. Below the subtotal, enter "U.S. Savings Bond Interest Previously Reported" and enter amounts previously reported or interest accrued before you received the bond.

3. Subtract these amounts from the subtotal and enter the result on line 2.

More information. For more information about how to report interest income, see chapter 1 of *IRS.gov/Pub550* or the instructions for the form you must file.

7.

Social Security and Equivalent Railroad Retirement Benefits

What's New

New lines 1a through 1z on Forms 1040 and 1040-SR. This year, line 1 is expanded and there are new lines 1a through 1z. Some amounts that in prior years were reported on Form 1040, and some amounts reported on Form 1040-SR, are now reported on Schedule 1.

- Scholarships and fellowship grants are now reported on Schedule 1, line 8r.

- Pension or annuity from a nonqualified deferred compensation plan or a nongovernmental section 457 plan is now reported on Schedule 1, line 8t.

- Wages earned while incarcerated are now reported on Schedule 1, line 8u.

New line 6c on Forms 1040 and 1040-SR. A checkbox was added on line 6c. Taxpayers who elect to use the lump-sum election method for their benefits will check this box. See *Lump-Sum Election* in Pub. 915, Social Security and Equivalent Railroad Retirement Benefits, for details.

Introduction

This chapter explains the federal income tax rules for social security benefits and equivalent tier 1 railroad retirement benefits. It explains the following topics.

- How to figure whether your benefits are taxable.

- How to report your taxable benefits.

- How to use the Social Security Benefits Worksheet (with examples).

- Deductions related to your benefits and how to treat repayments that are more than the benefits you received during the year.

Social security benefits include monthly retirement, survivor, and disability benefits. They don't include Supplemental Security Income (SSI) payments, which aren't taxable.

Equivalent tier 1 railroad retirement benefits are the part of tier 1 benefits that a railroad employee or beneficiary would have been entitled to receive under the social security system. They are commonly called the social security

equivalent benefit (SSEB) portion of tier 1 benefits.

If you received these benefits during 2022, you should have received a Form SSA-1099, Social Security Benefit Statement; or Form RRB-1099, Payments by the Railroad Retirement Board. These forms show the amounts received and repaid, and taxes withheld for the year. You may receive more than one of these forms for the same year. You should add the amounts shown on all the Forms SSA-1099 and Forms RRB-1099 you receive for the year to determine the total amounts received and repaid, and taxes withheld for that year. See the Appendix at the end of Pub. 915 for more information.

Note. When the term "benefits" is used in this chapter, it applies to both social security benefits and the SSEB portion of tier 1 railroad retirement benefits.

my Social Security account. Social security beneficiaries may quickly and easily obtain information from the SSA's website with a *my Social Security* account to:

- Keep track of your earnings and verify them every year,

- Get an estimate of your future benefits if you are still working,

- Get a letter with proof of your benefits if you currently receive them,

- Change your address,

- Start or change your direct deposit,

- Get a replacement Medicare card, and

- Get a replacement Form SSA-1099 for the tax season.

For more information and to set up an account, go to *SSA.gov/myaccount*.

What isn't covered in this chapter. This chapter doesn't cover the tax rules for the following railroad retirement benefits.

- Non-social security equivalent benefit (NSSEB) portion of tier 1 benefits.

- Tier 2 benefits.

- Vested dual benefits.

- Supplemental annuity benefits.

For information on these benefits, see Pub. 575, Pension and Annuity Income.

This chapter doesn't cover the tax rules for social security benefits reported on Form SSA-1042S, Social Security Benefit Statement; or Form RRB-1042S, Statement for Nonresident Alien Recipients of Payments by the Railroad Retirement Board. For information about these benefits, see Pub. 519, U.S. Tax Guide for Aliens; and Pub. 915.

This chapter also doesn't cover the tax rules for foreign social security benefits. These benefits are taxable as annuities, unless they are exempt from U.S. tax or treated as a U.S. social security benefit under a tax treaty.

Useful Items

You may want to see:

Publication

❑ **501** Dependents, Standard Deduction, and Filing Information

❑ **505** Tax Withholding and Estimated Tax

❑ **519** U.S. Tax Guide for Aliens

❑ **575** Pension and Annuity Income

❑ **590-A** Contributions to Individual Retirement Arrangements (IRAs)

❑ **915** Social Security and Equivalent Railroad Retirement Benefits

Form (and Instructions)

❑ **1040-ES** Estimated Tax for Individuals

❑ **SSA-1099** Social Security Benefit Statement

❑ **RRB-1099** Payments by the Railroad Retirement Board

❑ **W-4V** Voluntary Withholding Request

For these and other useful items, go to *IRS.gov/ Forms*.

Are Any of Your Benefits Taxable?

To find out whether any of your benefits may be taxable, compare the base amount (explained later) for your filing status with the total of:

1. One-half of your benefits; plus

2. All your other income, including tax-exempt interest.

Exclusions. When making this comparison, don't reduce your other income by any exclusions for:

- Interest from qualified U.S. savings bonds,

- Employer-provided adoption benefits,

- Interest on education loans,

- Foreign earned income or foreign housing, or

- Income earned by bona fide residents of American Samoa or Puerto Rico.

Children's benefits. The rules in this chapter apply to benefits received by children. See *Who is taxed*, later.

Figuring total income. To figure the total of one-half of your benefits plus your other income, use Worksheet 7-1, discussed later. If the total is more than your base amount, part of your benefits may be taxable.

If you are married and file a joint return for 2022, you and your spouse must combine your incomes and your benefits to figure whether any of your combined benefits are taxable. Even if your spouse didn't receive any benefits, you must add your spouse's income to yours to figure whether any of your benefits are taxable.

 If the only income you received during 2022 was your social security or the SSEB portion of tier 1 railroad

retirement benefits, your benefits generally aren't taxable and you probably don't have to file a return. If you have income in addition to your benefits, you may have to file a return even if none of your benefits are taxable. See *Do I Have To File a Return?* in chapter 1, earlier; Pub. 501; or your tax return instructions to find out if you have to file a return.

Base amount. Your base amount is:

- $25,000 if you are single, head of household, or qualifying surviving spouse;

- $25,000 if you are married filing separately and lived apart from your spouse for all of 2022;

- $32,000 if you are married filing jointly; or

- $0 if you are married filing separately and lived with your spouse at any time during 2022.

Worksheet 7-1. You can use Worksheet 7-1 to figure the amount of income to compare with your base amount. This is a quick way to check whether some of your benefits may be taxable.

Worksheet 7-1. **A Quick Way To Check if Your Benefits May Be Taxable**

Note. If you plan to file a joint income tax return, include your spouse's amounts, if any, on lines A, C, and D.

A. Enter the total amount from *box 5* of **all** your **Forms SSA-1099** and **RRB-1099**. Include the full amount of any lump-sum benefit payments received in 2022, for 2022 and earlier years. (If you received more than one form, combine the amounts from box 5 and enter the total) . . . . A. _____

Note. If the amount on line A is zero or less, stop here; none of your benefits are taxable this year.

B. Multiply line A by 50% (0.50) . . . . B. _____

C. Enter your total income that is taxable (excluding line A), such as pensions, wages, interest, ordinary dividends, and capital gain distributions. Don't reduce your income by any deductions, exclusions (listed earlier), or exemptions . . . . C. _____

D. Enter any tax-exempt interest income, such as interest on municipal bonds . . . . D. _____

E. Add lines B, C, and D . . . E. _____

Note. Compare the amount on line E to your **base amount** for your filing status. If the amount on line E equals or is less than the **base amount** for your filing status, none of your benefits are taxable this year. If the amount on line E is more than your **base amount,** some of your benefits may be taxable and you will need to complete Worksheet 1 in Pub. 915 (or the Social Security Benefits Worksheet in your tax form instructions). If none of your benefits are taxable, but you must otherwise file a tax return, see *Benefits not taxable*, later, under *How To Report Your Benefits*.

Example. You and your spouse (both over 65) are filing a joint return for 2022 and you both received social security benefits during the year. In January 2023, you received a Form SSA-1099 showing net benefits of $3,500 in box 5. Your spouse received a Form SSA-1099 showing net benefits of $2,500 in box 5. You also received a taxable pension of $28,100 and interest income of $700. You didn't have any tax-exempt interest income. Your benefits aren't taxable for 2022 because your income, as figured in Worksheet 7-1, isn't more than your base amount ($32,000) for married filing jointly.

Even though none of your benefits are taxable, you must file a return for 2022 because your taxable gross income ($28,800) exceeds the minimum filing requirement amount for your filing status.

Filled-in Worksheet 7-1. **A Quick Way To Check if Your Benefits May Be Taxable**

Note. If you plan to file a joint income tax return, include your spouse's amounts, if any, on lines A, C, and D.

A. Enter the total amount from **box 5** of **all** your **Forms SSA-1099 and RRB-1099.** Include the full amount of any lump-sum benefit payments received in 2022, for 2022 and earlier years. (If you received more than one form, combine the amounts from box 5 and enter the total.) . . . . . . A. $6,000

Note. If the amount on line A is zero or less, stop here; none of your benefits are taxable this year.

B. Multiply line A by 50% (0.50) . . . . B. 3,000

C. Enter your total income that is taxable (excluding line A), such as pensions, wages, interest, ordinary dividends, and capital gain distributions. Don't reduce your income by any deductions, exclusions (listed earlier), or exemptions . . . . C. 28,800

D. Enter any tax-exempt interest income, such as interest on municipal bonds . . . . D. -0-

E. Add lines B, C, and D . . . E. $31,800

Note. Compare the amount on line E to your **base amount** for your filing status. If the amount on line E equals or is less than the **base amount** for your filing status, none of your benefits are taxable this year. If the amount on line E is more than your **base amount,** some of your benefits may be taxable and you will need to complete Worksheet 1 in Pub. 915 (or the Social Security Benefits Worksheet in your tax form instructions). If none of your benefits are taxable, but you otherwise must file a tax return, see _Benefits not taxable_, later, under _How To Report Your Benefits_.

Who is taxed. Benefits are included in the taxable income (to the extent they are taxable) of the person who has the legal right to receive the benefits. For example, if you and your child receive benefits, but the check for your child is made out in your name, you must use only your part of the benefits to see whether any benefits are taxable to you. One-half of the part that belongs to your child must be added to your child's other income to see whether any of those benefits are taxable to your child.

Repayment of benefits. Any repayment of benefits you made during 2022 must be subtracted from the gross benefits you received in 2022. It doesn't matter whether the repayment was for a benefit you received in 2022 or in an earlier year. If you repaid more than the gross benefits you received in 2022, see _Repayments More Than Gross Benefits_, later.

Your gross benefits are shown in box 3 of Form SSA-1099 or RRB-1099. Your repayments are shown in box 4. The amount in box 5 shows your net benefits for 2022 (box 3 minus box 4). Use the amount in box 5 to figure whether any of your benefits are taxable.

Tax withholding and estimated tax. You can choose to have federal income tax withheld from your social security benefits and/or the SSEB portion of your tier 1 railroad retirement benefits. If you choose to do this, you must complete a Form W-4V.

If you don't choose to have income tax withheld, you may have to request additional withholding from other income or pay estimated tax during the year. For details, see chapter 4, earlier; Pub. 505; or the Instructions for Form 1040-ES.

How To Report Your Benefits

If part of your benefits are taxable, you must use Form 1040 or 1040-SR.

Reporting on Form 1040 or 1040-SR. Report your net benefits (the total amount from box 5 of all your Forms SSA-1099 and Forms RRB-1099) on line 6a and the taxable part on line 6b. If you are married filing separately and you lived apart from your spouse for all of 2022, also enter "D" to the right of the word "benefits" on line 6a.

Benefits not taxable. Report your net benefits (the total amount from box 5 of all your Forms SSA-1099 and Forms RRB-1099) on Form 1040 or 1040-SR, line 6a. Enter -0- on Form 1040 or 1040-SR, line 6b. If you are married filing separately and you lived apart from your spouse for all of 2022, also enter "D" to the right of the word "benefits" on Form 1040 or 1040-SR, line 6a.

How Much Is Taxable?

If part of your benefits are taxable, how much is taxable depends on the total amount of your benefits and other income. Generally, the higher that total amount, the greater the taxable part of your benefits.

Maximum taxable part. Generally, up to 50% of your benefits will be taxable. However, up to 85% of your benefits can be taxable if either of the following situations applies to you.

- The total of one-half of your benefits and all your other income is more than $34,000 ($44,000 if you are married filing jointly).

- You are married filing separately and lived with your spouse at any time during 2022.

Which worksheet to use. A worksheet you can use to figure your taxable benefits is in the Instructions for Form 1040. You can use either that worksheet or Worksheet 1 in Pub. 915, unless any of the following situations applies to you.

1. You contributed to a traditional individual retirement arrangement (IRA) and you or your spouse is covered by a retirement plan at work. In this situation, you must

use the special worksheets in Appendix B of Pub. 590-A to figure both your IRA deduction and your taxable benefits.

2. Situation 1 doesn't apply and you take an exclusion for interest from qualified U.S. savings bonds (Form 8815), for adoption benefits (Form 8839), for foreign earned income or housing (Form 2555), or for income earned in American Samoa (Form 4563) or Puerto Rico by bona fide residents. In this situation, you must use Worksheet 1 in Pub. 915 to figure your taxable benefits.

3. You received a lump-sum payment for an earlier year. In this situation, also complete Worksheet 2 or 3 and Worksheet 4 in Pub. 915. See _Lump-sum election_ next.

Lump-sum election. You must include the taxable part of a lump-sum (retroactive) payment of benefits received in 2022 in your 2022 income, even if the payment includes benefits for an earlier year.

 Line 6c: Check the box on line 6c if you elect to use the lump-sum election method for your benefits. If any of your benefits are taxable for 2022 and they include a lump-sum benefit payment that was for an earlier year, you may be able to reduce the taxable amount with the lump-sum election. See Lump-Sum Election in Pub. 915 for details.

 This type of lump-sum benefit payment shouldn't be confused with the lump-sum death benefit that both the SSA and RRB pay to many of their beneficiaries. No part of the lump-sum death benefit is subject to tax.

Generally, you use your 2022 income to figure the taxable part of the total benefits received in 2022. However, you may be able to figure the taxable part of a lump-sum payment for an earlier year separately, using your income for the earlier year. You can elect this method if it lowers your taxable benefits.

**Making the election.** If you received a lump-sum benefit payment in 2022 that includes benefits for one or more earlier years, follow the instructions in Pub. 915 under _Lump-Sum Election_ to see whether making the election will lower your taxable benefits. That discussion also explains how to make the election.

 Because the earlier year's taxable benefits are included in your 2022 income, no adjustment is made to the earlier year's return. Don't file an amended return for the earlier year.

Examples

The following are a few examples you can use as a guide to figure the taxable part of your benefits.

**Example 1.** George White is single and files Form 1040 for 2022. He received the following income in 2022.

Fully taxable pension	. . . .	$18,600
Wages from part-time job	. . . . .	9,400
Taxable interest income	. . . . . .	990
Total	. . . .	$28,990

George also received social security benefits during 2022. The Form SSA-1099 he received in January 2023 shows $5,980 in box 5. To figure his taxable benefits, George completes the worksheet shown here.

Filled-in Worksheet 1.
Figuring Your Taxable Benefits

1. Enter the total amount from **box 5** of **all** your **Forms SSA-1099** and **RRB-1099**. Also enter this amount on Form 1040 or 1040-SR, line 6a $5,980
2. Multiply line 1 by 50% (0.50) . . . . . . | 2,990
3. Combine the amounts from Form 1040 or 1040-SR, lines 1z, 2b, 3b, 4b, 5b, 7, and 8; and Schedule 1 (Form 1040), lines 8r, 8t, and 8u . . . . | 28,990
4. Enter the amount, if any, from Form 1040 or 1040-SR, line 2a . . . | -0-
5. Enter the total of any exclusions/ adjustments for:
   - Adoption benefits (Form 8839, line 28),
   - Foreign earned income or housing (Form 2555, lines 45 and 50), and
   - Certain income of bona fide residents of American Samoa (Form 4563, line 15) or Puerto Rico . . . . | -0-
6. Combine lines 2, 3, 4, and 5 above . . . | 31,980
7. Enter the total of the amounts from Schedule 1 (Form 1040), lines 11 through 20, and 23 and 25 . . . . | -0-
8. Is the amount on line 7 less than the amount on line 6?

   No. (STOP) None of your social security benefits are taxable. Enter -0- on Form 1040 or 1040-SR, line 6b.

   Yes. Subtract line 7 from line 6 . . . . | 31,980
9. If you are:
   - Married filing jointly, enter $32,000; or
   - Single, head of household, qualifying surviving spouse, or married filing separately and you **lived apart** from your spouse for all of 2022, enter $25,000 . . . . | 25,000

Note. If you are married filing separately and you lived with your spouse at any time in 2022, skip lines 9 through 16, multiply line 8 by 85% (0.85), and enter the result on line 17. Then, go to line 18.

10. Is the amount on line 9 less than the amount on line 8?

    No. (STOP) None of your benefits are taxable. Enter -0- on Form 1040 or 1040-SR, line 6b. If you are married filing separately and you **lived apart** from your spouse for all of 2022, be sure you entered "D" to the right of the word "benefits" on Form 1040 or 1040-SR, line 6a.

    Yes. Subtract line 9 from line 8 . . . . | 6,980
11. Enter $12,000 if married filing jointly; or $9,000 if single, head of household, qualifying surviving spouse, or married filing separately and you **lived apart** from your spouse for all of 2022 . . . . . | 9,000
12. Subtract line 11 from line 10. If zero or less, enter -0- . . . . | -0-
13. Enter the **smaller** of line 10 or line 11 . . . . | 6,980
14. Multiply line 13 by 50% (0.50) . . . . . | 3,490
15. Enter the **smaller** of line 2 or line 14 . . | 2,990
16. Multiply line 12 by 85% (0.85). If line 12 is zero, enter -0- . . . . | -0-
17. Add lines 15 and 16 . . . . | 2,990
18. Multiply line 1 by 85% (0.85) . . . . . . | 5,083
19. **Taxable benefits.** Enter the **smaller** of line 17 or line 18. Also enter this amount on Form 1040 or 1040-SR, line 6b . . . | $2,990

The amount on line 19 of George's worksheet shows that $2,990 of his social security benefits is taxable. On line 6a of his Form 1040, George enters his net benefits of $5,980. On line 6b, he enters his taxable benefits of $2,990.

Example 2. Ray and Alice Hopkins file a joint return on Form 1040 for 2022. Ray is retired and received a fully taxable pension of $15,500. He also received social security benefits, and his Form SSA-1099 for 2022 shows net benefits of $5,600 in box 5. Alice worked during the year and had wages of $14,000. She made a deductible payment to her IRA account of $1,000 and isn't covered by a retirement plan at work. Ray and Alice have two savings accounts with a total of $250 in taxable interest income. They complete Worksheet 1, shown below, entering $29,750 ($15,500 + $14,000 + $250) on line 3. They find none of Ray's social security benefits are taxable. On Form 1040, they enter $5,600 on line 6a and -0- on line 6b.

Filled-in Worksheet 1.
Figuring Your Taxable Benefits

1. Enter the total amount from **box 5** of **all** your **Forms SSA-1099** and **RRB-1099**. Also enter this amount on Form 1040 or 1040-SR, line 6a $5,600
2. Multiply line 1 by 50% (0.50) . . . | 2,800
3. Combine the amounts from Form 1040 or 1040-SR, lines 1z, 2b, 3b, 4b, 5b, 7, and 8; and Schedule 1 (Form 1040), lines 8r, 8t, and 8u . . . . | 29,750
4. Enter the amount, if any, from Form 1040 or 1040-SR, line 2a . . . . | -0-
5. Enter the total of any exclusions/ adjustments for:
   - Adoption benefits (Form 8839, line 28),
   - Foreign earned income or housing (Form 2555, lines 45 and 50), and
   - Certain income of bona fide residents of American Samoa (Form 4563, line 15) or Puerto Rico . . . . | -0-
6. Combine lines 2, 3, 4, and 5 above . . . . | 32,550
7. Enter the total of the amounts from Schedule 1 (Form 1040), lines 11 through 20, and 23 and 25 . . . . | 1,000
8. Is the amount on line 7 less than the amount on line 6?

   No. (STOP) None of your social security benefits are taxable. Enter -0- on Form 1040 or 1040-SR, line 6b.

   Yes. Subtract line 7 from line 6 . . . . | 31,550
9. If you are:
   - Married filing jointly, enter $32,000; or
   - Single, head of household, qualifying surviving spouse, or married filing separately and you **lived apart** from your spouse for all of 2022, enter $25,000 . . . . | 32,000

Note. If you are married filing separately and you lived with your spouse at any time in 2022, skip lines 9 through 16, multiply line 8 by 85% (0.85), and enter the result on line 17. Then, go to line 18.

10. Is the amount on line 9 less than the amount on line 8?

    No. (STOP) None of your benefits are taxable. Enter -0- on Form 1040 or 1040-SR, line 6b. If you are married filing separately and you **lived apart** from your spouse for all of 2022, be sure you entered "D" to the right of the word "benefits" on Form 1040 or 1040-SR, line 6a.

    Yes. Subtract line 9 from line 8 . . . . |

11. Enter $12,000 if married filing jointly; or $9,000 if single, head of household, qualifying surviving spouse, or married filing separately and you **lived apart** from your spouse for all of 2022 . . . . . _____

12. Subtract line 11 from line 10. If zero or less, enter -0- . . . . _____

13. Enter the **smaller** of line 10 or line 11 . . . . _____

14. Multiply line 13 by 50% (0.50) . . . . . . _____

15. Enter the **smaller** of line 2 or line 14 . . _____

16. Multiply line 12 by 85% (0.85). If line 12 is zero, enter -0- . . . . . . _____

17. Add lines 15 and 16 . . . . _____

18. Multiply line 1 by 85% (0.85) . . . . _____

19. **Taxable benefits.** Enter the **smaller** of line 17 or line 18. Also enter this amount on Form 1040 or 1040-SR, line 6b . . . _____

Example 3. Joe and Betty Johnson file a joint return on Form 1040 for 2022. Joe is a retired railroad worker and in 2022 received the SSEB portion of tier 1 railroad retirement benefits. Joe's Form RRB-1099 shows $10,000 in box 5. Betty is a retired government worker and received a fully taxable pension of $38,000. They had $2,300 in taxable interest income plus interest of $200 on a qualified U.S. savings bond. The savings bond interest qualified for the exclusion. They figure their taxable benefits by completing Worksheet 1, shown below. Because they have qualified U.S. savings bond interest, they follow the note at the beginning of the worksheet and use the amount from line 2 of their Schedule B (Form 1040) on line 3 of the worksheet instead of the amount from line 2b of their Form 1040. On line 3 of the worksheet, they enter $40,500 ($38,000 + $2,500).

Filled-in Worksheet 1.
Figuring Your Taxable Benefits

Before you begin:

- If you are married filing separately and you lived apart from your spouse for all of 2022, enter "D" to the right of the word "benefits" on Form 1040 or 1040-SR, line 6a.
- Don't use this worksheet if you repaid benefits in 2022 and your total repayments (box 4 of Forms SSA-1099 and RRB-1099) were more than your gross benefits for 2022 (box 3 of Forms SSA-1099 and RRB-1099). None of your benefits are taxable for 2022. For more information, see *Repayments More Than Gross Benefits*, later.
- If you are filing Form 8815, Exclusion of Interest From Series EE and I U.S. Savings Bonds Issued After 1989, don't include the amount from line 2b of Form 1040 or 1040-SR on line 3 of this worksheet. Instead, include the amount from Schedule B (Form 1040), line 2.

1. Enter the total amount from *box 5* of **all** your **Forms SSA-1099** and **RRB-1099**. Also enter this amount on Form 1040 or 1040-SR, line 6a $10,000

2. Multiply line 1 by 50% (0.50) 5,000

3. Combine the amounts from Form 1040 or 1040-SR, lines 1z, 2b, 3b, 4b, 5b, 7, and 8; and Schedule 1 (Form 1040), lines 8r, 8t, and 8u 40,500

4. Enter the amount, if any, from Form 1040 or 1040-SR, line 2a . . . . -0-

5. Enter the total of any exclusions/adjustments for:
   - Adoption benefits (Form 8839, line 28),
   - Foreign earned income or housing (Form 2555, lines 45 and 50), and
   - Certain income of bona fide residents of American Samoa (Form 4563, line 15) or Puerto Rico . . . . -0-

6. Combine lines 2, 3, 4, and 5 above . . . 45,500

7. Enter the total of the amounts from Schedule 1 (Form 1040), lines 11 through 20, and 23 and 25 . . . . -0-

8. Is the amount on line 7 less than the amount on line 6?

   No. (STOP) None of your social security benefits are taxable. Enter -0- on Form 1040 or 1040-SR, line 6b.

   Yes. Subtract line 7 from line 6 45,500

9. If you are:
   - Married filing jointly, enter $32,000; or
   - Single, head of household, qualifying surviving spouse, or married filing separately and you **lived apart** from your spouse for all of 2022, enter $25,000 32,000

Note. If you are married filing separately and you lived with your spouse at any time in 2022, skip lines 9 through 16, multiply line 8 by 85% (0.85), and enter the result on line 17. Then, go to line 18.

10. Is the amount on line 9 less than the amount on line 8?

    No. (STOP) None of your benefits are taxable. Enter -0- on Form 1040 or 1040-SR, line 6b. If you are married filing separately and you **lived apart** from your spouse for all of 2022, be sure you entered "D" to the right of the word "benefits" on Form 1040 or 1040-SR, line 6a.

    Yes. Subtract line 9 from line 8 13,500

11. Enter $12,000 if married filing jointly; or $9,000 if single, head of household, qualifying surviving spouse, or married filing separately and you **lived apart** from your spouse for all of 2022 12,000

12. Subtract line 11 from line 10. If zero or less, enter -0- 1,500

13. Enter the **smaller** of line 10 or line 11 12,000

14. Multiply line 13 by 50% (0.50) 6,000

15. Enter the **smaller** of line 2 or line 14 . . 5,000

16. Multiply line 12 by 85% (0.85). If line 12 is zero, enter -0- 1,275

17. Add lines 15 and 16 6,275

18. Multiply line 1 by 85% (0.85) 8,500

19. **Taxable benefits.** Enter the **smaller** of line 17 or line 18. Also enter this amount on Form 1040 or 1040-SR, line 6b . . . $6,275

More than 50% of Joe's net benefits are taxable because the income on line 8 of the worksheet ($45,500) is more than $44,000. (See *Maximum taxable part* under *How Much Is Taxable*, earlier.) Joe and Betty enter $10,000 on Form 1040, line 6a; and $6,275 on Form 1040, line 6b.

Deductions Related to Your Benefits

You may be entitled to deduct certain amounts related to the benefits you receive.

Disability payments. You may have received disability payments from your employer or an insurance company that you included as income on your tax return in an earlier year. If you received a lump-sum payment from the SSA or RRB, and you had to repay the employer or insurance company for the disability payments, you can take an itemized deduction for the part of the payments you included in gross income in the earlier year. If the amount you repay is more than $3,000, you may be able to claim a tax credit instead. Claim the deduction or credit in the same way explained under *Repayment of benefits received in an earlier year* under *Repayments More Than Gross Benefits* next.

Repayments More Than Gross Benefits

In some situations, your Form SSA-1099 or Form RRB-1099 will show that the total benefits you repaid (box 4) are more than the gross benefits (box 3) you received. If this occurred, your net benefits in box 5 will be a negative figure (a figure in parentheses) and none of your benefits will be taxable. Don't use a worksheet in this case. If you receive more than one form, a negative figure in box 5 of one form is used to offset a positive figure in box 5 of another form for that same year.

If you have any questions about this negative figure, contact your local *SSA office* or your local *RRB field office*.

Joint return. If you and your spouse file a joint return, and your Form SSA-1099 or RRB-1099 has a negative figure in box 5, but your spouse's doesn't, subtract the amount in box 5 of your form from the amount in box 5 of your spouse's form. You do this to get your net benefits when figuring if your combined benefits are taxable.

Example. John and Mary file a joint return for 2022. John received Form SSA-1099 showing $3,000 in box 5. Mary also received Form SSA-1099 and the amount in box 5 was ($500). John and Mary will use $2,500 ($3,000 minus $500) as the amount of their net benefits when figuring if any of their combined benefits are taxable.

Repayment of benefits received in an earlier year. If the total amount shown in box 5 of all of your Forms SSA-1099 and RRB-1099 is a negative figure, you may be able to deduct part of this negative figure that represents benefits you included in gross income in an earlier year if the figure is more than $3,000. If the figure is $3,000 or less, it is a miscellaneous itemized deduction and can no longer be deducted.

Deduction more than $3,000. If this deduction is more than $3,000, you should figure your tax two ways.

1. Figure your tax for 2022 with the itemized deduction included on Schedule A (Form 1040), line 16.

2. Figure your tax for 2022 in the following steps.

   a. Figure the tax without the itemized deduction included on Schedule A (Form 1040), line 16.

   b. For each year after 1983 for which part of the negative figure represents a repayment of benefits, refigure your taxable benefits as if your total benefits for the year were reduced by that part of the negative figure. Then refigure the tax for that year.

   c. Subtract the total of the refigured tax amounts in (b) from the total of your actual tax amounts.

   d. Subtract the result in (c) from the result in (a).

Compare the tax figured in methods 1 and 2. Your tax for 2022 is the smaller of the two amounts. If method 1 results in less tax, take the itemized deduction on Schedule A (Form 1040), line 16. If method 2 results in less tax, claim a credit for the amount from step 2c above on Schedule 3 (Form 1040), line 13z. Enter "I.R.C. 1341" on the entry line. If both methods produce the same tax, deduct the repayment on Schedule A (Form 1040), line 16.

8.

Other Income

What's New

Student loan forgiveness. The eligibility for student loan forgiveness has been expanded under the authority granted by the Higher Education Relief Opportunities for Students Act of 2003. Borrowers with annual income during the pandemic of under $125,000 (for individuals) or under $250,000 (for married couples or heads of households) who received a Pell Grant in college will be eligible for up to $20,000 in debt cancellation. Borrowers who met those income standards but did not receive a Pell Grant will be eligible for up to $10,000 in relief.

Reminders

Business meals. Section 210 of the Taxpayer Certainty and Disaster Tax Relief Act of 2020 provides for the temporary allowance of a 100% business meal deduction for food or beverages provided by a restaurant and paid or incurred after December 31, 2020, and before January 1, 2023.

Unemployment compensation. If you received unemployment compensation but did not receive Form 1099-G, Certain Government Payments, through the mail, you may need to access your information through your state's website to get your electronic Form 1099-G.

Introduction

You must include on your return all items of income you receive in the form of money, property, and services unless the tax law states that you don't include them. Some items, however, are only partly excluded from income. This chapter discusses many kinds of income and explains whether they're taxable or nontaxable.

- Income that's taxable must be reported on your tax return and is subject to tax.

- Income that's nontaxable may have to be shown on your tax return but isn't taxable.

This chapter begins with discussions of the following income items.

- Bartering.
- Canceled debts.
- Sales parties at which you're the host or hostess.
- Life insurance proceeds.
- Partnership income.
- S corporation income.
- Recoveries (including state income tax refunds).
- Rents from personal property.
- Repayments.

- Royalties.
- Unemployment benefits.
- Welfare and other public assistance benefits.

These discussions are followed by brief discussions of other income items.

Useful Items
You may want to see:

Publication

- ❑ **502** Medical and Dental Expenses
- ❑ **504** Divorced or Separated Individuals
- ❑ **523** Selling Your Home
- ❑ **525** Taxable and Nontaxable Income
- ❑ **544** Sales and Other Dispositions of Assets
- ❑ **547** Casualties, Disasters, and Thefts
- ❑ **550** Investment Income and Expenses
- ❑ **4681** Canceled Debts, Foreclosures, Repossessions, and Abandonments

For these and other useful items, go to *IRS.gov/ Forms*.

Bartering

Bartering is an exchange of property or services. You must include in your income, at the time received, the fair market value of property or services you receive in bartering. If you exchange services with another person and you both have agreed ahead of time on the value of the services, that value will be accepted as fair market value unless the value can be shown to be otherwise.

Generally, you report this income on Schedule C (Form 1040), Profit or Loss From Business. However, if the barter involves an exchange of something other than services, such as in *Example 3* below, you may have to use another form or schedule instead.

Example 1. You're a self-employed attorney who performs legal services for a client, a small corporation. The corporation gives you shares of its stock as payment for your services. You must include the fair market value of the shares in your income on Schedule C (Form 1040) in the year you receive them.

Example 2. You're self-employed and a member of a barter club. The club uses "credit units" as a means of exchange. It adds credit units to your account for goods or services you provide to members, which you can use to purchase goods or services offered by other members of the barter club. The club subtracts credit units from your account when you receive goods or services from other members. You must include in your income the value of the credit units that are added to your account, even though you may not actually receive goods or services from other members until a later tax year.

Example 3. You own a small apartment building. In return for 6 months rent-free use of an apartment, an artist gives you a work of art she created. You must report as rental income on Schedule E (Form 1040), Supplemental Income and Loss, the fair market value of the artwork, and the artist must report as income on Schedule C (Form 1040) the fair rental value of the apartment.

Form 1099-B from barter exchange. If you exchanged property or services through a barter exchange, Form 1099-B, Proceeds From Broker and Barter Exchange Transactions, or a similar statement from the barter exchange should be sent to you by February 15, 2023. It should show the value of cash, property, services, credits, or scrip you received from exchanges during 2022. The IRS will also receive a copy of Form 1099-B.

Canceled Debts

In most cases, if a debt you owe is canceled or forgiven, other than as a gift or bequest, you must include the canceled amount in your income. You have no income from the canceled debt if it's intended as a gift to you. A debt includes any indebtedness for which you're liable or which attaches to property you hold.

If the debt is a nonbusiness debt, report the canceled amount on Schedule 1 (Form 1040), line 8c. If it's a business debt, report the amount on Schedule C (Form 1040) (or on Schedule F (Form 1040), Profit or Loss From Farming, if the debt is farm debt and you're a farmer).

Form 1099-C. If a federal government agency, financial institution, or credit union cancels or forgives a debt you owe of $600 or more, you will receive a Form 1099-C, Cancellation of Debt. The amount of the canceled debt is shown in box 2.

Interest included in canceled debt. If any interest is forgiven and included in the amount of canceled debt in box 2, the amount of interest will also be shown in box 3. Whether or not you must include the interest portion of the canceled debt in your income depends on whether the interest would be deductible when you paid it. See *Deductible debt* under *Exceptions*, later.

If the interest wouldn't be deductible (such as interest on a personal loan), include in your income the amount from box 2 of Form 1099-C. If the interest would be deductible (such as on a business loan), include in your income the net amount of the canceled debt (the amount shown in box 2 less the interest amount shown in box 3).

Discounted mortgage loan. If your financial institution offers a discount for the early payment of your mortgage loan, the amount of the discount is canceled debt. You must include the canceled amount in your income.

Mortgage relief upon sale or other disposition. If you're personally liable for a mortgage (recourse debt), and you're relieved of the mortgage when you dispose of the property, you may realize gain or loss up to the fair market value of the property. Also, to the extent the mortgage discharge exceeds the fair market value of the property, it's income from discharge of indebtedness unless it qualifies for exclusion under *Excluded debt*, later. Report any income from discharge of indebtedness on

nonbusiness debt that doesn't qualify for exclusion as other income on Schedule 1 (Form 1040), line 8c.

If you aren't personally liable for a mortgage (nonrecourse debt), and you're relieved of the mortgage when you dispose of the property (such as through foreclosure), that relief is included in the amount you realize. You may have a taxable gain if the amount you realize exceeds your adjusted basis in the property. Report any gain on nonbusiness property as a capital gain.

See Pub. 4681 for more information.

Stockholder debt. If you're a stockholder in a corporation and the corporation cancels or forgives your debt to it, the canceled debt is a constructive distribution that's generally dividend income to you. For more information, see Pub. 542, Corporations.

If you're a stockholder in a corporation and you cancel a debt owed to you by the corporation, you generally don't realize income. This is because the canceled debt is considered as a contribution to the capital of the corporation equal to the amount of debt principal that you canceled.

Repayment of canceled debt. If you included a canceled amount in your income and later pay the debt, you may be able to file a claim for refund for the year the amount was included in income. You can file a claim on Form 1040-X, Amended U.S. Individual Income Tax Return, if the statute of limitations for filing a claim is still open. The statute of limitations generally doesn't end until 3 years after the due date of your original return.

Exceptions

There are several exceptions to the inclusion of canceled debt in income. These are explained next.

Student loans. Certain student loans contain a provision that all or part of the debt incurred to attend the qualified educational institution will be canceled if you work for a certain period of time in certain professions for any of a broad class of employers.

You don't have income if your student loan is canceled after you agreed to this provision and then performed the services required. To qualify, the loan must have been made by:

1. The federal government, a state or local government, or an instrumentality, agency, or subdivision thereof;

2. A tax-exempt public benefit corporation that has assumed control of a state, county, or municipal hospital, and whose employees are considered public employees under state law; or

3. An educational institution:

   a. Under an agreement with an entity described in (1) or (2) that provided the funds to the institution to make the loan, or

   b. As part of a program of the institution designed to encourage its students to serve in occupations with unmet needs or in areas with unmet needs

and under which the services provided by the students (or former students) are for or under the direction of a governmental unit or a tax-exempt organization described in section 501(c)(3).

A loan to refinance a qualified student loan will also qualify if it was made by an educational institution or a qualified tax-exempt organization under its program designed as described in item 3b above.

Special rule for student loan discharges for 2021 through 2025. The American Rescue Plan Act of 2021 modified the treatment of student loan forgiveness for discharges in 2021 through 2025. Generally, if you are responsible for making loan payments, and the loan is canceled or repaid by someone else, you must include the amount that was canceled or paid on your behalf in your gross income for tax purposes. However, in certain circumstances you may be able to exclude this amount from gross income if the loan was one of the following.

- A loan for postsecondary educational expenses.

- A private education loan.

- A loan from an educational organization described in section 170(b)(1)(A)(ii).

- A loan from an organization exempt from tax under section 501(a) to refinance a student loan.

See Pub. 4681 and Pub. 970 for more information.

Education loan repayment assistance. Education loan repayments made to you by the National Health Service Corps Loan Repayment Program (NHSC Loan Repayment Program), a state education loan repayment program eligible for funds under the Public Health Service Act, or any other state loan repayment or loan forgiveness program that's intended to provide for the increased availability of health services in underserved or health professional shortage areas aren't taxable.

Deductible debt. You don't have income from the cancellation of a debt if your payment of the debt would be deductible. This exception applies only if you use the cash method of accounting. For more information, see chapter 5 of Pub. 334, Tax Guide for Small Business.

Price reduced after purchase. In most cases, if the seller reduces the amount of debt you owe for property you purchased, you don't have income from the reduction. The reduction of the debt is treated as a purchase price adjustment and reduces your basis in the property.

Excluded debt. Don't include a canceled debt in your gross income in the following situations.

- The debt is canceled in a bankruptcy case under title 11 of the U.S. Code. See Pub. 908, Bankruptcy Tax Guide.

- The debt is canceled when you're insolvent. However, you can't exclude any amount of canceled debt that's more than the amount by which you're insolvent. See Pub. 908.

- The debt is qualified farm debt and is canceled by a qualified person. See chapter 3 of Pub. 225, Farmer's Tax Guide.
- The debt is qualified real property business debt. See chapter 5 of Pub. 334.
- The cancellation is intended as a gift.
- The debt is qualified principal residence indebtedness.

Host

If you host a party or event at which sales are made, any gift or gratuity you receive for giving the event is a payment for helping a direct seller make sales. You must report this item as income at its fair market value.

Your out-of-pocket party expenses are subject to the 50% limit for meal expenses. For tax years 2018 and after, no deduction is allowed for any expenses related to activities generally considered entertainment, amusement, or recreation. Taxpayers may continue to deduct 50% of the cost of business meals if the taxpayer (or an employee of the taxpayer) is present and the food or beverages are not considered lavish or extravagant. The meals may be provided to a current or potential business customer, client, consultant, or similar business contact. Food and beverages that are provided during entertainment events will not be considered entertainment if purchased separately from the event.

Section 210 of the Taxpayer Certainty and Disaster Tax Relief Act of 2020 provides for the temporary allowance of a 100% business meal deduction for food or beverages provided by a restaurant and paid or incurred after December 31, 2020, and before January 1, 2023.

For more information about the limit for meal expenses, see Pub. 463, Travel, Gift, and Car Expenses.

Life Insurance Proceeds

Life insurance proceeds paid to you because of the death of the insured person aren't taxable unless the policy was turned over to you for a price. This is true even if the proceeds were paid under an accident or health insurance policy or an endowment contract. However, interest income received as a result of life insurance proceeds may be taxable.

Proceeds not received in installments. If death benefits are paid to you in a lump sum or other than at regular intervals, include in your income only the benefits that are more than the amount payable to you at the time of the insured person's death. If the benefit payable at death isn't specified, you include in your income the benefit payments that are more than the present value of the payments at the time of death.

Proceeds received in installments. If you receive life insurance proceeds in installments, you can exclude part of each installment from your income.

To determine the excluded part, divide the amount held by the insurance company (generally, the total lump sum payable at the death of the insured person) by the number of installments to be paid. Include anything over this excluded part in your income as interest.

Surviving spouse. If your spouse died before October 23, 1986, and insurance proceeds paid to you because of the death of your spouse are received in installments, you can exclude up to $1,000 a year of the interest included in the installments. If you remarry, you can continue to take the exclusion.

Surrender of policy for cash. If you surrender a life insurance policy for cash, you must include in income any proceeds that are more than the cost of the life insurance policy. In most cases, your cost (or investment in the contract) is the total of premiums that you paid for the life insurance policy, less any refunded premiums, rebates, dividends, or unrepaid loans that weren't included in your income.

You should receive a Form 1099-R showing the total proceeds and the taxable part. Report these amounts on lines 5a and 5b of Form 1040 or 1040-SR.

More information. For more information, see *Life Insurance Proceeds* in Pub. 525.

Endowment Contract Proceeds

An endowment contract is a policy under which you're paid a specified amount of money on a certain date unless you die before that date, in which case the money is paid to your designated beneficiary. Endowment proceeds paid in a lump sum to you at maturity are taxable only if the proceeds are more than the cost of the policy. To determine your cost, subtract any amount that you previously received under the contract and excluded from your income from the total premiums (or other consideration) paid for the contract. Include in your income the part of the lump-sum payment that's more than your cost.

Accelerated Death Benefits

Certain amounts paid as accelerated death benefits under a life insurance contract or viatical settlement before the insured's death are excluded from income if the insured is terminally or chronically ill.

Viatical settlement. This is the sale or assignment of any part of the death benefit under a life insurance contract to a viatical settlement provider. A viatical settlement provider is a person who regularly engages in the business of buying or taking assignment of life insurance contracts on the lives of insured individuals who are terminally or chronically ill and who meets the requirements of section 101(g)(2)(B) of the Internal Revenue Code.

Exclusion for terminal illness. Accelerated death benefits are fully excludable if the insured is a terminally ill individual. This is a person who has been certified by a physician as having an illness or physical condition that can reasonably

be expected to result in death within 24 months from the date of the certification.

Exclusion for chronic illness. If the insured is a chronically ill individual who's not terminally ill, accelerated death benefits paid on the basis of costs incurred for qualified long-term care services are fully excludable. Accelerated death benefits paid on a per diem or other periodic basis are excludable up to a limit. For 2022, this limit is $390. It applies to the total of the accelerated death benefits and any periodic payments received from long-term care insurance contracts. For information on the limit and the definitions of chronically ill individual, qualified long-term care services, and long-term care insurance contracts, see *Long-Term Care Insurance Contracts* under *Sickness and Injury Benefits* in Pub. 525.

Exception. The exclusion doesn't apply to any amount paid to a person (other than the insured) who has an insurable interest in the life of the insured because the insured:

- Is a director, officer, or employee of the person; or
- Has a financial interest in the person's business.

Form 8853. To claim an exclusion for accelerated death benefits made on a per diem or other periodic basis, you must file Form 8853, Archer MSAs and Long-Term Care Insurance Contracts, with your return. You don't have to file Form 8853 to exclude accelerated death benefits paid on the basis of actual expenses incurred.

Public Safety Officer Killed or Injured in the Line of Duty

A spouse, former spouse, and child of a public safety officer killed in the line of duty can exclude from gross income survivor benefits received from a governmental section 401(a) plan attributable to the officer's service. See section 101(h).

A public safety officer who's permanently and totally disabled or killed in the line of duty and a surviving spouse or child can exclude from income death or disability benefits received from the federal Bureau of Justice Assistance or death benefits paid by a state program. See section 104(a)(6).

For this purpose, the term "public safety officer" includes law enforcement officers, firefighters, chaplains, and rescue squad and ambulance crew members. For more information, see Pub. 559, Survivors, Executors, and Administrators.

Partnership Income

A partnership generally isn't a taxable entity. The income, gains, losses, deductions, and credits of a partnership are passed through to the partners based on each partner's distributive share of these items.

Schedule K-1 (Form 1065). Although a partnership generally pays no tax, it must file an information return on Form 1065, U.S. Return of

Partnership Income, and send Schedule K-1 (Form 1065) to each partner. In addition, the partnership will send each partner a copy of the Partner's Instructions for Schedule K-1 (Form 1065) to help each partner report his or her share of the partnership's income, deductions, credits, and tax preference items.

 Keep Schedule K-1 (Form 1065) for your records. Don't attach it to your Form 1040 or 1040-SR, unless you're specifically required to do so.

For more information on partnerships, see Pub. 541, Partnerships.

Qualified joint venture. If you and your spouse each materially participate as the only members of a jointly owned and operated business, and you file a joint return for the tax year, you can make a joint election to be treated as a qualified joint venture instead of a partnership. To make this election, you must divide all items of income, gain, loss, deduction, and credit attributable to the business between you and your spouse in accordance with your respective interests in the venture. For further information on how to make the election and which schedule(s) to file, see the instructions for your individual tax return.

S Corporation Income

In most cases, an S corporation doesn't pay tax on its income. Instead, the income, losses, deductions, and credits of the corporation are passed through to the shareholders based on each shareholder's pro rata share.

Schedule K-1 (Form 1120-S). An S corporation must file a return on Form 1120-S, U.S. Income Tax Return for an S Corporation, and send Schedule K-1 (Form 1120-S) to each shareholder. In addition, the S corporation will send each shareholder a copy of the Shareholder's Instructions for Schedule K-1 (Form 1120-S) to help each shareholder report her or his share of the S corporation's income, losses, credits, and deductions.

 Keep Schedule K-1 (Form 1120-S) for your records. Don't attach it to your Form 1040 or 1040-SR, unless you're specifically required to do so.

For more information on S corporations and their shareholders, see the Instructions for Form 1120-S.

Recoveries

A recovery is a return of an amount you deducted or took a credit for in an earlier year. The most common recoveries are refunds, reimbursements, and rebates of deductions itemized on Schedule A (Form 1040). You may also have recoveries of nonitemized deductions (such as payments on previously deducted bad debts) and recoveries of items for which you previously claimed a tax credit.

Tax benefit rule. You must include a recovery in your income in the year you receive it up to the amount by which the deduction or credit you took for the recovered amount reduced your tax in the earlier year. For this purpose, any in-

crease to an amount carried over to the current year that resulted from the deduction or credit is considered to have reduced your tax in the earlier year. For more information, see Pub. 525.

Federal income tax refund. Refunds of federal income taxes aren't included in your income because they're never allowed as a deduction from income.

State tax refund. If you received a state or local income tax refund (or credit or offset) in 2022, you must generally include it in income if you deducted the tax in an earlier year. The payer should send Form 1099-G to you by January 31, 2023. The IRS will also receive a copy of the Form 1099-G. If you file Form 1040 or 1040-SR, use the State and Local Income Tax Refund Worksheet in the 2022 instructions for Schedule 1 (Form 1040) to figure the amount (if any) to include in your income. See Pub. 525 for when you must use another worksheet.

If you could choose to deduct for a tax year either:

- State and local income taxes, or
- State and local general sales taxes, then

the maximum refund that you may have to include in income is limited to the excess of the tax you chose to deduct for that year over the tax you didn't choose to deduct for that year. For examples, see Pub. 525.

Mortgage interest refund. If you received a refund or credit in 2022 of mortgage interest paid in an earlier year, the amount should be shown in box 4 of your Form 1098, Mortgage Interest Statement. Don't subtract the refund amount from the interest you paid in 2022. You may have to include it in your income under the rules explained in the following discussions.

Interest on recovery. Interest on any of the amounts you recover must be reported as interest income in the year received. For example, report any interest you received on state or local income tax refunds on Form 1040, 1040-SR, or 1040-NR, line 2b.

Recovery and expense in same year. If the refund or other recovery and the expense occur in the same year, the recovery reduces the deduction or credit and isn't reported as income.

Recovery for 2 or more years. If you receive a refund or other recovery that's for amounts you paid in 2 or more separate years, you must allocate, on a pro rata basis, the recovered amount between the years in which you paid it. This allocation is necessary to determine the amount of recovery from any earlier years and to determine the amount, if any, of your allowable deduction for this item for the current year. For information on how to figure the allocation, see Recoveries in Pub. 525.

Itemized Deduction Recoveries

If you recover any amount that you deducted in an earlier year on Schedule A (Form 1040), you must generally include the full amount of the recovery in your income in the year you receive it.

Where to report. Enter your state or local income tax refund on Schedule 1 (Form 1040),

line 1, and the total of all other recoveries as other income on Schedule 1 (Form 1040), line 8z.

Standard deduction limit. You are generally allowed to claim the standard deduction if you don't itemize your deductions. Only your itemized deductions that are more than your standard deduction are subject to the recovery rule (unless you're required to itemize your deductions). If your total deductions on the earlier year return weren't more than your income for that year, include in your income this year the lesser of:

- Your recoveries, or
- The amount by which your itemized deductions exceeded the standard deduction.

Example. For 2021, you filed a joint return. Your taxable income was $60,000 and you weren't entitled to any tax credits. Your standard deduction was $25,100, and you had itemized deductions of $26,600. In 2022, you received the following recoveries for amounts deducted on your 2021 return.

Medical expenses	$200
State and local income tax refund	400
Refund of mortgage interest	325
Total recoveries	$925

None of the recoveries were more than the deductions taken for 2021. The difference between the state and local income tax you deducted and your local general sales tax was more than $400.

Your total recoveries are less than the amount by which your itemized deductions exceeded the standard deduction ($26,600 − $25,100 = $1,500), so you must include your total recoveries in your income for 2022. Report the state and local income tax refund of $400 on Schedule 1 (Form 1040), line 1, and the balance of your recoveries, $525, on Schedule 1 (Form 1040), line 8z.

Standard deduction for earlier years. To determine if amounts recovered in the current year must be included in your income, you must know the standard deduction for your filing status for the year the deduction was claimed. Look in the instructions for your tax return from prior years to locate the standard deduction for the filing status for that prior year.

Example. You filed a joint return on Form 1040 for 2021 with taxable income of $45,000. Your itemized deductions were $25,350. The standard deduction that you could have claimed was $25,100. In 2022, you recovered $2,100 of your 2021 itemized deductions. None of the recoveries were more than the actual deductions for 2021. Include $250 of the recoveries in your 2022 income. This is the smaller of your recoveries ($2,100) or the amount by which your itemized deductions were more than the standard deduction ($25,350 − $25,100 = $250).

Recovery limited to deduction. You don't include in your income any amount of your recovery that's more than the amount you deducted in the earlier year. The amount you include in your income is limited to the smaller of:

- The amount deducted on Schedule A (Form 1040), or

- The amount recovered.

Example. During 2021, you paid $1,700 for medical expenses. Of this amount, you deducted $200 on your 2021 Schedule A (Form 1040). In 2022, you received a $500 reimbursement from your medical insurance for your 2021 expenses. The only amount of the $500 reimbursement that must be included in your income for 2022 is $200—the amount actually deducted.

Other recoveries. See *Recoveries* in Pub. 525 if:

- You have recoveries of items other than itemized deductions, or

- You received a recovery for an item for which you claimed a tax credit (other than investment credit or foreign tax credit) in a prior year.

Rents From Personal Property

If you rent out personal property, such as equipment or vehicles, how you report your income and expenses is in most cases determined by:

- Whether or not the rental activity is a business, and

- Whether or not the rental activity is conducted for profit.

In most cases, if your primary purpose is income or profit and you're involved in the rental activity with continuity and regularity, your rental activity is a business. See Pub. 535, Business Expenses, for details on deducting expenses for both business and not-for-profit activities.

Reporting business income and expenses. If you're in the business of renting personal property, report your income and expenses on Schedule C (Form 1040). The form instructions have information on how to complete them.

Reporting nonbusiness income. If you aren't in the business of renting personal property, report your rental income on Schedule 1 (Form 1040), line 8l.

Reporting nonbusiness expenses. If you rent personal property for profit, include your rental expenses in the total amount you enter on Schedule 1 (Form 1040), line 24b, and see the instructions there.

If you don't rent personal property for profit, your deductions are limited and you can't report a loss to offset other income. See *Activity not for profit* under *Other Income*, later.

Repayments

If you had to repay an amount that you included in your income in an earlier year, you may be able to deduct the amount repaid from your income for the year in which you repaid it. Or, if the amount you repaid is more than $3,000, you may be able to take a credit against your tax for the year in which you repaid it. Generally, you

can claim a deduction or credit only if the repayment qualifies as an expense or loss incurred in your trade or business or in a for-profit transaction.

Type of deduction. The type of deduction you're allowed in the year of repayment depends on the type of income you included in the earlier year. You generally deduct the repayment on the same form or schedule on which you previously reported it as income. For example, if you reported it as self-employment income, deduct it as a business expense on Schedule C (Form 1040) or Schedule F (Form 1040). If you reported it as a capital gain, deduct it as a capital loss as explained in the Instructions for Schedule D (Form 1040). If you reported it as wages, unemployment compensation, or other nonbusiness income, you may be able to deduct it as an other itemized deduction if the amount repaid is over $3,000.

 Beginning in 2018, you can no longer claim any miscellaneous itemized deductions, so if the amount repaid was $3,000 or less, you are not able to deduct it from your income in the year you repaid it.

Repaid social security benefits. If you repaid social security benefits or equivalent railroad retirement benefits, see *Repayment of benefits* in chapter 7.

Repayment of $3,000 or less. If the amount you repaid was $3,000 or less, deduct it from your income in the year you repaid it.

Repayment over $3,000. If the amount you repaid was more than $3,000, you can deduct the repayment as an other itemized deduction on Schedule A (Form 1040), line 16, if you included the income under a claim of right. This means that at the time you included the income, it appeared that you had an unrestricted right to it. However, you can choose to take a credit for the year of repayment. Figure your tax under both methods and compare the results. Use the method (deduction or credit) that results in less tax.

 When determining whether the amount you repaid was more or less than $3,000, consider the total amount being repaid on the return. Each instance of repayment isn't considered separately.

Method 1. Figure your tax for 2022 claiming a deduction for the repaid amount. If you deduct it as an other itemized deduction, enter it on Schedule A (Form 1040), line 16.

Method 2. Figure your tax for 2022 claiming a credit for the repaid amount. Follow these steps.

1. Figure your tax for 2022 without deducting the repaid amount.

2. Refigure your tax from the earlier year without including in income the amount you repaid in 2022.

3. Subtract the tax in (2) from the tax shown on your return for the earlier year. This is the credit.

4. Subtract the answer in (3) from the tax for 2022 figured without the deduction (step 1).

If method 1 results in less tax, deduct the amount repaid. If method 2 results in less tax, claim the credit figured in (3) above on Schedule 3 (Form 1040), line 13d, by adding the amount of the credit to any other credits on this line, and see the instructions there.

An example of this computation can be found in Pub. 525.

Repaid wages subject to social security and Medicare taxes. If you had to repay an amount that you included in your wages or compensation in an earlier year on which social security, Medicare, or tier 1 RRTA taxes were paid, ask your employer to refund the excess amount to you. If the employer refuses to refund the taxes, ask for a statement indicating the amount of the overcollection to support your claim. File a claim for refund using Form 843, Claim for Refund and Request for Abatement.

Repaid wages subject to Additional Medicare Tax. Employers can't make an adjustment or file a claim for refund for Additional Medicare Tax withholding when there is a repayment of wages received by an employee in a prior year because the employee determines liability for Additional Medicare Tax on the employee's income tax return for the prior year. If you had to repay an amount that you included in your wages or compensation in an earlier year, and on which Additional Medicare Tax was paid, you may be able to recover the Additional Medicare Tax paid on the amount. To recover Additional Medicare Tax on the repaid wages or compensation, you must file Form 1040-X for the prior year in which the wages or compensation was originally received. See the Instructions for Form 1040-X.

Royalties

Royalties from copyrights, patents, and oil, gas, and mineral properties are taxable as ordinary income.

In most cases, you report royalties in Part I of Schedule E (Form 1040). However, if you hold an operating oil, gas, or mineral interest or are in business as a self-employed writer, inventor, artist, etc., report your income and expenses on Schedule C (Form 1040).

Copyrights and patents. Royalties from copyrights on literary, musical, or artistic works, and similar property, or from patents on inventions, are amounts paid to you for the right to use your work over a specified period of time. Royalties are generally based on the number of units sold, such as the number of books, tickets to a performance, or machines sold.

Oil, gas, and minerals. Royalty income from oil, gas, and mineral properties is the amount you receive when natural resources are extracted from your property. The royalties are based on units, such as barrels, tons, etc., and are paid to you by a person or company that leases the property from you.

Depletion. If you're the owner of an economic interest in mineral deposits or oil and gas wells, you can recover your investment through the depletion allowance. For information on this subject, see chapter 9 of Pub. 535.

Coal and iron ore. Under certain circumstances, you can treat amounts you receive from the disposal of coal and iron ore as payments from the sale of a capital asset, rather than as royalty income. For information about gain or loss from the sale of coal and iron ore, see chapter 2 of Pub. 544.

Sale of property interest. If you sell your complete interest in oil, gas, or mineral rights, the amount you receive is considered payment for the sale of property used in a trade or business under section 1231, not royalty income. Under certain circumstances, the sale is subject to capital gain or loss treatment as explained in the Instructions for Schedule D (Form 1040). For more information on selling section 1231 property, see chapter 3 of Pub. 544.

If you retain a royalty, an overriding royalty, or a net profit interest in a mineral property for the life of the property, you have made a lease or a sublease, and any cash you receive for the assignment of other interests in the property is ordinary income subject to a depletion allowance.

Part of future production sold. If you own mineral property but sell part of the future production, in most cases you treat the money you receive from the buyer at the time of the sale as a loan from the buyer. Don't include it in your income or take depletion based on it.

When production begins, you include all the proceeds in your income, deduct all the production expenses, and deduct depletion from that amount to arrive at your taxable income from the property.

Unemployment Benefits

The tax treatment of unemployment benefits you receive depends on the type of program paying the benefits.

Unemployment compensation. You must include in income all unemployment compensation you receive. You should receive a Form 1099-G showing in box 1 the total unemployment compensation paid to you. In most cases, you enter unemployment compensation on Schedule 1 (Form 1040), line 7.

 If you received unemployment compensation but did not receive Form 1099-G through the mail, you may need to access your information through your state's website to get your electronic Form 1099-G.

Types of unemployment compensation. Unemployment compensation generally includes any amount received under an unemployment compensation law of the United States or of a state. It includes the following benefits.

- Benefits paid by a state or the District of Columbia from the Federal Unemployment Trust Fund.

- State unemployment insurance benefits.

- Railroad unemployment compensation benefits.

- Disability payments from a government program paid as a substitute for unemployment compensation. (Amounts received as workers' compensation for injuries or illness aren't unemployment compensation. See chapter 5 for more information.)

- Trade readjustment allowances under the Trade Act of 1974.

- Unemployment assistance under the Disaster Relief and Emergency Assistance Act.

- Unemployment assistance under the Airline Deregulation Act of 1978 Program.

Governmental program. If you contribute to a governmental unemployment compensation program and your contributions aren't deductible, amounts you receive under the program aren't included as unemployment compensation until you recover your contributions. If you deducted all of your contributions to the program, the entire amount you receive under the program is included in your income.

Repayment of unemployment compensation. If you repaid in 2022 unemployment compensation you received in 2022, subtract the amount you repaid from the total amount you received and enter the difference on Schedule 1 (Form 1040), line 7. On the dotted line next to your entry, enter "Repaid" and the amount you repaid. If you repaid unemployment compensation in 2022 that you included in income in an earlier year, you can deduct the amount repaid on Schedule A (Form 1040), line 16, if you itemize deductions and the amount is more than $3,000. See Repayments, earlier.

Tax withholding. You can choose to have federal income tax withheld from your unemployment compensation. To make this choice, complete Form W-4V, Voluntary Withholding Request, and give it to the paying office. Tax will be withheld at 10% of your payment.

 If you don't choose to have tax withheld from your unemployment compensation, you may be liable for estimated tax. If you don't pay enough tax, either through withholding or estimated tax, or a combination of both, you may have to pay a penalty. For more information on estimated tax, see chapter 4.

Supplemental unemployment benefits. Benefits received from an employer-financed fund (to which the employees didn't contribute) aren't unemployment compensation. They are taxable as wages. For more information, see Supplemental Unemployment Benefits in section 5 of Pub. 15-A, Employer's Supplemental Tax Guide. Report these payments on line 1a of Form 1040 or 1040-SR.

Repayment of benefits. You may have to repay some of your supplemental unemployment benefits to qualify for trade readjustment allowances under the Trade Act of 1974. If you repay supplemental unemployment benefits in the same year you receive them, reduce the total benefits by the amount you repay. If you repay the benefits in a later year, you must include the full amount of the benefits received in your income for the year you received them.

Deduct the repayment in the later year as an adjustment to gross income on Form 1040 or 1040-SR. Include the repayment on Schedule 1 (Form 1040), line 24e, and see the instructions there. If the amount you repay in a later year is more than $3,000, you may be able to take a credit against your tax for the later year instead of deducting the amount repaid. For more information on this, see Repayments, earlier.

Private unemployment fund. Unemployment benefit payments from a private (nonunion) fund to which you voluntarily contribute are taxable only if the amounts you receive are more than your total payments into the fund. Report the taxable amount on Schedule 1 (Form 1040), line 8z.

Payments by a union. Benefits paid to you as an unemployed member of a union from regular union dues are included in your income on Schedule 1 (Form 1040), line 8z. However, if you contribute to a special union fund and your payments to the fund aren't deductible, the unemployment benefits you receive from the fund are includible in your income only to the extent they're more than your contributions.

Guaranteed annual wage. Payments you receive from your employer during periods of unemployment, under a union agreement that guarantees you full pay during the year, are taxable as wages. Include them on line 1a of Form 1040 or 1040-SR.

State employees. Payments similar to a state's unemployment compensation may be made by the state to its employees who aren't covered by the state's unemployment compensation law. Although the payments are fully taxable, don't report them as unemployment compensation. Report these payments on Schedule 1 (Form 1040), line 8z.

Welfare and Other Public Assistance Benefits

Don't include in your income governmental benefit payments from a public welfare fund based upon need, such as payments to blind individuals under a state public assistance law. Payments from a state fund for the victims of crime shouldn't be included in the victims' incomes if they're in the nature of welfare payments. Don't deduct medical expenses that are reimbursed by such a fund. You must include in your income any welfare payments that are compensation for services or that are obtained fraudulently.

Reemployment Trade Adjustment Assistance (RTAA) payments. RTAA payments received from a state must be included in your income. The state must send you Form 1099-G to advise you of the amount you should include in income. The amount should be reported on Schedule 1 (Form 1040), line 8z.

Persons with disabilities. If you have a disability, you must include in income compensation you receive for services you perform unless the compensation is otherwise excluded. However, you don't include in income the value of goods, services, and cash that you receive, not in return for your services, but for your training and rehabilitation because you have a disability. Excludable amounts include payments for transportation and attendant care, such as interpreter services for the deaf, reader services for the blind, and services to help individuals with an intellectual disability do their work.

Disaster relief grants. Don't include post-disaster grants received under the Robert T. Stafford Disaster Relief and Emergency Assistance Act in your income if the grant payments are made to help you meet necessary expenses or serious needs for medical, dental, housing, personal property, transportation, childcare, or funeral expenses. Don't deduct casualty losses or medical expenses that are specifically reimbursed by these disaster relief grants. If you have deducted a casualty loss for the loss of your personal residence and you later receive a disaster relief grant for the loss of the same residence, you may have to include part or all of the grant in your taxable income. See *Recoveries*, earlier. Unemployment assistance payments under the Act are taxable unemployment compensation. See *Unemployment compensation* under *Unemployment Benefits*, earlier.

Disaster relief payments. You can exclude from income any amount you receive that's a qualified disaster relief payment. A qualified disaster relief payment is an amount paid to you:

1. To reimburse or pay reasonable and necessary personal, family, living, or funeral expenses that result from a qualified disaster;

2. To reimburse or pay reasonable and necessary expenses incurred for the repair or rehabilitation of your home or repair or replacement of its contents to the extent it's due to a qualified disaster;

3. By a person engaged in the furnishing or sale of transportation as a common carrier because of the death or personal physical injuries incurred as a result of a qualified disaster; or

4. By a federal, state, or local government, agency, or instrumentality in connection with a qualified disaster in order to promote the general welfare.

You can exclude this amount only to the extent any expense it pays for isn't paid for by insurance or otherwise. The exclusion doesn't apply if you were a participant or conspirator in a terrorist action or a representative of one.

A qualified disaster is:

- A disaster which results from a terrorist or military action;

- A federally declared disaster; or

- A disaster which results from an accident involving a common carrier, or from any other event, which is determined to be catastrophic by the Secretary of the Treasury or his or her delegate.

For amounts paid under item (4) above, a disaster is qualified if it's determined by an applicable federal, state, or local authority to warrant assistance from the federal, state, or local government, agency, or instrumentality.

Disaster mitigation payments. You can exclude from income any amount you receive that's a qualified disaster mitigation payment. Qualified disaster mitigation payments are most commonly paid to you in the period immediately following damage to property as a result of a natural disaster. However, disaster mitigation payments are used to mitigate (reduce the severity of) potential damage from future natural disasters. They're paid to you through state and local governments based on the provisions of the Robert T. Stafford Disaster Relief and Emergency Assistance Act or the National Flood Insurance Act.

You can't increase the basis or adjusted basis of your property for improvements made with nontaxable disaster mitigation payments.

Home Affordable Modification Program (HAMP). If you benefit from Pay-for-Performance Success Payments under HAMP, the payments aren't taxable.

Mortgage assistance payments under section 235 of the National Housing Act. Payments made under section 235 of the National Housing Act for mortgage assistance aren't included in the homeowner's income. Interest paid for the homeowner under the mortgage assistance program can't be deducted.

Medicare. Medicare benefits received under title XVIII of the Social Security Act aren't includible in the gross income of the individuals for whom they're paid. This includes basic (Part A (Hospital Insurance Benefits for the Aged)) and supplementary (Part B (Supplementary Medical Insurance Benefits for the Aged)).

Social security benefits (including lump-sum payments attributable to prior years), Supplemental Security Income (SSI) benefits, and lump-sum death benefits. The Social Security Administration (SSA) provides benefits such as old-age benefits, benefits to disabled workers, and benefits to spouses and dependents. These benefits may be subject to federal income tax depending on your filing status and other income. See chapter 7 in this publication and Pub. 915, Social Security and Equivalent Railroad Retirement Benefits, for more information. An individual originally denied benefits, but later approved, may receive a lump-sum payment for the period when benefits were denied (which may be prior years). See Pub. 915 for information on how to make a lump-sum election, which may reduce your tax liability. There are also other types of benefits paid by the SSA. However, SSI benefits and lump-sum death benefits (one-time payment to spouse and children of deceased) aren't subject to federal income tax. For more information on these benefits, go to SSA.gov.

Nutrition Program for the Elderly. Food benefits you receive under the Nutrition Program for the Elderly aren't taxable. If you prepare and serve free meals for the program, include in your income as wages the cash pay you receive, even if you're also eligible for food benefits.

Payments to reduce cost of winter energy. Payments made by a state to qualified people to reduce their cost of winter energy use aren't taxable.

Other Income

The following brief discussions are arranged in alphabetical order. Other income items briefly discussed below are referenced to publications which provide more topical information.

Activity not for profit. You must include on your return income from an activity from which you don't expect to make a profit. An example of this type of activity is a hobby or a farm you operate mostly for recreation and pleasure. Enter this income on Schedule 1 (Form 1040), line 8j. Deductions for expenses related to the activity are limited. They can't total more than the income you report and can be taken only if you itemize deductions on Schedule A (Form 1040). See *Not-for-Profit Activities* in chapter 1 of Pub. 535 for information on whether an activity is considered carried on for a profit.

Alaska Permanent Fund dividend. If you received a payment from Alaska's mineral income fund (Alaska Permanent Fund dividend), report it as income on Schedule 1 (Form 1040), line 8g. The state of Alaska sends each recipient a document that shows the amount of the payment with the check. The amount is also reported to the IRS.

Alimony. Include in your income on Schedule 1 (Form 1040), line 2a, any taxable alimony payments you receive. Amounts you receive for child support aren't income to you. Alimony and child support payments are discussed in Pub. 504.

 Don't include alimony payments you receive under a divorce or separation agreement (1) executed after 2018, or (2) executed before 2019 but later modified if the modification expressly states the repeal of the deduction for alimony payments applies to the modification.

Bribes. If you receive a bribe, include it in your income.

Campaign contributions. These contributions aren't income to a candidate unless they're diverted to her or his personal use. To be nontaxable, the contributions must be spent for campaign purposes or kept in a fund for use in future campaigns. However, interest earned on bank deposits, dividends received on contributed securities, and net gains realized on sales of contributed securities are taxable and must be reported on Form 1120-POL, U.S. Income Tax Return for Certain Political Organizations. Excess campaign funds transferred to an office account must be included in the officeholder's income on Schedule 1 (Form 1040), line 8z, in the year transferred.

Carpools. Don't include in your income amounts you receive from the passengers for driving a car in a carpool to and from work. These amounts are considered reimbursement for your expenses. However, this rule doesn't apply if you have developed carpool arrangements into a profit-making business of transporting workers for hire.

Cash rebates. A cash rebate you receive from a dealer or manufacturer of an item you buy isn't income, but you must reduce your basis by the amount of the rebate.

Example. You buy a new car for $24,000 cash and receive a $2,000 rebate check from the manufacturer. The $2,000 isn't income to you. Your basis in the car is $22,000. This is the basis on which you figure gain or loss if you sell the car and depreciation if you use it for business.

Casualty insurance and other reimbursements. You generally shouldn't report these reimbursements on your return unless you're figuring gain or loss from the casualty or theft. See Pub. 547 for more information.

Child support payments. You shouldn't report these payments on your return. See Pub. 504 for more information.

Court awards and damages. To determine if settlement amounts you receive by compromise or judgment must be included in your income, you must consider the item that the settlement replaces. The character of the income as ordinary income or capital gain depends on the nature of the underlying claim. Include the following as ordinary income.

1. Interest on any award.

2. Compensation for lost wages or lost profits in most cases.

3. Punitive damages, in most cases. It doesn't matter if they relate to a physical injury or physical sickness.

4. Amounts received in settlement of pension rights (if you didn't contribute to the plan).

5. Damages for:

   a. Patent or copyright infringement,

   b. Breach of contract, or

   c. Interference with business operations.

6. Back pay and damages for emotional distress received to satisfy a claim under title VII of the Civil Rights Act of 1964.

7. Attorney fees and costs (including contingent fees) where the underlying recovery is included in gross income.

8. Attorney fees and costs relating to whistleblower awards where the underlying recovery is included in gross income.

Don't include in your income compensatory damages for personal physical injury or physical sickness (whether received in a lump sum or installments).

Emotional distress. Emotional distress itself isn't a physical injury or physical sickness, but damages you receive for emotional distress due to a physical injury or sickness are treated as received for the physical injury or sickness. Don't include them in your income.

If the emotional distress is due to a personal injury that isn't due to a physical injury or sickness (for example, employment discrimination or injury to reputation), you must include the damages in your income, except for any damages that aren't more than amounts paid for medical care due to that emotional distress. Emotional distress includes physical symptoms

that result from emotional distress, such as headaches, insomnia, and stomach disorders.

Credit card insurance. In most cases, if you receive benefits under a credit card disability or unemployment insurance plan, the benefits are taxable to you. These plans make the minimum monthly payment on your credit card account if you can't make the payment due to injury, illness, disability, or unemployment. Report on Schedule 1 (Form 1040), line 8z, the amount of benefits you received during the year that's more than the amount of the premiums you paid during the year.

Down payment assistance. If you purchase a home and receive assistance from a nonprofit corporation to make the down payment, that assistance isn't included in your income. If the corporation qualifies as a tax-exempt charitable organization, the assistance is treated as a gift and is included in your basis of the house. If the corporation doesn't qualify, the assistance is treated as a rebate or reduction of the purchase price and isn't included in your basis.

Employment agency fees. If you get a job through an employment agency, and the fee is paid by your employer, the fee isn't includible in your income if you aren't liable for it. However, if you pay it and your employer reimburses you for it, it's includible in your income.

Energy conservation subsidies. You can exclude from gross income any subsidy provided, either directly or indirectly, by public utilities for the purchase or installation of an energy conservation measure for a dwelling unit.

Energy conservation measure. This includes installations or modifications that are primarily designed to reduce consumption of electricity or natural gas, or improve the management of energy demand.

Dwelling unit. This includes a house, apartment, condominium, mobile home, boat, or similar property. If a building or structure contains both dwelling and other units, any subsidy must be properly allocated.

Estate and trust income. An estate or trust, unlike a partnership, may have to pay federal income tax. If you're a beneficiary of an estate or trust, you may be taxed on your share of its income distributed or required to be distributed to you. However, there is never a double tax. Estates and trusts file their returns on Form 1041, U.S. Income Tax Return for Estates and Trusts, and your share of the income is reported to you on Schedule K-1 (Form 1041).

Current income required to be distributed. If you're the beneficiary of an estate or trust that must distribute all of its current income, you must report your share of the distributable net income, whether or not you actually received it.

Current income not required to be distributed. If you're the beneficiary of an estate or trust and the fiduciary has the choice of whether to distribute all or part of the current income, you must report:

- All income that's required to be distributed to you, whether or not it's actually distributed, plus

- All other amounts actually paid or credited to you,

up to the amount of your share of distributable net income.

How to report. Treat each item of income the same way that the estate or trust would treat it. For example, if a trust's dividend income is distributed to you, you report the distribution as dividend income on your return. The same rule applies to distributions of tax-exempt interest and capital gains.

The fiduciary of the estate or trust must tell you the type of items making up your share of the estate or trust income and any credits you're allowed on your individual income tax return.

Losses. Losses of estates and trusts generally aren't deductible by the beneficiaries.

Grantor trust. Income earned by a grantor trust is taxable to the grantor, not the beneficiary, if the grantor keeps certain control over the trust. (The grantor is the one who transferred property to the trust.) This rule applies if the property (or income from the property) put into the trust will or may revert (be returned) to the grantor or the grantor's spouse.

Generally, a trust is a grantor trust if the grantor has a reversionary interest valued (at the date of transfer) at more than 5% of the value of the transferred property.

Expenses paid by another. If your personal expenses are paid for by another person, such as a corporation, the payment may be taxable to you depending upon your relationship with that person and the nature of the payment. But if the payment makes up for a loss caused by that person, and only restores you to the position you were in before the loss, the payment isn't includible in your income.

Fees for services. Include all fees for your services in your income. Examples of these fees are amounts you receive for services you perform as:

- A corporate director;

- An executor, administrator, or personal representative of an estate;

- A manager of a trade or business you operated before declaring chapter 11 bankruptcy;

- A notary public; or

- An election precinct official.

Nonemployee compensation. If you aren't an employee and the fees for your services from a single payer in the course of the payer's trade or business total $600 or more for the year, the payer should send you a Form 1099-NEC. You may need to report your fees as self-employment income. See *Self-Employed Persons* in chapter 1 for a discussion of when you're considered self-employed.

Corporate director. Corporate director fees are self-employment income. Report these payments on Schedule C (Form 1040).

Personal representatives. All personal representatives must include in their gross income fees paid to them from an estate. If you aren't in the trade or business of being an executor (for instance, you're the executor of a friend's or relative's estate), report these fees on Schedule 1 (Form 1040), line 8z. If you're in the trade or business of being an executor, report these fees as self-employment income on Schedule C (Form 1040). The fee isn't includible in income if it's waived.

Manager of trade or business for bankruptcy estate. Include in your income all payments received from your bankruptcy estate for managing or operating a trade or business that you operated before you filed for bankruptcy. Report this income on Schedule 1 (Form 1040), line 8z.

Notary public. Report payments for these services on Schedule C (Form 1040). These payments aren't subject to self-employment tax. See the separate Instructions for Schedule SE (Form 1040) for details.

Election precinct official. You should receive a Form W-2 showing payments for services performed as an election official or election worker. Report these payments on line 1a of Form 1040 or 1040-SR.

Foster care providers. Generally, payment you receive from a state, a political subdivision, or a qualified foster care placement agency for caring for a qualified foster individual in your home is excluded from your income. However, you must include in your income payment to the extent it's received for the care of more than five qualified foster individuals age 19 years or older.

A qualified foster individual is a person who:

1. Is living in a foster family home; and

2. Was placed there by:

   a. An agency of a state or one of its political subdivisions, or

   b. A qualified foster care placement agency.

Difficulty-of-care payments. These are payments that are designated by the payer as compensation for providing the additional care that's required for physically, mentally, or emotionally handicapped qualified foster individuals. A state must determine that this compensation is needed, and the care for which the payments are made must be provided in the foster care provider's home in which the qualified foster individual was placed.

Certain Medicaid waiver payments are treated as difficulty-of-care payments when received by an individual care provider for caring for an eligible individual living in the provider's home. See Notice 2014-7, available at *IRS.gov/irb/2014-04_IRB#NOT-2014-7*, and related questions and answers, available at *IRS.gov/Individuals/Certain-Medicaid-Waiver-Payments-May-Be-Excludable-From-Income*, for more information.

You must include in your income difficulty-of-care payments to the extent they're received for more than:

- 10 qualified foster individuals under age 19, or

- Five qualified foster individuals age 19 or older.

Maintaining space in home. If you're paid to maintain space in your home for emergency foster care, you must include the payment in your income.

Reporting taxable payments. If you receive payments that you must include in your income and you're in business as a foster care provider, report the payments on Schedule C (Form 1040). See Pub. 587, Business Use of Your Home, to help you determine the amount you can deduct for the use of your home.

Found property. If you find and keep property that doesn't belong to you that has been lost or abandoned (treasure trove), it's taxable to you at its fair market value in the first year it's your undisputed possession.

Free tour. If you received a free tour from a travel agency for organizing a group of tourists, you must include its value in your income. Report the fair market value of the tour on Schedule 1 (Form 1040), line 8z, if you aren't in the trade or business of organizing tours. You can't deduct your expenses in serving as the voluntary leader of the group at the group's request. If you organize tours as a trade or business, report the tour's value on Schedule C (Form 1040).

Gambling winnings. You must include your gambling winnings in income on Schedule 1 (Form 1040), line 8b. Winnings from fantasy sports leagues are gambling winnings. If you itemize your deductions on Schedule A (Form 1040), you can deduct gambling losses you had during the year, but only up to the amount of your winnings. If you're in the trade or business of gambling, use Schedule C (Form 1040).

Lotteries and raffles. Winnings from lotteries and raffles are gambling winnings. In addition to cash winnings, you must include in your income the fair market value of bonds, cars, houses, and other noncash prizes.

 If you win a state lottery prize payable in installments, see Pub. 525 for more information.

Form W-2G. You may have received a Form W-2G, Certain Gambling Winnings, showing the amount of your gambling winnings and any tax taken out of them. Include the amount from box 1 on Schedule 1 (Form 1040), line 8b. Include the amount shown in box 4 on Form 1040 or 1040-SR, line 25c, as federal income tax withheld.

Reporting winnings and recordkeeping. For more information on reporting gambling winnings and recordkeeping, see *Gambling Losses up to the Amount of Gambling Winnings* in chapter 12.

Gifts and inheritances. In most cases, property you receive as a gift, bequest, or inheritance isn't included in your income. However, if property you receive this way later produces income such as interest, dividends, or rents, that income is taxable to you. If property is given to a trust and the income from it is paid, credited, or distributed to you, that income is also taxable to you. If the gift, bequest, or inheritance is the income from the property, that income is taxable to you.

Inherited pension or individual retirement arrangement (IRA). If you inherited a pension or an IRA, you may have to include part of the inherited amount in your income. See *Survivors and Beneficiaries* in Pub. 575 if you inherited a pension. See *What if You Inherit an IRA?* in Pubs. 590-A and 590-B if you inherited an IRA.

Hobby losses. Losses from a hobby aren't deductible from other income. A hobby is an activity from which you don't expect to make a profit. See *Activity not for profit*, earlier.

 If you collect stamps, coins, or other items as a hobby for recreation and pleasure, and you sell any of the items, your gain is taxable as a capital gain. (See Pub. 550.) However, if you sell items from your collection at a loss, you can't deduct the loss.

Illegal activities. Income from illegal activities, such as money from dealing illegal drugs, must be included in your income on Schedule 1 (Form 1040), line 8z, or on Schedule C (Form 1040) if from your self-employment activity.

Indian fishing rights. If you're a member of a qualified Indian tribe that has fishing rights secured by treaty, Executive order, or an Act of Congress as of March 17, 1988, don't include in your income amounts you receive from activities related to those fishing rights. The income isn't subject to income tax, self-employment tax, or employment taxes.

Interest on frozen deposits. In general, you exclude from your income the amount of interest earned on a frozen deposit. See *Interest income on frozen deposits* in chapter 6.

Interest on qualified savings bonds. You may be able to exclude from income the interest from qualified U.S. savings bonds you redeem if you pay qualified higher education expenses in the same year. For more information on this exclusion, see *Education Savings Bond Program* under *U.S. Savings Bonds* in chapter 6.

Job interview expenses. If a prospective employer asks you to appear for an interview and either pays you an allowance or reimburses you for your transportation and other travel expenses, the amount you receive is generally not taxable. You include in income only the amount you receive that's more than your actual expenses.

Jury duty. Jury duty pay you receive must be included in your income on Schedule 1 (Form 1040), line 8h. If you gave any of your jury duty pay to your employer because your employer continued to pay you while you served jury duty, include the amount you gave your employer as an income adjustment on Schedule 1 (Form 1040), line 24a, and see the instructions there.

Kickbacks. You must include kickbacks, side commissions, push money, or similar payments you receive in your income on Schedule 1 (Form 1040), line 8z, or on Schedule C (Form 1040) if from your self-employment activity.

Example. You sell cars and help arrange car insurance for buyers. Insurance brokers pay back part of their commissions to you for referring customers to them. You must include the kickbacks in your income.

Medical savings accounts (Archer MSAs and Medicare Advantage MSAs). In most cases, you don't include in income amounts you withdraw from your Archer MSA or Medicare Advantage MSA if you use the money to pay for qualified medical expenses. Generally, qualified medical expenses are those you can deduct on Schedule A (Form 1040). For more information about qualified medical expenses, see Pub. 502. For more information about Archer MSAs or Medicare Advantage MSAs, see Pub. 969, Health Savings Accounts and Other Tax-Favored Health Plans.

Prizes and awards. If you win a prize in a lucky number drawing, television or radio quiz program, beauty contest, or other event, you must include it in your income. For example, if you win a $50 prize in a photography contest, you must report this income on Schedule 1 (Form 1040), line 8i. If you refuse to accept a prize, don't include its value in your income.

Prizes and awards in goods or services must be included in your income at their fair market value.

Employee awards or bonuses. Cash awards or bonuses given to you by your employer for good work or suggestions must generally be included in your income as wages. However, certain noncash employee achievement awards can be excluded from income. See *Bonuses and awards* in chapter 5.

Pulitzer, Nobel, and similar prizes. If you were awarded a prize in recognition of accomplishments in religious, charitable, scientific, artistic, educational, literary, or civic fields, you must generally include the value of the prize in your income. However, you don't include this prize in your income if you meet all of the following requirements.

- You were selected without any action on your part to enter the contest or proceeding.

- You aren't required to perform substantial future services as a condition to receiving the prize or award.

- The prize or award is transferred by the payer directly to a governmental unit or tax-exempt charitable organization as designated by you.

See Pub. 525 for more information about the conditions that apply to the transfer.

Qualified Opportunity Fund (QOF). Effective December 22, 2017, Code section 1400Z-2 provides a temporary deferral on inclusion in gross income for capital gains invested in QOFs, and permanent exclusion of capital gains from the sale or exchange of an investment in the QOF if the investment is held for at least 10 years. See the Instructions for Form 8949 on how to report your election to defer eligible gains invested in a QOF. See the instructions for Form 8997, Initial and Annual Statement of Qualified Opportunity Fund (QOF) Investments, for reporting information. For additional information, see Opportunity Zones Frequently Asked Questions at *IRS.gov/ Newsroom/Opportunity-Zones-Frequently-Asked-Questions*.

Qualified tuition programs (QTPs). A QTP (also known as a 529 program) is a program set up to allow you to either prepay or contribute to an account established for paying a student's qualified higher education expenses at an eligible educational institution. A program can be established and maintained by a state, an agency or instrumentality of a state, or an eligible educational institution.

The part of a distribution representing the amount paid or contributed to a QTP isn't included in income. This is a return of the investment in the program.

In most cases, the beneficiary doesn't include in income any earnings distributed from a QTP if the total distribution is less than or equal to adjusted qualified higher education expenses. See Pub. 970 for more information.

Railroad retirement annuities. The following types of payments are treated as pension or annuity income and are taxable under the rules explained in Pub. 575, Pension and Annuity Income.

- Tier 1 railroad retirement benefits that are more than the social security equivalent benefit.

- Tier 2 benefits.

- Vested dual benefits.

Rewards. If you receive a reward for providing information, include it in your income.

Sale of home. You may be able to exclude from income all or part of any gain from the sale or exchange of your main home. See Pub. 523.

Sale of personal items. If you sold an item you owned for personal use, such as a car, refrigerator, furniture, stereo, jewelry, or silverware, your gain is taxable as a capital gain. Report it as explained in the Instructions for Schedule D (Form 1040). You can't deduct a loss.

However, if you sold an item you held for investment, such as gold or silver bullion, coins, or gems, any gain is taxable as a capital gain and any loss is deductible as a capital loss.

Example. You sold a painting on an online auction website for $100. You bought the painting for $20 at a garage sale years ago. Report your gain as a capital gain as explained in the Instructions for Schedule D (Form 1040).

Scholarships and fellowships. A candidate for a degree can exclude amounts received as a qualified scholarship or fellowship. A qualified scholarship or fellowship is any amount you receive that's for:

- Tuition and fees to enroll at or attend an educational institution; or

- Fees, books, supplies, and equipment required for courses at the educational institution.

Amounts used for room and board don't qualify for the exclusion. See Pub. 970 for more information on qualified scholarships and fellowship grants.

Payment for services. In most cases, you must include in income the part of any scholarship or fellowship that represents payment for past, present, or future teaching, research, or other services. This applies even if all candidates for a degree must perform the services to receive the degree.

For information about the rules that apply to a tax-free qualified tuition reduction provided to employees and their families by an educational institution, see Pub. 970.

Department of Veterans Affairs (VA) payments. Allowances paid by the VA aren't included in your income. These allowances aren't considered scholarship or fellowship grants.

Prizes. Scholarship prizes won in a contest aren't scholarships or fellowships if you don't have to use the prizes for educational purposes. You must include these amounts in your income on Schedule 1 (Form 1040), line 8i, whether or not you use the amounts for educational purposes.

Sharing/gig economy. Generally, if you work in the gig economy or did gig work, you must include all income received from all jobs whether you received a Form 1099-K, Payment Card and Third-Party Network Transactions, or not. See the Instructions for Schedule C (Form 1040) and the Instructions for Schedule SE (Form 1040).

Stolen property. If you steal property, you must report its fair market value in your income in the year you steal it unless you return it to its rightful owner in the same year.

Transporting school children. Don't include in your income a school board mileage allowance for taking children to and from school if you aren't in the business of taking children to school. You can't deduct expenses for providing this transportation.

Union benefits and dues. Amounts deducted from your pay for union dues, assessments, contributions, or other payments to a union can't be excluded from your income.

Strike and lockout benefits. Benefits paid to you by a union as strike or lockout benefits, including both cash and the fair market value of other property, are usually included in your income as compensation. You can exclude these benefits from your income only when the facts clearly show that the union intended them as gifts to you.

Utility rebates. If you're a customer of an electric utility company and you participate in the utility's energy conservation program, you may receive on your monthly electric bill either:

- A reduction in the purchase price of electricity furnished to you (rate reduction), or

- A nonrefundable credit against the purchase price of the electricity.

The amount of the rate reduction or nonrefundable credit isn't included in your income.

9.

Individual Retirement Arrangements (IRAs)

What's New

Modified AGI limit for traditional IRA contributions. For 2022, if you are covered by a retirement plan at work, your deduction for contributions to a traditional IRA is reduced (phased out) if your modified AGI is:

- More than $109,000 but less than $129,000 for a married couple filing a joint return or a qualifying surviving spouse,

- More than $68,000 but less than $78,000 for a single individual or head of household, or

- Less than $10,000 for a married individual filing a separate return.

If you either live with your spouse or file a joint return, and your spouse is covered by a retirement plan at work but you aren't, your deduction is phased out if your modified AGI is more than $204,000 but less than $214,000. If your modified AGI is $214,000 or more, you can't take a deduction for contributions to a traditional IRA. See *How Much Can You Deduct*, later.

Modified AGI limit for Roth IRA contributions. For 2022, your Roth IRA contribution limit is reduced (phased out) in the following situations.

- Your filing status is married filing jointly or qualifying surviving spouse and your modified AGI is at least $204,000. You can't make a Roth IRA contribution if your modified AGI is $214,000 or more.

- Your filing status is single, head of household, or married filing separately and you didn't live with your spouse at any time in 2022 and your modified AGI is at least $129,000. You can't make a Roth IRA contribution if your modified AGI is $144,000 or more.

- Your filing status is married filing separately, you lived with your spouse at any time during the year, and your modified AGI is more than zero. You can't make a Roth IRA contribution if your modified AGI is $10,000 or more.

See *Can You Contribute to a Roth IRA*, later.

2023 modified AGI limits. You can find information about the 2023 contribution and AGI limits in Pub. 590-A.

Reminders

Qualified disaster tax relief. Special rules provide for tax-favored withdrawals and repayments from certain retirement plans for taxpayers who suffered an economic loss as a result of a qualified disaster. A qualified disaster includes a major disaster that was declared by Presidential Declaration during the period between January 1, 2020, and February 25, 2021. However, in order to qualify under the latest legislation, the major disaster must have an incident period that began on or after December 28, 2019, and on or before December 27, 2020. A qualified disaster loss does not include any disaster that has been declared only by reason of COVID-19. See Form 8915-F, Qualified Disaster Plan Distributions and Repayments, for more information.

See Pub. 590-B, Distributions from Individual Retirement Arrangements (IRAs), for more information.

Maximum age for making traditional IRA contributions repealed. For tax years beginning after 2019, there is no age limit on making contributions to your traditional IRA. For more information, see Pub. 590-A.

Required minimum distributions (RMDs). For distributions required to be made after tax year 2019, the age for the required beginning date for mandatory distributions is changed to age 72 for taxpayers reaching age 70½ after 2019.

Contributions to both traditional and Roth IRAs. For information on your combined contribution limit if you contribute to both traditional and Roth IRAs, see *Roth IRAs and traditional IRAs*, later.

Statement of required minimum distribution. If a minimum distribution from your IRA is required, the trustee, custodian, or issuer that held the IRA at the end of the preceding year must either report the amount of the required minimum distribution to you, or offer to figure it for you. The report or offer must include the date by which the amount must be distributed. The report is due January 31 of the year in which the minimum distribution is required. It can be provided with the year-end fair market value statement that you normally get each year. No report is required for IRAs of owners who have died.

IRA interest. Although interest earned from your IRA is generally not taxed in the year earned, it isn't tax-exempt interest. Tax on your traditional IRA is generally deferred until you take a distribution. Don't report this interest on your tax return as tax-exempt interest.

Net Investment Income Tax (NIIT). For purposes of the NIIT, net investment income doesn't include distributions from a qualified retirement plan including IRAs (for example, 401(a), 403(a), 403(b), 408, 408A, or 457(b) plans). However, these distributions are taken into account when determining the modified AGI threshold. Distributions from a nonqualified

retirement plan are included in net investment income. See Form 8960, Net Investment Income Tax—Individuals, Estates, and Trusts, and its instructions for more information.

Form 8606. To designate contributions as nondeductible, you must file Form 8606.

 The term "50 or older" is used several times in this chapter. It refers to an IRA owner who is age 50 or older by the end of the tax year.

Introduction

An IRA is a personal savings plan that gives you tax advantages for setting aside money for your retirement.

This chapter discusses the following topics.

- The rules for a traditional IRA (any IRA that isn't a Roth or SIMPLE IRA).

- The Roth IRA, which features nondeductible contributions and tax-free distributions.

Simplified Employee Pensions (SEPs) and Savings Incentive Match Plans for Employees (SIMPLE) plans aren't discussed in this chapter. For more information on these plans and employees' SEP IRAs and SIMPLE IRAs that are part of these plans, see Pub. 560, Retirement Plans for Small Business.

For information about contributions, deductions, withdrawals, transfers, rollovers, and other transactions, see Pub. 590-A and Pub. 590-B.

Useful Items

You may want to see:

Publication

❏ **560** Retirement Plans for Small Business

❏ **575** Pension and Annuity Income

❏ **590-A** Contributions to Individual Retirement Arrangements (IRAs)

❏ **590-B** Distributions from Individual Retirement Arrangements (IRAs)

Form (and Instructions)

❏ **5329** Additional Taxes on Qualified Plans (Including IRAs) and Other Tax-Favored Accounts

❏ **8606** Nondeductible IRAs

❏ **8915-F** Qualified Disaster Retirement Plan Distributions and Repayments

For these and other useful items, go to *IRS.gov/ Forms*.

Traditional IRAs

In this chapter, the original IRA (sometimes called an ordinary or regular IRA) is referred to as a "traditional IRA." A traditional IRA is any IRA that isn't a Roth IRA or a SIMPLE IRA. Two advantages of a traditional IRA are:

- You may be able to deduct some or all of your contributions to it, depending on your circumstances; and

- Generally, amounts in your IRA, including earnings and gains, aren't taxed until they are distributed.

Who Can Open a Traditional IRA?

You can open and make contributions to a traditional IRA if you (or, if you file a joint return, your spouse) received taxable compensation during the year.

 For tax years beginning after 2019, there is no age limit on making contributions to your traditional IRA. For more information, see Pub. 590-A.

What is compensation? Generally, compensation is what you earn from working. Compensation includes wages, salaries, tips, professional fees, bonuses, and other amounts you receive for providing personal services. The IRS treats as compensation any amount properly shown in box 1 (Wages, tips, other compensation) of Form W-2, Wage and Tax Statement, provided that this amount is reduced by any amount properly shown in box 11 (Nonqualified plans).

Scholarship or fellowship payments are generally compensation for this purpose only if reported in box 1 of your Form W-2. However, for tax years beginning after 2019, certain non-tuition fellowship and stipend payments not reported to you on Form W-2 are treated as taxable compensation for IRA purposes. These amounts include taxable non-tuition fellowship and stipend payments made to aid you in the pursuit of graduate or postdoctoral study and included in your gross income under the rules discussed in chapter 1 of Pub. 970, Tax Benefits for Education.

Compensation also includes commissions and taxable alimony and separate maintenance payments.

Self-employment income. If you are self-employed (a sole proprietor or a partner), compensation is the net earnings from your trade or business (provided your personal services are a material income-producing factor) reduced by the total of:

- The deduction for contributions made on your behalf to retirement plans, and
- The deductible part of your self-employment tax.

Compensation includes earnings from self-employment even if they aren't subject to self-employment tax because of your religious beliefs.

Nontaxable combat pay. For IRA purposes, if you were a member of the U.S. Armed Forces, your compensation includes any nontaxable combat pay you receive.

What isn't compensation? Compensation doesn't include any of the following items.

- Earnings and profits from property, such as rental income, interest income, and dividend income.
- Pension or annuity income.

- Deferred compensation received (compensation payments postponed from a past year).
- Income from a partnership for which you don't provide services that are a material income-producing factor.
- Conservation Reserve Program (CRP) payments reported on Schedule SE (Form 1040), line 1b.
- Any amounts (other than combat pay) you exclude from income, such as foreign earned income and housing costs.

When and How Can a Traditional IRA Be Opened?

You can open a traditional IRA at any time. However, the time for making contributions for any year is limited. See *When Can Contributions Be Made*, later.

You can open different kinds of IRAs with a variety of organizations. You can open an IRA at a bank or other financial institution or with a mutual fund or life insurance company. You can also open an IRA through your stockbroker. Any IRA must meet Internal Revenue Code requirements.

Kinds of traditional IRAs. Your traditional IRA can be an individual retirement account or annuity. It can be part of either a SEP or an employer or employee association trust account.

How Much Can Be Contributed?

There are limits and other rules that affect the amount that can be contributed to a traditional IRA. These limits and other rules are explained below.

Community property laws. Except as discussed later under *Kay Bailey Hutchison Spousal IRA limit*, each spouse figures their limit separately, using their own compensation. This is the rule even in states with community property laws.

Brokers' commissions. Brokers' commissions paid in connection with your traditional IRA are subject to the contribution limit.

Trustees' fees. Trustees' administrative fees aren't subject to the contribution limit.

Qualified reservist repayments. If you are (or were) a member of a reserve component and you were ordered or called to active duty after September 11, 2001, you may be able to contribute (repay) to an IRA amounts equal to any qualified reservist distributions you received. You can make these repayment contributions even if they would cause your total contributions to the IRA to be more than the general limit on contributions. To be eligible to make these repayment contributions, you must have received a qualified reservist distribution from an IRA or from a section 401(k) or 403(b) plan or similar arrangement.

For more information, see *Qualified reservist repayments* under *How Much Can Be Contributed?* in chapter 1 of Pub. 590-A.

 Contributions on your behalf to a traditional IRA reduce your limit for contributions to a Roth IRA. (See Roth IRAs, later.)

General limit. For 2022, the most that can be contributed to your traditional IRA is generally the smaller of the following amounts.

- $6,000 ($7,000 if you are 50 or older).
- Your taxable compensation (defined earlier) for the year.

This is the most that can be contributed regardless of whether the contributions are to one or more traditional IRAs or whether all or part of the contributions are nondeductible. (See *Nondeductible Contributions*, later.) Qualified reservist repayments don't affect this limit.

Example 1. You are 34 years old and single and earned $24,000 in 2022. Your IRA contributions for 2022 are limited to $6,000.

Example 2. You are an unmarried college student working part time and earned $3,500 in 2022. Your IRA contributions for 2022 are limited to $3,500, the amount of your compensation.

Kay Bailey Hutchison Spousal IRA limit. For 2022, if you file a joint return and your taxable compensation is less than that of your spouse, the most that can be contributed for the year to your IRA is the smaller of the following amounts.

1. $6,000 ($7,000 if you are 50 or older).
2. The total compensation includible in the gross income of both you and your spouse for the year, reduced by the following two amounts.
   a. Your spouse's IRA contribution for the year to a traditional IRA.
   b. Any contribution for the year to a Roth IRA on behalf of your spouse.

This means that the total combined contributions that can be made for the year to your IRA and your spouse's IRA can be as much as $12,000 ($13,000 if only one of you is 50 or older, or $14,000 if both of you are 50 or older).

When Can Contributions Be Made?

As soon as you open your traditional IRA, contributions can be made to it through your chosen sponsor (trustee or other administrator). Contributions must be in the form of money (cash, check, or money order). Property can't be contributed.

Contributions must be made by due date. Contributions can be made to your traditional IRA for a year at any time during the year or by the due date for filing your return for that year, not including extensions.

Designating year for which contribution is made. If an amount is contributed to your traditional IRA between January 1 and April 15, you should tell the sponsor which year (the current year or the previous year) the contribution is for. If you don't tell the sponsor which year it is for, the sponsor can assume, and report to the IRS, that the contribution is for the current year (the year the sponsor received it).

Filing before a contribution is made. You can file your return claiming a traditional IRA contribution before the contribution is actually made. Generally, the contribution must be made by the due date of your return, not including extensions.

Contributions not required. You don't have to contribute to your traditional IRA for every tax year, even if you can.

How Much Can You Deduct?

Generally, you can deduct the lesser of:

- The contributions to your traditional IRA for the year, or
- The general limit (or the Kay Bailey Hutchison Spousal IRA limit, if it applies).

However, if you or your spouse was covered by an employer retirement plan, you may not be able to deduct this amount. See *Limit if Covered by Employer Plan*, later.

 You may be able to claim a credit for contributions to your traditional IRA. For more information, see chapter 3 of Pub. 590-A.

Trustees' fees. Trustees' administrative fees that are billed separately and paid in connection with your traditional IRA aren't deductible as IRA contributions. You are also not able to deduct these fees as an itemized deduction.

Brokers' commissions. Brokers' commissions are part of your IRA contribution and, as such, are deductible subject to the limits.

Full deduction. If neither you nor your spouse was covered for any part of the year by an employer retirement plan, you can take a deduction for total contributions to one or more traditional IRAs of up to the lesser of:

- $6,000 ($7,000 if you are 50 or older in 2022), or
- 100% of your compensation.

This limit is reduced by any contributions made to a 501(c)(18) plan on your behalf.

Kay Bailey Hutchison Spousal IRA. In the case of a married couple with unequal compensation who file a joint return, the deduction for contributions to the traditional IRA of the spouse with less compensation is limited to the lesser of the following amounts.

1. $6,000 ($7,000 if the spouse with the lower compensation is 50 or older in 2022).
2. The total compensation includible in the gross income of both spouses for the year reduced by the following three amounts.
   a. The IRA deduction for the year of the spouse with the greater compensation.
   b. Any designated nondeductible contribution for the year made on behalf of

the spouse with the greater compensation.
   c. Any contributions for the year to a Roth IRA on behalf of the spouse with the greater compensation.

This limit is reduced by any contributions to a 501(c)(18) plan on behalf of the spouse with the lesser compensation.

Note. If you were divorced or legally separated (and didn't remarry) before the end of the year, you can't deduct any contributions to your spouse's IRA. After a divorce or legal separation, you can deduct only contributions to your own IRA. Your deductions are subject to the rules for single individuals.

Covered by an employer retirement plan. If you or your spouse was covered by an employer retirement plan at any time during the year for which contributions were made, your deduction may be further limited. This is discussed later under *Limit if Covered by Employer Plan*. Limits on the amount you can deduct don't affect the amount that can be contributed. See *Nondeductible Contributions*, later.

Are You Covered by an Employer Plan?

The Form W-2 you receive from your employer has a box used to indicate whether you were covered for the year. The "Retirement plan" box should be checked if you were covered.

Reservists and volunteer firefighters should also see *Situations in Which You Aren't Covered*, later.

If you aren't certain whether you were covered by your employer's retirement plan, you should ask your employer.

Federal judges. For purposes of the IRA deduction, federal judges are covered by an employer retirement plan.

For Which Year(s) Are You Covered?

Special rules apply to determine the tax years for which you are covered by an employer plan. These rules differ depending on whether the plan is a defined contribution plan or a defined benefit plan.

Tax year. Your tax year is the annual accounting period you use to keep records and report income and expenses on your income tax return. For almost all people, the tax year is the calendar year.

Defined contribution plan. Generally, you are covered by a defined contribution plan for a tax year if amounts are contributed or allocated to your account for the plan year that ends with or within that tax year.

A defined contribution plan is a plan that provides for a separate account for each person covered by the plan. Types of defined contribution plans include profit-sharing plans, stock bonus plans, and money purchase pension plans. For additional information, see Pub. 590-A.

Defined benefit plan. If you are eligible to participate in your employer's defined benefit plan

for the plan year that ends within your tax year, you are covered by the plan. This rule applies even if you:

- Declined to participate in the plan,
- Didn't make a required contribution, or
- Didn't perform the minimum service required to accrue a benefit for the year.

A defined benefit plan is any plan that isn't a defined contribution plan. In a defined benefit plan, the level of benefits to be provided to each participant is spelled out in the plan. The plan administrator figures the amount needed to provide those benefits and those amounts are contributed to the plan. Defined benefit plans include pension plans and annuity plans.

No vested interest. If you accrue a benefit for a plan year, you are covered by that plan even if you have no vested interest in (legal right to) the accrual.

Situations in Which You Aren't Covered

Unless you are covered under another employer plan, you aren't covered by an employer plan if you are in one of the situations described below.

Social security or railroad retirement. Coverage under social security or railroad retirement isn't coverage under an employer retirement plan.

Benefits from a previous employer's plan. If you receive retirement benefits from a previous employer's plan, you aren't covered by that plan.

Reservists. If the only reason you participate in a plan is because you are a member of a reserve unit of the U.S. Armed Forces, you may not be covered by the plan. You aren't covered by the plan if both of the following conditions are met.

1. The plan you participate in is established for its employees by:
   a. The United States,
   b. A state or political subdivision of a state, or
   c. An instrumentality of either (a) or (b) above.
2. You didn't serve more than 90 days on active duty during the year (not counting duty for training).

Volunteer firefighters. If the only reason you participate in a plan is because you are a volunteer firefighter, you may not be covered by the plan. You aren't covered by the plan if both of the following conditions are met.

1. The plan you participate in is established for its employees by:
   a. The United States,
   b. A state or political subdivision of a state, or
   c. An instrumentality of either (a) or (b) above.

Table 9-1. Effect of Modified AGI[1] on Deduction if You Are Covered by Retirement Plan at Work

If you are covered by a retirement plan at work, use this table to determine if your modified AGI affects the amount of your deduction.

IF your filing status is...	AND your modified AGI is...	THEN you can take...
Single or **Head of household**	$68,000 or less	a full deduction.
	more than $68,000 but less than $78,000	a partial deduction.
	$78,000 or more	no deduction.
Married filing jointly or **Qualifying surviving spouse**	$109,000 or less	a full deduction.
	more than $109,000 but less than $129,000	a partial deduction.
	$129,000 or more	no deduction.
Married filing separately[2]	less than $10,000	a partial deduction.
	$10,000 or more	no deduction.

[1] Modified AGI (adjusted gross income). See *Modified adjusted gross income (AGI)*, later.

[2] If you didn't live with your spouse at any time during the year, your filing status is considered Single for this purpose (therefore, your IRA deduction is determined under the "Single" column).

Table 9-2. Effect of Modified AGI[1] on Deduction if You Aren't Covered by Retirement Plan at Work

If you aren't covered by a retirement plan at work, use this table to determine if your modified AGI affects the amount of your deduction.

IF your filing status is...	AND your modified AGI is...	THEN you can take...
Single, **Head of household,** or **Qualifying surviving spouse**	any amount	a full deduction.
Married filing jointly or **separately** with a spouse who *isn't* covered by a plan at work	any amount	a full deduction.
Married filing jointly with a spouse who *is* covered by a plan at work	$204,000 or less	a full deduction.
	more than $204,000 but less than $214,000	a partial deduction.
	$214,000 or more	no deduction.
Married filing separately with a spouse who *is* covered by a plan at work[2]	less than $10,000	a partial deduction.
	$10,000 or more	no deduction.

[1] Modified AGI (adjusted gross income). See *Modified adjusted gross income (AGI)*, later.

[2] You are entitled to the full deduction if you didn't live with your spouse at any time during the year.

2. Your accrued retirement benefits at the beginning of the year won't provide more than $1,800 per year at retirement.

Limit if Covered by Employer Plan

If either you or your spouse was covered by an employer retirement plan, you may be entitled to only a partial (reduced) deduction or no deduction at all, depending on your income and your filing status.

Your deduction begins to decrease (phase out) when your income rises above a certain amount and is eliminated altogether when it reaches a higher amount. These amounts vary depending on your filing status.

To determine if your deduction is subject to phaseout, you must determine your modified AGI and your filing status. See *Filing status* and *Modified adjusted gross income (AGI)*, later. Then use Table 9-1 or Table 9-2 to determine if the phaseout applies.

Social security recipients. Instead of using Table 9-1 or Table 9-2, use the worksheets in Appendix B of Pub. 590-A if, for the year, all of the following apply.

- You received social security benefits.
- You received taxable compensation.
- Contributions were made to your traditional IRA.
- You or your spouse was covered by an employer retirement plan.

Use those worksheets to figure your IRA deduction, your nondeductible contribution, and the taxable portion, if any, of your social security benefits.

Deduction phaseout. If you are covered by an employer retirement plan and you didn't receive any social security retirement benefits, your IRA deduction may be reduced or eliminated depending on your filing status and modified AGI as shown in Table 9-1.

If your spouse is covered. If you aren't covered by an employer retirement plan, but your spouse is, and you didn't receive any social security benefits, your IRA deduction may be reduced or eliminated entirely depending on your filing status and modified AGI as shown in Table 9-2.

Filing status. Your filing status depends primarily on your marital status. For this purpose, you need to know if your filing status is single, head of household, married filing jointly, qualifying surviving spouse, or married filing separately. If you need more information on filing status, see chapter 2.

Lived apart from spouse. If you didn't live with your spouse at any time during the year and you file a separate return, your filing status, for this purpose, is single.

Modified adjusted gross income (AGI). You may be able to use Worksheet 9-1 to figure your modified AGI. However, if you made contributions to your IRA for 2022 and received a distribution from your IRA in 2022, see Pub. 590-A.

 Don't assume that your modified AGI is the same as your compensation. Your modified AGI may include income in addition to your compensation (discussed earlier), such as interest, dividends, and income from IRA distributions.

When filing Form 1040 or 1040-SR, refigure the AGI amount on line 11 without taking into account any of the following amounts.

- IRA deduction.
- Student loan interest deduction.
- Foreign earned income exclusion.
- Foreign housing exclusion or deduction.
- Exclusion of qualified savings bond interest shown on Form 8815, Exclusion of Interest From Series EE and I U.S. Savings Bonds Issued After 1989.
- Exclusion of employer-provided adoption benefits shown on Form 8839, Qualified Adoption Expenses.

This is your modified AGI.

Worksheet 9-1. Figuring Your Modified AGI

Use this worksheet to figure your modified AGI for traditional IRA purposes.

1. Enter your adjusted gross income (AGI) from Form 1040 or 1040-SR, line 11, figured without taking into account the amount from Schedule 1 (Form 1040), line 20	1. _____
2. Enter any student loan interest deduction from Schedule 1 (Form 1040), line 21	2. _____
3. Enter any foreign earned income and/or housing exclusion from Form 2555, line 45	3. _____
4. Enter any foreign housing deduction from Form 2555, line 50	4. _____
5. Enter any excludable savings bond interest from Form 8815, line 14	5. _____
6. Enter any excluded employer-provided adoption benefits from Form 8839, line 28	6. _____
7. Add lines 1 through 6. This is your **modified AGI** for traditional IRA purposes	7. _____

Both contributions for 2022 and distributions in 2022. If all three of the following apply, any IRA distributions you received in 2022 may be partly tax free and partly taxable.

- You received distributions in 2022 from one or more traditional IRAs.

- You made contributions to a traditional IRA for 2022.

- Some of those contributions may be nondeductible contributions.

If this is your situation, you must figure the taxable part of the traditional IRA distribution before you can figure your modified AGI. To do this, you can use Worksheet 1-1 in Pub. 590-B.

If at least one of the above doesn't apply, figure your modified AGI using Worksheet 9-1.

How to figure your reduced IRA deduction. You can figure your reduced IRA deduction for Form 1040 or 1040-SR by using the worksheets in chapter 1 of Pub. 590-A. Also, the Instructions for Form 1040 include similar worksheets that you may be able to use instead.

Reporting Deductible Contributions

When filing Form 1040 or 1040-SR, enter your IRA deduction on Schedule 1 (Form 1040), line 20.

Nondeductible Contributions

Although your deduction for IRA contributions may be reduced or eliminated, contributions can be made to your IRA up to the general limit or, if it applies, the Kay Bailey Hutchison Spousal IRA limit. The difference between your total permitted contributions and your IRA deduction, if any, is your nondeductible contribution.

Example. You are 30 years old and single. In 2022, you were covered by a retirement plan at work. Your salary was $67,000. Your modified AGI was $80,000. You made a $6,000 IRA contribution for 2022. Because you were covered by a retirement plan and your modified AGI was over $78,000, you can't deduct the $6,000 IRA contribution. You must designate this contribution as a nondeductible contribution by reporting it on Form 8606, as explained next.

Form 8606. To designate contributions as nondeductible, you must file Form 8606.

You don't have to designate a contribution as nondeductible until you file your tax return. When you file, you can even designate otherwise deductible contributions as nondeductible.

You must file Form 8606 to report nondeductible contributions even if you don't have to file a tax return for the year.

 A Form 8606 isn't used for the year that you make a rollover from a qualified retirement plan to a traditional IRA and the rollover includes nontaxable amounts. In those situations, a Form 8606 is completed for the year you take a distribution from that IRA. See Form 8606 under Distributions Fully or Partly Taxable, later.

Failure to report nondeductible contributions. If you don't report nondeductible contributions, all of the contributions to your traditional IRA will be treated as deductible contributions when withdrawn. All distributions from your IRA will be taxed unless you can show, with satisfactory evidence, that nondeductible contributions were made.

Penalty for overstatement. If you overstate the amount of nondeductible contributions on your Form 8606 for any tax year, you must pay a penalty of $100 for each overstatement, unless it was due to reasonable cause.

Penalty for failure to file Form 8606. You will have to pay a $50 penalty if you don't file a required Form 8606, unless you can prove that the failure was due to reasonable cause.

Tax on earnings on nondeductible contributions. As long as contributions are within the contribution limits, none of the earnings or gains on contributions (deductible or nondeductible) will be taxed until they are distributed. See *When Can You Withdraw or Use IRA Assets*, later.

Cost basis. You will have a cost basis in your traditional IRA if you made any nondeductible contributions. Your cost basis is the sum of the nondeductible contributions to your IRA minus any withdrawals or distributions of nondeductible contributions.

Inherited IRAs

If you inherit a traditional IRA, you are called a "beneficiary." A beneficiary can be any person or entity the owner chooses to receive the benefits of the IRA after he or she dies. Beneficiaries of a traditional IRA must include in their gross income any taxable distributions they receive.

Inherited from spouse. If you inherit a traditional IRA from your spouse, you generally have the following three choices. You can do one of the following.

1. Treat it as your own IRA by designating yourself as the account owner.

2. Treat it as your own by rolling it over into your IRA, or to the extent it is taxable, into a:

   a. Qualified employer plan,

   b. Qualified employee annuity plan (section 403(a) plan),

   c. Tax-sheltered annuity plan (section 403(b) plan), or

   d. Deferred compensation plan of a state or local government (section 457 plan).

3. Treat yourself as the beneficiary rather than treating the IRA as your own.

Treating it as your own. You will be considered to have chosen to treat the IRA as your own if:

- Contributions (including rollover contributions) are made to the inherited IRA, or

- You don't take the required minimum distribution for a year as a beneficiary of the IRA.

You will only be considered to have chosen to treat the IRA as your own if:

- You are the sole beneficiary of the IRA, and

- You have an unlimited right to withdraw amounts from it.

However, if you receive a distribution from your deceased spouse's IRA, you can roll that distribution over into your own IRA within the 60-day time limit, as long as the distribution isn't a required distribution, even if you aren't the sole beneficiary of your deceased spouse's IRA.

Inherited from someone other than spouse. If you inherit a traditional IRA from anyone other than your deceased spouse, you can't treat the inherited IRA as your own. This means that you can't make any contributions to the IRA. It also means you can't roll over any amounts into or out of the inherited IRA. However, you can make a trustee-to-trustee transfer as long as the IRA into which amounts are being moved is set up and maintained in the name of the deceased IRA owner for the benefit of you as beneficiary.

For more information, see the discussion of *Inherited IRAs* under *Rollover From One IRA Into Another*, later.

Can You Move Retirement Plan Assets?

You can transfer, tax free, assets (money or property) from other retirement plans (including traditional IRAs) to a traditional IRA. You can make the following kinds of transfers.

- Transfers from one trustee to another.
- Rollovers.
- Transfers incident to a divorce.

Transfers to Roth IRAs. Under certain conditions, you can move assets from a traditional IRA or from a designated Roth account to a Roth IRA. You can also move assets from a qualified retirement plan to a Roth IRA. See *Can You Move Amounts Into a Roth IRA?* under *Roth IRAs*, later.

Trustee-to-Trustee Transfer

A transfer of funds in your traditional IRA from one trustee directly to another, either at your request or at the trustee's request, isn't a rollover. This includes the situation where the current trustee issues a check to the new trustee, but gives it to you to deposit. Because there is no distribution to you, the transfer is tax free. Because it isn't a rollover, it isn't affected by the 1-year waiting period required between rollovers, discussed later under *Rollover From One IRA Into Another*. For information about direct transfers to IRAs from retirement plans other than IRAs, see *Can You Move Retirement Plan Assets?* in chapter 1 and *Can You Move Amounts Into a Roth IRA?* in chapter 2 of Pub. 590-A.

Rollovers

Generally, a rollover is a tax-free distribution to you of cash or other assets from one retirement plan that you contribute (roll over) to another retirement plan. The contribution to the second retirement plan is called a "rollover contribution."

Note. An amount rolled over tax free from one retirement plan to another is generally includible in income when it is distributed from the second plan.

Kinds of rollovers to a traditional IRA. You can roll over amounts from the following plans into a traditional IRA.

- A traditional IRA.
- An employer's qualified retirement plan for its employees.

- A deferred compensation plan of a state or local government (section 457 plan).
- A tax-sheltered annuity plan (section 403(b) plan).

Treatment of rollovers. You can't deduct a rollover contribution, but you must report the rollover distribution on your tax return as discussed later under *Reporting rollovers from IRAs* and *Reporting rollovers from employer plans*.

Rollover notice. A written explanation of rollover treatment must be given to you by the plan (other than an IRA) making the distribution. See *Written explanation to recipients* in Pub. 590-A.

Kinds of rollovers from a traditional IRA. You may be able to roll over, tax free, a distribution from your traditional IRA into a qualified plan. These plans include the federal Thrift Savings Plan (for federal employees), deferred compensation plans of state or local governments (section 457 plans), and tax-sheltered annuity plans (section 403(b) plans). The part of the distribution that you can roll over is the part that would otherwise be taxable (includible in your income). Qualified plans may, but aren't required to, accept such rollovers.

Time limit for making a rollover contribution. You must generally make the rollover contribution by the 60th day after the day you receive the distribution from your traditional IRA or your employer's plan.

The IRS may waive the 60-day requirement where the failure to do so would be against equity or good conscience, such as in the event of a casualty, disaster, or other event beyond your reasonable control. For more information, see *Can You Move Retirement Plan Assets?* in chapter 1 of Pub. 590-A.

Extension of rollover period. If an amount distributed to you from a traditional IRA or a qualified employer retirement plan is a frozen deposit at any time during the 60-day period allowed for a rollover, special rules extend the rollover period. For more information, see *Can You Move Retirement Plan Assets?* in chapter 1 of Pub. 590-A.

Rollover From One IRA Into Another

You can withdraw, tax free, all or part of the assets from one traditional IRA if you reinvest them within 60 days in the same or another traditional IRA. Because this is a rollover, you can't deduct the amount that you reinvest in an IRA.

Waiting period between rollovers. Generally, if you make a tax-free rollover of any part of a distribution from a traditional IRA, you can't, within a 1-year period, make a tax-free rollover of any later distribution from that same IRA. You also can't make a tax-free rollover of any amount distributed, within the same 1-year period, from the IRA into which you made the tax-free rollover.

The 1-year period begins on the date you receive the IRA distribution, not on the date you roll it over into an IRA. Rules apply to the number of rollovers you can have with your

traditional IRAs. See *Application of one-rollover limitation* next.

Application of one-rollover limitation. You can make only one rollover from an IRA to another (or the same) IRA in any 1-year period, regardless of the number of IRAs you own. The limit applies by aggregating all of an individual's IRAs, including SEP and SIMPLE IRAs, as well as traditional and Roth IRAs, effectively treating them as one IRA for purposes of the limit. However, trustee-to-trustee transfers between IRAs aren't limited and rollovers from traditional IRAs to Roth IRAs (conversions) aren't limited.

Example. You have three traditional IRAs: IRA-1, IRA-2, and IRA-3. You didn't take any distributions from your IRAs in 2022. On January 1, 2023, you took a distribution from IRA-1 and rolled it over into IRA-2 on the same day. For 2023, you can't roll over any other 2022 IRA distribution, including a rollover distribution involving IRA-3. This wouldn't apply to a trustee-to-trustee transfer or a Roth IRA conversion.

Partial rollovers. If you withdraw assets from a traditional IRA, you can roll over part of the withdrawal tax free and keep the rest of it. The amount you keep will generally be taxable (except for the part that is a return of nondeductible contributions). The amount you keep may be subject to the 10% additional tax on early distributions, discussed later under *What Acts Result in Penalties or Additional Taxes*.

Required distributions. Amounts that must be distributed during a particular year under the required minimum distribution rules (discussed later) aren't eligible for rollover treatment.

Inherited IRAs. If you inherit a traditional IRA from your spouse, you can generally roll it over, or you can choose to make the inherited IRA your own. See *Treating it as your own*, earlier.

Not inherited from spouse. If you inherit a traditional IRA from someone other than your spouse, you can't roll it over or allow it to receive a rollover contribution. You must withdraw the IRA assets within a certain period. For more information, see *When Must You Withdraw Assets? (Required Minimum Distributions)* in chapter 1 of Pub. 590-B.

Reporting rollovers from IRAs. Report any rollover from one traditional IRA to the same or another traditional IRA on Form 1040 or 1040-SR as follows.

Enter the total amount of the distribution on Form 1040 or 1040-SR, line 4a. If the total amount on Form 1040 or 1040-SR, line 4a, was rolled over, enter zero on Form 1040 or 1040-SR, line 4b. If the total distribution wasn't rolled over, enter the taxable portion of the part that wasn't rolled over on Form 1040 or 1040-SR, line 4b. Enter "Rollover" next to Form 1040 or 1040-SR, line 4b. For more information, see the Instructions for Form 1040.

If you rolled over the distribution into a qualified plan (other than an IRA) or you make the rollover in 2023, attach a statement explaining what you did.

Rollover From Employer's Plan Into an IRA

You can roll over into a traditional IRA all or part of an eligible rollover distribution you receive from your (or your deceased spouse's):

- Employer's qualified pension, profit-sharing, or stock bonus plan;
- Annuity plan;
- Tax-sheltered annuity plan (section 403(b) plan); or
- Governmental deferred compensation plan (section 457 plan).

A qualified plan is one that meets the requirements of the Internal Revenue Code.

Eligible rollover distribution. Generally, an eligible rollover distribution is any distribution of all or part of the balance to your credit in a qualified retirement plan except the following.

1. A required minimum distribution (explained later under *When Must You Withdraw IRA Assets? (Required Minimum Distributions)*).
2. A hardship distribution.
3. Any of a series of substantially equal periodic distributions paid at least once a year over:
   a. Your lifetime or life expectancy,
   b. The lifetimes or life expectancies of you and your beneficiary, or
   c. A period of 10 years or more.
4. Corrective distributions of excess contributions or excess deferrals, and any income allocable to the excess, or of excess annual additions and any allocable gains.
5. A loan treated as a distribution because it doesn't satisfy certain requirements either when made or later (such as upon default), unless the participant's accrued benefits are reduced (offset) to repay the loan. For more information, see *Plan loan offsets* under *Time Limit for Making a Rollover Contribution* in Pub. 590-A.
6. Dividends on employer securities.
7. The cost of life insurance coverage.

Your rollover into a traditional IRA may include both amounts that would be taxable and amounts that wouldn't be taxable if they were distributed to you but not rolled over. To the extent the distribution is rolled over into a traditional IRA, it isn't includible in your income.

 Any nontaxable amounts that you roll over into your traditional IRA become part of your basis (cost) in your IRAs. To recover your basis when you take distributions from your IRA, you must complete Form 8606 for the year of the distribution. See Form 8606 *under* Distributions Fully or Partly Taxable, *later.*

Rollover by nonspouse beneficiary. A direct transfer from a deceased employee's qualified pension, profit-sharing, or stock bonus plan; annuity plan; tax-sheltered annuity (section 403(b)) plan; or governmental deferred compensation (section 457) plan to an IRA set up to

receive the distribution on your behalf can be treated as an eligible rollover distribution if you are the designated beneficiary of the plan and not the employee's spouse. The IRA is treated as an inherited IRA. For more information about inherited IRAs, see *Inherited IRAs*, earlier.

Reporting rollovers from employer plans. Enter the total distribution (before income tax or other deductions were withheld) on Form 1040 or 1040-SR, line 4a. This amount should be shown in box 1 of Form 1099-R. From this amount, subtract any contributions (usually shown in box 5 of Form 1099-R) that were taxable to you when made. From that result, subtract the amount that was rolled over either directly or within 60 days of receiving the distribution. Enter the remaining amount, even if zero, on Form 1040 or 1040-SR, line 4b. Also, enter "Rollover" next to Form 1040 or 1040-SR, line 4b.

Transfers Incident to Divorce

If an interest in a traditional IRA is transferred from your spouse or former spouse to you by a divorce or separate maintenance decree or a written document related to such a decree, the interest in the IRA, starting from the date of the transfer, is treated as your IRA. The transfer is tax free. For detailed information, see *Distributions under divorce or similar proceedings (alternate payees)* under *Rollover From Employer's Plan Into an IRA* in Pub. 590-A.

Converting From Any Traditional IRA to a Roth IRA

Allowable conversions. You can withdraw all or part of the assets from a traditional IRA and reinvest them (within 60 days) in a Roth IRA. The amount that you withdraw and timely contribute (convert) to the Roth IRA is called a "conversion contribution." If properly (and timely) rolled over, the 10% additional tax on early distributions won't apply. However, a part or all of the conversion contribution from your traditional IRA is included in your gross income.

Required distributions. You can't convert amounts that must be distributed from your traditional IRA for a particular year (including the calendar year in which you reach age 72 under the required minimum distribution rules (discussed later)).

Income. You must include in your gross income distributions from a traditional IRA that you would have had to include in income if you hadn't converted them into a Roth IRA. These amounts are normally included in income on your return for the year that you converted them from a traditional IRA to a Roth IRA.

You don't include in gross income any part of a distribution from a traditional IRA that is a return of your basis, as discussed later.

You must file Form 8606 to report 2022 conversions from traditional, SEP, or SIMPLE IRAs to a Roth IRA in 2022 (unless you recharacterized the entire amount) and to figure the amount to include in income.

If you must include any amount in your gross income, you may have to increase your withholding or make estimated tax payments. See chapter 4.

Recharacterizations

You may be able to treat a contribution made to one type of IRA as having been made to a different type of IRA. This is called "recharacterizing the contribution." See *Can You Move Retirement Plan Assets?* in chapter 1 of Pub. 590-A for more detailed information.

How to recharacterize a contribution. To recharacterize a contribution, you must generally have the contribution transferred from the first IRA (the one to which it was made) to the second IRA in a trustee-to-trustee transfer. If the transfer is made by the due date (including extensions) for your tax return for the year during which the contribution was made, you can elect to treat the contribution as having been originally made to the second IRA instead of to the first IRA. If you recharacterize your contribution, you must do all three of the following.

- Include in the transfer any net income allocable to the contribution. If there was a loss, the net income you must transfer may be a negative amount.
- Report the recharacterization on your tax return for the year during which the contribution was made.
- Treat the contribution as having been made to the second IRA on the date that it was actually made to the first IRA.

No recharacterizations of conversions made in 2018 or later. A conversion of a traditional IRA to a Roth IRA, and a rollover from any other eligible retirement plan to a Roth IRA, made in tax years beginning after tax year 2017, can't be recharacterized as having been made to a traditional IRA. If you made a conversion in the 2017 tax year, you had until the due date (with extensions) for filing the return for that tax year to recharacterize it.

No deduction allowed. You can't deduct the contribution to the first IRA. Any net income you transfer with the recharacterized contribution is treated as earned in the second IRA.

How do you recharacterize a contribution? To recharacterize a contribution, you must notify both the trustee of the first IRA (the one to which the contribution was actually made) and the trustee of the second IRA (the one to which the contribution is being moved) that you have elected to treat the contribution as having been made to the second IRA rather than the first. You must make the notifications by the date of the transfer. Only one notification is required if both IRAs are maintained by the same trustee. The notification(s) must include all of the following information.

- The type and amount of the contribution to the first IRA that is to be recharacterized.
- The date on which the contribution was made to the first IRA and the year for which it was made.
- A direction to the trustee of the first IRA to transfer in a trustee-to-trustee transfer the amount of the contribution and any net income (or loss) allocable to the contribution to the trustee of the second IRA.
- The name of the trustee of the first IRA and the name of the trustee of the second IRA.

- Any additional information needed to make the transfer.

Reporting a recharacterization. If you elect to recharacterize a contribution to one IRA as a contribution to another IRA, you must report the recharacterization on your tax return as directed by Form 8606 and its instructions. You must treat the contribution as having been made to the second IRA.

When Can You Withdraw or Use IRA Assets?

There are rules limiting use of your IRA assets and distributions from it. Violation of the rules generally results in additional taxes in the year of violation. See *What Acts Result in Penalties or Additional Taxes*, later.

Contributions returned before the due date of return. If you made IRA contributions in 2022, you can withdraw them tax free by the due date of your return. If you have an extension of time to file your return, you can withdraw them tax free by the extended due date. You can do this if, for each contribution you withdraw, both of the following conditions apply.

- You didn't take a deduction for the contribution.
- You withdraw any interest or other income earned on the contribution. You can take into account any loss on the contribution while it was in the IRA when figuring the amount that must be withdrawn. If there was a loss, the net income earned on the contribution may be a negative amount.

Note. To figure the amount you must withdraw, see Worksheet 1-4 under *When Can You Withdraw or Use Assets?* in chapter 1 of Pub. 590-A.

Earnings includible in income. You must include in income any earnings on the contributions you withdraw. Include the earnings in income for the year in which you made the contributions, not in the year in which you withdraw them.

 Generally, except for any part of a withdrawal that is a return of nondeductible contributions (basis), any withdrawal of your contributions after the due date (or extended due date) of your return will be treated as a taxable distribution. Excess contributions can also be recovered tax free as discussed under What Acts Result in Penalties or Additional Taxes, *later.*

Early distributions tax. The 10% additional tax on distributions made before you reach age 59½ doesn't apply to these tax-free withdrawals of your contributions. However, the distribution of interest or other income must be reported on Form 5329 and, unless the distribution qualifies as an exception to the age 59½ rule, it will be subject to this tax. See *Early Distributions* under *What Acts Result in Penalties or Additional Taxes?* in Pub. 590-B.

When Must You Withdraw IRA Assets? (Required Minimum Distributions)

You can't keep funds in a traditional IRA indefinitely. Eventually, they must be distributed. If there are no distributions, or if the distributions aren't large enough, you may have to pay a 50% excise tax on the amount not distributed as required. See *Excess Accumulations (Insufficient Distributions)*, later. The requirements for distributing IRA funds differ depending on whether you are the IRA owner or the beneficiary of a decedent's IRA.

Required minimum distribution. The amount that must be distributed each year is referred to as the "required minimum distribution."

Distributions not eligible for rollover. Amounts that must be distributed (required minimum distributions) during a particular year aren't eligible for rollover treatment.

IRA owners. If you are the owner of a traditional IRA, you must generally start receiving distributions from your IRA by April 1 of the year following the year in which you reach age 72. April 1 of the year following the year in which you reach age 72 is referred to as the "required beginning date."

Distributions by the required beginning date. You must receive at least a minimum amount for each year starting with the year you reach age 72. If you don't (or didn't) receive that minimum amount in the year you become age 72, then you must receive distributions for the year you become age 72 by April 1 of the next year.

If an IRA owner dies after reaching age 72 but before April 1 of the next year, no minimum distribution is required because death occurred before the required beginning date.

 Even if you begin receiving distributions before you attain age 72, you must begin figuring and receiving required minimum distributions by your required beginning date.

Distributions after the required beginning date. The required minimum distribution for any year after the year you turn age 72 must be made by December 31 of that later year.

Beneficiaries. If you are the beneficiary of a decedent's traditional IRA, the requirements for distributions from that IRA generally depend on whether the IRA owner died before or after the required beginning date for distributions.

More information. For more information, including how to figure your minimum required distribution each year and how to figure your required distribution if you are a beneficiary of a decedent's IRA, see *When Must You Withdraw Assets? (Required Minimum Distributions)* in chapter 1 of Pub. 590-B.

Are Distributions Taxable?

In general, distributions from a traditional IRA are taxable in the year you receive them.

Exceptions. Exceptions to distributions from traditional IRAs being taxable in the year you receive them are:

- Rollovers;
- Qualified charitable distributions (QCDs), discussed later;
- Tax-free withdrawals of contributions, discussed earlier; and
- The return of nondeductible contributions, discussed later under *Distributions Fully or Partly Taxable*.

 Although a conversion of a traditional IRA is considered a rollover for Roth IRA purposes, it isn't an exception to the rule that distributions from a traditional IRA are taxable in the year you receive them. Conversion distributions are includible in your gross income subject to this rule and the special rules for conversions explained in Converting From Any Traditional IRA Into a Roth IRA *under* Can You Move Retirement Plan Assets? *in chapter 1 of Pub. 590-A.*

Qualified charitable distributions (QCDs). A QCD is generally a nontaxable distribution made directly by the trustee of your IRA to an organization eligible to receive tax deductible contributions. See *Qualified Charitable Distributions* in Pub. 590-B for more information.

 A QCD will count towards your minimum required distribution. See Qualified charitable distributions *under* Are Distributions Taxable? *in chapter 1 of Pub. 590-B for more information.*

Ordinary income. Distributions from traditional IRAs that you include in income are taxed as ordinary income.

No special treatment. In figuring your tax, you can't use the 10-year tax option or capital gain treatment that applies to lump-sum distributions from qualified retirement plans.

Distributions Fully or Partly Taxable

Distributions from your traditional IRA may be fully or partly taxable, depending on whether your IRA includes any nondeductible contributions.

Fully taxable. If only deductible contributions were made to your traditional IRA (or IRAs, if you have more than one), you have no basis in your IRA. Because you have no basis in your IRA, any distributions are fully taxable when received. See *Reporting taxable distributions on your return*, later.

Partly taxable. If you made nondeductible contributions or rolled over any after-tax amounts to any of your traditional IRAs, you have a cost basis (investment in the contract) equal to the amount of those contributions. These nondeductible contributions aren't taxed when they are distributed to you. They are a return of your investment in your IRA.

Only the part of the distribution that represents nondeductible contributions and rolled over after-tax amounts (your cost basis) is tax free. If nondeductible contributions have been made or after-tax amounts have been rolled over to your IRA, distributions consist partly of nondeductible contributions (basis) and partly of deductible contributions, earnings, and gains (if there are any). Until all of your basis has been distributed, each distribution is partly nontaxable and partly taxable.

Form 8606. You must complete Form 8606 and attach it to your return if you receive a distribution from a traditional IRA and have ever made nondeductible contributions or rolled-over after-tax amounts to any of your traditional IRAs. Using the form, you will figure the nontaxable distributions for 2022 and your total IRA basis for 2022 and earlier years.

Note. If you are required to file Form 8606 but you aren't required to file an income tax return, you must still file Form 8606. Send it to the IRS at the time and place you would otherwise file an income tax return.

Distributions reported on Form 1099-R. If you receive a distribution from your traditional IRA, you will receive Form 1099-R, Distributions From Pensions, Annuities, Retirement or Profit-Sharing Plans, IRAs, Insurance Contracts, etc., or a similar statement. IRA distributions are shown in boxes 1 and 2a of Form 1099-R. The number or letter codes in box 7 tell you what type of distribution you received from your IRA.

Withholding. Federal income tax is withheld from distributions from traditional IRAs unless you choose not to have tax withheld. See chapter 4.

IRA distributions delivered outside the United States. In general, if you are a U.S. citizen or resident alien and your home address is outside the United States or its possessions, you can't choose exemption from withholding on distributions from your traditional IRA.

Reporting taxable distributions on your return. Report fully taxable distributions, including early distributions, on Form 1040 or 1040-SR, line 4b (no entry is required on Form 1040 or 1040-SR, line 4a). If only part of the distribution is taxable, enter the total amount on Form 1040 or 1040-SR, line 4a, and the taxable part on Form 1040 or 1040-SR, line 4b.

What Acts Result in Penalties or Additional Taxes?

The tax advantages of using traditional IRAs for retirement savings can be offset by additional taxes and penalties if you don't follow the rules.

There are additions to the regular tax for using your IRA funds in prohibited transactions. There are also additional taxes for the following activities.

- Investing in collectibles.
- Having unrelated business income; see Pub. 590-B.
- Making excess contributions.
- Taking early distributions.
- Allowing excess amounts to accumulate (failing to take required distributions).

There are penalties for overstating the amount of nondeductible contributions and for failure to file a Form 8606, if required.

Prohibited Transactions

Generally, a prohibited transaction is any improper use of your traditional IRA by you, your beneficiary, or any disqualified person.

Disqualified persons include your fiduciary and members of your family (spouse, ancestor, lineal descendent, and any spouse of a lineal descendent).

The following are examples of prohibited transactions with a traditional IRA.

- Borrowing money from it; see Pub. 590-B.
- Selling property to it.
- Using it as security for a loan.
- Buying property for personal use (present or future) with IRA funds.

Effect on an IRA account. Generally, if you or your beneficiary engages in a prohibited transaction in connection with your traditional IRA account at any time during the year, the account stops being an IRA as of the first day of that year.

Effect on you or your beneficiary. If your account stops being an IRA because you or your beneficiary engaged in a prohibited transaction, the account is treated as distributing all its assets to you at their fair market values on the first day of the year. If the total of those values is more than your basis in the IRA, you will have a taxable gain that is includible in your income. For information on figuring your gain and reporting it in income, see *Are Distributions Taxable*, earlier. The distribution may be subject to additional taxes or penalties.

Taxes on prohibited transactions. If someone other than the owner or beneficiary of a traditional IRA engages in a prohibited transaction, that person may be liable for certain taxes. In general, there is a 15% tax on the amount of the prohibited transaction and a 100% additional tax if the transaction isn't corrected.

More information. For more information on prohibited transactions, see *What Acts Result in Penalties or Additional Taxes?* in chapter 1 of Pub. 590-A.

Investment in Collectibles

If your traditional IRA invests in collectibles, the amount invested is considered distributed to you in the year invested. You may have to pay the 10% additional tax on early distributions, discussed later.

Collectibles. These include:

- Artworks,
- Rugs,
- Antiques,
- Metals,
- Gems,
- Stamps,
- Coins,
- Alcoholic beverages, and
- Certain other tangible personal property.

Exception. Your IRA can invest in one-, one-half-, one-quarter-, or one-tenth-ounce U.S. gold coins, or one-ounce silver coins minted by the Treasury Department. It can also invest in certain platinum coins and certain gold, silver, palladium, and platinum bullion.

Excess Contributions

Generally, an excess contribution is the amount contributed to your traditional IRA(s) for the year that is more than the smaller of:

- The maximum deductible amount for the year (for 2022, this is $6,000 ($7,000 if you are 50 or older)); or
- Your taxable compensation for the year.

An excess contribution could be the result of your contribution, your spouse's contribution, your employer's contribution, or an improper rollover contribution. If your employer makes contributions on your behalf to a SEP IRA, see chapter 2 of Pub. 560.

Tax on excess contributions. In general, if the excess contributions for a year aren't withdrawn by the date your return for the year is due (including extensions), you are subject to a 6% tax. You must pay the 6% tax each year on excess amounts that remain in your traditional IRA at the end of your tax year. The tax can't be more than 6% of the combined value of all your IRAs as of the end of your tax year. The additional tax is figured on Form 5329.

Excess contributions withdrawn by due date of return. You won't have to pay the 6% tax if you withdraw an excess contribution made during a tax year and you also withdraw interest or other income earned on the excess contribution. You must complete your withdrawal by the date your tax return for that year is due, including extensions.

How to treat withdrawn contributions. Don't include in your gross income an excess contribution that you withdraw from your traditional IRA before your tax return is due if both the following conditions are met.

- No deduction was allowed for the excess contribution.
- You withdraw the interest or other income earned on the excess contribution.

You can take into account any loss on the contribution while it was in the IRA when figuring the amount that must be withdrawn. If there was a loss, the net income you must withdraw may be a negative amount.

How to treat withdrawn interest or other income. You must include in your gross income the interest or other income that was earned on the excess contribution. Report it on your return for the year in which the excess contribution was made. Your withdrawal of interest or other income may be subject to an additional 10% tax on early distributions, discussed later.

Excess contributions withdrawn after due date of return. In general, you must include all distributions (withdrawals) from your traditional

IRA in your gross income. However, if the following conditions are met, you can withdraw excess contributions from your IRA and not include the amount withdrawn in your gross income.

- Total contributions (other than rollover contributions) for 2022 to your IRA weren't more than $6,000 ($7,000 if you are 50 or older).

- You didn't take a deduction for the excess contribution being withdrawn.

The withdrawal can take place at any time, even after the due date, including extensions, for filing your tax return for the year.

Excess contribution deducted in an earlier year. If you deducted an excess contribution in an earlier year for which the total contributions weren't more than the maximum deductible amount for that year (see the following table), you can still remove the excess from your traditional IRA and not include it in your gross income. To do this, file Form 1040-X for that year and don't deduct the excess contribution on the amended return. Generally, you can file an amended return within 3 years after you filed your return or 2 years from the time the tax was paid, whichever is later.

Year(s)	Contribution limit	Contribution limit if 50 or older at the end of the year
2019 through 2021	$6,000	$7,000
2013 through 2018	$5,500	$6,500
2008 through 2012	$5,000	$6,000
2006 or 2007	$4,000	$5,000
2005	$4,000	$4,500
2002 through 2004	$3,000	$3,500
1997 through 2001	$2,000	—
before 1997	$2,250	—

Excess due to incorrect rollover information. If an excess contribution in your traditional IRA is the result of a rollover and the excess occurred because the information the plan was required to give you was incorrect, you can withdraw the excess contribution. The limits mentioned above are increased by the amount of the excess that is due to the incorrect information. You will have to amend your return for the year in which the excess occurred to correct the reporting of the rollover amounts in that year. Don't include in your gross income the part of the excess contribution caused by the incorrect information. For more information, see *Excess Contributions* under *What Acts Result in Penalties or Additional Taxes?* in Pub. 590-A.

Early Distributions

You must include early distributions of taxable amounts from your traditional IRA in your gross income. Early distributions are also subject to an additional 10% tax. See the discussion of Form 5329 under *Reporting Additional Taxes*, later, to figure and report the tax.

Early distributions defined. Early distributions are generally amounts distributed from your traditional IRA account or annuity before you are age 59½.

Age 59½ rule. Generally, if you are under age 59½, you must pay a 10% additional tax on the distribution of any assets (money or other property) from your traditional IRA. Distributions before you are age 59½ are called "early distributions."

The 10% additional tax applies to the part of the distribution that you have to include in gross income. It is in addition to any regular income tax on that amount.

After age 59½ and before age 72. After you reach age 59½, you can receive distributions without having to pay the 10% additional tax. Even though you can receive distributions after you reach age 59½, distributions aren't required until you reach age 72. See *When Must You Withdraw IRA Assets? (Required Minimum Distributions)*, earlier.

Exceptions. There are several exceptions to the age 59½ rule. Even if you receive a distribution before you are age 59½, you may not have to pay the 10% additional tax if you are in one of the following situations.

- You have unreimbursed medical expenses that are more than 7.5% of your AGI.

- The distributions aren't more than the cost of your medical insurance due to a period of unemployment.

- You are totally and permanently disabled.

- You are the beneficiary of a deceased IRA owner.

- You are receiving distributions in the form of an annuity.

- The distributions aren't more than your qualified higher education expenses.

- You use the distributions to buy, build, or rebuild a first home.

- The distribution is due to an IRS levy of the IRA or retirement plan.

- The distribution is a qualified reservist distribution.

Most of these exceptions are explained under *Early Distributions* in *What Acts Result in Penalties or Additional Taxes?* in chapter 1 of Pub. 590-B.

Note. Distributions that are timely and properly rolled over, as discussed earlier, aren't subject to either regular income tax or the 10% additional tax. Certain withdrawals of excess contributions after the due date of your return are also tax free and therefore not subject to the 10% additional tax. (See *Excess contributions withdrawn after due date of return*, earlier.) This also applies to transfers incident to divorce, as discussed earlier.

Receivership distributions. Early distributions (with or without your consent) from savings institutions placed in receivership are subject to this tax unless one of the exceptions listed earlier applies. This is true even if the distribution is from a receiver that is a state agency.

Additional 10% tax. The additional tax on early distributions is 10% of the amount of the early distribution that you must include in your gross income. This tax is in addition to any regular income tax resulting from including the distribution in income.

Nondeductible contributions. The tax on early distributions doesn't apply to the part of a distribution that represents a return of your nondeductible contributions (basis).

More information. For more information on early distributions, see *What Acts Result in Penalties or Additional Taxes?* in chapter 1 of Pub. 590-B.

Excess Accumulations (Insufficient Distributions)

You can't keep amounts in your traditional IRA indefinitely. Generally, you must begin receiving distributions by April 1 of the year following the year in which you reach age 72. The required minimum distribution for any year after the year in which you reach age 72 must be made by December 31 of that later year.

Tax on excess. If distributions are less than the required minimum distribution for the year, you may have to pay a 50% excise tax for that year on the amount not distributed as required.

Request to waive the tax. If the excess accumulation is due to reasonable error, and you have taken, or are taking, steps to remedy the insufficient distribution, you can request that the tax be waived. If you believe you qualify for this relief, attach a statement of explanation and complete Form 5329 as instructed under *Waiver of tax for reasonable cause* in the Instructions for Form 5329.

Exemption from tax. If you are unable to take required distributions because you have a traditional IRA invested in a contract issued by an insurance company that is in state insurer delinquency proceedings, the 50% excise tax doesn't apply if the conditions and requirements of Revenue Procedure 92-10 are satisfied.

More information. For more information on excess accumulations, see *What Acts Result in Penalties or Additional Taxes?* in chapter 1 of Pub. 590-B.

Reporting Additional Taxes

Generally, you must use Form 5329 to report the tax on excess contributions, early distributions, and excess accumulations.

Filing a tax return. If you must file an individual income tax return, complete Form 5329 and attach it to your Form 1040 or 1040-SR. Enter the total additional taxes due on Schedule 2 (Form 1040), line 8.

Not filing a tax return. If you don't have to file a tax return but do have to pay one of the additional taxes mentioned earlier, file the completed Form 5329 with the IRS at the time and place you would have filed your Form 1040 or 1040-SR. Be sure to include your address on page 1 and your signature and date on page 2. Enclose, but don't attach, a check or money order payable to "United States Treasury" for the tax you owe, as shown on Form 5329. Enter your social security number and "2022 Form 5329" on your check or money order.

Form 5329 not required. You don't have to use Form 5329 if any of the following situations exists.

- Distribution code 1 (early distribution) is correctly shown in box 7 of all your Forms 1099-R. If you don't owe any other additional tax on a distribution, multiply the taxable part of the early distribution by 10% (0.10) and enter the result on Schedule 2 (Form 1040), line 8. Enter "No" to the left of the line to indicate that you don't have to file Form 5329. However, if you owe this tax and also owe any other additional tax on a distribution, don't enter this 10% additional tax directly on your Form 1040 or 1040-SR. You must file Form 5329 to report your additional taxes.

- If you rolled over part or all of a distribution from a qualified retirement plan, the part rolled over isn't subject to the tax on early distributions.

- If you have a qualified disaster distribution.

Roth IRAs

Regardless of your age, you may be able to establish and make nondeductible contributions to a retirement plan called a Roth IRA.

Contributions not reported. You don't report Roth IRA contributions on your return.

What Is a Roth IRA?

A Roth IRA is an individual retirement plan that, except as explained in this chapter, is subject to

the rules that apply to a traditional IRA (defined earlier). It can be either an account or an annuity. Individual retirement accounts and annuities are described under *How Can a Traditional IRA Be Opened?* in chapter 1 of Pub. 590-A.

To be a Roth IRA, the account or annuity must be designated as a Roth IRA when it is opened. A deemed IRA can be a Roth IRA, but neither a SEP IRA nor a SIMPLE IRA can be designated as a Roth IRA.

Unlike a traditional IRA, you can't deduct contributions to a Roth IRA. But, if you satisfy the requirements, qualified distributions (discussed later) are tax free. You can leave amounts in your Roth IRA as long as you live.

When Can a Roth IRA Be Opened?

You can open a Roth IRA at any time. However, the time for making contributions for any year is limited. See *When Can You Make Contributions* under *Can You Contribute to a Roth IRA?* next.

Can You Contribute to a Roth IRA?

Generally, you can contribute to a Roth IRA if you have taxable compensation (defined later) and your modified AGI (defined later) is less than:

- $214,000 for married filing jointly or qualifying surviving spouse;

- $144,000 for single, head of household, or married filing separately and you didn't live with your spouse at any time during the year; or

- $10,000 for married filing separately and you lived with your spouse at any time during the year.

 You may be eligible to claim a credit for contributions to your Roth IRA. For more information, see chapter 3 of Pub. 590-A.

Is there an age limit for contributions? Contributions can be made to your Roth IRA regardless of your age.

Can you contribute to a Roth IRA for your spouse? You can contribute to a Roth IRA for your spouse provided the contributions satisfy the Kay Bailey Hutchison Spousal IRA limit (discussed under *How Much Can Be Contributed*, earlier, under *Traditional IRAs*), you file jointly, and your modified AGI is less than $214,000.

Compensation. Compensation includes wages, salaries, tips, professional fees, bonuses, and other amounts received for providing personal services. It also includes commissions, self-employment income, nontaxable combat pay, military differential pay, and taxable alimony and separate maintenance payments.

See *What is compensation* for more information.

Modified AGI. Your modified AGI for Roth IRA purposes is your AGI as shown on your return with some adjustments. Use Worksheet 9-2 to determine your modified AGI.

Use this worksheet to figure your modified AGI for Roth IRA purposes.

1.	Enter your AGI from Form 1040 or 1040-SR, line 11	1. _____
2.	Enter any income resulting from the conversion of an IRA (other than a Roth IRA) to a Roth IRA (included on Form 1040 or 1040-SR, line 4b) and a rollover from a qualified retirement plan to a Roth IRA (included on Form 1040 or 1040-SR, line 5b)	2. _____
3.	Subtract line 2 from line 1	3. _____
4.	Enter any traditional IRA deduction from Schedule 1 (Form 1040), line 20	4. _____
5.	Enter any student loan interest deduction from Schedule 1 (Form 1040), line 21	5. _____
6.	Enter any foreign earned income and/or housing exclusion from Form 2555, line 45	6. _____
7.	Enter any foreign housing deduction from Form 2555, line 50	7. _____
8.	Enter any excludable savings bond interest from Form 8815, line 14	8. _____
9.	Enter any excluded employer-provided adoption benefits from Form 8839, line 28	9. _____
10.	Add the amounts on lines 3 through 9	10. _____
11.	Enter: • $214,000 if married filing jointly or qualifying surviving spouse, • $10,000 if married filing separately and you lived with your spouse at any time during the year, or • $144,000 for all others	11. _____

Is the amount on line 10 more than the amount on line 11?
If yes, then see the ***Note*** below.
If no, then the amount on line 10 is your **modified AGI** for Roth IRA purposes.

Note. If the amount on line 10 is more than the amount on line 11 and you have other income or loss items, such as social security income or passive activity losses, that are subject to AGI-based phaseouts, you can refigure your AGI solely for the purpose of figuring your modified AGI for Roth IRA purposes. (If you receive social security benefits, use Worksheet 1 in *Appendix B* of Pub. 590-A to refigure your AGI.) Then, go to line 3 above in this Worksheet 9-2 to refigure your modified AGI. If you don't have other income or loss items subject to AGI-based phaseouts, your modified AGI for Roth IRA purposes is the amount on line 10.

How Much Can Be Contributed?

The contribution limit for Roth IRAs generally depends on whether contributions are made only to Roth IRAs or to both traditional IRAs and Roth IRAs.

Roth IRAs only. If contributions are made only to Roth IRAs, your contribution limit is generally the lesser of the following amounts.

* $6,000 ($7,000 if you are 50 or older in 2022).
* Your taxable compensation.

However, if your modified AGI is above a certain amount, your contribution limit may be reduced, as explained later under *Contribution limit reduced*.

Roth IRAs and traditional IRAs. If contributions are made to both Roth IRAs and traditional IRAs established for your benefit, your contribution limit for Roth IRAs is generally the same as your limit would be if contributions were made only to Roth IRAs, but then reduced by all contributions for the year to all IRAs other than Roth IRAs. Employer contributions under a SEP or SIMPLE IRA plan don't affect this limit.

This means that your contribution limit is generally the lesser of the following amounts.

* $6,000 ($7,000 if you are 50 or older in 2022) minus all contributions (other than employer contributions under a SEP or SIMPLE IRA plan) for the year to all IRAs other than Roth IRAs.

* Your taxable compensation minus all contributions (other than employer contributions under a SEP or SIMPLE IRA plan) for the year to all IRAs other than Roth IRAs.

However, if your modified AGI is above a certain amount, your contribution limit may be reduced, as explained next under *Contribution limit reduced*.

Contribution limit reduced. If your modified AGI is above a certain amount, your contribution limit is gradually reduced. Use Table 9-3 to determine if this reduction applies to you.

Table 9-3. Effect of Modified AGI on Roth IRA Contribution

This table shows whether your contribution to a Roth IRA is affected by the amount of your modified AGI.

IF you have taxable compensation and your filing status is...	AND your modified AGI is...	THEN...
Married filing jointly or **Qualifying surviving spouse**	less than $204,000	you can contribute up to $6,000 ($7,000 if you are 50 or older in 2022).
	at least $204,000 but less than $214,000	the amount you can contribute is reduced as explained under *Contribution limit reduced* in chapter 2 of Pub. 590-A.
	$214,000 or more	you can't contribute to a Roth IRA.
Married filing separately and you lived with your spouse at any time during the year	zero (-0-)	you can contribute up to $6,000 ($7,000 if you are 50 or older in 2022).
	more than zero (-0-) but less than $10,000	the amount you can contribute is reduced as explained under *Contribution limit reduced* in chapter 2 of Pub. 590-A.
	$10,000 or more	you can't contribute to a Roth IRA.
Single, Head of household, or **Married filing separately** and you didn't live with your spouse at any time during the year	less than $129,000	you can contribute up to $6,000 ($7,000 if you are 50 or older in 2022).
	at least $129,000 but less than $144,000	the amount you can contribute is reduced as explained under *Contribution limit reduced* in chapter 2 of Pub. 590-A.
	$144,000 or more	you can't contribute to a Roth IRA.

Figuring the reduction. If the amount you can contribute to your Roth IRA is reduced, see Worksheet 2-2 under *Can You Contribute to a Roth IRA?* in chapter 2 of Pub. 590-A for how to figure the reduction.

When Can You Make Contributions?

You can make contributions to a Roth IRA for a year at any time during the year or by the due date of your return for that year (not including extensions).

You can make contributions for 2022 by the due date (not including extensions) for filing your 2022 tax return.

What if You Contribute Too Much?

A 6% excise tax applies to any excess contribution to a Roth IRA.

Excess contributions. These are the contributions to your Roth IRAs for a year that equal the total of:

1. Amounts contributed for the tax year to your Roth IRAs (other than amounts properly and timely rolled over from a Roth IRA or properly converted from a traditional IRA or rolled over from a qualified retirement plan, as described later) that are more than your contribution limit for the year; plus

2. Any excess contributions for the preceding year, reduced by the total of:

    a. Any distributions out of your Roth IRAs for the year, plus

    b. Your contribution limit for the year minus your contributions to all your IRAs for the year.

Withdrawal of excess contributions. For purposes of determining excess contributions, any contribution that is withdrawn on or before the due date (including extensions) for filing your tax return for the year is treated as an amount not contributed. This treatment applies only if any earnings on the contributions are also withdrawn. The earnings are considered to have been earned and received in the year the excess contribution was made.

Applying excess contributions. If contributions to your Roth IRA for a year were more than the limit, you can apply the excess contribution in one year to a later year if the contributions for that later year are less than the maximum allowed for that year.

Can You Move Amounts Into a Roth IRA?

You may be able to convert amounts from either a traditional, SEP, or SIMPLE IRA into a Roth IRA. You may be able to roll amounts over from a qualified retirement plan to a Roth IRA. You may be able to recharacterize contributions made to one IRA as having been made directly to a different IRA. You can roll amounts over from a designated Roth account or from one Roth IRA to another Roth IRA.

Conversions

You can convert a traditional IRA to a Roth IRA. The conversion is treated as a rollover, regardless of the conversion method used. Most of the rules for rollovers, described earlier under *Rollover From One IRA Into Another* under *Traditional IRAs*, apply to these rollovers. However, the 1-year waiting period doesn't apply.

Conversion methods. You can convert amounts from a traditional IRA to a Roth IRA in any of the following ways.

- *Rollover*. You can receive a distribution from a traditional IRA and roll it over (contribute it) to a Roth IRA within 60 days after the distribution.

- *Trustee-to-trustee transfer*. You can direct the trustee of the traditional IRA to transfer an amount from the traditional IRA to the trustee of the Roth IRA.

- *Same trustee transfer*. If the trustee of the traditional IRA also maintains the Roth IRA, you can direct the trustee to transfer an amount from the traditional IRA to the Roth IRA.

Same trustee. Conversions made with the same trustee can be made by redesignating the traditional IRA as a Roth IRA, rather than opening a new account or issuing a new contract.

Rollover from a qualified retirement plan into a Roth IRA. You can roll over into a Roth IRA all or part of an eligible rollover distribution you receive from your (or your deceased spouse's):

- Employer's qualified pension, profit-sharing, or stock bonus plan;

- Annuity plan;

- Tax-sheltered annuity plan (section 403(b) plan); or

- Governmental deferred compensation plan (section 457 plan).

Any amount rolled over is subject to the same rules as those for converting a traditional IRA into a Roth IRA. Also, the rollover contribution must meet the rollover requirements that apply to the specific type of retirement plan.

Income. You must include in your gross income distributions from a qualified retirement plan that you would have had to include in income if you hadn't rolled them over into a Roth IRA. You don't include in gross income any part of a distribution from a qualified retirement plan that is a return of basis (after-tax contributions) to the plan that was taxable to you when paid. These amounts are normally included in income on your return for the year of the rollover from the qualified employer plan to a Roth IRA.

 If you must include any amount in your gross income, you may have to increase your withholding or make estimated tax payments. See Pub. 505, Tax Withholding and Estimated Tax.

For more information, see *Rollover From Employer's Plan Into a Roth IRA* in chapter 2 of Pub. 590-A.

Converting from a SIMPLE IRA. Generally, you can convert an amount in your SIMPLE IRA to a Roth IRA under the same rules explained earlier under *Converting From Any Traditional IRA to a Roth IRA* under *Traditional IRAs*.

However, you can't convert any amount distributed from the SIMPLE IRA plan during the 2-year period beginning on the date you first participated in any SIMPLE IRA plan maintained by your employer.

More information. For more detailed information on conversions, see *Can You Move Amounts Into a Roth IRA?* of chapter 2 of Pub. 590-A.

Rollover From a Roth IRA

You can withdraw, tax free, all or part of the assets from one Roth IRA if you contribute them within 60 days to another Roth IRA. Most of the rules for rollovers, explained earlier under *Rollover From One IRA Into Another* under *Traditional IRAs*, apply to these rollovers.

Rollover from designated Roth account. A rollover from a designated Roth account can only be made to another designated Roth account or to a Roth IRA. For more information about designated Roth accounts, see *Designated Roth accounts* under *Rollovers* in Pub. 575.

Are Distributions Taxable?

You don't include in your gross income qualified distributions or distributions that are a return of your regular contributions from your Roth IRA(s). You also don't include distributions from your Roth IRA that you roll over tax free into another Roth IRA. You may have to include part of other distributions in your income. See *Ordering rules for distributions*, later.

What are qualified distributions? A qualified distribution is any payment or distribution from your Roth IRA that meets the following requirements.

1. It is made after the 5-year period beginning with the first tax year for which a contribution was made to a Roth IRA set up for your benefit.

2. The payment or distribution is:

   a. Made on or after the date you reach age 59¹/₂,

   b. Made because you are disabled,

   c. Made to a beneficiary or to your estate after your death, or

   d. To pay up to $10,000 (lifetime limit) of certain qualified first-time homebuyer amounts. See *First home* under *What Acts Result in Penalties or Additional Taxes?* in chapter 1 of Pub. 590-B for more information.

Additional tax on distributions of conversion and certain rollover contributions within 5-year period. If, within the 5-year period starting with the first day of your tax year in which you convert an amount from a traditional IRA or roll over an amount from a qualified retirement plan to a Roth IRA, you take a distribution from a Roth IRA, you may have to pay the 10% additional tax on early distributions. You must generally pay the 10% additional tax on any amount attributable to the part of the amount converted or rolled over (the conversion or rollover contribution) that you had to include in income. A separate 5-year period applies to each conversion and rollover. See *Ordering rules for distributions*, later, to determine the amount, if any, of the distribution that is attributable to the part of the conversion or rollover contribution that you had to include in income.

Additional tax on other early distributions. Unless an exception applies, you must pay the 10% additional tax on the taxable part of any distributions that aren't qualified distributions. See Pub. 590-B for more information.

Ordering rules for distributions. If you receive a distribution from your Roth IRA that isn't a qualified distribution, part of it may be taxable. There is a set order in which contributions (including conversion contributions and rollover contributions from qualified retirement plans) and earnings are considered to be distributed from your Roth IRA. Regular contributions are distributed first. See *Ordering Rules for Distributions* under *Are Distributions Taxable?* in chapter 2 of Pub. 590-B for more information.

Must you withdraw or use Roth IRA assets? You aren't required to take distributions from your Roth IRA at any age. The minimum distribution rules that apply to traditional IRAs don't apply to Roth IRAs while the owner is alive. However, after the death of a Roth IRA owner, certain minimum distribution rules that apply to traditional IRAs also apply to Roth IRAs.

More information. For more detailed information on Roth IRAs, see chapter 2 of Pub. 590-A and Pub. 590-B.

Part Three.

Standard Deduction, Itemized Deductions, and Other Deductions

After you have figured your adjusted gross income, you are ready to subtract the deductions used to figure taxable income. You can subtract either the standard deduction or itemized deductions, and, if you qualify, the qualified business income deduction. Itemized deductions are deductions for certain expenses that are listed on Schedule A (Form 1040). The three chapters in this part discuss the standard deduction and each itemized deduction. See chapter 10 for the factors to consider when deciding whether to take the standard deduction or itemized deductions.

The Form 1040 and 1040-SR schedules that are discussed in these chapters are:

- *Schedule 1, Additional Income and Adjustments to Income;*
- *Schedule 2 (Part II), Other Taxes; and*
- *Schedule 3 (Part I), Nonrefundable Credits.*

10.

Standard Deduction

What's New

Standard deduction increased. The standard deduction for taxpayers who don't itemize their deductions on Schedule A (Form 1040) has increased. The amount of your standard deduction depends on your filing status and other factors. Use the 2022 Standard Deduction Tables near the end of this chapter to figure your standard deduction.

Introduction

This chapter discusses the following topics.

- How to figure the amount of your standard deduction.
- The standard deduction for dependents.
- Who should itemize deductions.

Most taxpayers have a choice of either taking a standard deduction or itemizing their deductions. If you have a choice, you can use the method that gives you the lower tax.

The standard deduction is a dollar amount that reduces your taxable income. It is a benefit that eliminates the need for many taxpayers to itemize actual deductions, such as medical expenses, charitable contributions, and taxes, on Schedule A (Form 1040). The standard deduction is higher for taxpayers who:

- Are 65 or older, or
- Are blind.

 You benefit from the standard deduction if your standard deduction is more than the total of your allowable itemized deductions.

Persons not eligible for the standard deduction. Your standard deduction is zero and you should itemize any deductions you have if:

- Your filing status is married filing separately, and your spouse itemizes deductions on their return;
- You are filing a tax return for a short tax year because of a change in your annual accounting period; or
- You are a nonresident or dual-status alien during the year. You are considered a dual-status alien if you were both a nonresident and resident alien during the year.

If you are a nonresident alien who is married to a U.S. citizen or resident alien at the end of the year, you can choose to be treated as a U.S. resident. (See Pub. 519.) If you make this choice, you can take the standard deduction.

 If you can be claimed as a dependent on another person's return (such as your parents' return), your standard deduction may be limited. See Standard Deduction for Dependents, later.

Useful Items

You may want to see:

Publication

- ❏ **501** Dependents, Standard Deduction, and Filing Information
- ❏ **502** Medical and Dental Expenses
- ❏ **526** Charitable Contributions
- ❏ **530** Tax Information for Homeowners
- ❏ **547** Casualties, Disasters, and Thefts
- ❏ **550** Investment Income and Expenses
- ❏ **970** Tax Benefits for Education

- ❏ **936** Home Mortgage Interest Deduction

Form (and Instructions)

- ❏ **Schedule A (Form 1040)** Itemized Deductions

Standard Deduction Amount

The standard deduction amount depends on your filing status, whether you are 65 or older or blind, and whether another taxpayer can claim you as a dependent. Generally, the standard deduction amounts are adjusted each year for inflation. The standard deduction amounts for most people are shown in Table 10-1.

Decedent's final return. The standard deduction for a decedent's final tax return is the same as it would have been had the decedent continued to live. However, if the decedent wasn't 65 or older at the time of death, the higher standard deduction for age can't be claimed.

Higher Standard Deduction for Age (65 or Older)

If you are age 65 or older on the last day of the year and don't itemize deductions, you are entitled to a higher standard deduction. You are considered 65 on the day before your 65th birthday. Therefore, you can take a higher standard deduction for 2022 if you were born before January 2, 1958.

Use Table 10-2 to figure the standard deduction amount.

Death of a taxpayer. If you are preparing a return for someone who died in 2022, read this before using Table 10-2 or Table 10-3. Consider the taxpayer to be 65 or older at the end of 2022 only if they were 65 or older at the time of death. Even if the taxpayer was born before January 2, 1958, they are not considered 65 or older at the end of 2022 unless they were 65 or older at the time of death.

A person is considered to reach age 65 on the day before their 65th birthday.

Higher Standard Deduction for Blindness

If you are blind on the last day of the year and you don't itemize deductions, you are entitled to a higher standard deduction.

Not totally blind. If you aren't totally blind, you must get a certified statement from an eye doctor (ophthalmologist or optometrist) that:

- You can't see better than 20/200 in the better eye with glasses or contact lenses, or
- Your field of vision is 20 degrees or less.

If your eye condition isn't likely to improve beyond these limits, the statement should include this fact. Keep the statement in your records.

If your vision can be corrected beyond these limits only by contact lenses that you can wear only briefly because of pain, infection, or ulcers, you can take the higher standard deduction for blindness if you otherwise qualify.

Spouse 65 or Older or Blind

You can take the higher standard deduction if your spouse is age 65 or older or blind and:

- You file a joint return, or
- You file a separate return and your spouse had no gross income and can't be claimed as a dependent by another taxpayer.

Death of a spouse. If your spouse died in 2022 before reaching age 65, you can't take a higher standard deduction because of your spouse. Even if your spouse was born before January 2, 1958, your spouse isn't considered 65 or older at the end of 2022 unless your spouse was 65 or older at the time of death.

A person is considered to reach age 65 on the day before their 65th birthday.

Example. Your spouse was born on February 14, 1957, and died on February 13, 2022. Your spouse is considered age 65 at the time of death. However, if your spouse died on February 12, 2022, your spouse isn't considered age 65 at the time of death and isn't 65 or older at the end of 2022.

 You can't claim the higher standard deduction for an individual other than yourself and your spouse.

Higher Standard Deduction for Net Disaster Loss

Your standard deduction may be increased by any net qualified disaster loss.

See the Instructions for Form 1040 and the Instructions for Schedule A (Form 1040) for more information on how to figure your

increased standard deduction and how to report it on Form 1040 or 1040-SR.

Examples

The following examples illustrate how to determine your standard deduction using Tables 10-1 and 10-2.

Example 1. L, 46, and D, 33, are filing a joint return for 2022. Neither is blind, and neither can be claimed as a dependent. They decide not to itemize their deductions. They use Table 10-1. Their standard deduction is $25,900.

Example 2. The facts are the same as in Example 1, except that L is blind at the end of 2022. L and D use Table 10-2. Their standard deduction is $27,300.

Example 3. B and L are filing a joint return for 2022. Both are over age 65. Neither is blind, and neither can be claimed as a dependent. If they don't itemize deductions, they use Table 10-2. Their standard deduction is $28,700.

Standard Deduction for Dependents

The standard deduction for an individual who can be claimed as a dependent on another person's tax return is generally limited to the greater of:

- $1,150, or
- The individual's earned income for the year plus $400 (but not more than the regular standard deduction amount, generally $12,950).

However, if the individual is 65 or older or blind, the standard deduction may be higher.

If you (or your spouse, if filing jointly) can be claimed as a dependent on someone else's return, use Table 10-3 to determine your standard deduction.

Earned income defined. Earned income is salaries, wages, tips, professional fees, and other amounts received as pay for work you actually perform.

For purposes of the standard deduction, earned income also includes any part of a taxable scholarship or fellowship grant. See chapter 1 of Pub. 970, Tax Benefits for Education, for more information on what qualifies as a scholarship or fellowship grant.

Example 1. M is 16 years old and single. M's parents can claim M as a dependent on their 2022 tax return. M has interest income of $780 and wages of $150 and no itemized deductions. M uses Table 10-3 to find M's standard deduction. M enters $150 (earned income) on line 1, $550 ($150 + $400) on line 3, $1,150 (the larger of $550 and $1,150) on line 5, and $12,950 on line 6. M's standard deduction, on line 7a, is $1,150 (the smaller of $1,150 and $12,950).

Example 2. J, a 22-year-old college student, can be claimed as a dependent on J's parents' 2022 tax return. J is married and files a

separate return. J's spouse doesn't itemize deductions. J has $1,500 in interest income and wages of $3,800 and no itemized deductions. J finds J's standard deduction by using Table 10-3. J enters earned income, $3,800, on line 1. J adds lines 1 and 2 and enters $4,200 ($3,800 + $400) on line 3. On line 5, J enters $4,200, the larger of lines 3 and 4. Because J is married filing a separate return, J enters $12,950 on line 6. On line 7a, J enters $4,200 as the standard deduction amount because it is smaller than $12,950, the amount on line 6.

Example 3. A, who is single, can be claimed as a dependent on A's parents' 2022 tax return. A is 18 years old and blind. A has interest income of $1,300 and wages of $2,900 and no itemized deductions. A uses Table 10-3 to find the standard deduction amount. A enters wages of $2,900 on line 1 and adds lines 1 and 2 and enters $3,300 ($2,900 + 400) on line 3. On line 5, A enters $3,300, the larger of lines 3 and 4. Because A is single, A enters $12,950 on line 6. A enters $3,300 on line 7a. This is the smaller of the amounts on lines 5 and 6. Because A checked the box in the top part of the worksheet, indicating A is blind, A enters $1,750 on line 7b then adds the amounts on lines 7a and 7b and enters the standard deduction amount of $5,050 ($3,300 + $1,750) on line 7c.

Example 4. E is 18 years old and single and can be claimed as a dependent on E's parents' 2022 tax return. E has wages of $7,000, interest income of $500, a business loss of $3,000 and no itemized deductions. E uses Table 10-3 to figure the standard deduction amount. E enters $4,000 ($7,000 – $3,000) on line 1, adds lines 1 and 2 and enters $4,400 ($4,000 + $400) on line 3. On line 5, E enters $4,400, the larger of lines 3 and 4, and because E is single, $12,950 on line 6. On line 7a, E enters $4,400 as the standard deduction amount because it is smaller than $12,950, the amount on line 6.

Who Should Itemize

You should itemize deductions if your total deductions are more than your standard deduction amount. Also, you should itemize if you don't qualify for the standard deduction, as discussed earlier under *Persons not eligible for the standard deduction*.

You should first figure your itemized deductions and compare that amount to your standard deduction to make sure you are using the method that gives you the greater benefit.

When to itemize. You may benefit from itemizing your deductions on Schedule A (Form 1040) if you:

- Don't qualify for the standard deduction,
- Had large uninsured medical and dental expenses during the year,
- Paid interest and taxes on your home,
- Had large uninsured casualty or theft losses,
- Made large contributions to qualified charities, or

- Have total itemized deductions that are more than the standard deduction to which you are otherwise entitled.

These deductions are explained in chapter 11 and in the publications listed under *Useful Items*, earlier.

If you decide to itemize your deductions, complete Schedule A and attach it to your Form 1040 or 1040-SR. Enter the amount from Schedule A, line 17, on Form 1040 or Form 1040-SR, line 12.

Electing to itemize for state tax or other purposes. Even if your itemized deductions are less than your standard deduction, you can elect to itemize deductions on your federal re-turn rather than taking the standard deduction. You may want to do this if, for example, the tax benefit of itemizing your deductions on your state tax return is greater than the tax benefit you lose on your federal return by not taking the standard deduction. To make this election, you must check the box on line 18 of Schedule A.

Changing your mind. If you don't itemize your deductions and later find that you should have itemized—or if you itemize your deductions and later find you shouldn't have—you can change your return by filing Form 1040-X, Amended U.S. Individual Income Tax Return. See *Amended Returns and Claims for Refund* in chapter 1 for more information on amended returns.

Married persons who filed separate returns. You can change methods of taking deductions only if you and your spouse both make the same changes. Both of you must file a consent to assessment for any additional tax either one may owe as a result of the change.

You and your spouse can use the method that gives you the lower total tax, even though one of you may pay more tax than you would have paid by using the other method. You both must use the same method of claiming deductions. If one itemizes deductions, the other should itemize because they won't qualify for the standard deduction. See *Persons not eligible for the standard deduction*, earlier.

2022 Standard Deduction Tables

 If you are married filing a separate return and your spouse itemizes deductions, or if you are a dual-status alien, you can't take the standard deduction even if you were born before January 2, 1958, or are blind.

Table 10-1. Standard Deduction Chart for Most People*

IF your filing status is...	THEN your standard deduction is...
Single or Married filing separately	$12,950
Married filing jointly or Qualifying surviving spouse	25,900
Head of household	19,400

* Don't use this chart if you were born before January 2, 1958, are blind, or if someone else can claim you (or your spouse, if filing jointly) as a dependent. Use Table 10-2 or 10-3 instead.

Table 10-2. Standard Deduction Chart for People Born Before January 2, 1958, or Who Are Blind*

Check the correct number of boxes below. Then go to the chart.

You: Born before January 2, 1958 ☐   Blind ☐
Your spouse: Born before January 2, 1958 ☐   Blind ☐

Total number of boxes checked ☐

IF your filing status is...	AND the number in the box above is...	THEN your standard deduction is...
Single	1	$14,700
	2	16,450
Married filing jointly	1	$27,300
	2	28,700
	3	30,100
	4	31,500
Qualifying surviving spouse	1	$27,300
	2	28,700
Married filing separately**	1	$14,350
	2	15,750
	3	17,150
	4	18,550
Head of household	1	$21,150
	2	22,900

* If someone else can claim you (or your spouse, if filing jointly) as a dependent, use Table 10-3 instead.
** You can check the boxes for *Your Spouse* if your filing status is married filing separately and your spouse had no income, isn't filing a return, and can't be claimed as a dependent on another person's return.

Table 10-3. Standard Deduction Worksheet for Dependents

Use this worksheet only if someone else can claim you (or your spouse, if filing jointly) as a dependent.

Check the correct number of boxes below. Then go to the worksheet.

You: Born before January 2, 1958 ☐   Blind ☐
Your spouse: Born before January 2, 1958 ☐   Blind ☐

Total number of boxes checked ☐

1.	Enter your earned income (defined below). If none, enter -0-.	1. _____
2.	Additional amount.	2. _____ $400
3.	Add lines 1 and 2.	3. _____
4.	Minimum standard deduction.	4. _____ $1,150
5.	Enter the larger of line 3 or line 4.	5. _____
6.	Enter the amount shown below for your filing status. • Single or Married filing separately—$12,950 • Married filing jointly—$25,900 • Head of household—$19,400	6. _____
7.	**Standard deduction.** a. Enter the smaller of line 5 or line 6. If born after January 1, 1958, and not blind, stop here. This is your standard deduction. Otherwise, go on to line 7b. b. If born before January 2, 1958, or blind, multiply $1,750 ($1,400 if married) by the number in the box above. c. Add lines 7a and 7b. This is your standard deduction for 2022.	7a. _____ 7b. _____ 7c. _____

Earned income includes wages, salaries, tips, professional fees, and other compensation received for personal services you performed. It also includes any taxable scholarship or fellowship grant.

11.

Taxes

Reminders

Limitation on deduction for state and local taxes. The Tax Cuts and Jobs Act provided for a temporary limitation on the deduction for state and local taxes. See *Limitation on deduction for state and local taxes*, later.

No deduction for foreign taxes paid for real estate. You can no longer deduct foreign taxes you paid on real estate.

Introduction

This chapter discusses which taxes you can deduct if you itemize deductions on Schedule A (Form 1040). It also explains which taxes you can deduct on other schedules or forms and which taxes you can't deduct.

This chapter covers the following topics.

- Income taxes (federal, state, local, and foreign).
- General sales taxes (state and local).
- Real estate taxes (state, local, and foreign).
- Personal property taxes (state and local).
- Taxes and fees you can't deduct.

Use Table 11-1 as a guide to determine which taxes you can deduct.

The end of the chapter contains a section that explains which forms you use to deduct different types of taxes.

Business taxes. You can deduct certain taxes only if they are ordinary and necessary expenses of your trade or business or of producing income. For information on these taxes, see Pub. 535, Business Expenses.

State or local taxes. These are taxes imposed by the 50 states, U.S. possessions, or any of their political subdivisions (such as a county or city), or by the District of Columbia.

Indian tribal government. An Indian tribal government recognized by the Secretary of the Treasury as performing substantial government functions will be treated as a state for purposes of claiming a deduction for taxes. Income taxes, real estate taxes, and personal property taxes imposed by that Indian tribal government (or by any of its subdivisions that are treated as political subdivisions of a state) are deductible.

General sales taxes. These are taxes imposed at one rate on retail sales of a broad range of classes of items.

Foreign taxes. These are taxes imposed by a foreign country or any of its political subdivisions.

Useful Items

You may want to see:

Publication

- ❏ **502** Medical and Dental Expenses
- ❏ **503** Child and Dependent Care Expenses
- ❏ **504** Divorced or Separated Individuals
- ❏ **514** Foreign Tax Credit for Individuals
- ❏ **525** Taxable and Nontaxable Income
- ❏ **530** Tax Information for Homeowners

Form (and Instructions)

- ❏ **Schedule A (Form 1040)** Itemized Deductions
- ❏ **Schedule E (Form 1040)** Supplemental Income and Loss
- ❏ **1116** Foreign Tax Credit

For these and other useful items, go to *IRS.gov/Forms*.

Tests To Deduct Any Tax

The following two tests must be met for you to deduct any tax.

- The tax must be imposed on you.
- You must pay the tax during your tax year.

The tax must be imposed on you. In general, you can deduct only taxes imposed on you.

Generally, you can deduct property taxes only if you are an owner of the property. If your spouse owns the property and pays the real estate taxes, the taxes are deductible on your spouse's separate return or on your joint return.

You must pay the tax during your tax year. If you are a cash basis taxpayer, you can deduct only those taxes you actually paid during your tax year. If you pay your taxes by check and the check is honored by your financial institution, the day you mail or deliver the check is the date of payment. If you use a pay-by-phone account (such as a credit card or electronic funds withdrawal), the date reported on the statement of the financial institution showing when payment was made is the date of payment. If you contest a tax liability and are a cash basis taxpayer, you can deduct the tax only in the year you actually pay it (or transfer money or other property to provide for satisfaction of the contested liability). See Pub. 538, Accounting Periods and Methods, for details.

If you use an accrual method of accounting, see Pub. 538 for more information.

Income Taxes

This section discusses the deductibility of state and local income taxes (including employee contributions to state benefit funds) and foreign income taxes.

State and Local Income Taxes

You can deduct state and local income taxes.

Exception. You can't deduct state and local income taxes you pay on income that is exempt from federal income tax, unless the exempt income is interest income. For example, you can't deduct the part of a state's income tax that is on a cost-of-living allowance exempt from federal income tax.

What To Deduct

Your deduction may be for withheld taxes, estimated tax payments, or other tax payments as follows.

Withheld taxes. You can deduct state and local income taxes withheld from your salary in the year they are withheld. Your Form(s) W-2 will show these amounts. Forms W-2G, 1099-B, 1099-DIV, 1099-G, 1099-K, 1099-MISC, 1099-NEC, 1099-OID, and 1099-R may also show state and local income taxes withheld.

Estimated tax payments. You can deduct estimated tax payments you made during the year to a state or local government. However, you must have a reasonable basis for making the estimated tax payments. Any estimated state or local tax payments that aren't made in good faith at the time of payment aren't deductible.

Example. You made an estimated state income tax payment. However, the estimate of your state tax liability shows that you will get a refund of the full amount of your estimated payment. You had no reasonable basis to believe you had any additional liability for state income taxes and you can't deduct the estimated tax payment.

Refund applied to taxes. You can deduct any part of a refund of prior-year state or local income taxes that you chose to have credited to your 2022 estimated state or local income taxes.

Don't reduce your deduction by either of the following items.

- Any state or local income tax refund (or credit) you expect to receive for 2022.
- Any refund of (or credit for) prior-year state and local income taxes you actually received in 2022.

However, part or all of this refund (or credit) may be taxable. See *Refund (or credit) of state or local income taxes*, later.

Separate federal returns. If you and your spouse file separate state, local, and federal income tax returns, each of you can deduct on your federal return only the amount of your own state and local income tax that you paid during the tax year.

Joint state and local returns. If you and your spouse file joint state and local returns and separate federal returns, each of you can deduct on your separate federal return a part of the state and local income taxes paid during the tax year. You can deduct only the amount of the total taxes that is proportionate to your gross income compared to the combined gross income of you and your spouse. However, you can't deduct more than the amount you actually paid during the year. You can avoid this calculation if you and your spouse are jointly and individually liable for the full amount of the state and local income taxes. If so, you and your spouse can deduct on your separate federal returns the amount you each actually paid.

Joint federal return. If you file a joint federal return, you can deduct the state and local income taxes both of you paid.

Contributions to state benefit funds. As an employee, you can deduct mandatory contributions to state benefit funds withheld from your wages that provide protection against loss of wages. For example, certain states require employees to make contributions to state funds providing disability or unemployment insurance benefits. Mandatory payments made to the following state benefit funds are deductible as state income taxes on Schedule A (Form 1040), line 5a.

- Alaska Unemployment Compensation Fund.
- California Nonoccupational Disability Benefit Fund.
- New Jersey Nonoccupational Disability Benefit Fund.
- New Jersey Unemployment Compensation Fund.
- New York Nonoccupational Disability Benefit Fund.
- Pennsylvania Unemployment Compensation Fund.
- Rhode Island Temporary Disability Benefit Fund.
- Washington State Supplemental Workmen's Compensation Fund.

 Employee contributions to private or voluntary disability plans aren't deductible.

Refund (or credit) of state or local income taxes. If you receive a refund of (or credit for) state or local income taxes in a year after the year in which you paid them, you may have to include the refund in income on Schedule 1 (Form 1040), line 1, in the year you receive it. This includes refunds resulting from taxes that were overwithheld, applied from a prior-year return, not figured correctly, or figured again because of an amended return. If you didn't itemize your deductions in the previous year, don't include the refund in income. If you deducted the taxes in the previous year, include all or part of the refund on Schedule 1 (Form 1040), line 1, in the year you receive the refund. For a discussion of how much to include, see *Recoveries* in Pub. 525, Taxable and Nontaxable Income, for more information.

Foreign Income Taxes

Generally, you can take either a deduction or a credit for income taxes imposed on you by a foreign country or a U.S. possession. However, you can't take a deduction or credit for foreign income taxes paid on income that is exempt from U.S. tax under the foreign earned income exclusion or the foreign housing exclusion. For information on these exclusions, see Pub. 54, Tax Guide for U.S. Citizens and Resident Aliens Abroad. For information on the foreign tax credit, see Pub. 514.

State and Local General Sales Taxes

You can elect to deduct state and local general sales taxes, instead of state and local income taxes, as an itemized deduction on Schedule A (Form 1040), line 5a. You can use either your actual expenses or the state and local sales tax tables to figure your sales tax deduction.

Actual expenses. Generally, you can deduct the actual state and local general sales taxes (including compensating use taxes) if the tax rate was the same as the general sales tax rate.

Food, clothing, and medical supplies. Sales taxes on food, clothing, and medical supplies are deductible as a general sales tax even if the tax rate was less than the general sales tax rate.

Motor vehicles. Sales taxes on motor vehicles are deductible as a general sales tax even if the tax rate was less than the general sales tax rate. However, if you paid sales tax on a motor vehicle at a rate higher than the general sales tax, you can deduct only the amount of the tax that you would have paid at the general sales tax rate on that vehicle. Include any state and local general sales taxes paid for a leased motor vehicle. For purposes of this section, motor vehicles include cars, motorcycles, motor homes, recreational vehicles, sport utility vehicles, trucks, vans, and off-road vehicles.

 If you use the actual expenses method, you must have receipts to show the general sales taxes paid.

Trade or business items. Don't include sales taxes paid on items used in your trade or business on Schedule A (Form 1040). Instead, go to the instructions for the form you are using to report business income and expenses to see if you can deduct these taxes.

Optional sales tax tables. Instead of using your actual expenses, you can figure your state and local general sales tax deduction using the state and local sales tax tables in the Instructions for Schedule A (Form 1040). You may also be able to add the state and local general sales taxes paid on certain specified items.

Your applicable table amount is based on the state where you live, your income, and your family size. Your income is your adjusted gross income plus any nontaxable items such as the following.

- Tax-exempt interest.
- Veterans' benefits.
- Nontaxable combat pay.
- Workers' compensation.
- Nontaxable part of social security and railroad retirement benefits.
- Nontaxable part of IRA, pension, or annuity distributions, excluding rollovers.
- Public assistance payments.

If you lived in different states during the same tax year, you must prorate your applicable table amount for each state based on the days you lived in each state. See the

instructions for Schedule A (Form 1040), line 5a, for details.

State and Local Real Estate Taxes

Deductible real estate taxes are any state and local taxes on real property levied for the general public welfare. You can deduct these taxes only if they are assessed uniformly against all property under the jurisdiction of the taxing authority. The proceeds must be for general community or governmental purposes and not be a payment for a special privilege granted or service rendered to you.

Deductible real estate taxes generally don't include taxes charged for local benefits and improvements that increase the value of the property. They also don't include itemized charges for services (such as trash collection) assessed against specific property or certain people, even if the charge is paid to the taxing authority. For more information about taxes and charges that aren't deductible, see *Real Estate-Related Items You Can't Deduct*, later.

Tenant-shareholders in a cooperative housing corporation. Generally, if you are a tenant-stockholder in a cooperative housing corporation, you can deduct the amount paid to the corporation that represents your share of the real estate taxes the corporation paid or incurred for your dwelling unit. The corporation should provide you with a statement showing your share of the taxes. For more information, see *Special Rules for Cooperatives* in Pub. 530.

Division of real estate taxes between buyers and sellers. If you bought or sold real estate during the year, the real estate taxes must be divided between the buyer and the seller.

The buyer and the seller must divide the real estate taxes according to the number of days in the real property tax year (the period to which the tax is imposed relates) that each owned the property. The seller is treated as paying the taxes up to, but not including, the date of sale. The buyer is treated as paying the taxes beginning with the date of sale. This applies regardless of the lien dates under local law. Generally, this information is included on the settlement statement provided at the closing.

If you (the seller) can't deduct taxes until they are paid because you use the cash method of accounting, and the buyer of your property is personally liable for the tax, you are considered to have paid your part of the tax at the time of the sale. This lets you deduct the part of the tax to the date of sale even though you didn't actually pay it. However, you must also include the amount of that tax in the selling price of the property. The buyer must include the same amount in his or her cost of the property.

You figure your deduction for taxes on each property bought or sold during the real property tax year as follows.

Worksheet 11-1. **Figuring Your State and Local Real Estate Tax Deduction**
Keep for Your Records

1. Enter the total state and local real estate taxes for the real property tax year . . . . _____

2. Enter the number of days in the real property tax year that you owned the property . . . . _____

3. Divide line 2 by 365 (for leap years, divide line 2 by 366) . . . . _____

4. Multiply line 1 by line 3. This is your deduction. Enter it on Schedule A (Form 1040), line 5b . . . . _____

Note. Repeat steps 1 through 4 for each property you bought or sold during the real property tax year. Your total deduction is the sum of the line 4 amounts for all of the properties.

Real estate taxes for prior years. Don't divide delinquent taxes between the buyer and seller if the taxes are for any real property tax year before the one in which the property is sold. Even if the buyer agrees to pay the delinquent taxes, the buyer can't deduct them. The buyer must add them to the cost of the property. The seller can deduct these taxes paid by the buyer. However, the seller must include them in the selling price.

Examples. The following examples illustrate how real estate taxes are divided between buyer and seller.

Example 1. Dennis and Beth White's real property tax year for both their old home and their new home is the calendar year, with payment due August 1. The tax on their old home, sold on May 7, was $620. The tax on their new home, bought on May 3, was $732. Dennis and Beth are considered to have paid a proportionate share of the real estate taxes on the old home even though they didn't actually pay them to the taxing authority. On the other hand, they can claim only a proportionate share of the taxes they paid on their new property even though they paid the entire amount.

Dennis and Beth owned their old home during the real property tax year for 126 days (January 1 to May 6, the day before the sale). They figure their deduction for taxes on their old home as follows.

Worksheet 11-1. **Figuring Your State and Local Real Estate Tax Deduction — Taxes on Old Home**

1. Enter the total state and local real estate taxes for the real property tax year $620

2. Enter the number of days in the real property tax year that you owned the property 126

3. Divide line 2 by 365 (for leap years, divide line 2 by 366) 0.3452

4. Multiply line 1 by line 3. This is your deduction. Enter it on Schedule A (Form 1040), line 5b $214

Since the buyers of their old home paid all of the taxes, Dennis and Beth also include the $214 in the selling price of the old home. (The buyers add the $214 to their cost of the home.)

Dennis and Beth owned their new home during the real property tax year for 243 days

(May 3 to December 31, including their date of purchase). They figure their deduction for taxes on their new home as follows.

Worksheet 11-1. **Figuring Your State and Local Real Estate Tax Deduction — Taxes on New Home**

1. Enter the total state and local real estate taxes for the real property tax year . . . $732

2. Enter the number of days in the real property tax year that you owned the property 243

3. Divide line 2 by 365 (for leap years, divide line 2 by 366) 0.6658

4. Multiply line 1 by line 3. This is your deduction. Enter it on Schedule A (Form 1040), line 5b $487

Since Dennis and Beth paid all of the taxes on the new home, they add $245 ($732 paid less $487 deduction) to their cost of the new home. (The sellers add this $245 to their selling price and deduct the $245 as a real estate tax.)

Dennis and Beth's real estate tax deduction for their old and new homes is the sum of $214 and $487, or $701. They will enter this amount on Schedule A (Form 1040), line 5b.

Example 2. George and Helen Brown bought a new home on May 3, 2022. Their real property tax year for the new home is the calendar year. Real estate taxes for 2021 were assessed in their state on January 1, 2022. The taxes became due on May 31, 2022, and October 31, 2022.

The Browns agreed to pay all taxes due after the date of purchase. Real estate taxes for 2021 were $680. They paid $340 on May 31, 2022, and $340 on October 31, 2022. These taxes were for the 2021 real property tax year. The Browns can't deduct them since they didn't own the property until 2022. Instead, they must add $680 to the cost of their new home.

In January 2023, the Browns receive their 2022 property tax statement for $752, which they will pay in 2023. The Browns owned their new home during the 2022 real property tax year for 243 days (May 3 to December 31). They will figure their 2023 deduction for taxes as follows.

Worksheet 11-1. **Figuring Your State and Local Real Estate Tax Deduction — Taxes on New Home**

1. Enter the total state and local real estate taxes for the real property tax year $752

2. Enter the number of days in the real property tax year that you owned the property 243

3. Divide line 2 by 365 (for leap years, divide line 2 by 366) 0.6658

4. Multiply line 1 by line 3. This is your deduction. Claim it on Schedule A (Form 1040), line 5b $501

The remaining $251 ($752 paid less $501 deduction) of taxes paid in 2023, along with the $680 paid in 2022, is added to the cost of their new home.

Because the taxes up to the date of sale are considered paid by the seller on the date of

sale, the seller is entitled to a 2022 tax deduction of $931. This is the sum of the $680 for 2021 and the $251 for the 122 days the seller owned the home in 2022. The seller must also include the $931 in the selling price when they figure the gain or loss on the sale. The seller should contact the Browns in January 2023 to find out how much real estate tax is due for 2022.

Form 1099-S. For certain sales or exchanges of real estate, the person responsible for closing the sale (generally, the settlement agent) prepares Form 1099-S, Proceeds From Real Estate Transactions, to report certain information to the IRS and to the seller of the property. Box 2 of Form 1099-S is for the gross proceeds from the sale and should include the portion of the seller's real estate tax liability that the buyer will pay after the date of sale. The buyer includes these taxes in the cost basis of the property, and the seller both deducts this amount as a tax paid and includes it in the sales price of the property.

For a real estate transaction that involves a home, any real estate tax the seller paid in advance but that is the liability of the buyer appears on Form 1099-S, box 6. The buyer deducts this amount as a real estate tax, and the seller reduces their real estate tax deduction (or includes it in income) by the same amount. See *Refund (or rebate)*, later.

Taxes placed in escrow. If your monthly mortgage payment includes an amount placed in escrow (put in the care of a third party) for real estate taxes, you may not be able to deduct the total amount placed in escrow. You can deduct only the real estate tax that the third party actually paid to the taxing authority. If the third party doesn't notify you of the amount of real estate tax that was paid for you, contact the third party or the taxing authority to find the proper amount to show on your return.

Tenants by the entirety. If you and your spouse held property as tenants by the entirety and you file separate federal returns, each of you can deduct only the taxes each of you paid on the property.

Divorced individuals. If your divorce or separation agreement states that you must pay the real estate taxes for a home owned by you and your spouse, part of your payments may be deductible as alimony and part as real estate taxes. See *Payments to a third party* in Pub. 504, Divorced or Separated Individuals, for more information.

Ministers' and military housing allowances. If you are a minister or a member of the uniformed services and receive a housing allowance that you can exclude from income, you still can deduct all of the real estate taxes you pay on your home.

Refund (or rebate). If you received a refund or rebate in 2022 of real estate taxes you paid in 2022, you must reduce your deduction by the amount refunded to you. If you received a refund or rebate in 2022 of real estate taxes you deducted in an earlier year, you generally must include the refund or rebate in income in the year you receive it. However, the amount you include in income is limited to the amount of the deduction that reduced your tax in the earlier

Table 11-1. **Which Taxes Can You Deduct?**

Type of Tax	You Can Deduct	You Can't Deduct
Fees and Charges	Fees and charges that are expenses of your trade or business or of producing income.	Fees and charges that aren't expenses of your trade or business or of producing income, such as fees for driver's licenses, car inspections, parking, or charges for water bills (see *Taxes and Fees You Can't Deduct*). Fines and penalties.
Income Taxes	State and local income taxes. Foreign income taxes. Employee contributions to state funds listed under *Contributions to state benefit funds*.	Federal income taxes. Employee contributions to private or voluntary disability plans. State and local general sales taxes if you choose to deduct state and local income taxes.
General Sales Taxes	State and local general sales taxes, including compensating use taxes.	State and local income taxes if you choose to deduct state and local general sales taxes.
Other Taxes	Taxes that are expenses of your trade or business. Taxes on property producing rent or royalty income. One-half of self-employment tax paid.	Federal excise taxes, such as tax on gasoline, that aren't expenses of your trade or business or of producing income. Per capita taxes.
Personal Property Taxes	State and local personal property taxes.	Customs duties that aren't expenses of your trade or business or of producing income.
Real Estate Taxes	State and local real estate taxes. Tenant's share of real estate taxes paid by a cooperative housing corporation.	Real estate taxes that are treated as imposed on someone else (see *Division of real estate taxes between buyers and sellers*). Foreign real estate taxes. Taxes for local benefits (with exceptions). See *Real Estate-Related Items You Can't Deduct*. Trash and garbage pickup fees (with exceptions). See *Real Estate-Related Items You Can't Deduct*. Rent increase due to higher real estate taxes. Homeowners' association charges.

year. For more information, see *Recoveries* in Pub. 525.

Real Estate-Related Items You Can't Deduct

Payments for the following items generally aren't deductible as real estate taxes.

- Taxes for local benefits.
- Itemized charges for services (such as trash and garbage pickup fees).
- Transfer taxes (or stamp taxes).
- Rent increases due to higher real estate taxes.
- Homeowners' association charges.

Taxes for local benefits. Deductible real estate taxes generally don't include taxes charged for local benefits and improvements tending to increase the value of your property. These include assessments for streets, sidewalks, water mains, sewer lines, public parking facilities, and similar improvements. You should increase the basis of your property by the amount of the assessment.

Local benefit taxes are deductible only if they are for maintenance, repair, or interest charges related to those benefits. If only a part of the taxes is for maintenance, repair, or interest, you must be able to show the amount of that part to claim the deduction. If you can't determine what part of the tax is for maintenance, repair, or interest, none of it is deductible.

 Taxes for local benefits may be included in your real estate tax bill. If your taxing authority (or mortgage lender) doesn't furnish you a copy of your real estate tax bill, ask for it. You should use the rules above to determine if the local benefit tax is deductible. Contact the taxing authority if you need additional information about a specific charge on your real estate tax bill.

Itemized charges for services. An itemized charge for services assessed against specific property or certain people isn't a tax, even if the charge is paid to the taxing authority. For example, you can't deduct the charge as a real estate tax if it is:

- A unit fee for the delivery of a service (such as a $5 fee charged for every 1,000 gallons of water you use),

- A periodic charge for a residential service (such as a $20 per month or $240 annual fee charged to each homeowner for trash collection), or

- A flat fee charged for a single service provided by your government (such as a $30 charge for mowing your lawn because it was allowed to grow higher than permitted under your local ordinance).

 You must look at your real estate tax bill to determine if any nondeductible itemized charges, such as those listed above, are included in the bill. If your taxing authority (or mortgage lender) doesn't furnish you a copy of your real estate tax bill, ask for it.

Exception. Service charges used to maintain or improve services (such as trash collection or police and fire protection) are deductible as real estate taxes if:

- The fees or charges are imposed at a like rate against all property in the taxing jurisdiction;

- The funds collected aren't earmarked; instead, they are commingled with general revenue funds; and

• Funds used to maintain or improve services aren't limited to or determined by the amount of these fees or charges collected.

Transfer taxes (or stamp taxes). Transfer taxes and similar taxes and charges on the sale of a personal home aren't deductible. If they are paid by the seller, they are expenses of the sale and reduce the amount realized on the sale. If paid by the buyer, they are included in the cost basis of the property.

Rent increase due to higher real estate taxes. If your landlord increases your rent in the form of a tax surcharge because of increased real estate taxes, you can't deduct the increase as taxes.

Homeowners' association charges. These charges aren't deductible because they are imposed by the homeowners' association, rather than the state or local government.

Personal Property Taxes

Personal property tax is deductible if it is a state or local tax that is:

• Charged on personal property;

• Based only on the value of the personal property; and

• Charged on a yearly basis, even if it is collected more or less than once a year.

A tax that meets the above requirements can be considered charged on personal property even if it is for the exercise of a privilege. For example, a yearly tax based on value qualifies as a personal property tax even if it is called a registration fee and is for the privilege of registering motor vehicles or using them on the highways.

If the tax is partly based on value and partly based on other criteria, it may qualify in part.

Example. Your state charges a yearly motor vehicle registration tax of 1% of value plus 50 cents per hundredweight. You paid $32 based on the value ($1,500) and weight (3,400 lbs.) of your car. You can deduct $15 (1% × $1,500) as a personal property tax because it is based on the value. The remaining $17 ($0.50 × 34), based on the weight, isn't deductible.

Taxes and Fees You Can't Deduct

Many federal, state, and local government taxes aren't deductible because they don't fall within the categories discussed earlier. Other taxes and fees, such as federal income taxes, aren't deductible because the tax law specifically prohibits a deduction for them. See Table 11-1.

Taxes and fees that are generally not deductible include the following items.

• *Employment taxes.* This includes social security, Medicare, and railroad retirement taxes withheld from your pay. However, one-half of self-employment tax you pay is deductible. In addition, the social security

and other employment taxes you pay on the wages of a household worker may be included in medical expenses that you can deduct, or childcare expenses that allow you to claim the child and dependent care credit. For more information, see Pub. 502, Medical and Dental Expenses, and Pub. 503, Child and Dependent Care Expenses.

• *Estate, inheritance, legacy, or succession taxes.* You can deduct the estate tax attributable to income in respect of a decedent if you, as a beneficiary, must include that income in your gross income. In that case, deduct the estate tax on Schedule A (Form 1040), line 16. For more information, see Pub. 559, Survivors, Executors, and Administrators.

• *Federal income taxes.* This includes income taxes withheld from your pay.

• *Fines and penalties.* You can't deduct fines and penalties paid to a government for violation of any law, including related amounts forfeited as collateral deposits.

• *Foreign personal or real property taxes.*

• *Gift taxes.*

• *License fees.* You can't deduct license fees for personal purposes (such as marriage, driver's, and pet license fees).

• *Per capita taxes.* You can't deduct state or local per capita taxes.

Many taxes and fees other than those listed above are also nondeductible, unless they are ordinary and necessary expenses of a business or income-producing activity. For other nondeductible items, see *Real Estate-Related Items You Can't Deduct*, earlier.

Where To Deduct

You deduct taxes on the following schedules.

State and local income taxes. These taxes are deducted on Schedule A (Form 1040), line 5a, even if your only source of income is from business, rents, or royalties.

Limitation on deduction for state and local taxes. The deduction for state and local taxes is limited to $10,000 ($5,000 if married filing married separately). State and local taxes are the taxes that you include on Schedule A (Form 1040), lines 5a, 5b, and 5c. Include taxes imposed by a U.S. possession with your state and local taxes on Schedule A (Form 1040), lines 5a, 5b, and 5c. However, don't include any U.S. possession taxes you paid that are allocable to excluded income.

 You may want to take a credit for U.S. possession tax instead of a deduction. See the instructions for Schedule 3 (Form 1040), line 1, for details.

General sales taxes. Sales taxes are deducted on Schedule A (Form 1040), line 5a. You must check the box on line 5a. If you elect to deduct sales taxes, you can't deduct state and local income taxes on Schedule A (Form 1040), line 5a.

Foreign income taxes. Generally, income taxes you pay to a foreign country or U.S. possession can be claimed as an itemized deduction on Schedule A (Form 1040), line 6, or as a credit against your U.S. income tax on Schedule 3 (Form 1040), line 1. To claim the credit, you may have to complete and attach Form 1116. For more information, see the Instructions for Form 1040 or Pub. 514.

Real estate taxes and personal property taxes. Real estate and personal property taxes are deducted on Schedule A (Form 1040), lines 5b and 5c, respectively, unless they are paid on property used in your business, in which case they are deducted on Schedule C (Form 1040) or Schedule F (Form 1040). Taxes on property that produces rent or royalty income are deducted on Schedule E (Form 1040).

Self-employment tax. Deduct one-half of your self-employment tax on Schedule 1 (Form 1040), line 15.

Other taxes. All other deductible taxes are deducted on Schedule A (Form 1040), line 6.

12.

Other Itemized Deductions

What's New

Standard mileage rate. The 2022 rate for business use of a vehicle is 58.5 cents a mile from January 1, 2022 to June 30, 2022, and 62.5 cents a mile from July 1, 2022 to December 31, 2022.

Reminders

Educator expenses. Educator expenses include amounts paid or incurred after March 12, 2020, for personal protective equipment, disinfectant, and other supplies used for the prevention of the spread of coronavirus. For more information, see the instructions for Schedule 1 (Form 1040), line 11, and *Educator Expenses* in Pub. 529, Miscellaneous Deductions.

No miscellaneous itemized deductions allowed. You can no longer claim any miscellaneous itemized deductions. Miscellaneous itemized deductions are those deductions that would have been subject to the 2%-of-adjusted-gross-income (AGI) limitation. See *Miscellaneous Itemized Deductions*, later.

Fines and penalties. Rules regarding deducting fines and penalties have changed. See *Fines and Penalties*, later.

Introduction

This chapter explains that you can no longer claim any miscellaneous itemized deductions, unless you fall into one of the qualified categories of employment claiming a deduction relating to unreimbursed employee expenses. Miscellaneous itemized deductions are those deductions that would have been subject to the 2%-of-AGI limitation. You can still claim certain expenses as itemized deductions on Schedule A (Form 1040), Schedule A (Form 1040-NR), or as an adjustment to income on Form 1040 or 1040-SR. This chapter covers the following topics.

- Miscellaneous itemized deductions.
- Expenses you can't deduct.
- Expenses you can deduct.
- How to report your deductions.

 You must keep records to verify your deductions. You should keep receipts, canceled checks, substitute checks, financial account statements, and other documentary evidence. For more information on recordkeeping, see *What Records Should I Keep?* in chapter 1.

Useful Items

You may want to see:

Publication

❏ **463** Travel, Gift, and Car Expenses

❏ **525** Taxable and Nontaxable Income

❏ **529** Miscellaneous Deductions

❏ **535** Business Expenses

❏ **547** Casualties, Disasters, and Thefts

❏ **575** Pension and Annuity Income

❏ **587** Business Use of Your Home

❏ **946** How To Depreciate Property

Form (and Instructions)

❏ **Schedule A (Form 1040)** Itemized Deductions

❏ **2106** Employee Business Expenses

❏ **8839** Qualified Adoption Expenses

❏ **Schedule K-1 (Form 1041)** Beneficiary's Share of Income, Deductions, Credits, etc.

For these and other useful items, go to *IRS.gov/Forms*.

Miscellaneous Itemized Deductions

You can no longer claim any miscellaneous itemized deductions that are subject to the 2%-of-AGI limitation, including unreimbursed employee expenses. However, you may be able to deduct certain unreimbursed employee business expenses if you fall into one of the following categories of employment listed under *Unreimbursed Employee Expenses* next.

Unreimbursed Employee Expenses

You can no longer claim a deduction for unreimbursed employee expenses unless you fall into one of the following categories of employment.

- Armed Forces reservists.
- Qualified performing artists.
- Fee-basis state or local government officials.
- Employees with impairment-related work expenses.

Categories of Employment

You can deduct unreimbursed employee expenses only if you qualify as an Armed Forces reservist, a qualified performing artist, a fee-basis state or local government official, or an employee with impairment-related work expenses.

Armed Forces reservist (member of a reserve component). You are a member of a reserve component of the Armed Forces of the United States if you are in the Army, Navy, Marine Corps, Air Force, or Coast Guard Reserve; the Army National Guard of the United States; or the Reserve Corps of the Public Health Service.

Qualified performing artist. You are a qualified performing artist if you:

1. Performed services in the performing arts as an employee for at least two employers during the tax year,

2. Received from at least two of the employers wages of $200 or more per employer,

3. Had allowable business expenses attributable to the performing arts of more than 10% of gross income from the performing arts, and

4. Had AGI of $16,000 or less before deducting expenses as a performing artist.

Fee-basis state or local government official. You are a qualifying fee-basis official if you are employed by a state or political subdivision of a state and are compensated, in whole or in part, on a fee basis.

Employee with impairment-related work expenses. Impairment-related work expenses are the allowable expenses of an individual with physical or mental disabilities for attendant care at their place of employment. They also include other expenses in connection with the place of employment that enable the employee to work. See Pub. 463, Travel, Gift, and Car Expenses, for more details.

Allowable unreimbursed employee expenses. If you qualify as an employee in one of the categories mentioned above, you may be able to deduct the following items as unreimbursed employee expenses.

Unreimbursed employee expenses for individuals in these categories of employment are deducted as adjustments to gross income. Qualified employees listed in one of the categories above must complete Form 2106, Employee Business Expenses, to take the deduction.

You can deduct only unreimbursed employee expenses that are paid or incurred during your tax year, for carrying on your trade or business of being an employee, and ordinary and necessary.

An expense is ordinary if it's common and accepted in your trade, business, or profession. An expense is necessary if it's appropriate and helpful to your business. An expense doesn't have to be required to be considered necessary.

Educator Expenses

If you were an eligible educator in 2022, you can deduct up to $300 of qualified expenses you paid in 2022 as an adjustment to gross income on Schedule 1 (Form 1040), line 11, rather than as a miscellaneous itemized deduction. If you and your spouse are filing jointly and both of you were eligible educators, the maximum deduction is $600. However, neither spouse can deduct more than $300 of their qualified expenses. For additional information, see *Educator Expenses* in Pub. 529, Miscellaneous Deductions.

 Educator expenses include amounts paid or incurred after March 12, 2020, for personal protective equipment, disinfectant, and other supplies used for the prevention of the spread of coronavirus. For more information, see the instructions for Schedule 1 (Form 1040), line 11, and Educator Expenses *in Pub. 529, Miscellaneous Deductions.*

Expenses You Can't Deduct

Because of the suspension of miscellaneous itemized deductions, there are two categories of expenses you can't deduct: miscellaneous itemized deductions subject to the 2%-of-AGI limitation, and those expenses that are traditionally nondeductible under the Internal Revenue Code. Both categories of deduction are discussed next.

Miscellaneous Deductions Subject to 2% AGI

Unless you fall into one of the qualified categories of employment under *Unreimbursed Employee Expenses*, earlier, miscellaneous itemized deductions that are subject to the 2%-of-AGI limitation can no longer be claimed. For expenses not related to unreimbursed employee expenses, you generally can't deduct the following expenses, even if you fall into one of the qualified categories of employment listed earlier.

Appraisal Fees

Appraisal fees you pay to figure a casualty loss or the fair market value of donated property are miscellaneous itemized deductions and can no longer be deducted.

Casualty and Theft Losses

Damaged or stolen property used in performing services as an employee is a miscellaneous deduction and can no longer be deducted. For other casualty and theft losses, see Pub. 547, Casualties, Disasters, and Thefts.

Clerical Help and Office Rent

Office expenses, such as rent and clerical help, you pay in connection with your investments and collecting taxable income on those investments are miscellaneous itemized deductions and are no longer deductible.

Credit or Debit Card Convenience Fees

The convenience fee charged by the card processor for paying your income tax (including estimated tax payments) by credit or debit card is a miscellaneous itemized deduction and is no longer deductible.

Depreciation on Home Computer

If you use your home computer to produce income (for example, to manage your investments that produce taxable income), the depreciation of the computer for that part of the usage of the computer is a miscellaneous itemized deduction and is no longer deductible.

Fees To Collect Interest and Dividends

Fees you pay to a broker, bank, trustee, or similar agent to collect your taxable bond interest or dividends on shares of stock are miscellaneous itemized deductions and can no longer be deducted.

Hobby Expenses

A hobby isn't a business because it isn't carried on to make a profit. Hobby expenses are miscellaneous itemized deductions and can no longer be deducted. See *Not-for-Profit Activities* in chapter 1 of Pub. 535, Business Expenses.

Indirect Deductions of Pass-Through Entities

Pass-through entities include partnerships, S corporations, and mutual funds that aren't publicly offered. Deductions of pass-through entities are passed through to the partners or shareholders. The partner's or shareholder's share of passed-through deductions for investment expenses are miscellaneous itemized deductions and can no longer be deducted.

Nonpublicly offered mutual funds. These funds will send you a Form 1099-DIV, Dividends and Distributions, or a substitute form, showing your share of gross income and investment expenses. The investment expenses reported on Form 1099-DIV are a miscellaneous itemized deduction and are no longer deductible.

Investment Fees and Expenses

Investment fees, custodial fees, trust administration fees, and other expenses you paid for managing your investments that produce taxable income are miscellaneous itemized deductions and are no longer deductible.

Legal Expenses

You can usually deduct legal expenses that you incur in attempting to produce or collect taxable income or that you pay in connection with the determination, collection, or refund of any tax.

Legal expenses that you incur in attempting to produce or collect taxable income, or that you pay in connection with the determination, collection, or refund of any tax are miscellaneous itemized deductions and are no longer deductible.

You can deduct expenses of resolving tax issues relating to profit or loss from business reported on Schedule C (Form 1040), Profit or Loss From Business, from rentals or royalties reported on Schedule E (Form 1040), Supplemental Income and Loss, or from farm income and expenses reported on Schedule F (Form 1040), Profit or Loss From Farming, on that schedule. Expenses for resolving nonbusiness tax issues are miscellaneous itemized deductions and are no longer deductible.

Loss on Deposits

For information on whether, and if so, how, you may deduct a loss on your deposit in a qualified financial institution, see *Loss on Deposits* in Pub. 547.

Repayments of Income

Generally, repayments of amounts that you included in income in an earlier year is a miscellaneous itemized deduction and can no longer be deducted. If you had to repay more than $3,000 that you included in your income in an earlier year, you may be able to deduct the amount. See *Repayments Under Claim of Right*, later.

Repayments of Social Security Benefits

For information on how to deduct your repayments of certain social security benefits, see *Repayments More Than Gross Benefits* in chapter 7.

Safe Deposit Box Rent

Rent you pay for a safe deposit box you use to store taxable income-producing stocks, bonds, or investment-related papers is a miscellaneous itemized deduction and can no longer be deducted. You also can't deduct the rent if you use the box for jewelry, other personal items, or tax-exempt securities.

Service Charges on Dividend Reinvestment Plans

Service charges you pay as a subscriber in a dividend reinvestment plan are a miscellaneous

itemized deduction and can no longer be deducted. These service charges include payments for:

- Holding shares acquired through a plan,
- Collecting and reinvesting cash dividends, and
- Keeping individual records and providing detailed statements of accounts.

Tax Preparation Fees

Tax preparation fees on the return for the year in which you pay them are a miscellaneous itemized deduction and can no longer be deducted. These fees include the cost of tax preparation software programs and tax publications. They also include any fee you paid for electronic filing of your return.

Trustee's Administrative Fees for IRA

Trustee's administrative fees that are billed separately and paid by you in connection with your IRA are a miscellaneous itemized deduction and can no longer be deducted. For more information about IRAs, see chapter 9.

Nondeductible Expenses

In addition to the miscellaneous itemized deductions discussed earlier, you can't deduct the following expenses.

List of Nondeductible Expenses

- Adoption expenses.
- Broker's commissions.
- Burial or funeral expenses, including the cost of a cemetery lot.
- Campaign expenses.
- Capital expenses.
- Check-writing fees.
- Club dues.
- Commuting expenses.
- Fees and licenses, such as car licenses, marriage licenses, and dog tags.
- Fines or penalties.
- Health spa expenses.
- Hobby losses, but see *Hobby Expenses*, earlier.
- Home repairs, insurance, and rent.
- Home security system.
- Illegal bribes and kickbacks. See *Bribes and kickbacks* in chapter 11 of Pub. 535.
- Investment-related seminars.
- Life insurance premiums paid by the insured.
- Lobbying expenses.
- Losses from the sale of your home, furniture, personal car, etc.
- Lost or misplaced cash or property.

- Lunches with co-workers.
- Meals while working late.
- Medical expenses as business expenses other than medical examinations required by your employer.
- Personal disability insurance premiums.
- Personal legal expenses.
- Personal, living, or family expenses.
- Political contributions.
- Professional accreditation fees.
- Professional reputation improvement expense.
- Relief fund contributions.
- Residential telephone line.
- Stockholders' meeting attendance expenses.
- Tax-exempt income earning/collecting expenses.
- The value of wages never received or lost vacation time.
- Travel expenses for another individual.
- Voluntary unemployment benefit fund contributions.
- Wristwatches.

Adoption Expenses

You can't deduct the expenses of adopting a child, but you may be able to take a credit for those expenses. See the Instructions for Form 8839, Qualified Adoption Expenses, for more information.

Campaign Expenses

You can't deduct campaign expenses of a candidate for any office, even if the candidate is running for reelection to the office. These include qualification and registration fees for primary elections.

Legal fees. You can't deduct legal fees paid to defend charges that arise from participation in a political campaign.

Check-Writing Fees on Personal Account

If you have a personal checking account, you can't deduct fees charged by the bank for the privilege of writing checks, even if the account pays interest.

Club Dues

Generally, you can't deduct the cost of membership in any club organized for business, pleasure, recreation, or other social purpose. This includes business, social, athletic, luncheon, sporting, airline, hotel, golf, and country clubs.

You can't deduct dues paid to an organization if one of its main purposes is to:

- Conduct entertainment activities for members or their guests, or
- Provide members or their guests with access to entertainment facilities.

Dues paid to airline, hotel, and luncheon clubs aren't deductible.

Commuting Expenses

You can't deduct commuting expenses (the cost of transportation between your home and your main or regular place of work). If you haul tools, instruments, or other items in your car to and from work, you can deduct only the additional cost of hauling the items such as the rent on a trailer to carry the items.

Fines and Penalties

Generally, no deduction is allowed for fines and penalties paid to a government or specified nongovernmental entity for the violation of any law except in the following situations.

- Amounts that constitute restitution.
- Amounts paid to come into compliance with the law.
- Amounts paid or incurred as the result of certain court orders in which no government or specified nongovernmental agency is a party.
- Amounts paid or incurred for taxes due.

Nondeductible amounts include an amount paid in settlement of your actual or potential liability for a fine or penalty (civil or criminal). Fines or penalties include amounts paid such as parking tickets, tax penalties, and penalties deducted from teachers' paychecks after an illegal strike.

No deduction is allowed for the restitution amount or amount paid to come into compliance with the law unless the amounts are specifically identified in the settlement agreement or court order. Also, any amount paid or incurred as reimbursement to the government for the costs of any investigation or litigation are not eligible for the exceptions and are nondeductible.

Health Spa Expenses

You can't deduct health spa expenses, even if there is a job requirement to stay in excellent physical condition, such as might be required of a law enforcement officer.

Home Security System

You can't deduct the cost of a home security system as a miscellaneous deduction. However, you may be able to claim a deduction for a home security system as a business expense if you have a home office. See *Security system* under *Figuring the Deduction* in Pub. 587.

Investment-Related Seminars

You can't deduct any expenses for attending a convention, seminar, or similar meeting for investment purposes.

Life Insurance Premiums

You can't deduct premiums you pay on your life insurance. You may be able to deduct, as alimony, premiums you pay on life insurance policies assigned to your former spouse. See Pub. 504, Divorced or Separated Individuals, for information on alimony.

Lobbying Expenses

You generally can't deduct amounts paid or incurred for lobbying expenses. These include expenses to:

- Influence legislation;
- Participate or intervene in any political campaign for, or against, any candidate for public office;
- Attempt to influence the general public, or segments of the public, about elections, legislative matters, or referendums; or
- Communicate directly with covered executive branch officials in any attempt to influence the official actions or positions of those officials.

Lobbying expenses also include any amounts paid or incurred for research, preparation, planning, or coordination of any of these activities.

Dues used for lobbying. If a tax-exempt organization notifies you that part of the dues or other amounts you pay to the organization are used to pay nondeductible lobbying expenses, you can't deduct that part. See *Lobbying Expenses* in Pub. 529 for information on exceptions.

Lost or Mislaid Cash or Property

You can't deduct a loss based on the mere disappearance of money or property. However, an accidental loss or disappearance of property can qualify as a casualty if it results from an identifiable event that is sudden, unexpected, or unusual. See Pub. 547 for more information.

Lunches With Co-Workers

You can't deduct the expenses of lunches with co-workers, except while traveling away from home on business. See Pub. 463 for information on deductible expenses while traveling away from home.

Meals While Working Late

You can't deduct the cost of meals while working late. However, you may be able to claim a deduction if the cost of meals is a deductible entertainment expense, or if you're traveling away from home. See Pub. 463 for information on deductible entertainment expenses and expenses while traveling away from home.

Personal Legal Expenses

You can't deduct personal legal expenses such as those for the following.

- Custody of children.
- Breach of promise to marry suit.
- Civil or criminal charges resulting from a personal relationship.
- Damages for personal injury, except for certain unlawful discrimination and whistle-blower claims.
- Preparation of a title (or defense or perfection of a title).
- Preparation of a will.
- Property claims or property settlement in a divorce.

You can't deduct these expenses even if a result of the legal proceeding is the loss of income-producing property.

Political Contributions

You can't deduct contributions made to a political candidate, a campaign committee, or a newsletter fund. Advertisements in convention bulletins and admissions to dinners or programs that benefit a political party or political candidate aren't deductible.

Professional Accreditation Fees

You can't deduct professional accreditation fees such as the following.

- Accounting certificate fees paid for the initial right to practice accounting.
- Bar exam fees and incidental expenses in securing initial admission to the bar.
- Medical and dental license fees paid to get initial licensing.

Professional Reputation

You can't deduct expenses of radio and TV appearances to increase your personal prestige or establish your professional reputation.

Relief Fund Contributions

You can't deduct contributions paid to a private plan that pays benefits to any covered employee who can't work because of any injury or illness not related to the job.

Residential Telephone Service

You can't deduct any charge (including taxes) for basic local telephone service for the first telephone line to your residence, even if it's used in a trade or business.

Stockholders' Meetings

You can't deduct transportation and other expenses you pay to attend stockholders' meetings of companies in which you own stock but have no other interest. You can't deduct these expenses even if you're attending the meeting to get information that would be useful in making further investments.

Tax-Exempt Income Expenses

You can't deduct expenses to produce tax-exempt income. You can't deduct interest on a debt incurred or continued to buy or carry tax-exempt securities.

If you have expenses to produce both taxable and tax-exempt income, but you can't identify the expenses that produce each type of income, you must divide the expenses based on the amount of each type of income to determine the amount that you can deduct.

Travel Expenses for Another Individual

You generally can't deduct travel expenses you pay or incur for a spouse, dependent, or other individual who accompanies you (or your employee) on business or personal travel unless the spouse, dependent, or other individual is an employee of the taxpayer, the travel is for a bona fide business purpose, and such expenses would otherwise be deductible by the spouse, dependent, or other individual. See Pub. 463 for more information on deductible travel expenses.

Voluntary Unemployment Benefit Fund Contributions

You can't deduct voluntary unemployment benefit fund contributions you make to a union fund or a private fund. However, you can deduct contributions as taxes if state law requires you to make them to a state unemployment fund that covers you for the loss of wages from unemployment caused by business conditions.

Wristwatches

You can't deduct the cost of a wristwatch, even if there is a job requirement that you know the correct time to properly perform your duties.

Expenses You Can Deduct

You can deduct the items listed below as itemized deductions. Report these items on Schedule A (Form 1040), line 16, or Schedule A (Form 1040-NR), line 7.

List of Deductions

Each of the following items is discussed in detail after the list (except where indicated).

- Amortizable premium on taxable bonds.
- Casualty and theft losses from income-producing property.
- Excess deductions of an estate or trust.
- Federal estate tax on income in respect of a decedent.
- Gambling losses up to the amount of gambling winnings.
- Impairment-related work expenses of persons with disabilities.
- Losses from Ponzi-type investment schemes (see Pub. 547 for more information).
- Repayments of more than $3,000 under a claim of right.
- Unlawful discrimination claims.
- Unrecovered investment in an annuity.

Amortizable Premium on Taxable Bonds

In general, if the amount you pay for a bond is greater than its stated principal amount, the excess is bond premium. You can elect to amortize the premium on taxable bonds. The amortization of the premium is generally an offset to interest income on the bond rather than a separate deduction item.

Part of the premium on some bonds may be an itemized deduction on Schedule A (Form 1040). For more information, see *Amortizable Premium on Taxable Bonds* in Pub. 529, and *Bond Premium Amortization* in chapter 3 of Pub. 550, Investment Income and Expenses.

Casualty and Theft Losses of Income-Producing Property

You can deduct a casualty or theft loss as an itemized deduction on Schedule A (Form 1040), line 16, if the damaged or stolen property was income-producing property (property held for investment, such as stocks, notes, bonds, gold, silver, vacant lots, and works of art). First, report the loss in Form 4684, Section B. You may also have to include the loss on Form 4797 if you're otherwise required to file that form. To figure your deduction, add all casualty or theft losses from this type of property included on Form 4684, lines 32 and 38b, or Form 4797, line 18a. For more information on casualty and theft losses, see Pub. 547.

Excess Deductions of an Estate or Trust

Generally, if an estate or trust has an excess deduction resulting from total deductions being greater than its gross income, in the estate's or trust's last tax year, a beneficiary can deduct the excess deductions, depending on its character. The excess deductions retain their character as an adjustment to arrive at adjusted gross income on Schedule 1 (Form 1040), as a non-miscellaneous itemized deduction reported on Schedule A (Form 1040), or as a miscellaneous itemized deduction. For more information on excess deductions of an estate or trust, see the Instructions for Schedule K-1 (Form 1041) for a Beneficiary Filing Form 1040.

Federal Estate Tax on Income in Respect of a Decedent

You can deduct the federal estate tax attributable to income in respect of a decedent that you as a beneficiary include in your gross income. Income in respect of the decedent is gross income that the decedent would have received had death not occurred and that wasn't properly includible in the decedent's final income tax return. See Pub. 559, Survivors, Executors, and Administrators, for more information.

Gambling Losses up to the Amount of Gambling Winnings

You must report the full amount of your gambling winnings for the year on Schedule 1 (Form 1040), line 8b. You deduct your gambling losses for the year on Schedule A (Form 1040), line 16. You can't deduct gambling losses that are more than your winnings.

 You can't reduce your gambling winnings by your gambling losses and report the difference. You must report the full amount of your winnings as income and claim your losses (up to the amount of winnings) as an itemized deduction. Therefore, your records should show your winnings separately from your losses.

 Diary of winnings and losses. You must keep an accurate diary or similar record of your losses and winnings.

Your diary should contain at least the following information.

- The date and type of your specific wager or wagering activity.
- The name and address or location of the gambling establishment.
- The names of other persons present with you at the gambling establishment.
- The amount(s) you won or lost.

See Pub. 529 for more information.

Impairment-Related Work Expenses

If you have a physical or mental disability that limits your being employed, or substantially limits one or more of your major life activities, such as performing manual tasks, walking, speaking, breathing, learning, and working, you can deduct your impairment-related work expenses.

Impairment-related work expenses are ordinary and necessary business expenses for attendant care services at your place of work and for other expenses in connection with your place of work that are necessary for you to be able to work.

Self-employed. If you're self-employed, enter your impairment-related work expenses on the appropriate form (Schedule C (Form 1040), Schedule E (Form 1040), or Schedule F (Form 1040)) used to report your business income and expenses.

Repayments Under Claim of Right

If you had to repay more than $3,000 that you included in your income in an earlier year because at the time you thought you had an unrestricted right to it, you may be able to deduct the amount you repaid or take a credit against your tax. See *Repayments* in chapter 8 for more information.

Unlawful Discrimination Claims

You may be able to deduct, as an adjustment to income on Schedule 1 (Form 1040), line 24h, attorney fees and court costs for actions settled or decided after October 22, 2004, involving a claim of unlawful discrimination, a claim against the U.S. Government, or a claim made under section 1862(b)(3)(A) of the Social Security Act. However, the amount you can deduct on Schedule 1 (Form 1040), line 24h, is limited to the amount of the judgment or settlement you are including in income for the tax year. See Pub. 525, Taxable and Nontaxable Income, for more information.

Unrecovered Investment in Annuity

A retiree who contributed to the cost of an annuity can exclude from income a part of each payment received as a tax-free return of the retiree's investment. If the retiree dies before the entire investment is recovered tax free, any unrecovered investment can be deducted on the retiree's final income tax return. See Pub. 575, Pension and Annuity Income, for more information about the tax treatment of pensions and annuities.

Part Four.

Figuring Your Taxes, and Refundable and Nonrefundable Credits

The two chapters in this part explain how to figure your tax. They also discuss tax credits that, unlike deductions, are subtracted directly from your tax and reduce your tax dollar for dollar.

The Form 1040 and 1040-SR schedules that are discussed in these chapters are:

- Schedule 1, Additional Income and Adjustments to Income;
- Schedule 2, Additional Taxes; and
- Schedule 3, Additional Credits and Payments.

13.

How To Figure Your Tax

Introduction

After you have figured your income and deductions your next step is to figure your tax. This chapter discusses:

- The general steps you take to figure your tax,
- An additional tax you may have to pay called the alternative minimum tax (AMT), and
- The conditions you must meet if you want the IRS to figure your tax.

Useful Items

You may want to see:

Publication

- ❏ **503** Child and Dependent Care Expenses
- ❏ **505** Tax Withholding and Estimated Tax
- ❏ **524** Credit for the Elderly or Disabled
- ❏ **525** Taxable and Nontaxable Income
- ❏ **531** Reporting Tip Income
- ❏ **550** Investment Income and Expenses
- ❏ **560** Retirement Plans for Small Business (SEP, SIMPLE, and Qualified Plans)
- ❏ **575** Pension and Annuity Income
- ❏ **596** Earned Income Credit (EIC)
- ❏ **926** Household Employer's Tax Guide
- ❏ **929** Tax Rules for Children and Dependents
- ❏ **969** Health Savings Accounts and Other Tax-Favored Health Plans
- ❏ **970** Tax Benefits for Education

- ❏ **974** Premium Tax Credit (PTC)

Form (and Instructions)

- ❏ **W-2** Wage and Tax Statement
- ❏ **Schedule SE (Form 1040)** Self-Employment Tax
- ❏ **Schedule 8812 (Form 1040)** Credits for Qualifying Children and Other Dependents
- ❏ **1116** Foreign Tax Credit
- ❏ **3800** General Business Credit
- ❏ **4136** Credit for Federal Tax Paid on Fuels
- ❏ **4970** Tax on Accumulation Distribution of Trusts
- ❏ **5329** Additional Taxes on Qualified Plans (Including IRAs) and Other Tax-Favored Accounts
- ❏ **5405** Repayment of the First-Time Homebuyer Credit
- ❏ **5695** Residential Energy Credit
- ❏ **5884** Work Opportunity Credit
- ❏ **8396** Mortgage Interest Credit
- ❏ **8801** Credit for Prior Year Minimum Tax—Individuals, Estates, and Trusts
- ❏ **8835** Renewable Electricity Production Credit
- ❏ **8839** Qualified Adoption Expenses
- ❏ **8846** Credit for Employer Social Security and Medicare Taxes Paid on Certain Employee Tips
- ❏ **8853** Archer MSAs and Long-Term Care Insurance Contracts
- ❏ **8880** Credit for Qualified Retirement Savings Contributions
- ❏ **8889** Health Savings Accounts (HSAs)
- ❏ **8910** Alternative Motor Vehicle Credit
- ❏ **8912** Credit to Holders of Tax Credit Bonds
- ❏ **8936** Qualified Plug-In Electric Drive Motor Vehicle Credit (Including Qualified Two-Wheeled Plug-In Electric Vehicle)

- ❏ **8959** Additional Medicare Tax
- ❏ **8960** Net Investment Income Tax—Individuals, Estates, and Trusts
- ❏ **8962** Premium Tax Credit (PTC)

Figuring Your Tax

Your income tax is based on your taxable income. After you figure your income tax and AMT, if any, subtract your tax credits and add any other taxes you may owe. The result is your total tax. Compare your total tax with your total payments to determine whether you are entitled to a refund or must make a payment.

This section provides a general outline of how to figure your tax. You can find step-by-step directions in the Instructions for Form 1040.

Tax. Most taxpayers use either the Tax Table or the Tax Computation Worksheet to figure their income tax. However, there are special methods if your income includes any of the following items.

- A net capital gain. See Pub. 550.
- Qualified dividends taxed at the same rates as a net capital gain. See Pub. 550.
- Lump-sum distributions. See Pub. 575.
- Farming or fishing income. See Schedule J (Form 1040).
- Tax for certain children who have unearned income. See Pub. 929.
- Parent's election to report child's interest and dividends. See Pub. 929.
- Foreign earned income exclusion or the housing exclusion. (See Form 2555, Foreign Earned Income, and the Foreign Earned Income Tax Worksheet in the Instructions for Form 1040.)

Credits. After you figure your income tax and any AMT (discussed later), determine if you are eligible for any tax credits. Eligibility information for these tax credits is discussed in other publications and your form instructions. The following items are some of the credits you may be able to subtract from your tax and shows where you can find more information on each credit.

- Adoption credit. See Form 8839.

- Alternative motor vehicle credit. See Form 8910.
- Child and dependent care credit. See Pub. 503.
- Child tax credit. See Schedule 8812 (Form 1040).
- Credit for employer social security and Medicare taxes paid on certain employee tips. See Form 8846.
- Credit to holders of tax credit bonds. See Form 8912.
- Education credit. See Pub. 970.
- Elderly or disabled credit. See Pub. 524.
- Foreign tax credit. See Form 1116.
- General business credit. See Form 3800.
- Mortgage interest credit. See Form 8396.
- Plug-in electric drive motor credit. See Form 8936.
- Premium tax credit. See Pub. 974.
- Prior year minimum tax credit. See Form 8801.
- Renewable electricity production credit. See Form 8835.
- Residential clean energy credit. See Form 5695.
- Retirement savings contribution credit. See Form 8880.
- Work opportunity credit. See Form 5884.

Some credits (such as the earned income credit) aren't listed because they are treated as payments. See *Payments*, later.

Other taxes. After you subtract your tax credits, determine whether there are any other taxes you must pay. This chapter doesn't explain these other taxes. You can find that information in other publications and your form instructions. See the following list for other taxes you may need to add to your income tax.

- Additional Medicare tax. See Form 8959.
- Additional tax on ABLE accounts. See Pub. 969.
- Additional tax on Archer MSAs and long-term care insurance contracts. See Form 8853.
- Additional tax on Coverdell ESAs. See Form 5329.
- Additional tax on HSAs. See Form 8889.
- Additional tax on income you received from a nonqualified deferred compensation plan that fails to meet certain requirements. See the Instructions for Form 1040.
- Additional tax on qualified plans and other tax-favored accounts. See Form 5329.
- Additional tax on qualified retirement plans and IRAs. See Form 5329.
- Additional tax on qualified tuition programs. See Pub. 970.
- Excise tax on insider stock compensation from an expatriated corporation. See the Instructions for Form 1040.
- Household employment taxes. See Pub. 926.

- Interest on the deferred tax on gain from certain installment sales with a sales price over $150,000. See the Instructions for Form 1040.
- Interest on the tax due on installment income from the sale of certain residential lots and timeshares. See the Instructions for Form 1040.
- Net investment income tax. See Form 8960.
- Recapture of an education credit. See Pub. 970.
- Recapture of other credits. See the Instructions for Form 1040.
- Repayment of first-time homebuyer credit. See Form 5405.
- Section 72(m)(5) excess benefits tax. See Pub. 560.
- Self-employment tax. See the Schedule SE (Form 1040).
- Social security and Medicare tax on tips. See Pub. 531.
- Social security and Medicare tax on wages. See Pub. 525.
- Tax on accumulation distribution of trusts. See Form 4970.
- Tax on golden parachute payments. See the Instructions for Form 1040.
- Uncollected social security and Medicare tax on group-term life insurance. See Form W-2.
- Uncollected social security and Medicare tax on tips. See Pub. 531.

You may also have to pay AMT (discussed later in this chapter).

Payments. After you determine your total tax, figure the total payments you have already made for the year. Include credits that are treated as payments. This chapter doesn't explain these payments and credits. You can find that information in other publications and your form instructions. See the following list of payments and credits that you may be able to include in your total payments.

- American opportunity credit. See Pub. 970.
- Additional child tax credit. See Schedule 8812 (Form 1040).
- Credit for federal tax on fuels. See Form 4136.
- Credit for tax on undistributed capital gain. See the Instructions for Form 1040.
- Earned income credit. See Pub. 596.
- Estimated tax paid. See Pub. 505.
- Excess social security and RRTA tax withheld. See the Instructions for Form 1040.
- Federal income tax withheld. See Pub. 505.
- Net premium tax credit. See the Instructions for Form 8962 or the Instructions for Form 1040.
- Qualified sick and family leave credits. See the Instructions for Form 1040.
- Tax paid with extension. See the Instructions for Form 1040.

Refund or balance due. To determine whether you are entitled to a refund or whether you must make a payment, compare your total payments with your total tax. If you are entitled to a refund, see your form instructions for information on having it directly deposited into one or more of your accounts (including a traditional IRA, Roth IRA, or a SEP-IRA), or to purchase U.S. savings bonds instead of receiving a paper check.

Alternative Minimum Tax (AMT)

This section briefly discusses an additional tax you may have to pay.

The tax law gives special treatment to some kinds of income and allows special deductions and credits for some kinds of expenses. Taxpayers who benefit from this special treatment may have to pay at least a minimum amount of tax through an additional tax called AMT.

You may have to pay the AMT if your taxable income for regular tax purposes, combined with certain adjustments and tax preference items, is more than a certain amount. See Form 6251, Alternative Minimum Tax—Individuals.

Adjustments and tax preference items. The more common adjustments and tax preference items include:

- Addition of the standard deduction (if claimed);
- Addition of itemized deductions claimed for state and local taxes and certain interest;
- Subtraction of any refund of state and local taxes included in gross income;
- Changes to accelerated depreciation of certain property;
- Difference between gain or loss on the sale of property reported for regular tax purposes and AMT purposes;
- Addition of certain income from incentive stock options;
- Change in certain passive activity loss deductions;
- Addition of certain depletion that is more than the adjusted basis of the property;
- Addition of part of the deduction for certain intangible drilling costs; and
- Addition of tax-exempt interest on certain private activity bonds.

More information. For more information about the AMT, see the Instructions for Form 6251.

Tax Figured by IRS

If you file by the due date of your return (not counting extensions) — April 18, 2023, for most people — you can have the IRS figure your tax for you on Form 1040 or 1040-SR.

If the IRS figures your tax and you paid too much, you will receive a refund. If you didn't pay enough, you will receive a bill for the balance. To avoid interest or the penalty for late payment, you must pay the bill within 30 days of the date of the bill or by the due date for your return, whichever is later.

The IRS can also figure the credit for the elderly or the disabled and the earned income credit for you.

When the IRS cannot figure your tax. The IRS can't figure your tax for you if any of the following apply.

1. You want your refund directly deposited into your checking or savings account.

2. You want any part of your refund applied to your 2023 estimated tax.

3. You had income for the year from sources other than wages, salaries, tips, interest, dividends, taxable social security benefits, unemployment compensation, IRA distributions, pensions, and annuities.

4. Your taxable income is $100,000 or more.

5. You itemize deductions.

6. You file any of the following forms.

   a. Form 2555, Foreign Earned Income.

   b. Form 4137, Social Security and Medicare Tax on Unreported Tip Income.

   c. Form 4970, Tax on Accumulation Distribution of Trusts.

   d. Form 4972, Tax on Lump-Sum Distributions.

   e. Form 6198, At-Risk Limitations.

   f. Form 6251, Alternative Minimum Tax—Individuals.

   g. Form 8606, Nondeductible IRAs.

   h. Form 8615, Tax for Certain Children Who Have Unearned Income.

   i. Form 8814, Parents' Election To Report Child's Interest and Dividends.

   j. Form 8839, Qualified Adoption Expenses.

   k. Form 8853, Archer MSAs and Long-Term Care Insurance Contracts.

   l. Form 8889, Health Savings Accounts (HSAs).

   m. Form 8919, Uncollected Social Security and Medicare Tax on Wages.

Filing the Return

After you complete the line entries for the tax form you are filing, fill in your name and address. Enter your social security number in the space provided. If you are married, enter the social security numbers of you and your spouse, even if you file separately. Sign and date your return and enter your occupation(s). If you are filing a joint return, both you and your spouse must sign it. Enter your daytime phone number in the space provided. This may help speed the processing of your return if we have a question that can be answered over the phone. If you are filing a joint return, you may enter either your or your spouse's daytime phone number.

If you want to allow your preparer, a friend, a family member, or any other person you choose

to discuss your 2022 tax return with the IRS, check the "Yes" box in the "Third Party Designee" area on your return. Also, enter the designee's name, phone number, and any five digits the designee chooses as their personal identification number (PIN). If you check the "Yes" box, you, and your spouse if filing a joint return, are authorizing the IRS to call the designee to answer any questions that may arise during the processing of your return.

Fill in and attach any schedules and forms asked for on the lines you completed to your paper return. Attach a copy of each of your Forms W-2 to your paper return. Also, attach to your paper return any Form 1099-R you received that has withholding tax in box 4.

Mail your return to the Internal Revenue Service Center for the area where you live. A list of Service Center addresses is in the instructions for your tax return.

Form 1040 or 1040-SR Line Entries

If you want the IRS to figure your tax. Read Form 1040 or 1040-SR, lines 1 through 15, and Schedule 1 (Form 1040), if applicable. Fill in the lines that apply to you and attach Schedule 1 (Form 1040), if applicable. Don't complete Form 1040 or 1040-SR, line 16 or 17.

If you are filing a joint return, use the space on the dotted line next to the words "Adjusted Gross Income" on the first page of your return to separately show your taxable income and your spouse's taxable income.

Read Form 1040 or 1040-SR, lines 19 through 33, and Schedules 2 and 3 (Form 1040), if applicable. Fill in the lines that apply to you and attach Schedules 2 and 3 (Form 1040), if applicable. Don't fill in Form 1040 or 1040-SR, lines 22, 24, 33, or 34 through 38. Don't fill in Schedule 2 (Form 1040), line 1 or 3. Also, don't complete Schedule 3 (Form 1040), line 6d, if you are completing Schedule R (Form 1040), or Form 1040 or 1040-SR, line 27, if you want the IRS to figure the credits shown on those lines.

Payments. If you have federal income tax withheld that is shown on Form W-2, box 2, Form 1099, box 4, Form W-2G, box 4, or another form (see Instructions for Form 1040 for more information) enter the amount on Form 1040 or 1040-SR, line 25. Enter any estimated tax payments you made on Form 1040 or 1040-SR, line 26.

Credit for child and dependent care expenses. If you can take this credit, complete Form 2441 and attach it to your paper return. Enter the amount of the credit on Schedule 3 (Form 1040), line 2. The IRS will not figure this credit.

Net premium tax credit. If you take this credit, complete Form 8962, Premium Tax Credit (PTC), and attach it to your return. Enter the amount of the credit on Schedule 3 (Form 1040), line 9. The IRS will not figure this credit.

Credit for the elderly or the disabled. If you can take this credit, the IRS can figure it for you. Enter "CFE" on the line next to Schedule 3 (Form 1040), line 6d, and attach Schedule R (Form 1040) to your paper return. On Schedule R (Form 1040), check the box in Part I for your filing status and age. Complete Parts II and III, lines 11 and 13, if they apply.

Earned income credit. If you can take this credit, the IRS can figure it for you. Enter "EIC" on the dotted line on Form 1040 or 1040-SR, line 27. If you elect to use your nontaxable combat pay in figuring your EIC, enter the amount on Form 1040 or 1040-SR, line 1i.

If you have a qualifying child, you must fill in Schedule EIC (Form 1040), Earned Income Credit, and attach it to your paper return. If you don't provide the child's social security number on Schedule EIC, line 2, the credit will be reduced or disallowed unless the child was born and died in 2022.

If your credit for any year after 1996 was reduced or disallowed by the IRS, you may also have to file Form 8862 with your return. For details, see the Instructions for Form 1040.

14.

Child Tax Credit and Credit for Other Dependents

What's New

Child tax credit enhancements have expired. Many changes to the child tax credit (CTC) for 2021 implemented by the American Rescue Plan Act of 2021, have expired. For tax year 2022:

- The enhanced credit allowed for qualifying children under age 6 and children under age 18 has expired. For 2022, the initial amount of the CTC is $2,000 for each qualifying child. The credit amount begins to phase out where modified adjusted gross income exceeds $200,000 ($400,000 in case of a joint return). The amount of the CTC that can be claimed as a refundable credit is limited as it was in 2020 except that the maximum additional child tax credit (ACTC) amount for each qualifying child increased to $1,500.

- The increased age allowance for a qualifying child has expired. A child must be under age 17 at the end of 2022 to be a qualifying child.

ACTC and bona fide residents of Puerto Rico. Bona fide residents of Puerto Rico are no longer required to have three or more qualifying children to be eligible to claim the ACTC. Bona fide residents of Puerto Rico may be eligible to claim the ACTC if they have one or more qualifying children.

Reminders

Advance child tax credit payments. Advance child tax credit payments have not been issued for 2022.

Reminders

Schedule 8812 (Form 1040). The Schedule 8812 (Form 1040) and its instructions are the single source for figuring and reporting the child tax credit and credit for other dependents. The instructions now include all applicable worksheets for figuring these credits. As a result, Pub. 972, Child Tax Credit, won't be revised. For prior-year versions of Pub. 972, go to *IRS.gov/Pub972*.

Abbreviations used throughout this chapter. The following abbreviations will be used in this chapter when appropriate.

- ACTC means additional child tax credit.
- ATIN means adoption taxpayer identification number.
- CTC means child tax credit.
- ITIN means individual taxpayer identification number.
- ODC means credit for other dependents.
- SSN means social security number.
- TIN means taxpayer identification number. A TIN may be an ATIN, an ITIN, or an SSN.

Other abbreviations may be used in this chapter and will be defined as needed.

Delayed refund for returns claiming the ACTC. The IRS can't issue refunds before mid-February 2023 for returns that properly claim the ACTC. This time frame applies to the entire refund, not just the portion associated with the ACTC.

Introduction

The CTC is a credit that may reduce your tax by as much as $2,000 for each child who qualifies you for the credit. See *Limits on the CTC and ODC*, later.

The ACTC is a credit you may be able to take if you are not able to claim the full amount of the CTC.

The ODC is a credit that may reduce your tax by as much as $500 for each eligible dependent.

 The CTC and the ACTC shouldn't be confused with the child and dependent care credit discussed in Pub. 503.

Useful Items

You may want to see:

Form (and Instructions)

❏ **Schedule 8812 (Form 1040)** Credits for Qualifying Children and Other Dependents

❏ **8862** Information To Claim Certain Credits After Disallowance

For these and other useful items, go to *IRS.gov/Forms*.

Taxpayer Identification Number Requirements

You must have a TIN by the due date of your return. If you, or your spouse if filing jointly, don't have an SSN or ITIN issued on or before the due date of your 2022 return (including extensions), you can't claim the CTC, ODC, or ACTC on either your original or amended 2022 tax return.

If you apply for an ITIN on or before the due date of your 2022 return (including extensions) and the IRS issues you an ITIN as a result of the application, the IRS will consider your ITIN as issued on or before the due date of your return.

Each qualifying child you use for CTC or ACTC must have the required SSN. If you have a qualifying child who doesn't have the required SSN, you can't use the child to claim the CTC or ACTC on either your original or amended 2022 tax return. The required SSN is one that is valid for employment and is issued before the due date of your 2022 return (including extensions).

If your qualifying child was born and died in 2022 and you don't have an SSN for the child, attach a copy of the child's birth certificate, death certificate, or hospital records. The document must show the child was born alive.

If your qualifying child doesn't have the required SSN but has another type of TIN issued on or before the due date of your 2022 return (including extensions), you may be able to claim the ODC for that child. See *Credit for Other Dependents (ODC)*, later.

Each dependent you use for the ODC must have a TIN by the due date of your return. If you have a dependent who doesn't have an SSN, ITIN, or ATIN issued on or before the due date of your 2022 return (including extensions), you can't use that dependent to claim the ODC on either your original or amended 2022 tax return.

If you apply for an ITIN or ATIN for the dependent on or before the due date of your 2022 return (including extensions) and the IRS issues the ITIN or ATIN as a result of the application, the IRS will consider the ITIN or ATIN as issued on or before the due date of your return.

Improper Claims

If you erroneously claim the CTC, RCTC (refundable child tax credit for tax year 2021), ACTC, or ODC, and it is later determined that your error was due to reckless or intentional disregard of the CTC, ACTC, or ODC rules, you will not be allowed to claim any of these credits for 2 years. If it is determined that your error was due to fraud, you will not be allowed to claim any of these credits for 10 years. You may also have to pay penalties.

Form 8862 may be required. If your CTC, RCTC (refundable child tax credit for tax year 2021), ACTC, or ODC for a year after 2015 was denied or reduced for any reason other than a math or clerical error, you must attach Form 8862 to your tax return to claim the CTC, ACTC, or ODC, unless an exception applies. See Form 8862, Information To Claim Certain Credits After Disallowance, and its instructions for more information, including whether an exception applies.

Child Tax Credit (CTC)

The CTC is for individuals who claim a child as a dependent if the child meets additional conditions (described later).

Note. This credit is different from and in addition to the credit for child and dependent care expenses and the earned income credit that you may also be eligible to claim.

The maximum amount you can claim for the credit is $2,000 for each child who qualifies you for the CTC. But, see *Limits on the CTC and ODC*, later.

For more information about claiming the CTC, see *Claiming the CTC and ODC*, later.

Qualifying Child for the CTC

A child qualifies you for the CTC if the child meets all of the following conditions.

1. The child is your son, daughter, stepchild, foster child, brother, sister, stepbrother, stepsister, half brother, half sister, or a descendant of any of them (for example, your grandchild, niece, or nephew).

2. The child was under age 17 at the end of 2022.

3. The child didn't provide over half the child's own support for 2022.

4. The child lived with you for more than half of 2022 (see *Exceptions to time lived with you*, later).

5. The child is claimed as a dependent on your return. See chapter 3 for more information about claiming someone as a dependent.

6. The child doesn't file a joint return for the year (or files it only to claim a refund of withheld income tax or estimated tax paid).

7. The child was a U.S. citizen, U.S. national, or U.S. resident alien. For more information, see Pub. 519. If the child was adopted, see *Adopted child*, later.

Example. Your child, B, turned 17 on December 30, 2022. B is a citizen of the United States and can be claimed as a dependent on your return. You can't use B to claim the CTC or ACTC because B was not **under** age 17 at the end of 2022.

 If your child is age 17 or older at the end of 2022, see Credit for Other Dependents (ODC), *later.*

Adopted child. An adopted child is always treated as your own child. An adopted child includes a child lawfully placed with you for legal adoption.

If you are a U.S. citizen or U.S. national and your adopted child lived with you all year as a member of your household in 2022, that child meets condition 7, earlier, to be a qualifying child for the child tax credit (or condition 3, later, to be a qualifying person for the ODC).

Exceptions to time lived with you. A child is considered to have lived with you for more than half of 2022 if the child was born or died in 2022 and your home was this child's home for more than half the time the child was alive. Temporary absences by you or the child for special circumstances, such as school, vacation, business, medical care, military service, or detention in a juvenile facility, count as time the child lived with you.

There are also exceptions for kidnapped children and children of divorced or separated parents. For details, see *Residency Test* in chapter 3.

Qualifying child of more than one person. A special rule applies if your qualifying child is the qualifying child of more than one person. For details, see *Qualifying Child of More Than One Person* in chapter 3.

Required SSN

In addition to being a qualifying child for the CTC, your child must have the required SSN. The required SSN is one that is valid for employment and that is issued by the Social Security Administration (SSA) before the due date of your 2022 return (including extensions).

 If your qualifying child does not have the required SSN, see Credit for Other Dependents (ODC), *later.*

If your child was a U.S. citizen when the child received the SSN, the SSN is valid for employment. If "Not Valid for Employment" is printed on your child's social security card and your child's immigration status has changed so that your child is now a U.S. citizen or permanent resident, ask the SSA for a new social security card without the legend. However, if "Valid for Work Only With DHS Authorization" is printed on your child's social security card, your child has the required SSN only as long as the Department of Homeland Security (DHS) authorization is valid.

If your child doesn't have the required SSN, you can't use the child to claim the CTC (or ACTC) on either your original or amended 2022 tax return.

Credit for Other Dependents (ODC)

This credit is for individuals with a dependent who meets additional conditions (described later).

Note. This credit is different from and in addition to the credit for child and dependent care expenses that you may also be eligible to claim.

The maximum amount you can claim for this credit is $500 for each qualifying dependent. See *Limits on the CTC and ODC*, later.

For more information about claiming the ODC, see *Claiming the CTC and ODC*, later.

Qualifying Person for the ODC

A person qualifies you for the ODC if the person meets all of the following conditions.

1. The person is claimed as a dependent on your return. See chapter 3 for more information about claiming someone as a dependent.

2. The person can't be used by you to claim the CTC or ACTC. See *Child Tax Credit (CTC)*, earlier.

3. The person was a U.S. citizen, U.S. national, or U.S. resident alien. For more information, see Pub. 519. If the person is your adopted child, see *Adopted child*, earlier.

Example. Your 10-year-old dependent, L, lives in Mexico. L is not a U.S. citizen, U.S. national, or U.S. resident alien. You can't use L to claim the ODC.

 You can't use the same child to claim the CTC or ACTC, and the ODC.

Timely Issued TIN

In addition to being a qualifying person for the ODC, the person must have an SSN, ITIN, or ATIN issued to the dependent on or before the due date of your 2022 return (including extensions). If the person has not been issued an SSN, ITIN, or ATIN by that date, you can't use the person to claim the ODC on either your original or amended 2022 return. For more information, see *Taxpayer Identification Number Requirements*, earlier.

Limits on the CTC and ODC

The credit amount of your CTC or ODC may be reduced if your modified adjusted gross income (AGI) is more than the amounts shown below for your filing status.

- Married filing jointly — $400,000.

- All other filing statuses — $200,000.

AGI. Your AGI is the amount on line 11 of your Form 1040, 1040-SR, or 1040-NR.

For more information about limits on the CTC and ODC, see the Instructions for Schedule 8812 (Form 1040).

Claiming the CTC and ODC

To claim the CTC or ODC, be sure you meet the following requirements.

- You must file Form 1040, 1040-SR, or 1040-NR and include the name and TIN of each dependent for whom you are claiming the CTC or ODC.

- You must file Schedule 8812 (Form 1040).

- You must file Form 8862, if applicable. See *Improper Claims*, earlier.

- You must enter a timely issued TIN on your tax return for you and your spouse (if filing jointly). See *Taxpayer Identification Number Requirements*, earlier.

- For each qualifying child under 17 for whom you are claiming the CTC, you must enter the required SSN for the child in column (2) of the *Dependents* section of your tax return and check the Child tax credit box in column (4). See *Child Tax Credit (CTC)*, earlier.

- For each dependent for whom you are claiming the ODC, you must enter the timely issued TIN for the dependent in column (2) of the *Dependents* section of your tax return and check the Credit for other dependents box in column (4). See *Credit for Other Dependents (ODC)*, earlier.

 Don't check both the Child tax credit box and the Credit for other dependents box for the same person.

Additional Child Tax Credit (ACTC)

This credit is for certain individuals who get less than the full amount of the CTC.

 The ODC can't be used to figure the ACTC. Only your CTC can be used to figure your ACTC. If you are claiming the ODC but not the CTC, you can't claim the ACTC.

Foreign earned income. If you file Form 2555 (relating to foreign earned income), you can't claim the ACTC.

Bona fide residents of Puerto Rico. Bona fide residents of Puerto Rico are no longer required to have three or more qualifying children to be eligible to claim the ACTC. See Schedule 8812 (Form 1040) and its instructions.

How to claim the ACTC. To claim the ACTC, see Schedule 8812 (Form 1040) and its instructions.

See the instructions for line 16 to see if you must use the Tax Table below to figure your tax.

Example. A married couple are filing a joint return. Their taxable income on Form 1040, line 15, is $25,300. First, they find the $25,300-25,350 taxable income line. Next, they find the column for married filing jointly and read down the column. The amount shown where the taxable income line and filing status column meet is $2,628. This is the tax amount they should enter in the entry space on Form 1040, line 16.

Sample Table

At Least	But Less Than	Single	Married filing jointly*	Married filing separately	Head of a household
			Your tax is—		
25,200	25,250	2,822	2,616	2,822	2,734
25,250	25,300	2,828	2,622	2,828	2,740
25,300	25,350	2,834	(2,628)	2,834	2,746
25,350	25,400	2,840	2,634	2,840	2,752

If line 15 (taxable income) is—		And you are—			
At least	But less than	Single	Married filing jointly *	Married filing sepa-rately	Head of a house-hold
			Your tax is—		
0	5	0	0	0	0
5	15	1	1	1	1
15	25	2	2	2	2
25	50	4	4	4	4
50	75	6	6	6	6
75	100	9	9	9	9
100	125	11	11	11	11
125	150	14	14	14	14
150	175	16	16	16	16
175	200	19	19	19	19
200	225	21	21	21	21
225	250	24	24	24	24
250	275	26	26	26	26
275	300	29	29	29	29
300	325	31	31	31	31
325	350	34	34	34	34
350	375	36	36	36	36
375	400	39	39	39	39
400	425	41	41	41	41
425	450	44	44	44	44
450	475	46	46	46	46
475	500	49	49	49	49
500	525	51	51	51	51
525	550	54	54	54	54
550	575	56	56	56	56
575	600	59	59	59	59
600	625	61	61	61	61
625	650	64	64	64	64
650	675	66	66	66	66
675	700	69	69	69	69
700	725	71	71	71	71
725	750	74	74	74	74
750	775	76	76	76	76
775	800	79	79	79	79
800	825	81	81	81	81
825	850	84	84	84	84
850	875	86	86	86	86
875	900	89	89	89	89
900	925	91	91	91	91
925	950	94	94	94	94
950	975	96	96	96	96
975	1,000	99	99	99	99

1,000

At least	But less than	Single	Married filing jointly *	Married filing sepa-rately	Head of a house-hold
			Your tax is—		
1,000	1,025	101	101	101	101
1,025	1,050	104	104	104	104
1,050	1,075	106	106	106	106
1,075	1,100	109	109	109	109
1,100	1,125	111	111	111	111
1,125	1,150	114	114	114	114
1,150	1,175	116	116	116	116
1,175	1,200	119	119	119	119
1,200	1,225	121	121	121	121
1,225	1,250	124	124	124	124
1,250	1,275	126	126	126	126
1,275	1,300	129	129	129	129
1,300	1,325	131	131	131	131
1,325	1,350	134	134	134	134
1,350	1,375	136	136	136	136
1,375	1,400	139	139	139	139
1,400	1,425	141	141	141	141
1,425	1,450	144	144	144	144
1,450	1,475	146	146	146	146
1,475	1,500	149	149	149	149
1,500	1,525	151	151	151	151
1,525	1,550	154	154	154	154
1,550	1,575	156	156	156	156
1,575	1,600	159	159	159	159
1,600	1,625	161	161	161	161
1,625	1,650	164	164	164	164
1,650	1,675	166	166	166	166
1,675	1,700	169	169	169	169
1,700	1,725	171	171	171	171
1,725	1,750	174	174	174	174
1,750	1,775	176	176	176	176
1,775	1,800	179	179	179	179
1,800	1,825	181	181	181	181
1,825	1,850	184	184	184	184
1,850	1,875	186	186	186	186
1,875	1,900	189	189	189	189
1,900	1,925	191	191	191	191
1,925	1,950	194	194	194	194
1,950	1,975	196	196	196	196
1,975	2,000	199	199	199	199

2,000

At least	But less than	Single	Married filing jointly *	Married filing sepa-rately	Head of a house-hold
			Your tax is—		
2,000	2,025	201	201	201	201
2,025	2,050	204	204	204	204
2,050	2,075	206	206	206	206
2,075	2,100	209	209	209	209
2,100	2,125	211	211	211	211
2,125	2,150	214	214	214	214
2,150	2,175	216	216	216	216
2,175	2,200	219	219	219	219
2,200	2,225	221	221	221	221
2,225	2,250	224	224	224	224
2,250	2,275	226	226	226	226
2,275	2,300	229	229	229	229
2,300	2,325	231	231	231	231
2,325	2,350	234	234	234	234
2,350	2,375	236	236	236	236
2,375	2,400	239	239	239	239
2,400	2,425	241	241	241	241
2,425	2,450	244	244	244	244
2,450	2,475	246	246	246	246
2,475	2,500	249	249	249	249
2,500	2,525	251	251	251	251
2,525	2,550	254	254	254	254
2,550	2,575	256	256	256	256
2,575	2,600	259	259	259	259
2,600	2,625	261	261	261	261
2,625	2,650	264	264	264	264
2,650	2,675	266	266	266	266
2,675	2,700	269	269	269	269
2,700	2,725	271	271	271	271
2,725	2,750	274	274	274	274
2,750	2,775	276	276	276	276
2,775	2,800	279	279	279	279
2,800	2,825	281	281	281	281
2,825	2,850	284	284	284	284
2,850	2,875	286	286	286	286
2,875	2,900	289	289	289	289
2,900	2,925	291	291	291	291
2,925	2,950	294	294	294	294
2,950	2,975	296	296	296	296
2,975	3,000	299	299	299	299

(Continued)

* This column must also be used by a qualifying surviving spouse.

If line 15 (taxable income) is—		And you are—			
At least	But less than	Single	Married filing jointly *	Married filing separately	Head of a household
		Your tax is—			

3,000

At least	But less than	Single	MFJ*	MFS	HoH
3,000	3,050	303	303	303	303
3,050	3,100	308	308	308	308
3,100	3,150	313	313	313	313
3,150	3,200	318	318	318	318
3,200	3,250	323	323	323	323
3,250	3,300	328	328	328	328
3,300	3,350	333	333	333	333
3,350	3,400	338	338	338	338
3,400	3,450	343	343	343	343
3,450	3,500	348	348	348	348
3,500	3,550	353	353	353	353
3,550	3,600	358	358	358	358
3,600	3,650	363	363	363	363
3,650	3,700	368	368	368	368
3,700	3,750	373	373	373	373
3,750	3,800	378	378	378	378
3,800	3,850	383	383	383	383
3,850	3,900	388	388	388	388
3,900	3,950	393	393	393	393
3,950	4,000	398	398	398	398

4,000

At least	But less than	Single	MFJ*	MFS	HoH
4,000	4,050	403	403	403	403
4,050	4,100	408	408	408	408
4,100	4,150	413	413	413	413
4,150	4,200	418	418	418	418
4,200	4,250	423	423	423	423
4,250	4,300	428	428	428	428
4,300	4,350	433	433	433	433
4,350	4,400	438	438	438	438
4,400	4,450	443	443	443	443
4,450	4,500	448	448	448	448
4,500	4,550	453	453	453	453
4,550	4,600	458	458	458	458
4,600	4,650	463	463	463	463
4,650	4,700	468	468	468	468
4,700	4,750	473	473	473	473
4,750	4,800	478	478	478	478
4,800	4,850	483	483	483	483
4,850	4,900	488	488	488	488
4,900	4,950	493	493	493	493
4,950	5,000	498	498	498	498

5,000

At least	But less than	Single	MFJ*	MFS	HoH
5,000	5,050	503	503	503	503
5,050	5,100	508	508	508	508
5,100	5,150	513	513	513	513
5,150	5,200	518	518	518	518
5,200	5,250	523	523	523	523
5,250	5,300	528	528	528	528
5,300	5,350	533	533	533	533
5,350	5,400	538	538	538	538
5,400	5,450	543	543	543	543
5,450	5,500	548	548	548	548
5,500	5,550	553	553	553	553
5,550	5,600	558	558	558	558
5,600	5,650	563	563	563	563
5,650	5,700	568	568	568	568
5,700	5,750	573	573	573	573
5,750	5,800	578	578	578	578
5,800	5,850	583	583	583	583
5,850	5,900	588	588	588	588
5,900	5,950	593	593	593	593
5,950	6,000	598	598	598	598

6,000

At least	But less than	Single	MFJ*	MFS	HoH
6,000	6,050	603	603	603	603
6,050	6,100	608	608	608	608
6,100	6,150	613	613	613	613
6,150	6,200	618	618	618	618
6,200	6,250	623	623	623	623
6,250	6,300	628	628	628	628
6,300	6,350	633	633	633	633
6,350	6,400	638	638	638	638
6,400	6,450	643	643	643	643
6,450	6,500	648	648	648	648
6,500	6,550	653	653	653	653
6,550	6,600	658	658	658	658
6,600	6,650	663	663	663	663
6,650	6,700	668	668	668	668
6,700	6,750	673	673	673	673
6,750	6,800	678	678	678	678
6,800	6,850	683	683	683	683
6,850	6,900	688	688	688	688
6,900	6,950	693	693	693	693
6,950	7,000	698	698	698	698

7,000

At least	But less than	Single	MFJ*	MFS	HoH
7,000	7,050	703	703	703	703
7,050	7,100	708	708	708	708
7,100	7,150	713	713	713	713
7,150	7,200	718	718	718	718
7,200	7,250	723	723	723	723
7,250	7,300	728	728	728	728
7,300	7,350	733	733	733	733
7,350	7,400	738	738	738	738
7,400	7,450	743	743	743	743
7,450	7,500	748	748	748	748
7,500	7,550	753	753	753	753
7,550	7,600	758	758	758	758
7,600	7,650	763	763	763	763
7,650	7,700	768	768	768	768
7,700	7,750	773	773	773	773
7,750	7,800	778	778	778	778
7,800	7,850	783	783	783	783
7,850	7,900	788	788	788	788
7,900	7,950	793	793	793	793
7,950	8,000	798	798	798	798

8,000

At least	But less than	Single	MFJ*	MFS	HoH
8,000	8,050	803	803	803	803
8,050	8,100	808	808	808	808
8,100	8,150	813	813	813	813
8,150	8,200	818	818	818	818
8,200	8,250	823	823	823	823
8,250	8,300	828	828	828	828
8,300	8,350	833	833	833	833
8,350	8,400	838	838	838	838
8,400	8,450	843	843	843	843
8,450	8,500	848	848	848	848
8,500	8,550	853	853	853	853
8,550	8,600	858	858	858	858
8,600	8,650	863	863	863	863
8,650	8,700	868	868	868	868
8,700	8,750	873	873	873	873
8,750	8,800	878	878	878	878
8,800	8,850	883	883	883	883
8,850	8,900	888	888	888	888
8,900	8,950	893	893	893	893
8,950	9,000	898	898	898	898

9,000

At least	But less than	Single	MFJ*	MFS	HoH
9,000	9,050	903	903	903	903
9,050	9,100	908	908	908	908
9,100	9,150	913	913	913	913
9,150	9,200	918	918	918	918
9,200	9,250	923	923	923	923
9,250	9,300	928	928	928	928
9,300	9,350	933	933	933	933
9,350	9,400	938	938	938	938
9,400	9,450	943	943	943	943
9,450	9,500	948	948	948	948
9,500	9,550	953	953	953	953
9,550	9,600	958	958	958	958
9,600	9,650	963	963	963	963
9,650	9,700	968	968	968	968
9,700	9,750	973	973	973	973
9,750	9,800	978	978	978	978
9,800	9,850	983	983	983	983
9,850	9,900	988	988	988	988
9,900	9,950	993	993	993	993
9,950	10,000	998	998	998	998

10,000

At least	But less than	Single	MFJ*	MFS	HoH
10,000	10,050	1,003	1,003	1,003	1,003
10,050	10,100	1,008	1,008	1,008	1,008
10,100	10,150	1,013	1,013	1,013	1,013
10,150	10,200	1,018	1,018	1,018	1,018
10,200	10,250	1,023	1,023	1,023	1,023
10,250	10,300	1,028	1,028	1,028	1,028
10,300	10,350	1,034	1,033	1,034	1,033
10,350	10,400	1,040	1,038	1,040	1,038
10,400	10,450	1,046	1,043	1,046	1,043
10,450	10,500	1,052	1,048	1,052	1,048
10,500	10,550	1,058	1,053	1,058	1,053
10,550	10,600	1,064	1,058	1,064	1,058
10,600	10,650	1,070	1,063	1,070	1,063
10,650	10,700	1,076	1,068	1,076	1,068
10,700	10,750	1,082	1,073	1,082	1,073
10,750	10,800	1,088	1,078	1,088	1,078
10,800	10,850	1,094	1,083	1,094	1,083
10,850	10,900	1,100	1,088	1,100	1,088
10,900	10,950	1,106	1,093	1,106	1,093
10,950	11,000	1,112	1,098	1,112	1,098

11,000

At least	But less than	Single	MFJ*	MFS	HoH
11,000	11,050	1,118	1,103	1,118	1,103
11,050	11,100	1,124	1,108	1,124	1,108
11,100	11,150	1,130	1,113	1,130	1,113
11,150	11,200	1,136	1,118	1,136	1,118
11,200	11,250	1,142	1,123	1,142	1,123
11,250	11,300	1,148	1,128	1,148	1,128
11,300	11,350	1,154	1,133	1,154	1,133
11,350	11,400	1,160	1,138	1,160	1,138
11,400	11,450	1,166	1,143	1,166	1,143
11,450	11,500	1,172	1,148	1,172	1,148
11,500	11,550	1,178	1,153	1,178	1,153
11,550	11,600	1,184	1,158	1,184	1,158
11,600	11,650	1,190	1,163	1,190	1,163
11,650	11,700	1,196	1,168	1,196	1,168
11,700	11,750	1,202	1,173	1,202	1,173
11,750	11,800	1,208	1,178	1,208	1,178
11,800	11,850	1,214	1,183	1,214	1,183
11,850	11,900	1,220	1,188	1,220	1,188
11,900	11,950	1,226	1,193	1,226	1,193
11,950	12,000	1,232	1,198	1,232	1,198

(Continued)

* This column must also be used by a qualifying surviving spouse.

At least	But less than	Single	Married filing jointly *	Married filing separately	Head of a household

12,000

At least	But less than	Single	Married filing jointly *	Married filing separately	Head of a household
12,000	12,050	1,238	1,203	1,238	1,203
12,050	12,100	1,244	1,208	1,244	1,208
12,100	12,150	1,250	1,213	1,250	1,213
12,150	12,200	1,256	1,218	1,256	1,218
12,200	12,250	1,262	1,223	1,262	1,223
12,250	12,300	1,268	1,228	1,268	1,228
12,300	12,350	1,274	1,233	1,274	1,233
12,350	12,400	1,280	1,238	1,280	1,238
12,400	12,450	1,286	1,243	1,286	1,243
12,450	12,500	1,292	1,248	1,292	1,248
12,500	12,550	1,298	1,253	1,298	1,253
12,550	12,600	1,304	1,258	1,304	1,258
12,600	12,650	1,310	1,263	1,310	1,263
12,650	12,700	1,316	1,268	1,316	1,268
12,700	12,750	1,322	1,273	1,322	1,273
12,750	12,800	1,328	1,278	1,328	1,278
12,800	12,850	1,334	1,283	1,334	1,283
12,850	12,900	1,340	1,288	1,340	1,288
12,900	12,950	1,346	1,293	1,346	1,293
12,950	13,000	1,352	1,298	1,352	1,298

13,000

At least	But less than	Single	Married filing jointly *	Married filing separately	Head of a household
13,000	13,050	1,358	1,303	1,358	1,303
13,050	13,100	1,364	1,308	1,364	1,308
13,100	13,150	1,370	1,313	1,370	1,313
13,150	13,200	1,376	1,318	1,376	1,318
13,200	13,250	1,382	1,323	1,382	1,323
13,250	13,300	1,388	1,328	1,388	1,328
13,300	13,350	1,394	1,333	1,394	1,333
13,350	13,400	1,400	1,338	1,400	1,338
13,400	13,450	1,406	1,343	1,406	1,343
13,450	13,500	1,412	1,348	1,412	1,348
13,500	13,550	1,418	1,353	1,418	1,353
13,550	13,600	1,424	1,358	1,424	1,358
13,600	13,650	1,430	1,363	1,430	1,363
13,650	13,700	1,436	1,368	1,436	1,368
13,700	13,750	1,442	1,373	1,442	1,373
13,750	13,800	1,448	1,378	1,448	1,378
13,800	13,850	1,454	1,383	1,454	1,383
13,850	13,900	1,460	1,388	1,460	1,388
13,900	13,950	1,466	1,393	1,466	1,393
13,950	14,000	1,472	1,398	1,472	1,398

14,000

At least	But less than	Single	Married filing jointly *	Married filing separately	Head of a household
14,000	14,050	1,478	1,403	1,478	1,403
14,050	14,100	1,484	1,408	1,484	1,408
14,100	14,150	1,490	1,413	1,490	1,413
14,150	14,200	1,496	1,418	1,496	1,418
14,200	14,250	1,502	1,423	1,502	1,423
14,250	14,300	1,508	1,428	1,508	1,428
14,300	14,350	1,514	1,433	1,514	1,433
14,350	14,400	1,520	1,438	1,520	1,438
14,400	14,450	1,526	1,443	1,526	1,443
14,450	14,500	1,532	1,448	1,532	1,448
14,500	14,550	1,538	1,453	1,538	1,453
14,550	14,600	1,544	1,458	1,544	1,458
14,600	14,650	1,550	1,463	1,550	1,463
14,650	14,700	1,556	1,468	1,556	1,468
14,700	14,750	1,562	1,473	1,562	1,474
14,750	14,800	1,568	1,478	1,568	1,480
14,800	14,850	1,574	1,483	1,574	1,486
14,850	14,900	1,580	1,488	1,580	1,492
14,900	14,950	1,586	1,493	1,586	1,498
14,950	15,000	1,592	1,498	1,592	1,504

15,000

At least	But less than	Single	Married filing jointly *	Married filing separately	Head of a household
15,000	15,050	1,598	1,503	1,598	1,510
15,050	15,100	1,604	1,508	1,604	1,516
15,100	15,150	1,610	1,513	1,610	1,522
15,150	15,200	1,616	1,518	1,616	1,528
15,200	15,250	1,622	1,523	1,622	1,534
15,250	15,300	1,628	1,528	1,628	1,540
15,300	15,350	1,634	1,533	1,634	1,546
15,350	15,400	1,640	1,538	1,640	1,552
15,400	15,450	1,646	1,543	1,646	1,558
15,450	15,500	1,652	1,548	1,652	1,564
15,500	15,550	1,658	1,553	1,658	1,570
15,550	15,600	1,664	1,558	1,664	1,576
15,600	15,650	1,670	1,563	1,670	1,582
15,650	15,700	1,676	1,568	1,676	1,588
15,700	15,750	1,682	1,573	1,682	1,594
15,750	15,800	1,688	1,578	1,688	1,600
15,800	15,850	1,694	1,583	1,694	1,606
15,850	15,900	1,700	1,588	1,700	1,612
15,900	15,950	1,706	1,593	1,706	1,618
15,950	16,000	1,712	1,598	1,712	1,624

16,000

At least	But less than	Single	Married filing jointly *	Married filing separately	Head of a household
16,000	16,050	1,718	1,603	1,718	1,630
16,050	16,100	1,724	1,608	1,724	1,636
16,100	16,150	1,730	1,613	1,730	1,642
16,150	16,200	1,736	1,618	1,736	1,648
16,200	16,250	1,742	1,623	1,742	1,654
16,250	16,300	1,748	1,628	1,748	1,660
16,300	16,350	1,754	1,633	1,754	1,666
16,350	16,400	1,760	1,638	1,760	1,672
16,400	16,450	1,766	1,643	1,766	1,678
16,450	16,500	1,772	1,648	1,772	1,684
16,500	16,550	1,778	1,653	1,778	1,690
16,550	16,600	1,784	1,658	1,784	1,696
16,600	16,650	1,790	1,663	1,790	1,702
16,650	16,700	1,796	1,668	1,796	1,708
16,700	16,750	1,802	1,673	1,802	1,714
16,750	16,800	1,808	1,678	1,808	1,720
16,800	16,850	1,814	1,683	1,814	1,726
16,850	16,900	1,820	1,688	1,820	1,732
16,900	16,950	1,826	1,693	1,826	1,738
16,950	17,000	1,832	1,698	1,832	1,744

17,000

At least	But less than	Single	Married filing jointly *	Married filing separately	Head of a household
17,000	17,050	1,838	1,703	1,838	1,750
17,050	17,100	1,844	1,708	1,844	1,756
17,100	17,150	1,850	1,713	1,850	1,762
17,150	17,200	1,856	1,718	1,856	1,768
17,200	17,250	1,862	1,723	1,862	1,774
17,250	17,300	1,868	1,728	1,868	1,780
17,300	17,350	1,874	1,733	1,874	1,786
17,350	17,400	1,880	1,738	1,880	1,792
17,400	17,450	1,886	1,743	1,886	1,798
17,450	17,500	1,892	1,748	1,892	1,804
17,500	17,550	1,898	1,753	1,898	1,810
17,550	17,600	1,904	1,758	1,904	1,816
17,600	17,650	1,910	1,763	1,910	1,822
17,650	17,700	1,916	1,768	1,916	1,828
17,700	17,750	1,922	1,773	1,922	1,834
17,750	17,800	1,928	1,778	1,928	1,840
17,800	17,850	1,934	1,783	1,934	1,846
17,850	17,900	1,940	1,788	1,940	1,852
17,900	17,950	1,946	1,793	1,946	1,858
17,950	18,000	1,952	1,798	1,952	1,864

18,000

At least	But less than	Single	Married filing jointly *	Married filing separately	Head of a household
18,000	18,050	1,958	1,803	1,958	1,870
18,050	18,100	1,964	1,808	1,964	1,876
18,100	18,150	1,970	1,813	1,970	1,882
18,150	18,200	1,976	1,818	1,976	1,888
18,200	18,250	1,982	1,823	1,982	1,894
18,250	18,300	1,988	1,828	1,988	1,900
18,300	18,350	1,994	1,833	1,994	1,906
18,350	18,400	2,000	1,838	2,000	1,912
18,400	18,450	2,006	1,843	2,006	1,918
18,450	18,500	2,012	1,848	2,012	1,924
18,500	18,550	2,018	1,853	2,018	1,930
18,550	18,600	2,024	1,858	2,024	1,936
18,600	18,650	2,030	1,863	2,030	1,942
18,650	18,700	2,036	1,868	2,036	1,948
18,700	18,750	2,042	1,873	2,042	1,954
18,750	18,800	2,048	1,878	2,048	1,960
18,800	18,850	2,054	1,883	2,054	1,966
18,850	18,900	2,060	1,888	2,060	1,972
18,900	18,950	2,066	1,893	2,066	1,978
18,950	19,000	2,072	1,898	2,072	1,984

19,000

At least	But less than	Single	Married filing jointly *	Married filing separately	Head of a household
19,000	19,050	2,078	1,903	2,078	1,990
19,050	19,100	2,084	1,908	2,084	1,996
19,100	19,150	2,090	1,913	2,090	2,002
19,150	19,200	2,096	1,918	2,096	2,008
19,200	19,250	2,102	1,923	2,102	2,014
19,250	19,300	2,108	1,928	2,108	2,020
19,300	19,350	2,114	1,933	2,114	2,026
19,350	19,400	2,120	1,938	2,120	2,032
19,400	19,450	2,126	1,943	2,126	2,038
19,450	19,500	2,132	1,948	2,132	2,044
19,500	19,550	2,138	1,953	2,138	2,050
19,550	19,600	2,144	1,958	2,144	2,056
19,600	19,650	2,150	1,963	2,150	2,062
19,650	19,700	2,156	1,968	2,156	2,068
19,700	19,750	2,162	1,973	2,162	2,074
19,750	19,800	2,168	1,978	2,168	2,080
19,800	19,850	2,174	1,983	2,174	2,086
19,850	19,900	2,180	1,988	2,180	2,092
19,900	19,950	2,186	1,993	2,186	2,098
19,950	20,000	2,192	1,998	2,192	2,104

20,000

At least	But less than	Single	Married filing jointly *	Married filing separately	Head of a household
20,000	20,050	2,198	2,003	2,198	2,110
20,050	20,100	2,204	2,008	2,204	2,116
20,100	20,150	2,210	2,013	2,210	2,122
20,150	20,200	2,216	2,018	2,216	2,128
20,200	20,250	2,222	2,023	2,222	2,134
20,250	20,300	2,228	2,028	2,228	2,140
20,300	20,350	2,234	2,033	2,234	2,146
20,350	20,400	2,240	2,038	2,240	2,152
20,400	20,450	2,246	2,043	2,246	2,158
20,450	20,500	2,252	2,048	2,252	2,164
20,500	20,550	2,258	2,053	2,258	2,170
20,550	20,600	2,264	2,058	2,264	2,176
20,600	20,650	2,270	2,064	2,270	2,182
20,650	20,700	2,276	2,070	2,276	2,188
20,700	20,750	2,282	2,076	2,282	2,194
20,750	20,800	2,288	2,082	2,288	2,200
20,800	20,850	2,294	2,088	2,294	2,206
20,850	20,900	2,300	2,094	2,300	2,212
20,900	20,950	2,306	2,100	2,306	2,218
20,950	21,000	2,312	2,106	2,312	2,224

(Continued)

* This column must also be used by a qualifying surviving spouse.

21,000

At least	But less than	Single	Married filing jointly *	Married filing separately	Head of a household
21,000	21,050	2,318	2,112	2,318	2,230
21,050	21,100	2,324	2,118	2,324	2,236
21,100	21,150	2,330	2,124	2,330	2,242
21,150	21,200	2,336	2,130	2,336	2,248
21,200	21,250	2,342	2,136	2,342	2,254
21,250	21,300	2,348	2,142	2,348	2,260
21,300	21,350	2,354	2,148	2,354	2,266
21,350	21,400	2,360	2,154	2,360	2,272
21,400	21,450	2,366	2,160	2,366	2,278
21,450	21,500	2,372	2,166	2,372	2,284
21,500	21,550	2,378	2,172	2,378	2,290
21,550	21,600	2,384	2,178	2,384	2,296
21,600	21,650	2,390	2,184	2,390	2,302
21,650	21,700	2,396	2,190	2,396	2,308
21,700	21,750	2,402	2,196	2,402	2,314
21,750	21,800	2,408	2,202	2,408	2,320
21,800	21,850	2,414	2,208	2,414	2,326
21,850	21,900	2,420	2,214	2,420	2,332
21,900	21,950	2,426	2,220	2,426	2,338
21,950	22,000	2,432	2,226	2,432	2,344

22,000

At least	But less than	Single	Married filing jointly *	Married filing separately	Head of a household
22,000	22,050	2,438	2,232	2,438	2,350
22,050	22,100	2,444	2,238	2,444	2,356
22,100	22,150	2,450	2,244	2,450	2,362
22,150	22,200	2,456	2,250	2,456	2,368
22,200	22,250	2,462	2,256	2,462	2,374
22,250	22,300	2,468	2,262	2,468	2,380
22,300	22,350	2,474	2,268	2,474	2,386
22,350	22,400	2,480	2,274	2,480	2,392
22,400	22,450	2,486	2,280	2,486	2,398
22,450	22,500	2,492	2,286	2,492	2,404
22,500	22,550	2,498	2,292	2,498	2,410
22,550	22,600	2,504	2,298	2,504	2,416
22,600	22,650	2,510	2,304	2,510	2,422
22,650	22,700	2,516	2,310	2,516	2,428
22,700	22,750	2,522	2,316	2,522	2,434
22,750	22,800	2,528	2,322	2,528	2,440
22,800	22,850	2,534	2,328	2,534	2,446
22,850	22,900	2,540	2,334	2,540	2,452
22,900	22,950	2,546	2,340	2,546	2,458
22,950	23,000	2,552	2,346	2,552	2,464

23,000

At least	But less than	Single	Married filing jointly *	Married filing separately	Head of a household
23,000	23,050	2,558	2,352	2,558	2,470
23,050	23,100	2,564	2,358	2,564	2,476
23,100	23,150	2,570	2,364	2,570	2,482
23,150	23,200	2,576	2,370	2,576	2,488
23,200	23,250	2,582	2,376	2,582	2,494
23,250	23,300	2,588	2,382	2,588	2,500
23,300	23,350	2,594	2,388	2,594	2,506
23,350	23,400	2,600	2,394	2,600	2,512
23,400	23,450	2,606	2,400	2,606	2,518
23,450	23,500	2,612	2,406	2,612	2,524
23,500	23,550	2,618	2,412	2,618	2,530
23,550	23,600	2,624	2,418	2,624	2,536
23,600	23,650	2,630	2,424	2,630	2,542
23,650	23,700	2,636	2,430	2,636	2,548
23,700	23,750	2,642	2,436	2,642	2,554
23,750	23,800	2,648	2,442	2,648	2,560
23,800	23,850	2,654	2,448	2,654	2,566
23,850	23,900	2,660	2,454	2,660	2,572
23,900	23,950	2,666	2,460	2,666	2,578
23,950	24,000	2,672	2,466	2,672	2,584

24,000

At least	But less than	Single	Married filing jointly *	Married filing separately	Head of a household
24,000	24,050	2,678	2,472	2,678	2,590
24,050	24,100	2,684	2,478	2,684	2,596
24,100	24,150	2,690	2,484	2,690	2,602
24,150	24,200	2,696	2,490	2,696	2,608
24,200	24,250	2,702	2,496	2,702	2,614
24,250	24,300	2,708	2,502	2,708	2,620
24,300	24,350	2,714	2,508	2,714	2,626
24,350	24,400	2,720	2,514	2,720	2,632
24,400	24,450	2,726	2,520	2,726	2,638
24,450	24,500	2,732	2,526	2,732	2,644
24,500	24,550	2,738	2,532	2,738	2,650
24,550	24,600	2,744	2,538	2,744	2,656
24,600	24,650	2,750	2,544	2,750	2,662
24,650	24,700	2,756	2,550	2,756	2,668
24,700	24,750	2,762	2,556	2,762	2,674
24,750	24,800	2,768	2,562	2,768	2,680
24,800	24,850	2,774	2,568	2,774	2,686
24,850	24,900	2,780	2,574	2,780	2,692
24,900	24,950	2,786	2,580	2,786	2,698
24,950	25,000	2,792	2,586	2,792	2,704

25,000

At least	But less than	Single	Married filing jointly *	Married filing separately	Head of a household
25,000	25,050	2,798	2,592	2,798	2,710
25,050	25,100	2,804	2,598	2,804	2,716
25,100	25,150	2,810	2,604	2,810	2,722
25,150	25,200	2,816	2,610	2,816	2,728
25,200	25,250	2,822	2,616	2,822	2,734
25,250	25,300	2,828	2,622	2,828	2,740
25,300	25,350	2,834	2,628	2,834	2,746
25,350	25,400	2,840	2,634	2,840	2,752
25,400	25,450	2,846	2,640	2,846	2,758
25,450	25,500	2,852	2,646	2,852	2,764
25,500	25,550	2,858	2,652	2,858	2,770
25,550	25,600	2,864	2,658	2,864	2,776
25,600	25,650	2,870	2,664	2,870	2,782
25,650	25,700	2,876	2,670	2,876	2,788
25,700	25,750	2,882	2,676	2,882	2,794
25,750	25,800	2,888	2,682	2,888	2,800
25,800	25,850	2,894	2,688	2,894	2,806
25,850	25,900	2,900	2,694	2,900	2,812
25,900	25,950	2,906	2,700	2,906	2,818
25,950	26,000	2,912	2,706	2,912	2,824

26,000

At least	But less than	Single	Married filing jointly *	Married filing separately	Head of a household
26,000	26,050	2,918	2,712	2,918	2,830
26,050	26,100	2,924	2,718	2,924	2,836
26,100	26,150	2,930	2,724	2,930	2,842
26,150	26,200	2,936	2,730	2,936	2,848
26,200	26,250	2,942	2,736	2,942	2,854
26,250	26,300	2,948	2,742	2,948	2,860
26,300	26,350	2,954	2,748	2,954	2,866
26,350	26,400	2,960	2,754	2,960	2,872
26,400	26,450	2,966	2,760	2,966	2,878
26,450	26,500	2,972	2,766	2,972	2,884
26,500	26,550	2,978	2,772	2,978	2,890
26,550	26,600	2,984	2,778	2,984	2,896
26,600	26,650	2,990	2,784	2,990	2,902
26,650	26,700	2,996	2,790	2,996	2,908
26,700	26,750	3,002	2,796	3,002	2,914
26,750	26,800	3,008	2,802	3,008	2,920
26,800	26,850	3,014	2,808	3,014	2,926
26,850	26,900	3,020	2,814	3,020	2,932
26,900	26,950	3,026	2,820	3,026	2,938
26,950	27,000	3,032	2,826	3,032	2,944

27,000

At least	But less than	Single	Married filing jointly *	Married filing separately	Head of a household
27,000	27,050	3,038	2,832	3,038	2,950
27,050	27,100	3,044	2,838	3,044	2,956
27,100	27,150	3,050	2,844	3,050	2,962
27,150	27,200	3,056	2,850	3,056	2,968
27,200	27,250	3,062	2,856	3,062	2,974
27,250	27,300	3,068	2,862	3,068	2,980
27,300	27,350	3,074	2,868	3,074	2,986
27,350	27,400	3,080	2,874	3,080	2,992
27,400	27,450	3,086	2,880	3,086	2,998
27,450	27,500	3,092	2,886	3,092	3,004
27,500	27,550	3,098	2,892	3,098	3,010
27,550	27,600	3,104	2,898	3,104	3,016
27,600	27,650	3,110	2,904	3,110	3,022
27,650	27,700	3,116	2,910	3,116	3,028
27,700	27,750	3,122	2,916	3,122	3,034
27,750	27,800	3,128	2,922	3,128	3,040
27,800	27,850	3,134	2,928	3,134	3,046
27,850	27,900	3,140	2,934	3,140	3,052
27,900	27,950	3,146	2,940	3,146	3,058
27,950	28,000	3,152	2,946	3,152	3,064

28,000

At least	But less than	Single	Married filing jointly *	Married filing separately	Head of a household
28,000	28,050	3,158	2,952	3,158	3,070
28,050	28,100	3,164	2,958	3,164	3,076
28,100	28,150	3,170	2,964	3,170	3,082
28,150	28,200	3,176	2,970	3,176	3,088
28,200	28,250	3,182	2,976	3,182	3,094
28,250	28,300	3,188	2,982	3,188	3,100
28,300	28,350	3,194	2,988	3,194	3,106
28,350	28,400	3,200	2,994	3,200	3,112
28,400	28,450	3,206	3,000	3,206	3,118
28,450	28,500	3,212	3,006	3,212	3,124
28,500	28,550	3,218	3,012	3,218	3,130
28,550	28,600	3,224	3,018	3,224	3,136
28,600	28,650	3,230	3,024	3,230	3,142
28,650	28,700	3,236	3,030	3,236	3,148
28,700	28,750	3,242	3,036	3,242	3,154
28,750	28,800	3,248	3,042	3,248	3,160
28,800	28,850	3,254	3,048	3,254	3,166
28,850	28,900	3,260	3,054	3,260	3,172
28,900	28,950	3,266	3,060	3,266	3,178
28,950	29,000	3,272	3,066	3,272	3,184

29,000

At least	But less than	Single	Married filing jointly *	Married filing separately	Head of a household
29,000	29,050	3,278	3,072	3,278	3,190
29,050	29,100	3,284	3,078	3,284	3,196
29,100	29,150	3,290	3,084	3,290	3,202
29,150	29,200	3,296	3,090	3,296	3,208
29,200	29,250	3,302	3,096	3,302	3,214
29,250	29,300	3,308	3,102	3,308	3,220
29,300	29,350	3,314	3,108	3,314	3,226
29,350	29,400	3,320	3,114	3,320	3,232
29,400	29,450	3,326	3,120	3,326	3,238
29,450	29,500	3,332	3,126	3,332	3,244
29,500	29,550	3,338	3,132	3,338	3,250
29,550	29,600	3,344	3,138	3,344	3,256
29,600	29,650	3,350	3,144	3,350	3,262
29,650	29,700	3,356	3,150	3,356	3,268
29,700	29,750	3,362	3,156	3,362	3,274
29,750	29,800	3,368	3,162	3,368	3,280
29,800	29,850	3,374	3,168	3,374	3,286
29,850	29,900	3,380	3,174	3,380	3,292
29,900	29,950	3,386	3,180	3,386	3,298
29,950	30,000	3,392	3,186	3,392	3,304

(Continued)

* This column must also be used by a qualifying surviving spouse.

30,000

At least	But less than	Single	Married filing jointly *	Married filing separately	Head of a household
30,000	30,050	3,398	3,192	3,398	3,310
30,050	30,100	3,404	3,198	3,404	3,316
30,100	30,150	3,410	3,204	3,410	3,322
30,150	30,200	3,416	3,210	3,416	3,328
30,200	30,250	3,422	3,216	3,422	3,334
30,250	30,300	3,428	3,222	3,428	3,340
30,300	30,350	3,434	3,228	3,434	3,346
30,350	30,400	3,440	3,234	3,440	3,352
30,400	30,450	3,446	3,240	3,446	3,358
30,450	30,500	3,452	3,246	3,452	3,364
30,500	30,550	3,458	3,252	3,458	3,370
30,550	30,600	3,464	3,258	3,464	3,376
30,600	30,650	3,470	3,264	3,470	3,382
30,650	30,700	3,476	3,270	3,476	3,388
30,700	30,750	3,482	3,276	3,482	3,394
30,750	30,800	3,488	3,282	3,488	3,400
30,800	30,850	3,494	3,288	3,494	3,406
30,850	30,900	3,500	3,294	3,500	3,412
30,900	30,950	3,506	3,300	3,506	3,418
30,950	31,000	3,512	3,306	3,512	3,424

31,000

At least	But less than	Single	Married filing jointly *	Married filing separately	Head of a household
31,000	31,050	3,518	3,312	3,518	3,430
31,050	31,100	3,524	3,318	3,524	3,436
31,100	31,150	3,530	3,324	3,530	3,442
31,150	31,200	3,536	3,330	3,536	3,448
31,200	31,250	3,542	3,336	3,542	3,454
31,250	31,300	3,548	3,342	3,548	3,460
31,300	31,350	3,554	3,348	3,554	3,466
31,350	31,400	3,560	3,354	3,560	3,472
31,400	31,450	3,566	3,360	3,566	3,478
31,450	31,500	3,572	3,366	3,572	3,484
31,500	31,550	3,578	3,372	3,578	3,490
31,550	31,600	3,584	3,378	3,584	3,496
31,600	31,650	3,590	3,384	3,590	3,502
31,650	31,700	3,596	3,390	3,596	3,508
31,700	31,750	3,602	3,396	3,602	3,514
31,750	31,800	3,608	3,402	3,608	3,520
31,800	31,850	3,614	3,408	3,614	3,526
31,850	31,900	3,620	3,414	3,620	3,532
31,900	31,950	3,626	3,420	3,626	3,538
31,950	32,000	3,632	3,426	3,632	3,544

32,000

At least	But less than	Single	Married filing jointly *	Married filing separately	Head of a household
32,000	32,050	3,638	3,432	3,638	3,550
32,050	32,100	3,644	3,438	3,644	3,556
32,100	32,150	3,650	3,444	3,650	3,562
32,150	32,200	3,656	3,450	3,656	3,568
32,200	32,250	3,662	3,456	3,662	3,574
32,250	32,300	3,668	3,462	3,668	3,580
32,300	32,350	3,674	3,468	3,674	3,586
32,350	32,400	3,680	3,474	3,680	3,592
32,400	32,450	3,686	3,480	3,686	3,598
32,450	32,500	3,692	3,486	3,692	3,604
32,500	32,550	3,698	3,492	3,698	3,610
32,550	32,600	3,704	3,498	3,704	3,616
32,600	32,650	3,710	3,504	3,710	3,622
32,650	32,700	3,716	3,510	3,716	3,628
32,700	32,750	3,722	3,516	3,722	3,634
32,750	32,800	3,728	3,522	3,728	3,640
32,800	32,850	3,734	3,528	3,734	3,646
32,850	32,900	3,740	3,534	3,740	3,652
32,900	32,950	3,746	3,540	3,746	3,658
32,950	33,000	3,752	3,546	3,752	3,664

33,000

At least	But less than	Single	Married filing jointly *	Married filing separately	Head of a household
33,000	33,050	3,758	3,552	3,758	3,670
33,050	33,100	3,764	3,558	3,764	3,676
33,100	33,150	3,770	3,564	3,770	3,682
33,150	33,200	3,776	3,570	3,776	3,688
33,200	33,250	3,782	3,576	3,782	3,694
33,250	33,300	3,788	3,582	3,788	3,700
33,300	33,350	3,794	3,588	3,794	3,706
33,350	33,400	3,800	3,594	3,800	3,712
33,400	33,450	3,806	3,600	3,806	3,718
33,450	33,500	3,812	3,606	3,812	3,724
33,500	33,550	3,818	3,612	3,818	3,730
33,550	33,600	3,824	3,618	3,824	3,736
33,600	33,650	3,830	3,624	3,830	3,742
33,650	33,700	3,836	3,630	3,836	3,748
33,700	33,750	3,842	3,636	3,842	3,754
33,750	33,800	3,848	3,642	3,848	3,760
33,800	33,850	3,854	3,648	3,854	3,766
33,850	33,900	3,860	3,654	3,860	3,772
33,900	33,950	3,866	3,660	3,866	3,778
33,950	34,000	3,872	3,666	3,872	3,784

34,000

At least	But less than	Single	Married filing jointly *	Married filing separately	Head of a household
34,000	34,050	3,878	3,672	3,878	3,790
34,050	34,100	3,884	3,678	3,884	3,796
34,100	34,150	3,890	3,684	3,890	3,802
34,150	34,200	3,896	3,690	3,896	3,808
34,200	34,250	3,902	3,696	3,902	3,814
34,250	34,300	3,908	3,702	3,908	3,820
34,300	34,350	3,914	3,708	3,914	3,826
34,350	34,400	3,920	3,714	3,920	3,832
34,400	34,450	3,926	3,720	3,926	3,838
34,450	34,500	3,932	3,726	3,932	3,844
34,500	34,550	3,938	3,732	3,938	3,850
34,550	34,600	3,944	3,738	3,944	3,856
34,600	34,650	3,950	3,744	3,950	3,862
34,650	34,700	3,956	3,750	3,956	3,868
34,700	34,750	3,962	3,756	3,962	3,874
34,750	34,800	3,968	3,762	3,968	3,880
34,800	34,850	3,974	3,768	3,974	3,886
34,850	34,900	3,980	3,774	3,980	3,892
34,900	34,950	3,986	3,780	3,986	3,898
34,950	35,000	3,992	3,786	3,992	3,904

35,000

At least	But less than	Single	Married filing jointly *	Married filing separately	Head of a household
35,000	35,050	3,998	3,792	3,998	3,910
35,050	35,100	4,004	3,798	4,004	3,916
35,100	35,150	4,010	3,804	4,010	3,922
35,150	35,200	4,016	3,810	4,016	3,928
35,200	35,250	4,022	3,816	4,022	3,934
35,250	35,300	4,028	3,822	4,028	3,940
35,300	35,350	4,034	3,828	4,034	3,946
35,350	35,400	4,040	3,834	4,040	3,952
35,400	35,450	4,046	3,840	4,046	3,958
35,450	35,500	4,052	3,846	4,052	3,964
35,500	35,550	4,058	3,852	4,058	3,970
35,550	35,600	4,064	3,858	4,064	3,976
35,600	35,650	4,070	3,864	4,070	3,982
35,650	35,700	4,076	3,870	4,076	3,988
35,700	35,750	4,082	3,876	4,082	3,994
35,750	35,800	4,088	3,882	4,088	4,000
35,800	35,850	4,094	3,888	4,094	4,006
35,850	35,900	4,100	3,894	4,100	4,012
35,900	35,950	4,106	3,900	4,106	4,018
35,950	36,000	4,112	3,906	4,112	4,024

36,000

At least	But less than	Single	Married filing jointly *	Married filing separately	Head of a household
36,000	36,050	4,118	3,912	4,118	4,030
36,050	36,100	4,124	3,918	4,124	4,036
36,100	36,150	4,130	3,924	4,130	4,042
36,150	36,200	4,136	3,930	4,136	4,048
36,200	36,250	4,142	3,936	4,142	4,054
36,250	36,300	4,148	3,942	4,148	4,060
36,300	36,350	4,154	3,948	4,154	4,066
36,350	36,400	4,160	3,954	4,160	4,072
36,400	36,450	4,166	3,960	4,166	4,078
36,450	36,500	4,172	3,966	4,172	4,084
36,500	36,550	4,178	3,972	4,178	4,090
36,550	36,600	4,184	3,978	4,184	4,096
36,600	36,650	4,190	3,984	4,190	4,102
36,650	36,700	4,196	3,990	4,196	4,108
36,700	36,750	4,202	3,996	4,202	4,114
36,750	36,800	4,208	4,002	4,208	4,120
36,800	36,850	4,214	4,008	4,214	4,126
36,850	36,900	4,220	4,014	4,220	4,132
36,900	36,950	4,226	4,020	4,226	4,138
36,950	37,000	4,232	4,026	4,232	4,144

37,000

At least	But less than	Single	Married filing jointly *	Married filing separately	Head of a household
37,000	37,050	4,238	4,032	4,238	4,150
37,050	37,100	4,244	4,038	4,244	4,156
37,100	37,150	4,250	4,044	4,250	4,162
37,150	37,200	4,256	4,050	4,256	4,168
37,200	37,250	4,262	4,056	4,262	4,174
37,250	37,300	4,268	4,062	4,268	4,180
37,300	37,350	4,274	4,068	4,274	4,186
37,350	37,400	4,280	4,074	4,280	4,192
37,400	37,450	4,286	4,080	4,286	4,198
37,450	37,500	4,292	4,086	4,292	4,204
37,500	37,550	4,298	4,092	4,298	4,210
37,550	37,600	4,304	4,098	4,304	4,216
37,600	37,650	4,310	4,104	4,310	4,222
37,650	37,700	4,316	4,110	4,316	4,228
37,700	37,750	4,322	4,116	4,322	4,234
37,750	37,800	4,328	4,122	4,328	4,240
37,800	37,850	4,334	4,128	4,334	4,246
37,850	37,900	4,340	4,134	4,340	4,252
37,900	37,950	4,346	4,140	4,346	4,258
37,950	38,000	4,352	4,146	4,352	4,264

38,000

At least	But less than	Single	Married filing jointly *	Married filing separately	Head of a household
38,000	38,050	4,358	4,152	4,358	4,270
38,050	38,100	4,364	4,158	4,364	4,276
38,100	38,150	4,370	4,164	4,370	4,282
38,150	38,200	4,376	4,170	4,376	4,288
38,200	38,250	4,382	4,176	4,382	4,294
38,250	38,300	4,388	4,182	4,388	4,300
38,300	38,350	4,394	4,188	4,394	4,306
38,350	38,400	4,400	4,194	4,400	4,312
38,400	38,450	4,406	4,200	4,406	4,318
38,450	38,500	4,412	4,206	4,412	4,324
38,500	38,550	4,418	4,212	4,418	4,330
38,550	38,600	4,424	4,218	4,424	4,336
38,600	38,650	4,430	4,224	4,430	4,342
38,650	38,700	4,436	4,230	4,436	4,348
38,700	38,750	4,442	4,236	4,442	4,354
38,750	38,800	4,448	4,242	4,448	4,360
38,800	38,850	4,454	4,248	4,454	4,366
38,850	38,900	4,460	4,254	4,460	4,372
38,900	38,950	4,466	4,260	4,466	4,378
38,950	39,000	4,472	4,266	4,472	4,384

(Continued)

* This column must also be used by a qualifying surviving spouse.

If line 15 (taxable income) is— At least	But less than	Single	Married filing jointly *	Married filing separately	Head of a household
			Your tax is—		

39,000

At least	But less than	Single	Married filing jointly *	Married filing separately	Head of a household
39,000	39,050	4,478	4,272	4,478	4,390
39,050	39,100	4,484	4,278	4,484	4,396
39,100	39,150	4,490	4,284	4,490	4,402
39,150	39,200	4,496	4,290	4,496	4,408
39,200	39,250	4,502	4,296	4,502	4,414
39,250	39,300	4,508	4,302	4,508	4,420
39,300	39,350	4,514	4,308	4,514	4,426
39,350	39,400	4,520	4,314	4,520	4,432
39,400	39,450	4,526	4,320	4,526	4,438
39,450	39,500	4,532	4,326	4,532	4,444
39,500	39,550	4,538	4,332	4,538	4,450
39,550	39,600	4,544	4,338	4,544	4,456
39,600	39,650	4,550	4,344	4,550	4,462
39,650	39,700	4,556	4,350	4,556	4,468
39,700	39,750	4,562	4,356	4,562	4,474
39,750	39,800	4,568	4,362	4,568	4,480
39,800	39,850	4,574	4,368	4,574	4,486
39,850	39,900	4,580	4,374	4,580	4,492
39,900	39,950	4,586	4,380	4,586	4,498
39,950	40,000	4,592	4,386	4,592	4,504

40,000

At least	But less than	Single	Married filing jointly *	Married filing separately	Head of a household
40,000	40,050	4,598	4,392	4,598	4,510
40,050	40,100	4,604	4,398	4,604	4,516
40,100	40,150	4,610	4,404	4,610	4,522
40,150	40,200	4,616	4,410	4,616	4,528
40,200	40,250	4,622	4,416	4,622	4,534
40,250	40,300	4,628	4,422	4,628	4,540
40,300	40,350	4,634	4,428	4,634	4,546
40,350	40,400	4,640	4,434	4,640	4,552
40,400	40,450	4,646	4,440	4,646	4,558
40,450	40,500	4,652	4,446	4,652	4,564
40,500	40,550	4,658	4,452	4,658	4,570
40,550	40,600	4,664	4,458	4,664	4,576
40,600	40,650	4,670	4,464	4,670	4,582
40,650	40,700	4,676	4,470	4,676	4,588
40,700	40,750	4,682	4,476	4,682	4,594
40,750	40,800	4,688	4,482	4,688	4,600
40,800	40,850	4,694	4,488	4,694	4,606
40,850	40,900	4,700	4,494	4,700	4,612
40,900	40,950	4,706	4,500	4,706	4,618
40,950	41,000	4,712	4,506	4,712	4,624

41,000

At least	But less than	Single	Married filing jointly *	Married filing separately	Head of a household
41,000	41,050	4,718	4,512	4,718	4,630
41,050	41,100	4,724	4,518	4,724	4,636
41,100	41,150	4,730	4,524	4,730	4,642
41,150	41,200	4,736	4,530	4,736	4,648
41,200	41,250	4,742	4,536	4,742	4,654
41,250	41,300	4,748	4,542	4,748	4,660
41,300	41,350	4,754	4,548	4,754	4,666
41,350	41,400	4,760	4,554	4,760	4,672
41,400	41,450	4,766	4,560	4,766	4,678
41,450	41,500	4,772	4,566	4,772	4,684
41,500	41,550	4,778	4,572	4,778	4,690
41,550	41,600	4,784	4,578	4,784	4,696
41,600	41,650	4,790	4,584	4,790	4,702
41,650	41,700	4,796	4,590	4,796	4,708
41,700	41,750	4,802	4,596	4,802	4,714
41,750	41,800	4,808	4,602	4,808	4,720
41,800	41,850	4,819	4,608	4,819	4,726
41,850	41,900	4,830	4,614	4,830	4,732
41,900	41,950	4,841	4,620	4,841	4,738
41,950	42,000	4,852	4,626	4,852	4,744

42,000

At least	But less than	Single	Married filing jointly *	Married filing separately	Head of a household
42,000	42,050	4,863	4,632	4,863	4,750
42,050	42,100	4,874	4,638	4,874	4,756
42,100	42,150	4,885	4,644	4,885	4,762
42,150	42,200	4,896	4,650	4,896	4,768
42,200	42,250	4,907	4,656	4,907	4,774
42,250	42,300	4,918	4,662	4,918	4,780
42,300	42,350	4,929	4,668	4,929	4,786
42,350	42,400	4,940	4,674	4,940	4,792
42,400	42,450	4,951	4,680	4,951	4,798
42,450	42,500	4,962	4,686	4,962	4,804
42,500	42,550	4,973	4,692	4,973	4,810
42,550	42,600	4,984	4,698	4,984	4,816
42,600	42,650	4,995	4,704	4,995	4,822
42,650	42,700	5,006	4,710	5,006	4,828
42,700	42,750	5,017	4,716	5,017	4,834
42,750	42,800	5,028	4,722	5,028	4,840
42,800	42,850	5,039	4,728	5,039	4,846
42,850	42,900	5,050	4,734	5,050	4,852
42,900	42,950	5,061	4,740	5,061	4,858
42,950	43,000	5,072	4,746	5,072	4,864

43,000

At least	But less than	Single	Married filing jointly *	Married filing separately	Head of a household
43,000	43,050	5,083	4,752	5,083	4,870
43,050	43,100	5,094	4,758	5,094	4,876
43,100	43,150	5,105	4,764	5,105	4,882
43,150	43,200	5,116	4,770	5,116	4,888
43,200	43,250	5,127	4,776	5,127	4,894
43,250	43,300	5,138	4,782	5,138	4,900
43,300	43,350	5,149	4,788	5,149	4,906
43,350	43,400	5,160	4,794	5,160	4,912
43,400	43,450	5,171	4,800	5,171	4,918
43,450	43,500	5,182	4,806	5,182	4,924
43,500	43,550	5,193	4,812	5,193	4,930
43,550	43,600	5,204	4,818	5,204	4,936
43,600	43,650	5,215	4,824	5,215	4,942
43,650	43,700	5,226	4,830	5,226	4,948
43,700	43,750	5,237	4,836	5,237	4,954
43,750	43,800	5,248	4,842	5,248	4,960
43,800	43,850	5,259	4,848	5,259	4,966
43,850	43,900	5,270	4,854	5,270	4,972
43,900	43,950	5,281	4,860	5,281	4,978
43,950	44,000	5,292	4,866	5,292	4,984

44,000

At least	But less than	Single	Married filing jointly *	Married filing separately	Head of a household
44,000	44,050	5,303	4,872	5,303	4,990
44,050	44,100	5,314	4,878	5,314	4,996
44,100	44,150	5,325	4,884	5,325	5,002
44,150	44,200	5,336	4,890	5,336	5,008
44,200	44,250	5,347	4,896	5,347	5,014
44,250	44,300	5,358	4,902	5,358	5,020
44,300	44,350	5,369	4,908	5,369	5,026
44,350	44,400	5,380	4,914	5,380	5,032
44,400	44,450	5,391	4,920	5,391	5,038
44,450	44,500	5,402	4,926	5,402	5,044
44,500	44,550	5,413	4,932	5,413	5,050
44,550	44,600	5,424	4,938	5,424	5,056
44,600	44,650	5,435	4,944	5,435	5,062
44,650	44,700	5,446	4,950	5,446	5,068
44,700	44,750	5,457	4,956	5,457	5,074
44,750	44,800	5,468	4,962	5,468	5,080
44,800	44,850	5,479	4,968	5,479	5,086
44,850	44,900	5,490	4,974	5,490	5,092
44,900	44,950	5,501	4,980	5,501	5,098
44,950	45,000	5,512	4,986	5,512	5,104

45,000

At least	But less than	Single	Married filing jointly *	Married filing separately	Head of a household
45,000	45,050	5,523	4,992	5,523	5,110
45,050	45,100	5,534	4,998	5,534	5,116
45,100	45,150	5,545	5,004	5,545	5,122
45,150	45,200	5,556	5,010	5,556	5,128
45,200	45,250	5,567	5,016	5,567	5,134
45,250	45,300	5,578	5,022	5,578	5,140
45,300	45,350	5,589	5,028	5,589	5,146
45,350	45,400	5,600	5,034	5,600	5,152
45,400	45,450	5,611	5,040	5,611	5,158
45,450	45,500	5,622	5,046	5,622	5,164
45,500	45,550	5,633	5,052	5,633	5,170
45,550	45,600	5,644	5,058	5,644	5,176
45,600	45,650	5,655	5,064	5,655	5,182
45,650	45,700	5,666	5,070	5,666	5,188
45,700	45,750	5,677	5,076	5,677	5,194
45,750	45,800	5,688	5,082	5,688	5,200
45,800	45,850	5,699	5,088	5,699	5,206
45,850	45,900	5,710	5,094	5,710	5,212
45,900	45,950	5,721	5,100	5,721	5,218
45,950	46,000	5,732	5,106	5,732	5,224

46,000

At least	But less than	Single	Married filing jointly *	Married filing separately	Head of a household
46,000	46,050	5,743	5,112	5,743	5,230
46,050	46,100	5,754	5,118	5,754	5,236
46,100	46,150	5,765	5,124	5,765	5,242
46,150	46,200	5,776	5,130	5,776	5,248
46,200	46,250	5,787	5,136	5,787	5,254
46,250	46,300	5,798	5,142	5,798	5,260
46,300	46,350	5,809	5,148	5,809	5,266
46,350	46,400	5,820	5,154	5,820	5,272
46,400	46,450	5,831	5,160	5,831	5,278
46,450	46,500	5,842	5,166	5,842	5,284
46,500	46,550	5,853	5,172	5,853	5,290
46,550	46,600	5,864	5,178	5,864	5,296
46,600	46,650	5,875	5,184	5,875	5,302
46,650	46,700	5,886	5,190	5,886	5,308
46,700	46,750	5,897	5,196	5,897	5,314
46,750	46,800	5,908	5,202	5,908	5,320
46,800	46,850	5,919	5,208	5,919	5,326
46,850	46,900	5,930	5,214	5,930	5,332
46,900	46,950	5,941	5,220	5,941	5,338
46,950	47,000	5,952	5,226	5,952	5,344

47,000

At least	But less than	Single	Married filing jointly *	Married filing separately	Head of a household
47,000	47,050	5,963	5,232	5,963	5,350
47,050	47,100	5,974	5,238	5,974	5,356
47,100	47,150	5,985	5,244	5,985	5,362
47,150	47,200	5,996	5,250	5,996	5,368
47,200	47,250	6,007	5,256	6,007	5,374
47,250	47,300	6,018	5,262	6,018	5,380
47,300	47,350	6,029	5,268	6,029	5,386
47,350	47,400	6,040	5,274	6,040	5,392
47,400	47,450	6,051	5,280	6,051	5,398
47,450	47,500	6,062	5,286	6,062	5,404
47,500	47,550	6,073	5,292	6,073	5,410
47,550	47,600	6,084	5,298	6,084	5,416
47,600	47,650	6,095	5,304	6,095	5,422
47,650	47,700	6,106	5,310	6,106	5,428
47,700	47,750	6,117	5,316	6,117	5,434
47,750	47,800	6,128	5,322	6,128	5,440
47,800	47,850	6,139	5,328	6,139	5,446
47,850	47,900	6,150	5,334	6,150	5,452
47,900	47,950	6,161	5,340	6,161	5,458
47,950	48,000	6,172	5,346	6,172	5,464

(Continued)

* This column must also be used by a qualifying surviving spouse.

If line 15 (taxable income) is—		And you are—			
At least	But less than	Single	Married filing jointly *	Married filing separately	Head of a household
		Your tax is—			

48,000

At least	But less than	Single	Married filing jointly *	Married filing separately	Head of a household
48,000	48,050	6,183	5,352	6,183	5,470
48,050	48,100	6,194	5,358	6,194	5,476
48,100	48,150	6,205	5,364	6,205	5,482
48,150	48,200	6,216	5,370	6,216	5,488
48,200	48,250	6,227	5,376	6,227	5,494
48,250	48,300	6,238	5,382	6,238	5,500
48,300	48,350	6,249	5,388	6,249	5,506
48,350	48,400	6,260	5,394	6,260	5,512
48,400	48,450	6,271	5,400	6,271	5,518
48,450	48,500	6,282	5,406	6,282	5,524
48,500	48,550	6,293	5,412	6,293	5,530
48,550	48,600	6,304	5,418	6,304	5,536
48,600	48,650	6,315	5,424	6,315	5,542
48,650	48,700	6,326	5,430	6,326	5,548
48,700	48,750	6,337	5,436	6,337	5,554
48,750	48,800	6,348	5,442	6,348	5,560
48,800	48,850	6,359	5,448	6,359	5,566
48,850	48,900	6,370	5,454	6,370	5,572
48,900	48,950	6,381	5,460	6,381	5,578
48,950	49,000	6,392	5,466	6,392	5,584

49,000

At least	But less than	Single	Married filing jointly *	Married filing separately	Head of a household
49,000	49,050	6,403	5,472	6,403	5,590
49,050	49,100	6,414	5,478	6,414	5,596
49,100	49,150	6,425	5,484	6,425	5,602
49,150	49,200	6,436	5,490	6,436	5,608
49,200	49,250	6,447	5,496	6,447	5,614
49,250	49,300	6,458	5,502	6,458	5,620
49,300	49,350	6,469	5,508	6,469	5,626
49,350	49,400	6,480	5,514	6,480	5,632
49,400	49,450	6,491	5,520	6,491	5,638
49,450	49,500	6,502	5,526	6,502	5,644
49,500	49,550	6,513	5,532	6,513	5,650
49,550	49,600	6,524	5,538	6,524	5,656
49,600	49,650	6,535	5,544	6,535	5,662
49,650	49,700	6,546	5,550	6,546	5,668
49,700	49,750	6,557	5,556	6,557	5,674
49,750	49,800	6,568	5,562	6,568	5,680
49,800	49,850	6,579	5,568	6,579	5,686
49,850	49,900	6,590	5,574	6,590	5,692
49,900	49,950	6,601	5,580	6,601	5,698
49,950	50,000	6,612	5,586	6,612	5,704

50,000

At least	But less than	Single	Married filing jointly *	Married filing separately	Head of a household
50,000	50,050	6,623	5,592	6,623	5,710
50,050	50,100	6,634	5,598	6,634	5,716
50,100	50,150	6,645	5,604	6,645	5,722
50,150	50,200	6,656	5,610	6,656	5,728
50,200	50,250	6,667	5,616	6,667	5,734
50,250	50,300	6,678	5,622	6,678	5,740
50,300	50,350	6,689	5,628	6,689	5,746
50,350	50,400	6,700	5,634	6,700	5,752
50,400	50,450	6,711	5,640	6,711	5,758
50,450	50,500	6,722	5,646	6,722	5,764
50,500	50,550	6,733	5,652	6,733	5,770
50,550	50,600	6,744	5,658	6,744	5,776
50,600	50,650	6,755	5,664	6,755	5,782
50,650	50,700	6,766	5,670	6,766	5,788
50,700	50,750	6,777	5,676	6,777	5,794
50,750	50,800	6,788	5,682	6,788	5,800
50,800	50,850	6,799	5,688	6,799	5,806
50,850	50,900	6,810	5,694	6,810	5,812
50,900	50,950	6,821	5,700	6,821	5,818
50,950	51,000	6,832	5,706	6,832	5,824

51,000

At least	But less than	Single	Married filing jointly *	Married filing separately	Head of a household
51,000	51,050	6,843	5,712	6,843	5,830
51,050	51,100	6,854	5,718	6,854	5,836
51,100	51,150	6,865	5,724	6,865	5,842
51,150	51,200	6,876	5,730	6,876	5,848
51,200	51,250	6,887	5,736	6,887	5,854
51,250	51,300	6,898	5,742	6,898	5,860
51,300	51,350	6,909	5,748	6,909	5,866
51,350	51,400	6,920	5,754	6,920	5,872
51,400	51,450	6,931	5,760	6,931	5,878
51,450	51,500	6,942	5,766	6,942	5,884
51,500	51,550	6,953	5,772	6,953	5,890
51,550	51,600	6,964	5,778	6,964	5,896
51,600	51,650	6,975	5,784	6,975	5,902
51,650	51,700	6,986	5,790	6,986	5,908
51,700	51,750	6,997	5,796	6,997	5,914
51,750	51,800	7,008	5,802	7,008	5,920
51,800	51,850	7,019	5,808	7,019	5,926
51,850	51,900	7,030	5,814	7,030	5,932
51,900	51,950	7,041	5,820	7,041	5,938
51,950	52,000	7,052	5,826	7,052	5,944

52,000

At least	But less than	Single	Married filing jointly *	Married filing separately	Head of a household
52,000	52,050	7,063	5,832	7,063	5,950
52,050	52,100	7,074	5,838	7,074	5,956
52,100	52,150	7,085	5,844	7,085	5,962
52,150	52,200	7,096	5,850	7,096	5,968
52,200	52,250	7,107	5,856	7,107	5,974
52,250	52,300	7,118	5,862	7,118	5,980
52,300	52,350	7,129	5,868	7,129	5,986
52,350	52,400	7,140	5,874	7,140	5,992
52,400	52,450	7,151	5,880	7,151	5,998
52,450	52,500	7,162	5,886	7,162	6,004
52,500	52,550	7,173	5,892	7,173	6,010
52,550	52,600	7,184	5,898	7,184	6,016
52,600	52,650	7,195	5,904	7,195	6,022
52,650	52,700	7,206	5,910	7,206	6,028
52,700	52,750	7,217	5,916	7,217	6,034
52,750	52,800	7,228	5,922	7,228	6,040
52,800	52,850	7,239	5,928	7,239	6,046
52,850	52,900	7,250	5,934	7,250	6,052
52,900	52,950	7,261	5,940	7,261	6,058
52,950	53,000	7,272	5,946	7,272	6,064

53,000

At least	But less than	Single	Married filing jointly *	Married filing separately	Head of a household
53,000	53,050	7,283	5,952	7,283	6,070
53,050	53,100	7,294	5,958	7,294	6,076
53,100	53,150	7,305	5,964	7,305	6,082
53,150	53,200	7,316	5,970	7,316	6,088
53,200	53,250	7,327	5,976	7,327	6,094
53,250	53,300	7,338	5,982	7,338	6,100
53,300	53,350	7,349	5,988	7,349	6,106
53,350	53,400	7,360	5,994	7,360	6,112
53,400	53,450	7,371	6,000	7,371	6,118
53,450	53,500	7,382	6,006	7,382	6,124
53,500	53,550	7,393	6,012	7,393	6,130
53,550	53,600	7,404	6,018	7,404	6,136
53,600	53,650	7,415	6,024	7,415	6,142
53,650	53,700	7,426	6,030	7,426	6,148
53,700	53,750	7,437	6,036	7,437	6,154
53,750	53,800	7,448	6,042	7,448	6,160
53,800	53,850	7,459	6,048	7,459	6,166
53,850	53,900	7,470	6,054	7,470	6,172
53,900	53,950	7,481	6,060	7,481	6,178
53,950	54,000	7,492	6,066	7,492	6,184

54,000

At least	But less than	Single	Married filing jointly *	Married filing separately	Head of a household
54,000	54,050	7,503	6,072	7,503	6,190
54,050	54,100	7,514	6,078	7,514	6,196
54,100	54,150	7,525	6,084	7,525	6,202
54,150	54,200	7,536	6,090	7,536	6,208
54,200	54,250	7,547	6,096	7,547	6,214
54,250	54,300	7,558	6,102	7,558	6,220
54,300	54,350	7,569	6,108	7,569	6,226
54,350	54,400	7,580	6,114	7,580	6,232
54,400	54,450	7,591	6,120	7,591	6,238
54,450	54,500	7,602	6,126	7,602	6,244
54,500	54,550	7,613	6,132	7,613	6,250
54,550	54,600	7,624	6,138	7,624	6,256
54,600	54,650	7,635	6,144	7,635	6,262
54,650	54,700	7,646	6,150	7,646	6,268
54,700	54,750	7,657	6,156	7,657	6,274
54,750	54,800	7,668	6,162	7,668	6,280
54,800	54,850	7,679	6,168	7,679	6,286
54,850	54,900	7,690	6,174	7,690	6,292
54,900	54,950	7,701	6,180	7,701	6,298
54,950	55,000	7,712	6,186	7,712	6,304

55,000

At least	But less than	Single	Married filing jointly *	Married filing separately	Head of a household
55,000	55,050	7,723	6,192	7,723	6,310
55,050	55,100	7,734	6,198	7,734	6,316
55,100	55,150	7,745	6,204	7,745	6,322
55,150	55,200	7,756	6,210	7,756	6,328
55,200	55,250	7,767	6,216	7,767	6,334
55,250	55,300	7,778	6,222	7,778	6,340
55,300	55,350	7,789	6,228	7,789	6,346
55,350	55,400	7,800	6,234	7,800	6,352
55,400	55,450	7,811	6,240	7,811	6,358
55,450	55,500	7,822	6,246	7,822	6,364
55,500	55,550	7,833	6,252	7,833	6,370
55,550	55,600	7,844	6,258	7,844	6,376
55,600	55,650	7,855	6,264	7,855	6,382
55,650	55,700	7,866	6,270	7,866	6,388
55,700	55,750	7,877	6,276	7,877	6,394
55,750	55,800	7,888	6,282	7,888	6,400
55,800	55,850	7,899	6,288	7,899	6,406
55,850	55,900	7,910	6,294	7,910	6,412
55,900	55,950	7,921	6,300	7,921	6,421
55,950	56,000	7,932	6,306	7,932	6,432

56,000

At least	But less than	Single	Married filing jointly *	Married filing separately	Head of a household
56,000	56,050	7,943	6,312	7,943	6,443
56,050	56,100	7,954	6,318	7,954	6,454
56,100	56,150	7,965	6,324	7,965	6,465
56,150	56,200	7,976	6,330	7,976	6,476
56,200	56,250	7,987	6,336	7,987	6,487
56,250	56,300	7,998	6,342	7,998	6,498
56,300	56,350	8,009	6,348	8,009	6,509
56,350	56,400	8,020	6,354	8,020	6,520
56,400	56,450	8,031	6,360	8,031	6,531
56,450	56,500	8,042	6,366	8,042	6,542
56,500	56,550	8,053	6,372	8,053	6,553
56,550	56,600	8,064	6,378	8,064	6,564
56,600	56,650	8,075	6,384	8,075	6,575
56,650	56,700	8,086	6,390	8,086	6,586
56,700	56,750	8,097	6,396	8,097	6,597
56,750	56,800	8,108	6,402	8,108	6,608
56,800	56,850	8,119	6,408	8,119	6,619
56,850	56,900	8,130	6,414	8,130	6,630
56,900	56,950	8,141	6,420	8,141	6,641
56,950	57,000	8,152	6,426	8,152	6,652

(Continued)

* This column must also be used by a qualifying surviving spouse.

If line 15 (taxable income) is—		And you are—			
At least	But less than	Single	Married filing jointly *	Married filing separately	Head of a household
		Your tax is—			

57,000

At least	But less than	Single	Married filing jointly *	Married filing separately	Head of a household
57,000	57,050	8,163	6,432	8,163	6,663
57,050	57,100	8,174	6,438	8,174	6,674
57,100	57,150	8,185	6,444	8,185	6,685
57,150	57,200	8,196	6,450	8,196	6,696
57,200	57,250	8,207	6,456	8,207	6,707
57,250	57,300	8,218	6,462	8,218	6,718
57,300	57,350	8,229	6,468	8,229	6,729
57,350	57,400	8,240	6,474	8,240	6,740
57,400	57,450	8,251	6,480	8,251	6,751
57,450	57,500	8,262	6,486	8,262	6,762
57,500	57,550	8,273	6,492	8,273	6,773
57,550	57,600	8,284	6,498	8,284	6,784
57,600	57,650	8,295	6,504	8,295	6,795
57,650	57,700	8,306	6,510	8,306	6,806
57,700	57,750	8,317	6,516	8,317	6,817
57,750	57,800	8,328	6,522	8,328	6,828
57,800	57,850	8,339	6,528	8,339	6,839
57,850	57,900	8,350	6,534	8,350	6,850
57,900	57,950	8,361	6,540	8,361	6,861
57,950	58,000	8,372	6,546	8,372	6,872

58,000

At least	But less than	Single	Married filing jointly *	Married filing separately	Head of a household
58,000	58,050	8,383	6,552	8,383	6,883
58,050	58,100	8,394	6,558	8,394	6,894
58,100	58,150	8,405	6,564	8,405	6,905
58,150	58,200	8,416	6,570	8,416	6,916
58,200	58,250	8,427	6,576	8,427	6,927
58,250	58,300	8,438	6,582	8,438	6,938
58,300	58,350	8,449	6,588	8,449	6,949
58,350	58,400	8,460	6,594	8,460	6,960
58,400	58,450	8,471	6,600	8,471	6,971
58,450	58,500	8,482	6,606	8,482	6,982
58,500	58,550	8,493	6,612	8,493	6,993
58,550	58,600	8,504	6,618	8,504	7,004
58,600	58,650	8,515	6,624	8,515	7,015
58,650	58,700	8,526	6,630	8,526	7,026
58,700	58,750	8,537	6,636	8,537	7,037
58,750	58,800	8,548	6,642	8,548	7,048
58,800	58,850	8,559	6,648	8,559	7,059
58,850	58,900	8,570	6,654	8,570	7,070
58,900	58,950	8,581	6,660	8,581	7,081
58,950	59,000	8,592	6,666	8,592	7,092

59,000

At least	But less than	Single	Married filing jointly *	Married filing separately	Head of a household
59,000	59,050	8,603	6,672	8,603	7,103
59,050	59,100	8,614	6,678	8,614	7,114
59,100	59,150	8,625	6,684	8,625	7,125
59,150	59,200	8,636	6,690	8,636	7,136
59,200	59,250	8,647	6,696	8,647	7,147
59,250	59,300	8,658	6,702	8,658	7,158
59,300	59,350	8,669	6,708	8,669	7,169
59,350	59,400	8,680	6,714	8,680	7,180
59,400	59,450	8,691	6,720	8,691	7,191
59,450	59,500	8,702	6,726	8,702	7,202
59,500	59,550	8,713	6,732	8,713	7,213
59,550	59,600	8,724	6,738	8,724	7,224
59,600	59,650	8,735	6,744	8,735	7,235
59,650	59,700	8,746	6,750	8,746	7,246
59,700	59,750	8,757	6,756	8,757	7,257
59,750	59,800	8,768	6,762	8,768	7,268
59,800	59,850	8,779	6,768	8,779	7,279
59,850	59,900	8,790	6,774	8,790	7,290
59,900	59,950	8,801	6,780	8,801	7,301
59,950	60,000	8,812	6,786	8,812	7,312

60,000

At least	But less than	Single	Married filing jointly *	Married filing separately	Head of a household
60,000	60,050	8,823	6,792	8,823	7,323
60,050	60,100	8,834	6,798	8,834	7,334
60,100	60,150	8,845	6,804	8,845	7,345
60,150	60,200	8,856	6,810	8,856	7,356
60,200	60,250	8,867	6,816	8,867	7,367
60,250	60,300	8,878	6,822	8,878	7,378
60,300	60,350	8,889	6,828	8,889	7,389
60,350	60,400	8,900	6,834	8,900	7,400
60,400	60,450	8,911	6,840	8,911	7,411
60,450	60,500	8,922	6,846	8,922	7,422
60,500	60,550	8,933	6,852	8,933	7,433
60,550	60,600	8,944	6,858	8,944	7,444
60,600	60,650	8,955	6,864	8,955	7,455
60,650	60,700	8,966	6,870	8,966	7,466
60,700	60,750	8,977	6,876	8,977	7,477
60,750	60,800	8,988	6,882	8,988	7,488
60,800	60,850	8,999	6,888	8,999	7,499
60,850	60,900	9,010	6,894	9,010	7,510
60,900	60,950	9,021	6,900	9,021	7,521
60,950	61,000	9,032	6,906	9,032	7,532

61,000

At least	But less than	Single	Married filing jointly *	Married filing separately	Head of a household
61,000	61,050	9,043	6,912	9,043	7,543
61,050	61,100	9,054	6,918	9,054	7,554
61,100	61,150	9,065	6,924	9,065	7,565
61,150	61,200	9,076	6,930	9,076	7,576
61,200	61,250	9,087	6,936	9,087	7,587
61,250	61,300	9,098	6,942	9,098	7,598
61,300	61,350	9,109	6,948	9,109	7,609
61,350	61,400	9,120	6,954	9,120	7,620
61,400	61,450	9,131	6,960	9,131	7,631
61,450	61,500	9,142	6,966	9,142	7,642
61,500	61,550	9,153	6,972	9,153	7,653
61,550	61,600	9,164	6,978	9,164	7,664
61,600	61,650	9,175	6,984	9,175	7,675
61,650	61,700	9,186	6,990	9,186	7,686
61,700	61,750	9,197	6,996	9,197	7,697
61,750	61,800	9,208	7,002	9,208	7,708
61,800	61,850	9,219	7,008	9,219	7,719
61,850	61,900	9,230	7,014	9,230	7,730
61,900	61,950	9,241	7,020	9,241	7,741
61,950	62,000	9,252	7,026	9,252	7,752

62,000

At least	But less than	Single	Married filing jointly *	Married filing separately	Head of a household
62,000	62,050	9,263	7,032	9,263	7,763
62,050	62,100	9,274	7,038	9,274	7,774
62,100	62,150	9,285	7,044	9,285	7,785
62,150	62,200	9,296	7,050	9,296	7,796
62,200	62,250	9,307	7,056	9,307	7,807
62,250	62,300	9,318	7,062	9,318	7,818
62,300	62,350	9,329	7,068	9,329	7,829
62,350	62,400	9,340	7,074	9,340	7,840
62,400	62,450	9,351	7,080	9,351	7,851
62,450	62,500	9,362	7,086	9,362	7,862
62,500	62,550	9,373	7,092	9,373	7,873
62,550	62,600	9,384	7,098	9,384	7,884
62,600	62,650	9,395	7,104	9,395	7,895
62,650	62,700	9,406	7,110	9,406	7,906
62,700	62,750	9,417	7,116	9,417	7,917
62,750	62,800	9,428	7,122	9,428	7,928
62,800	62,850	9,439	7,128	9,439	7,939
62,850	62,900	9,450	7,134	9,450	7,950
62,900	62,950	9,461	7,140	9,461	7,961
62,950	63,000	9,472	7,146	9,472	7,972

63,000

At least	But less than	Single	Married filing jointly *	Married filing separately	Head of a household
63,000	63,050	9,483	7,152	9,483	7,983
63,050	63,100	9,494	7,158	9,494	7,994
63,100	63,150	9,505	7,164	9,505	8,005
63,150	63,200	9,516	7,170	9,516	8,016
63,200	63,250	9,527	7,176	9,527	8,027
63,250	63,300	9,538	7,182	9,538	8,038
63,300	63,350	9,549	7,188	9,549	8,049
63,350	63,400	9,560	7,194	9,560	8,060
63,400	63,450	9,571	7,200	9,571	8,071
63,450	63,500	9,582	7,206	9,582	8,082
63,500	63,550	9,593	7,212	9,593	8,093
63,550	63,600	9,604	7,218	9,604	8,104
63,600	63,650	9,615	7,224	9,615	8,115
63,650	63,700	9,626	7,230	9,626	8,126
63,700	63,750	9,637	7,236	9,637	8,137
63,750	63,800	9,648	7,242	9,648	8,148
63,800	63,850	9,659	7,248	9,659	8,159
63,850	63,900	9,670	7,254	9,670	8,170
63,900	63,950	9,681	7,260	9,681	8,181
63,950	64,000	9,692	7,266	9,692	8,192

64,000

At least	But less than	Single	Married filing jointly *	Married filing separately	Head of a household
64,000	64,050	9,703	7,272	9,703	8,203
64,050	64,100	9,714	7,278	9,714	8,214
64,100	64,150	9,725	7,284	9,725	8,225
64,150	64,200	9,736	7,290	9,736	8,236
64,200	64,250	9,747	7,296	9,747	8,247
64,250	64,300	9,758	7,302	9,758	8,258
64,300	64,350	9,769	7,308	9,769	8,269
64,350	64,400	9,780	7,314	9,780	8,280
64,400	64,450	9,791	7,320	9,791	8,291
64,450	64,500	9,802	7,326	9,802	8,302
64,500	64,550	9,813	7,332	9,813	8,313
64,550	64,600	9,824	7,338	9,824	8,324
64,600	64,650	9,835	7,344	9,835	8,335
64,650	64,700	9,846	7,350	9,846	8,346
64,700	64,750	9,857	7,356	9,857	8,357
64,750	64,800	9,868	7,362	9,868	8,368
64,800	64,850	9,879	7,368	9,879	8,379
64,850	64,900	9,890	7,374	9,890	8,390
64,900	64,950	9,901	7,380	9,901	8,401
64,950	65,000	9,912	7,386	9,912	8,412

65,000

At least	But less than	Single	Married filing jointly *	Married filing separately	Head of a household
65,000	65,050	9,923	7,392	9,923	8,423
65,050	65,100	9,934	7,398	9,934	8,434
65,100	65,150	9,945	7,404	9,945	8,445
65,150	65,200	9,956	7,410	9,956	8,456
65,200	65,250	9,967	7,416	9,967	8,467
65,250	65,300	9,978	7,422	9,978	8,478
65,300	65,350	9,989	7,428	9,989	8,489
65,350	65,400	10,000	7,434	10,000	8,500
65,400	65,450	10,011	7,440	10,011	8,511
65,450	65,500	10,022	7,446	10,022	8,522
65,500	65,550	10,033	7,452	10,033	8,533
65,550	65,600	10,044	7,458	10,044	8,544
65,600	65,650	10,055	7,464	10,055	8,555
65,650	65,700	10,066	7,470	10,066	8,566
65,700	65,750	10,077	7,476	10,077	8,577
65,750	65,800	10,088	7,482	10,088	8,588
65,800	65,850	10,099	7,488	10,099	8,599
65,850	65,900	10,110	7,494	10,110	8,610
65,900	65,950	10,121	7,500	10,121	8,621
65,950	66,000	10,132	7,506	10,132	8,632

(Continued)

* This column must also be used by a qualifying surviving spouse.

If line 15 (taxable income) is— / And you are—

Columns: At least | But less than | Single | Married filing jointly * | Married filing separately | Head of a household — Your tax is—

66,000

At least	But less than	Single	MFJ *	MFS	HoH
66,000	66,050	10,143	7,512	10,143	8,643
66,050	66,100	10,154	7,518	10,154	8,654
66,100	66,150	10,165	7,524	10,165	8,665
66,150	66,200	10,176	7,530	10,176	8,676
66,200	66,250	10,187	7,536	10,187	8,687
66,250	66,300	10,198	7,542	10,198	8,698
66,300	66,350	10,209	7,548	10,209	8,709
66,350	66,400	10,220	7,554	10,220	8,720
66,400	66,450	10,231	7,560	10,231	8,731
66,450	66,500	10,242	7,566	10,242	8,742
66,500	66,550	10,253	7,572	10,253	8,753
66,550	66,600	10,264	7,578	10,264	8,764
66,600	66,650	10,275	7,584	10,275	8,775
66,650	66,700	10,286	7,590	10,286	8,786
66,700	66,750	10,297	7,596	10,297	8,797
66,750	66,800	10,308	7,602	10,308	8,808
66,800	66,850	10,319	7,608	10,319	8,819
66,850	66,900	10,330	7,614	10,330	8,830
66,900	66,950	10,341	7,620	10,341	8,841
66,950	67,000	10,352	7,626	10,352	8,852

67,000

At least	But less than	Single	MFJ *	MFS	HoH
67,000	67,050	10,363	7,632	10,363	8,863
67,050	67,100	10,374	7,638	10,374	8,874
67,100	67,150	10,385	7,644	10,385	8,885
67,150	67,200	10,396	7,650	10,396	8,896
67,200	67,250	10,407	7,656	10,407	8,907
67,250	67,300	10,418	7,662	10,418	8,918
67,300	67,350	10,429	7,668	10,429	8,929
67,350	67,400	10,440	7,674	10,440	8,940
67,400	67,450	10,451	7,680	10,451	8,951
67,450	67,500	10,462	7,686	10,462	8,962
67,500	67,550	10,473	7,692	10,473	8,973
67,550	67,600	10,484	7,698	10,484	8,984
67,600	67,650	10,495	7,704	10,495	8,995
67,650	67,700	10,506	7,710	10,506	9,006
67,700	67,750	10,517	7,716	10,517	9,017
67,750	67,800	10,528	7,722	10,528	9,028
67,800	67,850	10,539	7,728	10,539	9,039
67,850	67,900	10,550	7,734	10,550	9,050
67,900	67,950	10,561	7,740	10,561	9,061
67,950	68,000	10,572	7,746	10,572	9,072

68,000

At least	But less than	Single	MFJ *	MFS	HoH
68,000	68,050	10,583	7,752	10,583	9,083
68,050	68,100	10,594	7,758	10,594	9,094
68,100	68,150	10,605	7,764	10,605	9,105
68,150	68,200	10,616	7,770	10,616	9,116
68,200	68,250	10,627	7,776	10,627	9,127
68,250	68,300	10,638	7,782	10,638	9,138
68,300	68,350	10,649	7,788	10,649	9,149
68,350	68,400	10,660	7,794	10,660	9,160
68,400	68,450	10,671	7,800	10,671	9,171
68,450	68,500	10,682	7,806	10,682	9,182
68,500	68,550	10,693	7,812	10,693	9,193
68,550	68,600	10,704	7,818	10,704	9,204
68,600	68,650	10,715	7,824	10,715	9,215
68,650	68,700	10,726	7,830	10,726	9,226
68,700	68,750	10,737	7,836	10,737	9,237
68,750	68,800	10,748	7,842	10,748	9,248
68,800	68,850	10,759	7,848	10,759	9,259
68,850	68,900	10,770	7,854	10,770	9,270
68,900	68,950	10,781	7,860	10,781	9,281
68,950	69,000	10,792	7,866	10,792	9,292

69,000

At least	But less than	Single	MFJ *	MFS	HoH
69,000	69,050	10,803	7,872	10,803	9,303
69,050	69,100	10,814	7,878	10,814	9,314
69,100	69,150	10,825	7,884	10,825	9,325
69,150	69,200	10,836	7,890	10,836	9,336
69,200	69,250	10,847	7,896	10,847	9,347
69,250	69,300	10,858	7,902	10,858	9,358
69,300	69,350	10,869	7,908	10,869	9,369
69,350	69,400	10,880	7,914	10,880	9,380
69,400	69,450	10,891	7,920	10,891	9,391
69,450	69,500	10,902	7,926	10,902	9,402
69,500	69,550	10,913	7,932	10,913	9,413
69,550	69,600	10,924	7,938	10,924	9,424
69,600	69,650	10,935	7,944	10,935	9,435
69,650	69,700	10,946	7,950	10,946	9,446
69,700	69,750	10,957	7,956	10,957	9,457
69,750	69,800	10,968	7,962	10,968	9,468
69,800	69,850	10,979	7,968	10,979	9,479
69,850	69,900	10,990	7,974	10,990	9,490
69,900	69,950	11,001	7,980	11,001	9,501
69,950	70,000	11,012	7,986	11,012	9,512

70,000

At least	But less than	Single	MFJ *	MFS	HoH
70,000	70,050	11,023	7,992	11,023	9,523
70,050	70,100	11,034	7,998	11,034	9,534
70,100	70,150	11,045	8,004	11,045	9,545
70,150	70,200	11,056	8,010	11,056	9,556
70,200	70,250	11,067	8,016	11,067	9,567
70,250	70,300	11,078	8,022	11,078	9,578
70,300	70,350	11,089	8,028	11,089	9,589
70,350	70,400	11,100	8,034	11,100	9,600
70,400	70,450	11,111	8,040	11,111	9,611
70,450	70,500	11,122	8,046	11,122	9,622
70,500	70,550	11,133	8,052	11,133	9,633
70,550	70,600	11,144	8,058	11,144	9,644
70,600	70,650	11,155	8,064	11,155	9,655
70,650	70,700	11,166	8,070	11,166	9,666
70,700	70,750	11,177	8,076	11,177	9,677
70,750	70,800	11,188	8,082	11,188	9,688
70,800	70,850	11,199	8,088	11,199	9,699
70,850	70,900	11,210	8,094	11,210	9,710
70,900	70,950	11,221	8,100	11,221	9,721
70,950	71,000	11,232	8,106	11,232	9,732

71,000

At least	But less than	Single	MFJ *	MFS	HoH
71,000	71,050	11,243	8,112	11,243	9,743
71,050	71,100	11,254	8,118	11,254	9,754
71,100	71,150	11,265	8,124	11,265	9,765
71,150	71,200	11,276	8,130	11,276	9,776
71,200	71,250	11,287	8,136	11,287	9,787
71,250	71,300	11,298	8,142	11,298	9,798
71,300	71,350	11,309	8,148	11,309	9,809
71,350	71,400	11,320	8,154	11,320	9,820
71,400	71,450	11,331	8,160	11,331	9,831
71,450	71,500	11,342	8,166	11,342	9,842
71,500	71,550	11,353	8,172	11,353	9,853
71,550	71,600	11,364	8,178	11,364	9,864
71,600	71,650	11,375	8,184	11,375	9,875
71,650	71,700	11,386	8,190	11,386	9,886
71,700	71,750	11,397	8,196	11,397	9,897
71,750	71,800	11,408	8,202	11,408	9,908
71,800	71,850	11,419	8,208	11,419	9,919
71,850	71,900	11,430	8,214	11,430	9,930
71,900	71,950	11,441	8,220	11,441	9,941
71,950	72,000	11,452	8,226	11,452	9,952

72,000

At least	But less than	Single	MFJ *	MFS	HoH
72,000	72,050	11,463	8,232	11,463	9,963
72,050	72,100	11,474	8,238	11,474	9,974
72,100	72,150	11,485	8,244	11,485	9,985
72,150	72,200	11,496	8,250	11,496	9,996
72,200	72,250	11,507	8,256	11,507	10,007
72,250	72,300	11,518	8,262	11,518	10,018
72,300	72,350	11,529	8,268	11,529	10,029
72,350	72,400	11,540	8,274	11,540	10,040
72,400	72,450	11,551	8,280	11,551	10,051
72,450	72,500	11,562	8,286	11,562	10,062
72,500	72,550	11,573	8,292	11,573	10,073
72,550	72,600	11,584	8,298	11,584	10,084
72,600	72,650	11,595	8,304	11,595	10,095
72,650	72,700	11,606	8,310	11,606	10,106
72,700	72,750	11,617	8,316	11,617	10,117
72,750	72,800	11,628	8,322	11,628	10,128
72,800	72,850	11,639	8,328	11,639	10,139
72,850	72,900	11,650	8,334	11,650	10,150
72,900	72,950	11,661	8,340	11,661	10,161
72,950	73,000	11,672	8,346	11,672	10,172

73,000

At least	But less than	Single	MFJ *	MFS	HoH
73,000	73,050	11,683	8,352	11,683	10,183
73,050	73,100	11,694	8,358	11,694	10,194
73,100	73,150	11,705	8,364	11,705	10,205
73,150	73,200	11,716	8,370	11,716	10,216
73,200	73,250	11,727	8,376	11,727	10,227
73,250	73,300	11,738	8,382	11,738	10,238
73,300	73,350	11,749	8,388	11,749	10,249
73,350	73,400	11,760	8,394	11,760	10,260
73,400	73,450	11,771	8,400	11,771	10,271
73,450	73,500	11,782	8,406	11,782	10,282
73,500	73,550	11,793	8,412	11,793	10,293
73,550	73,600	11,804	8,418	11,804	10,304
73,600	73,650	11,815	8,424	11,815	10,315
73,650	73,700	11,826	8,430	11,826	10,326
73,700	73,750	11,837	8,436	11,837	10,337
73,750	73,800	11,848	8,442	11,848	10,348
73,800	73,850	11,859	8,448	11,859	10,359
73,850	73,900	11,870	8,454	11,870	10,370
73,900	73,950	11,881	8,460	11,881	10,381
73,950	74,000	11,892	8,466	11,892	10,392

74,000

At least	But less than	Single	MFJ *	MFS	HoH
74,000	74,050	11,903	8,472	11,903	10,403
74,050	74,100	11,914	8,478	11,914	10,414
74,100	74,150	11,925	8,484	11,925	10,425
74,150	74,200	11,936	8,490	11,936	10,436
74,200	74,250	11,947	8,496	11,947	10,447
74,250	74,300	11,958	8,502	11,958	10,458
74,300	74,350	11,969	8,508	11,969	10,469
74,350	74,400	11,980	8,514	11,980	10,480
74,400	74,450	11,991	8,520	11,991	10,491
74,450	74,500	12,002	8,526	12,002	10,502
74,500	74,550	12,013	8,532	12,013	10,513
74,550	74,600	12,024	8,538	12,024	10,524
74,600	74,650	12,035	8,544	12,035	10,535
74,650	74,700	12,046	8,550	12,046	10,546
74,700	74,750	12,057	8,556	12,057	10,557
74,750	74,800	12,068	8,562	12,068	10,568
74,800	74,850	12,079	8,568	12,079	10,579
74,850	74,900	12,090	8,574	12,090	10,590
74,900	74,950	12,101	8,580	12,101	10,601
74,950	75,000	12,112	8,586	12,112	10,612

(Continued)

* This column must also be used by a qualifying surviving spouse.

If line 15 (taxable income) is— And you are— Your tax is—

75,000

At least	But less than	Single	Married filing jointly *	Married filing separately	Head of a household
75,000	75,050	12,123	8,592	12,123	10,623
75,050	75,100	12,134	8,598	12,134	10,634
75,100	75,150	12,145	8,604	12,145	10,645
75,150	75,200	12,156	8,610	12,156	10,656
75,200	75,250	12,167	8,616	12,167	10,667
75,250	75,300	12,178	8,622	12,178	10,678
75,300	75,350	12,189	8,628	12,189	10,689
75,350	75,400	12,200	8,634	12,200	10,700
75,400	75,450	12,211	8,640	12,211	10,711
75,450	75,500	12,222	8,646	12,222	10,722
75,500	75,550	12,233	8,652	12,233	10,733
75,550	75,600	12,244	8,658	12,244	10,744
75,600	75,650	12,255	8,664	12,255	10,755
75,650	75,700	12,266	8,670	12,266	10,766
75,700	75,750	12,277	8,676	12,277	10,777
75,750	75,800	12,288	8,682	12,288	10,788
75,800	75,850	12,299	8,688	12,299	10,799
75,850	75,900	12,310	8,694	12,310	10,810
75,900	75,950	12,321	8,700	12,321	10,821
75,950	76,000	12,332	8,706	12,332	10,832

76,000

At least	But less than	Single	Married filing jointly *	Married filing separately	Head of a household
76,000	76,050	12,343	8,712	12,343	10,843
76,050	76,100	12,354	8,718	12,354	10,854
76,100	76,150	12,365	8,724	12,365	10,865
76,150	76,200	12,376	8,730	12,376	10,876
76,200	76,250	12,387	8,736	12,387	10,887
76,250	76,300	12,398	8,742	12,398	10,898
76,300	76,350	12,409	8,748	12,409	10,909
76,350	76,400	12,420	8,754	12,420	10,920
76,400	76,450	12,431	8,760	12,431	10,931
76,450	76,500	12,442	8,766	12,442	10,942
76,500	76,550	12,453	8,772	12,453	10,953
76,550	76,600	12,464	8,778	12,464	10,964
76,600	76,650	12,475	8,784	12,475	10,975
76,650	76,700	12,486	8,790	12,486	10,986
76,700	76,750	12,497	8,796	12,497	10,997
76,750	76,800	12,508	8,802	12,508	11,008
76,800	76,850	12,519	8,808	12,519	11,019
76,850	76,900	12,530	8,814	12,530	11,030
76,900	76,950	12,541	8,820	12,541	11,041
76,950	77,000	12,552	8,826	12,552	11,052

77,000

At least	But less than	Single	Married filing jointly *	Married filing separately	Head of a household
77,000	77,050	12,563	8,832	12,563	11,063
77,050	77,100	12,574	8,838	12,574	11,074
77,100	77,150	12,585	8,844	12,585	11,085
77,150	77,200	12,596	8,850	12,596	11,096
77,200	77,250	12,607	8,856	12,607	11,107
77,250	77,300	12,618	8,862	12,618	11,118
77,300	77,350	12,629	8,868	12,629	11,129
77,350	77,400	12,640	8,874	12,640	11,140
77,400	77,450	12,651	8,880	12,651	11,151
77,450	77,500	12,662	8,886	12,662	11,162
77,500	77,550	12,673	8,892	12,673	11,173
77,550	77,600	12,684	8,898	12,684	11,184
77,600	77,650	12,695	8,904	12,695	11,195
77,650	77,700	12,706	8,910	12,706	11,206
77,700	77,750	12,717	8,916	12,717	11,217
77,750	77,800	12,728	8,922	12,728	11,228
77,800	77,850	12,739	8,928	12,739	11,239
77,850	77,900	12,750	8,934	12,750	11,250
77,900	77,950	12,761	8,940	12,761	11,261
77,950	78,000	12,772	8,946	12,772	11,272

78,000

At least	But less than	Single	Married filing jointly *	Married filing separately	Head of a household
78,000	78,050	12,783	8,952	12,783	11,283
78,050	78,100	12,794	8,958	12,794	11,294
78,100	78,150	12,805	8,964	12,805	11,305
78,150	78,200	12,816	8,970	12,816	11,316
78,200	78,250	12,827	8,976	12,827	11,327
78,250	78,300	12,838	8,982	12,838	11,338
78,300	78,350	12,849	8,988	12,849	11,349
78,350	78,400	12,860	8,994	12,860	11,360
78,400	78,450	12,871	9,000	12,871	11,371
78,450	78,500	12,882	9,006	12,882	11,382
78,500	78,550	12,893	9,012	12,893	11,393
78,550	78,600	12,904	9,018	12,904	11,404
78,600	78,650	12,915	9,024	12,915	11,415
78,650	78,700	12,926	9,030	12,926	11,426
78,700	78,750	12,937	9,036	12,937	11,437
78,750	78,800	12,948	9,042	12,948	11,448
78,800	78,850	12,959	9,048	12,959	11,459
78,850	78,900	12,970	9,054	12,970	11,470
78,900	78,950	12,981	9,060	12,981	11,481
78,950	79,000	12,992	9,066	12,992	11,492

79,000

At least	But less than	Single	Married filing jointly *	Married filing separately	Head of a household
79,000	79,050	13,003	9,072	13,003	11,503
79,050	79,100	13,014	9,078	13,014	11,514
79,100	79,150	13,025	9,084	13,025	11,525
79,150	79,200	13,036	9,090	13,036	11,536
79,200	79,250	13,047	9,096	13,047	11,547
79,250	79,300	13,058	9,102	13,058	11,558
79,300	79,350	13,069	9,108	13,069	11,569
79,350	79,400	13,080	9,114	13,080	11,580
79,400	79,450	13,091	9,120	13,091	11,591
79,450	79,500	13,102	9,126	13,102	11,602
79,500	79,550	13,113	9,132	13,113	11,613
79,550	79,600	13,124	9,138	13,124	11,624
79,600	79,650	13,135	9,144	13,135	11,635
79,650	79,700	13,146	9,150	13,146	11,646
79,700	79,750	13,157	9,156	13,157	11,657
79,750	79,800	13,168	9,162	13,168	11,668
79,800	79,850	13,179	9,168	13,179	11,679
79,850	79,900	13,190	9,174	13,190	11,690
79,900	79,950	13,201	9,180	13,201	11,701
79,950	80,000	13,212	9,186	13,212	11,712

80,000

At least	But less than	Single	Married filing jointly *	Married filing separately	Head of a household
80,000	80,050	13,223	9,192	13,223	11,723
80,050	80,100	13,234	9,198	13,234	11,734
80,100	80,150	13,245	9,204	13,245	11,745
80,150	80,200	13,256	9,210	13,256	11,756
80,200	80,250	13,267	9,216	13,267	11,767
80,250	80,300	13,278	9,222	13,278	11,778
80,300	80,350	13,289	9,228	13,289	11,789
80,350	80,400	13,300	9,234	13,300	11,800
80,400	80,450	13,311	9,240	13,311	11,811
80,450	80,500	13,322	9,246	13,322	11,822
80,500	80,550	13,333	9,252	13,333	11,833
80,550	80,600	13,344	9,258	13,344	11,844
80,600	80,650	13,355	9,264	13,355	11,855
80,650	80,700	13,366	9,270	13,366	11,866
80,700	80,750	13,377	9,276	13,377	11,877
80,750	80,800	13,388	9,282	13,388	11,888
80,800	80,850	13,399	9,288	13,399	11,899
80,850	80,900	13,410	9,294	13,410	11,910
80,900	80,950	13,421	9,300	13,421	11,921
80,950	81,000	13,432	9,306	13,432	11,932

81,000

At least	But less than	Single	Married filing jointly *	Married filing separately	Head of a household
81,000	81,050	13,443	9,312	13,443	11,943
81,050	81,100	13,454	9,318	13,454	11,954
81,100	81,150	13,465	9,324	13,465	11,965
81,150	81,200	13,476	9,330	13,476	11,976
81,200	81,250	13,487	9,336	13,487	11,987
81,250	81,300	13,498	9,342	13,498	11,998
81,300	81,350	13,509	9,348	13,509	12,009
81,350	81,400	13,520	9,354	13,520	12,020
81,400	81,450	13,531	9,360	13,531	12,031
81,450	81,500	13,542	9,366	13,542	12,042
81,500	81,550	13,553	9,372	13,553	12,053
81,550	81,600	13,564	9,378	13,564	12,064
81,600	81,650	13,575	9,384	13,575	12,075
81,650	81,700	13,586	9,390	13,586	12,086
81,700	81,750	13,597	9,396	13,597	12,097
81,750	81,800	13,608	9,402	13,608	12,108
81,800	81,850	13,619	9,408	13,619	12,119
81,850	81,900	13,630	9,414	13,630	12,130
81,900	81,950	13,641	9,420	13,641	12,141
81,950	82,000	13,652	9,426	13,652	12,152

82,000

At least	But less than	Single	Married filing jointly *	Married filing separately	Head of a household
82,000	82,050	13,663	9,432	13,663	12,163
82,050	82,100	13,674	9,438	13,674	12,174
82,100	82,150	13,685	9,444	13,685	12,185
82,150	82,200	13,696	9,450	13,696	12,196
82,200	82,250	13,707	9,456	13,707	12,207
82,250	82,300	13,718	9,462	13,718	12,218
82,300	82,350	13,729	9,468	13,729	12,229
82,350	82,400	13,740	9,474	13,740	12,240
82,400	82,450	13,751	9,480	13,751	12,251
82,450	82,500	13,762	9,486	13,762	12,262
82,500	82,550	13,773	9,492	13,773	12,273
82,550	82,600	13,784	9,498	13,784	12,284
82,600	82,650	13,795	9,504	13,795	12,295
82,650	82,700	13,806	9,510	13,806	12,306
82,700	82,750	13,817	9,516	13,817	12,317
82,750	82,800	13,828	9,522	13,828	12,328
82,800	82,850	13,839	9,528	13,839	12,339
82,850	82,900	13,850	9,534	13,850	12,350
82,900	82,950	13,861	9,540	13,861	12,361
82,950	83,000	13,872	9,546	13,872	12,372

83,000

At least	But less than	Single	Married filing jointly *	Married filing separately	Head of a household
83,000	83,050	13,883	9,552	13,883	12,383
83,050	83,100	13,894	9,558	13,894	12,394
83,100	83,150	13,905	9,564	13,905	12,405
83,150	83,200	13,916	9,570	13,916	12,416
83,200	83,250	13,927	9,576	13,927	12,427
83,250	83,300	13,938	9,582	13,938	12,438
83,300	83,350	13,949	9,588	13,949	12,449
83,350	83,400	13,960	9,594	13,960	12,460
83,400	83,450	13,971	9,600	13,971	12,471
83,450	83,500	13,982	9,606	13,982	12,482
83,500	83,550	13,993	9,612	13,993	12,493
83,550	83,600	14,004	9,621	14,004	12,504
83,600	83,650	14,015	9,632	14,015	12,515
83,650	83,700	14,026	9,643	14,026	12,526
83,700	83,750	14,037	9,654	14,037	12,537
83,750	83,800	14,048	9,665	14,048	12,548
83,800	83,850	14,059	9,676	14,059	12,559
83,850	83,900	14,070	9,687	14,070	12,570
83,900	83,950	14,081	9,698	14,081	12,581
83,950	84,000	14,092	9,709	14,092	12,592

* This column must also be used by a qualifying surviving spouse.

(Continued)

If line 15 (taxable income) is—		And you are—				If line 15 (taxable income) is—		And you are—				If line 15 (taxable income) is—		And you are—			
At least	But less than	Single	Married filing jointly *	Married filing sepa-rately	Head of a house-hold	At least	But less than	Single	Married filing jointly *	Married filing sepa-rately	Head of a house-hold	At least	But less than	Single	Married filing jointly *	Married filing sepa-rately	Head of a house-hold
		Your tax is—						Your tax is—						Your tax is—			
84,000						**87,000**						**90,000**					
84,000	84,050	14,103	9,720	14,103	12,603	87,000	87,050	14,763	10,380	14,763	13,263	90,000	90,050	15,442	11,040	15,442	13,942
84,050	84,100	14,114	9,731	14,114	12,614	87,050	87,100	14,774	10,391	14,774	13,274	90,050	90,100	15,454	11,051	15,454	13,954
84,100	84,150	14,125	9,742	14,125	12,625	87,100	87,150	14,785	10,402	14,785	13,285	90,100	90,150	15,466	11,062	15,466	13,966
84,150	84,200	14,136	9,753	14,136	12,636	87,150	87,200	14,796	10,413	14,796	13,296	90,150	90,200	15,478	11,073	15,478	13,978
84,200	84,250	14,147	9,764	14,147	12,647	87,200	87,250	14,807	10,424	14,807	13,307	90,200	90,250	15,490	11,084	15,490	13,990
84,250	84,300	14,158	9,775	14,158	12,658	87,250	87,300	14,818	10,435	14,818	13,318	90,250	90,300	15,502	11,095	15,502	14,002
84,300	84,350	14,169	9,786	14,169	12,669	87,300	87,350	14,829	10,446	14,829	13,329	90,300	90,350	15,514	11,106	15,514	14,014
84,350	84,400	14,180	9,797	14,180	12,680	87,350	87,400	14,840	10,457	14,840	13,340	90,350	90,400	15,526	11,117	15,526	14,026
84,400	84,450	14,191	9,808	14,191	12,691	87,400	87,450	14,851	10,468	14,851	13,351	90,400	90,450	15,538	11,128	15,538	14,038
84,450	84,500	14,202	9,819	14,202	12,702	87,450	87,500	14,862	10,479	14,862	13,362	90,450	90,500	15,550	11,139	15,550	14,050
84,500	84,550	14,213	9,830	14,213	12,713	87,500	87,550	14,873	10,490	14,873	13,373	90,500	90,550	15,562	11,150	15,562	14,062
84,550	84,600	14,224	9,841	14,224	12,724	87,550	87,600	14,884	10,501	14,884	13,384	90,550	90,600	15,574	11,161	15,574	14,074
84,600	84,650	14,235	9,852	14,235	12,735	87,600	87,650	14,895	10,512	14,895	13,395	90,600	90,650	15,586	11,172	15,586	14,086
84,650	84,700	14,246	9,863	14,246	12,746	87,650	87,700	14,906	10,523	14,906	13,406	90,650	90,700	15,598	11,183	15,598	14,098
84,700	84,750	14,257	9,874	14,257	12,757	87,700	87,750	14,917	10,534	14,917	13,417	90,700	90,750	15,610	11,194	15,610	14,110
84,750	84,800	14,268	9,885	14,268	12,768	87,750	87,800	14,928	10,545	14,928	13,428	90,750	90,800	15,622	11,205	15,622	14,122
84,800	84,850	14,279	9,896	14,279	12,779	87,800	87,850	14,939	10,556	14,939	13,439	90,800	90,850	15,634	11,216	15,634	14,134
84,850	84,900	14,290	9,907	14,290	12,790	87,850	87,900	14,950	10,567	14,950	13,450	90,850	90,900	15,646	11,227	15,646	14,146
84,900	84,950	14,301	9,918	14,301	12,801	87,900	87,950	14,961	10,578	14,961	13,461	90,900	90,950	15,658	11,238	15,658	14,158
84,950	85,000	14,312	9,929	14,312	12,812	87,950	88,000	14,972	10,589	14,972	13,472	90,950	91,000	15,670	11,249	15,670	14,170
85,000						**88,000**						**91,000**					
85,000	85,050	14,323	9,940	14,323	12,823	88,000	88,050	14,983	10,600	14,983	13,483	91,000	91,050	15,682	11,260	15,682	14,182
85,050	85,100	14,334	9,951	14,334	12,834	88,050	88,100	14,994	10,611	14,994	13,494	91,050	91,100	15,694	11,271	15,694	14,194
85,100	85,150	14,345	9,962	14,345	12,845	88,100	88,150	15,005	10,622	15,005	13,505	91,100	91,150	15,706	11,282	15,706	14,206
85,150	85,200	14,356	9,973	14,356	12,856	88,150	88,200	15,016	10,633	15,016	13,516	91,150	91,200	15,718	11,293	15,718	14,218
85,200	85,250	14,367	9,984	14,367	12,867	88,200	88,250	15,027	10,644	15,027	13,527	91,200	91,250	15,730	11,304	15,730	14,230
85,250	85,300	14,378	9,995	14,378	12,878	88,250	88,300	15,038	10,655	15,038	13,538	91,250	91,300	15,742	11,315	15,742	14,242
85,300	85,350	14,389	10,006	14,389	12,889	88,300	88,350	15,049	10,666	15,049	13,549	91,300	91,350	15,754	11,326	15,754	14,254
85,350	85,400	14,400	10,017	14,400	12,900	88,350	88,400	15,060	10,677	15,060	13,560	91,350	91,400	15,766	11,337	15,766	14,266
85,400	85,450	14,411	10,028	14,411	12,911	88,400	88,450	15,071	10,688	15,071	13,571	91,400	91,450	15,778	11,348	15,778	14,278
85,450	85,500	14,422	10,039	14,422	12,922	88,450	88,500	15,082	10,699	15,082	13,582	91,450	91,500	15,790	11,359	15,790	14,290
85,500	85,550	14,433	10,050	14,433	12,933	88,500	88,550	15,093	10,710	15,093	13,593	91,500	91,550	15,802	11,370	15,802	14,302
85,550	85,600	14,444	10,061	14,444	12,944	88,550	88,600	15,104	10,721	15,104	13,604	91,550	91,600	15,814	11,381	15,814	14,314
85,600	85,650	14,455	10,072	14,455	12,955	88,600	88,650	15,115	10,732	15,115	13,615	91,600	91,650	15,826	11,392	15,826	14,326
85,650	85,700	14,466	10,083	14,466	12,966	88,650	88,700	15,126	10,743	15,126	13,626	91,650	91,700	15,838	11,403	15,838	14,338
85,700	85,750	14,477	10,094	14,477	12,977	88,700	88,750	15,137	10,754	15,137	13,637	91,700	91,750	15,850	11,414	15,850	14,350
85,750	85,800	14,488	10,105	14,488	12,988	88,750	88,800	15,148	10,765	15,148	13,648	91,750	91,800	15,862	11,425	15,862	14,362
85,800	85,850	14,499	10,116	14,499	12,999	88,800	88,850	15,159	10,776	15,159	13,659	91,800	91,850	15,874	11,436	15,874	14,374
85,850	85,900	14,510	10,127	14,510	13,010	88,850	88,900	15,170	10,787	15,170	13,670	91,850	91,900	15,886	11,447	15,886	14,386
85,900	85,950	14,521	10,138	14,521	13,021	88,900	88,950	15,181	10,798	15,181	13,681	91,900	91,950	15,898	11,458	15,898	14,398
85,950	86,000	14,532	10,149	14,532	13,032	88,950	89,000	15,192	10,809	15,192	13,692	91,950	92,000	15,910	11,469	15,910	14,410
86,000						**89,000**						**92,000**					
86,000	86,050	14,543	10,160	14,543	13,043	89,000	89,050	15,203	10,820	15,203	13,703	92,000	92,050	15,922	11,480	15,922	14,422
86,050	86,100	14,554	10,171	14,554	13,054	89,050	89,100	15,214	10,831	15,214	13,714	92,050	92,100	15,934	11,491	15,934	14,434
86,100	86,150	14,565	10,182	14,565	13,065	89,100	89,150	15,226	10,842	15,226	13,726	92,100	92,150	15,946	11,502	15,946	14,446
86,150	86,200	14,576	10,193	14,576	13,076	89,150	89,200	15,238	10,853	15,238	13,738	92,150	92,200	15,958	11,513	15,958	14,458
86,200	86,250	14,587	10,204	14,587	13,087	89,200	89,250	15,250	10,864	15,250	13,750	92,200	92,250	15,970	11,524	15,970	14,470
86,250	86,300	14,598	10,215	14,598	13,098	89,250	89,300	15,262	10,875	15,262	13,762	92,250	92,300	15,982	11,535	15,982	14,482
86,300	86,350	14,609	10,226	14,609	13,109	89,300	89,350	15,274	10,886	15,274	13,774	92,300	92,350	15,994	11,546	15,994	14,494
86,350	86,400	14,620	10,237	14,620	13,120	89,350	89,400	15,286	10,897	15,286	13,786	92,350	92,400	16,006	11,557	16,006	14,506
86,400	86,450	14,631	10,248	14,631	13,131	89,400	89,450	15,298	10,908	15,298	13,798	92,400	92,450	16,018	11,568	16,018	14,518
86,450	86,500	14,642	10,259	14,642	13,142	89,450	89,500	15,310	10,919	15,310	13,810	92,450	92,500	16,030	11,579	16,030	14,530
86,500	86,550	14,653	10,270	14,653	13,153	89,500	89,550	15,322	10,930	15,322	13,822	92,500	92,550	16,042	11,590	16,042	14,542
86,550	86,600	14,664	10,281	14,664	13,164	89,550	89,600	15,334	10,941	15,334	13,834	92,550	92,600	16,054	11,601	16,054	14,554
86,600	86,650	14,675	10,292	14,675	13,175	89,600	89,650	15,346	10,952	15,346	13,846	92,600	92,650	16,066	11,612	16,066	14,566
86,650	86,700	14,686	10,303	14,686	13,186	89,650	89,700	15,358	10,963	15,358	13,858	92,650	92,700	16,078	11,623	16,078	14,578
86,700	86,750	14,697	10,314	14,697	13,197	89,700	89,750	15,370	10,974	15,370	13,870	92,700	92,750	16,090	11,634	16,090	14,590
86,750	86,800	14,708	10,325	14,708	13,208	89,750	89,800	15,382	10,985	15,382	13,882	92,750	92,800	16,102	11,645	16,102	14,602
86,800	86,850	14,719	10,336	14,719	13,219	89,800	89,850	15,394	10,996	15,394	13,894	92,800	92,850	16,114	11,656	16,114	14,614
86,850	86,900	14,730	10,347	14,730	13,230	89,850	89,900	15,406	11,007	15,406	13,906	92,850	92,900	16,126	11,667	16,126	14,626
86,900	86,950	14,741	10,358	14,741	13,241	89,900	89,950	15,418	11,018	15,418	13,918	92,900	92,950	16,138	11,678	16,138	14,638
86,950	87,000	14,752	10,369	14,752	13,252	89,950	90,000	15,430	11,029	15,430	13,930	92,950	93,000	16,150	11,689	16,150	14,650

(Continued)

* This column must also be used by a qualifying surviving spouse.

93,000

At least	But less than	Single	Married filing jointly *	Married filing separately	Head of a household
93,000	93,050	16,162	11,700	16,162	14,662
93,050	93,100	16,174	11,711	16,174	14,674
93,100	93,150	16,186	11,722	16,186	14,686
93,150	93,200	16,198	11,733	16,198	14,698
93,200	93,250	16,210	11,744	16,210	14,710
93,250	93,300	16,222	11,755	16,222	14,722
93,300	93,350	16,234	11,766	16,234	14,734
93,350	93,400	16,246	11,777	16,246	14,746
93,400	93,450	16,258	11,788	16,258	14,758
93,450	93,500	16,270	11,799	16,270	14,770
93,500	93,550	16,282	11,810	16,282	14,782
93,550	93,600	16,294	11,821	16,294	14,794
93,600	93,650	16,306	11,832	16,306	14,806
93,650	93,700	16,318	11,843	16,318	14,818
93,700	93,750	16,330	11,854	16,330	14,830
93,750	93,800	16,342	11,865	16,342	14,842
93,800	93,850	16,354	11,876	16,354	14,854
93,850	93,900	16,366	11,887	16,366	14,866
93,900	93,950	16,378	11,898	16,378	14,878
93,950	94,000	16,390	11,909	16,390	14,890

94,000

At least	But less than	Single	Married filing jointly *	Married filing separately	Head of a household
94,000	94,050	16,402	11,920	16,402	14,902
94,050	94,100	16,414	11,931	16,414	14,914
94,100	94,150	16,426	11,942	16,426	14,926
94,150	94,200	16,438	11,953	16,438	14,938
94,200	94,250	16,450	11,964	16,450	14,950
94,250	94,300	16,462	11,975	16,462	14,962
94,300	94,350	16,474	11,986	16,474	14,974
94,350	94,400	16,486	11,997	16,486	14,986
94,400	94,450	16,498	12,008	16,498	14,998
94,450	94,500	16,510	12,019	16,510	15,010
94,500	94,550	16,522	12,030	16,522	15,022
94,550	94,600	16,534	12,041	16,534	15,034
94,600	94,650	16,546	12,052	16,546	15,046
94,650	94,700	16,558	12,063	16,558	15,058
94,700	94,750	16,570	12,074	16,570	15,070
94,750	94,800	16,582	12,085	16,582	15,082
94,800	94,850	16,594	12,096	16,594	15,094
94,850	94,900	16,606	12,107	16,606	15,106
94,900	94,950	16,618	12,118	16,618	15,118
94,950	95,000	16,630	12,129	16,630	15,130

95,000

At least	But less than	Single	Married filing jointly *	Married filing separately	Head of a household
95,000	95,050	16,642	12,140	16,642	15,142
95,050	95,100	16,654	12,151	16,654	15,154
95,100	95,150	16,666	12,162	16,666	15,166
95,150	95,200	16,678	12,173	16,678	15,178
95,200	95,250	16,690	12,184	16,690	15,190
95,250	95,300	16,702	12,195	16,702	15,202
95,300	95,350	16,714	12,206	16,714	15,214
95,350	95,400	16,726	12,217	16,726	15,226
95,400	95,450	16,738	12,228	16,738	15,238
95,450	95,500	16,750	12,239	16,750	15,250
95,500	95,550	16,762	12,250	16,762	15,262
95,550	95,600	16,774	12,261	16,774	15,274
95,600	95,650	16,786	12,272	16,786	15,286
95,650	95,700	16,798	12,283	16,798	15,298
95,700	95,750	16,810	12,294	16,810	15,310
95,750	95,800	16,822	12,305	16,822	15,322
95,800	95,850	16,834	12,316	16,834	15,334
95,850	95,900	16,846	12,327	16,846	15,346
95,900	95,950	16,858	12,338	16,858	15,358
95,950	96,000	16,870	12,349	16,870	15,370

96,000

At least	But less than	Single	Married filing jointly *	Married filing separately	Head of a household
96,000	96,050	16,882	12,360	16,882	15,382
96,050	96,100	16,894	12,371	16,894	15,394
96,100	96,150	16,906	12,382	16,906	15,406
96,150	96,200	16,918	12,393	16,918	15,418
96,200	96,250	16,930	12,404	16,930	15,430
96,250	96,300	16,942	12,415	16,942	15,442
96,300	96,350	16,954	12,426	16,954	15,454
96,350	96,400	16,966	12,437	16,966	15,466
96,400	96,450	16,978	12,448	16,978	15,478
96,450	96,500	16,990	12,459	16,990	15,490
96,500	96,550	17,002	12,470	17,002	15,502
96,550	96,600	17,014	12,481	17,014	15,514
96,600	96,650	17,026	12,492	17,026	15,526
96,650	96,700	17,038	12,503	17,038	15,538
96,700	96,750	17,050	12,514	17,050	15,550
96,750	96,800	17,062	12,525	17,062	15,562
96,800	96,850	17,074	12,536	17,074	15,574
96,850	96,900	17,086	12,547	17,086	15,586
96,900	96,950	17,098	12,558	17,098	15,598
96,950	97,000	17,110	12,569	17,110	15,610

97,000

At least	But less than	Single	Married filing jointly *	Married filing separately	Head of a household
97,000	97,050	17,122	12,580	17,122	15,622
97,050	97,100	17,134	12,591	17,134	15,634
97,100	97,150	17,146	12,602	17,146	15,646
97,150	97,200	17,158	12,613	17,158	15,658
97,200	97,250	17,170	12,624	17,170	15,670
97,250	97,300	17,182	12,635	17,182	15,682
97,300	97,350	17,194	12,646	17,194	15,694
97,350	97,400	17,206	12,657	17,206	15,706
97,400	97,450	17,218	12,668	17,218	15,718
97,450	97,500	17,230	12,679	17,230	15,730
97,500	97,550	17,242	12,690	17,242	15,742
97,550	97,600	17,254	12,701	17,254	15,754
97,600	97,650	17,266	12,712	17,266	15,766
97,650	97,700	17,278	12,723	17,278	15,778
97,700	97,750	17,290	12,734	17,290	15,790
97,750	97,800	17,302	12,745	17,302	15,802
97,800	97,850	17,314	12,756	17,314	15,814
97,850	97,900	17,326	12,767	17,326	15,826
97,900	97,950	17,338	12,778	17,338	15,838
97,950	98,000	17,350	12,789	17,350	15,850

98,000

At least	But less than	Single	Married filing jointly *	Married filing separately	Head of a household
98,000	98,050	17,362	12,800	17,362	15,862
98,050	98,100	17,374	12,811	17,374	15,874
98,100	98,150	17,386	12,822	17,386	15,886
98,150	98,200	17,398	12,833	17,398	15,898
98,200	98,250	17,410	12,844	17,410	15,910
98,250	98,300	17,422	12,855	17,422	15,922
98,300	98,350	17,434	12,866	17,434	15,934
98,350	98,400	17,446	12,877	17,446	15,946
98,400	98,450	17,458	12,888	17,458	15,958
98,450	98,500	17,470	12,899	17,470	15,970
98,500	98,550	17,482	12,910	17,482	15,982
98,550	98,600	17,494	12,921	17,494	15,994
98,600	98,650	17,506	12,932	17,506	16,006
98,650	98,700	17,518	12,943	17,518	16,018
98,700	98,750	17,530	12,954	17,530	16,030
98,750	98,800	17,542	12,965	17,542	16,042
98,800	98,850	17,554	12,976	17,554	16,054
98,850	98,900	17,566	12,987	17,566	16,066
98,900	98,950	17,578	12,998	17,578	16,078
98,950	99,000	17,590	13,009	17,590	16,090

99,000

At least	But less than	Single	Married filing jointly *	Married filing separately	Head of a household
99,000	99,050	17,602	13,020	17,602	16,102
99,050	99,100	17,614	13,031	17,614	16,114
99,100	99,150	17,626	13,042	17,626	16,126
99,150	99,200	17,638	13,053	17,638	16,138
99,200	99,250	17,650	13,064	17,650	16,150
99,250	99,300	17,662	13,075	17,662	16,162
99,300	99,350	17,674	13,086	17,674	16,174
99,350	99,400	17,686	13,097	17,686	16,186
99,400	99,450	17,698	13,108	17,698	16,198
99,450	99,500	17,710	13,119	17,710	16,210
99,500	99,550	17,722	13,130	17,722	16,222
99,550	99,600	17,734	13,141	17,734	16,234
99,600	99,650	17,746	13,152	17,746	16,246
99,650	99,700	17,758	13,163	17,758	16,258
99,700	99,750	17,770	13,174	17,770	16,270
99,750	99,800	17,782	13,185	17,782	16,282
99,800	99,850	17,794	13,196	17,794	16,294
99,850	99,900	17,806	13,207	17,806	16,306
99,900	99,950	17,818	13,218	17,818	16,318
99,950	100,000	17,830	13,229	17,830	16,330

$100,000 or over use the Tax Computation Worksheet

* This column must also be used by a qualifying surviving spouse.

2022 Tax Computation Worksheet—Line 16

See Line 16 in the Instructions for Form 1040 to see if you must use the worksheet below to figure your tax.

Note. If you're required to use this worksheet to figure the tax on an amount from another form or worksheet, such as the Qualified Dividends and Capital Gain Tax Worksheet, the Schedule D Tax Worksheet, Schedule J, Form 8615, or the Foreign Earned Income Tax Worksheet, enter the amount from that form or worksheet in column (a) of the row that applies to the amount you're looking up. Enter the result on the appropriate line of the form or worksheet that you're completing.

Section A—Use if your filing status is **Single.** Complete the row below that applies to you.

Taxable income. If line 15 is—	(a) Enter the amount from line 15	(b) Multiplication amount	(c) Multiply (a) by (b)	(d) Subtraction amount	Tax. Subtract (d) from (c). Enter the result here and on Form 1040 or 1040-SR, line 16
At least $100,000 but not over $170,050	$	× 24% (0.24)	$	$ 6,164.50	$
Over $170,050 but not over $215,950	$	× 32% (0.32)	$	$ 19,768.50	$
Over $215,950 but not over $539,900	$	× 35% (0.35)	$	$ 26,247.00	$
Over $539,900	$	× 37% (0.37)	$	$ 37,045.00	$

Section B—Use if your filing status is **Married filing jointly** or **Qualifying surviving spouse.** Complete the row below that applies to you.

Taxable income. If line 15 is—	(a) Enter the amount from line 15	(b) Multiplication amount	(c) Multiply (a) by (b)	(d) Subtraction amount	Tax. Subtract (d) from (c). Enter the result here and on Form 1040 or 1040-SR, line 16
At least $100,000 but not over $178,150	$	× 22% (0.22)	$	$ 8,766.00	$
Over $178,150 but not over $340,100	$	× 24% (0.24)	$	$ 12,329.00	$
Over $340,100 but not over $431,900	$	× 32% (0.32)	$	$ 39,537.00	$
Over $431,900 but not over $647,850	$	× 35% (0.35)	$	$ 52,494.00	$
Over $647,850	$	× 37% (0.37)	$	$ 65,451.00	$

Section C—Use if your filing status is **Married filing separately.** Complete the row below that applies to you.

Taxable income. If line 15 is—	(a) Enter the amount from line 15	(b) Multiplication amount	(c) Multiply (a) by (b)	(d) Subtraction amount	Tax. Subtract (d) from (c). Enter the result here and on Form 1040 or 1040-SR, line 16
At least $100,000 but not over $170,050	$	× 24% (0.24)	$	$ 6,164.50	$
Over $170,050 but not over $215,950	$	× 32% (0.32)	$	$ 19,768.50	$
Over $215,950 but not over $323,925	$	× 35% (0.35)	$	$ 26,247.00	$
Over $323,925	$	× 37% (0.37)	$	$ 32,725.50	$

Section D—Use if your filing status is **Head of household.** Complete the row below that applies to you.

Taxable income. If line 15 is—	(a) Enter the amount from line 15	(b) Multiplication amount	(c) Multiply (a) by (b)	(d) Subtraction amount	Tax. Subtract (d) from (c). Enter the result here and on Form 1040 or 1040-SR, line 16
At least $100,000 but not over $170,050	$	× 24% (0.24)	$	$ 7,664.00	$
Over $170,050 but not over $215,950	$	× 32% (0.32)	$	$ 21,268.00	$
Over $215,950 but not over $539,900	$	× 35% (0.35)	$	$ 27,746.50	$
Over $539,900	$	× 37% (0.37)	$	$ 38,544.50	$

2022 Tax Rate Schedules

The Tax Rate Schedules are shown so you can see the tax rate that applies to all levels of taxable income. Don't use them to figure your tax. Instead, see Chapter 13.

Schedule X —If your filing status is **Single**

If your taxable income is: Over—	But not over—	The tax is:	of the amount over—
$0	$10,275	- - - - - - 10%	$0
10,275	41,775	$1,027.50 + 12%	10,275
41,775	89,075	4,807.50 + 22%	41,775
89,075	170,050	15,213.50 + 24%	89,075
170,050	215,950	34,647.50 + 32%	170,050
215,950	539,900	49,335.50 + 35%	215,950
539,900	- - - - - - -	162,718.00 + 37%	539,900

Schedule Y-1 —If your filing status is **Married filing jointly** or **Qualifying surviving spouse**

If your taxable income is: Over—	But not over—	The tax is:	of the amount over—
$0	$20,550	- - - - - - 10%	$0
20,550	83,550	$2,055.00 + 12%	20,550
83,550	178,150	9,615.00 + 22%	83,550
178,150	340,100	30,427.00 + 24%	178,150
340,100	431,900	69,295.00 + 32%	340,100
431,900	647,850	98,671.00 + 35%	431,900
647,850	- - - - - - -	174,253.50 + 37%	647,850

Schedule Y-2 —If your filing status is **Married filing separately**

If your taxable income is: Over—	But not over—	The tax is:	of the amount over—
$0	$10,275	- - - - - - 10%	$0
10,275	41,775	$1,027.50 + 12%	10,275
41,775	89,075	4,807.50 + 22%	41,775
89,075	170,050	15,213.50 + 24%	89,075
170,050	215,950	34,647.50 + 32%	170,050
215,950	323,925	49,335.50 + 35%	215,950
323,925	- - - - - - -	87,126.75 + 37%	323,925

Schedule Z —If your filing status is **Head of household**

If your taxable income is: Over—	But not over—	The tax is:	of the amount over—
$0	$14,650	- - - - - - 10%	$0
14,650	55,900	$1,465.00 + 12%	14,650
55,900	89,050	6,415.00 + 22%	55,900
89,050	170,050	13,708.00 + 24%	89,050
170,050	215,950	33,148.00 + 32%	170,050
215,950	539,900	47,836.00 + 35%	215,950
539,900	- - - - - - -	161,218.50 + 37%	539,900

Your Rights as a Taxpayer

This section explains your rights as a taxpayer and the processes for examination, appeal, collection, and refunds.

The Taxpayer Bill of Rights

1. The Right to Be Informed. Taxpayers have the right to know what they need to do to comply with the tax laws. They are entitled to clear explanations of the laws and IRS procedures in all tax forms, instructions, publications, notices, and correspondence. They have the right to be informed of IRS decisions about their tax accounts and to receive clear explanations of the outcomes.

2. The Right to Quality Service. Taxpayers have the right to receive prompt, courteous, and professional assistance in their dealings with the IRS, to be spoken to in a way they can easily understand, to receive clear and easily understandable communications from the IRS, and to speak to a supervisor about inadequate service.

3. The Right to Pay No More than the Correct Amount of Tax. Taxpayers have the right to pay only the amount of tax legally due, including interest and penalties, and to have the IRS apply all tax payments properly.

4. The Right to Challenge the IRS's Position and Be Heard. Taxpayers have the right to raise objections and provide additional documentation in response to formal IRS actions or proposed actions, to expect that the IRS will consider their timely objections and documentation promptly and fairly, and to receive a response if the IRS does not agree with their position.

5. The Right to Appeal an IRS Decision in an Independent Forum. Taxpayers are entitled to a fair and impartial administrative appeal of most IRS decisions, including many penalties, and have the right to receive a written response regarding the Office of Appeals' decision. Taxpayers generally have the right to take their cases to court.

6. The Right to Finality. Taxpayers have the right to know the maximum amount of time they have to challenge the IRS's position as well as the maximum amount of time the IRS has to audit a particular tax year or collect a tax debt. Taxpayers have the right to know when the IRS has finished an audit.

7. The Right to Privacy. Taxpayers have the right to expect that any IRS inquiry, examination, or enforcement action will comply with the law and be no more intrusive than necessary, and will respect all due process rights, including search and seizure protections, and will provide, where applicable, a collection due process hearing.

8. The Right to Confidentiality. Taxpayers have the right to expect that any information they provide to the IRS will not be disclosed unless authorized by the taxpayer or by law. Taxpayers have the right to expect appropriate action will be taken against employees, return preparers, and others who wrongfully use or disclose taxpayer return information.

9. The Right to Retain Representation. Taxpayers have the right to retain an authorized representative of their choice to represent them in their dealings with the IRS. Taxpayers have the right to seek assistance from a Low Income Taxpayer Clinic if they cannot afford representation.

10. The Right to a Fair and Just Tax System. Taxpayers have the right to expect the tax system to consider facts and circumstances that might affect their underlying liabilities, ability to pay, or ability to provide information timely. Taxpayers have the right to receive assistance from the Taxpayer Advocate Service if they are experiencing financial difficulty or if the IRS has not resolved their tax issues properly and timely through its normal channels.

Examinations (Audits)

We accept most taxpayers' returns as filed. If we inquire about your return or select it for examination, it does not suggest that you are dishonest. The inquiry or examination may or may not result in more tax. We may close your case without change; or, you may receive a refund.

The process of selecting a return for examination usually begins in one of two ways. First, we use computer programs to identify returns that may have incorrect amounts. These programs may be based on information returns, such as Forms 1099 and W-2, on studies of past examinations, or on certain issues identified by compliance projects. Second, we use information from outside sources that indicates that a return may have incorrect amounts. These sources may include newspapers, public records, and individuals. If we determine that the information is accurate and reliable, we may use it to select a return for examination.

Publication 556, Examination of Returns, Appeal Rights, and Claims for Refund, explains the rules and procedures that we follow in examinations. The following sections give an overview of how we conduct examinations.

By mail. We handle many examinations and inquiries by mail. We will send you a letter with either a request for more information or a reason why we believe a change to your return may be needed. You can respond by mail or you can request a personal interview with an examiner. If you mail us the requested information or provide an explanation, we may or may not agree with you, and we will explain the reasons for any changes. Please do not hesitate to write to us about anything you do not understand.

By interview. If we notify you that we will conduct your examination through a personal interview, or you request such an interview, you have the right to ask that the examination take place at a reasonable time and place that is convenient for both you and the IRS. If our examiner proposes any changes to your return, he or she will explain the reasons for the changes. If you do not agree with these changes, you can meet with the examiner's supervisor.

Repeat examinations. If we examined your return for the same items in either of the 2 previous years and proposed no change to your tax liability, please contact us as soon as possible so we can see if we should discontinue the examination.

Appeals

If you do not agree with the examiner's proposed changes, you can appeal them to the Appeals Office of the IRS. Most differences can be settled without expensive and time-consuming court trials. Your appeal rights are explained in detail in both Publication 5, Your Appeal Rights and How To Prepare a Protest If You Don't Agree, and Publication 556, Examination of Returns, Appeal Rights, and Claims for Refund.

If you do not wish to use the Appeals Office or disagree with its findings, you may be able to take your case to the U.S. Tax Court, U.S. Court of Federal Claims, or the U.S. District Court where you live. If you take your case to court, the IRS will have the burden of proving certain facts if you kept adequate records to show your tax liability, cooperated with the IRS, and meet certain other conditions. If the court agrees with you on most issues in your case and finds that our position was largely unjustified, you may be able to recover some of your administrative and litigation costs. You will not be eligible to recover these costs unless you tried to resolve your case administratively, including going through the appeals system, and you gave us the information necessary to resolve the case.

Collections

Publication 594, The IRS Collection Process, explains your rights and responsibilities regarding payment of federal taxes. It describes:

- What to do when you owe taxes. It describes what to do if you get a tax bill and what to do if you think your bill is wrong. It also covers making installment payments, delaying collection action, and submitting an offer in compromise.

- IRS collection actions. It covers liens, releasing a lien, levies, releasing a levy, seizures and sales, and release of property.

- IRS certification to the State Department of a seriously delinquent tax debt, which will generally result in denial of a passport application and may lead to revocation of a passport.

Your collection appeal rights are explained in detail in Publication 1660, Collection Appeal Rights.

Innocent spouse relief. Generally, both you and your spouse are each responsible for paying the full amount of tax, interest, and penalties due on your joint return. However, if you qualify for innocent spouse relief, you may be relieved of part or all of the joint liability. To request relief, you must file Form 8857, Request for Innocent Spouse Relief. For more information on innocent spouse relief, see Publication 971, Innocent Spouse Relief, and Form 8857.

Potential third party contacts. Generally, the IRS will deal directly with you or your duly authorized representative. However, we sometimes talk with other persons if we need information that you have been unable to provide, or to verify information we have received. If we do contact other persons, such as a neighbor, bank, employer, or employees, we will generally need to tell them limited information, such as your name. The law prohibits us from disclosing any more information than is necessary to obtain or verify the information we are seeking. Our need to contact other persons may continue as long as there is activity in your case. If we do contact other persons, you have a right to request a list of those contacted. Your request can be made by telephone, in writing, or during a personal interview.

Refunds

You may file a claim for refund if you think you paid too much tax. You must generally file the claim within 3 years from the date you filed your original return or 2 years from the date you paid the tax, whichever is later. The law generally provides for interest on your refund if it is not paid within 45 days of the date you filed your return or claim for refund. Publication 556, Examination of Returns, Appeal Rights, and Claims for Refund, has more information on refunds.

If you were due a refund but you did not file a return, you generally must file your return within 3 years from the date the return was due (including extensions) to get that refund.

Taxpayer Advocate Service

TAS is an *independent* organization within the IRS that can help protect your taxpayer rights. We can offer you help if your tax problem is causing a hardship, or you've tried but haven't been able to resolve your problem with the IRS. If you qualify for our assistance, which is always free, we will do everything possible to help you. Visit *TaxpayerAdvocate.IRS.gov* or call 1-877-777-4778.

Tax Information

The IRS provides the following sources for forms, publications, and additional information.

- *Internet*: IRS.gov.
- *Tax Questions*:

IRS.gov/help/tax-law-questions and *How To Get Tax Help*.

- *Forms and Publications*: *IRS.gov/Forms* and *IRS.gov/OrderForms*.
- *Small Business Ombudsman*: A small business entity can participate in the regulatory process and comment on enforcement actions of the IRS by calling 1-888-REG-FAIR.
- *Treasury Inspector General for Tax Administration*: You can confidentially report misconduct, waste, fraud, or abuse by an IRS employee by calling 1-800-366-4484. People who are deaf, hard of hearing, or have a speech disability and who have access to TTY/TDD equipment can call 1-800-877-8339. You can remain anonymous.

How To Get Tax Help

If you have questions about a tax issue; need help preparing your tax return; or want to download free publications, forms, or instructions, go to *IRS.gov* to find resources that can help you right away.

Preparing and filing your tax return. After receiving all your wage and earnings statements (Forms W-2, W-2G, 1099-R, 1099-MISC, 1099-NEC, etc.); unemployment compensation statements (by mail or in a digital format) or other government payment statements (Form 1099-G); and interest, dividend, and retirement statements from banks and investment firms (Forms 1099), you have several options to choose from to prepare and file your tax return. You can prepare the tax return yourself, see if you qualify for free tax preparation, or hire a tax professional to prepare your return.

Free options for tax preparation. Go to *IRS.gov* to see your options for preparing and filing your return online or in your local community, if you qualify, which include the following.

- **Free File.** This program lets you prepare and file your federal individual income tax return for free using brand-name tax-preparation-and-filing software or Free File fillable forms. However, state tax preparation may not be available through Free File. Go to *IRS.gov/FreeFile* to see if you qualify for free online federal tax preparation, e-filing, and direct deposit or payment options.

- **VITA.** The Volunteer Income Tax Assistance (VITA) program offers free tax help to people with low-to-moderate incomes, persons with disabilities, and limited-English-speaking taxpayers who need help preparing their own tax returns. Go to *IRS.gov/VITA*, download the free IRS2Go app, or call 800-906-9887 for information on free tax return preparation.

- **TCE.** The Tax Counseling for the Elderly (TCE) program offers free tax help for all taxpayers, particularly those who are 60 years of age and older. TCE volunteers specialize in answering questions about pensions and retirement-related issues unique to seniors. Go to *IRS.gov/TCE*, download the free IRS2Go app, or call 888-227-7669 for information on free tax return preparation.

- **MilTax.** Members of the U.S. Armed Forces and qualified veterans may use MilTax, a free tax service offered by the Department of Defense through Military OneSource. For more information, go to *MilitaryOneSource* (*MilitaryOneSource.mil/MilTax*).

Also, the IRS offers Free Fillable Forms, which can be completed online and then filed electronically regardless of income.

Using online tools to help prepare your return. Go to *IRS.gov/Tools* for the following.

- The *Earned Income Tax Credit Assistant* (*IRS.gov/EITCAssistant*) determines if you're eligible for the earned income credit (EIC).

- The *Online EIN Application* (*IRS.gov/EIN*) helps you get an employer identification number (EIN) at no cost.

- The *Tax Withholding Estimator* (*IRS.gov/W4app*) makes it easier for you to estimate the federal income tax you want your employer to withhold from your paycheck. This is tax withholding. See how your withholding affects your refund, take-home pay, or tax due.

- The *First-Time Homebuyer Credit Account Look-up* (*IRS.gov/HomeBuyer*) tool provides information on your repayments and account balance.

- The *Sales Tax Deduction Calculator* (*IRS.gov/SalesTax*) figures the amount you can claim if you itemize deductions on Schedule A (Form 1040).

Getting answers to your tax questions. On IRS.gov, you can get up-to-date information on current events and changes in tax law.

- *IRS.gov/Help*: A variety of tools to help you get answers to some of the most common tax questions.

- *IRS.gov/ITA*: The Interactive Tax Assistant, a tool that will ask you questions and, based on your input, provide answers on a number of tax law topics.

- *IRS.gov/Forms*: Find forms, instructions, and publications. You will find details on the most recent tax changes and interactive links to help you find answers to your questions.

You may also be able to access tax law information in your electronic filing software.

Need someone to prepare your tax return? There are various types of tax return preparers, including enrolled agents, certified public accountants (CPAs), accountants, and many others who don't have professional credentials. If you choose to have someone prepare your tax return, choose that preparer wisely. A paid tax preparer is:

- Primarily responsible for the overall substantive accuracy of your return,

- Required to sign the return, and

- Required to include their preparer tax identification number (PTIN).

Although the tax preparer always signs the return, you're ultimately responsible for providing all the information required for the preparer to accurately prepare your return. Anyone paid to prepare tax returns for others should have a thorough understanding of tax matters. For more information on how to choose a tax preparer, go to *Tips for Choosing a Tax Preparer* on IRS.gov.

Coronavirus. Go to *IRS.gov/Coronavirus* for links to information on the impact of the coronavirus, as well as tax relief available for individuals and families, small and large businesses, and tax-exempt organizations.

Employers can register to use Business Services Online. The Social Security Administration (SSA) offers online service at *SSA.gov/employer* for fast, free, and secure online W-2 filing options to CPAs, accountants, enrolled agents, and individuals who process Form W-2, Wage and Tax Statement, and Form W-2c, Corrected Wage and Tax Statement.

IRS social media. Go to *IRS.gov/SocialMedia* to see the various social media tools the IRS uses to share the latest information on tax changes, scam alerts, initiatives, products, and services. At the IRS, privacy and security are our highest priority. We use these tools to share public information with you. **Don't** post your social security number (SSN) or other confidential information on social media sites. Always protect your identity when using any social networking site.

The following IRS YouTube channels provide short, informative videos on various tax-related topics in English, Spanish, and ASL.

- *Youtube.com/irsvideos*.
- *Youtube.com/irsvideosmultilingua*.
- *Youtube.com/irsvideosASL*.

Watching IRS videos. The IRS Video portal (*IRSVideos.gov*) contains video and audio presentations for individuals, small businesses, and tax professionals.

Online tax information in other languages. You can find information on *IRS.gov/MyLanguage* if English isn't your native language.

Free Over-the-Phone Interpreter (OPI) Service. The IRS is committed to serving our multilingual customers by offering OPI services. The OPI Service is a federally funded program and is available at Taxpayer Assistance Centers (TACs), other IRS offices, and every VITA/TCE return site. The OPI Service is accessible in more than 350 languages.

Accessibility Helpline available for taxpayers with disabilities. Taxpayers who need information about accessibility services can call 833-690-0598. The Accessibility Helpline can answer questions related to current and future accessibility products and services available in alternative media formats (for example, braille, large print, audio, etc.). The Accessibility Helpline does not have access to your IRS account. For help with tax law, refunds, or account-related issues, go to *IRS.gov/LetUsHelp*.

Note. Form 9000, Alternative Media Preference, or Form 9000(SP) allows you to elect to receive certain types of written correspondence in the following formats.

- Standard Print.
- Large Print.
- Braille.
- Audio (MP3).
- Plain Text File (TXT).
- Braille Ready File (BRF).

Disasters. Go to *Disaster Assistance and Emergency Relief for Individuals and Businesses* to review the available disaster tax relief.

Getting tax forms and publications. Go to *IRS.gov/Forms* to view, download, or print all the forms, instructions, and publications you may need. Or, you can go to *IRS.gov/OrderForms* to place an order.

Getting tax publications and instructions in eBook format. You can also download and view popular tax publications and instructions (including the Instructions for Form 1040) on mobile devices as eBooks at *IRS.gov/eBooks*.

Note. IRS eBooks have been tested using Apple's iBooks for iPad. Our eBooks haven't been tested on other dedicated eBook readers, and eBook functionality may not operate as intended.

Access your online account (individual taxpayers only). Go to *IRS.gov/Account* to securely access information about your federal tax account.

- View the amount you owe and a breakdown by tax year.

- See payment plan details or apply for a new payment plan.

- Make a payment or view 5 years of payment history and any pending or scheduled payments.

- Access your tax records, including key data from your most recent tax return, and transcripts.

- View digital copies of select notices from the IRS.

- Approve or reject authorization requests from tax professionals.

- View your address on file or manage your communication preferences.

Tax Pro Account. This tool lets your tax professional submit an authorization request to access your individual taxpayer *IRS online account*. For more information, go to *IRS.gov/TaxProAccount*.

Using direct deposit. The fastest way to receive a tax refund is to file electronically and choose direct deposit, which securely and electronically transfers your refund directly into your financial account. Direct deposit also avoids the possibility that your check could be lost, stolen, destroyed, or returned undeliverable to the IRS. Eight in 10 taxpayers use direct deposit to receive their refunds. If you don't have a bank account, go to *IRS.gov/DirectDeposit* for more information on where to find a bank or credit union that can open an account online.

Getting a transcript of your return. The quickest way to get a copy of your tax transcript is to go to *IRS.gov/Transcripts*. Click on either "Get Transcript Online" or "Get Transcript by Mail" to order a free copy of your transcript. If you prefer, you can order your transcript by calling 800-908-9946.

Reporting and resolving your tax-related identity theft issues.

- Tax-related identity theft happens when someone steals your personal information to commit tax fraud. Your taxes can be affected if your SSN is

used to file a fraudulent return or to claim a refund or credit.

- The IRS doesn't initiate contact with taxpayers by email, text messages (including shortened links), telephone calls, or social media channels to request or verify personal or financial information. This includes requests for personal identification numbers (PINs), passwords, or similar information for credit cards, banks, or other financial accounts.

- Go to *IRS.gov/IdentityTheft*, the IRS Identity Theft Central webpage, for information on identity theft and data security protection for taxpayers, tax professionals, and businesses. If your SSN has been lost or stolen or you suspect you're a victim of tax-related identity theft, you can learn what steps you should take.

- Get an Identity Protection PIN (IP PIN). IP PINs are six-digit numbers assigned to taxpayers to help prevent the misuse of their SSNs on fraudulent federal income tax returns. When you have an IP PIN, it prevents someone else from filing a tax return with your SSN. To learn more, go to *IRS.gov/IPPIN*.

Ways to check on the status of your refund.

- Go to *IRS.gov/Refunds*.

- Download the official IRS2Go app to your mobile device to check your refund status.

- Call the automated refund hotline at 800-829-1954.

Note. The IRS can't issue refunds before mid-February for returns that claimed the EIC or the additional child tax credit (ACTC). This applies to the entire refund, not just the portion associated with these credits.

Making a tax payment. Go to *IRS.gov/Payments* for information on how to make a payment using any of the following options.

- *IRS Direct Pay*: Pay your individual tax bill or estimated tax payment directly from your checking or savings account at no cost to you.

- *Debit or Credit Card*: Choose an approved payment processor to pay online or by phone.

- *Electronic Funds Withdrawal*: Schedule a payment when filing your federal taxes using tax return preparation software or through a tax professional.

- *Electronic Federal Tax Payment System*: Best option for businesses. Enrollment is required.

- *Check or Money Order*: Mail your payment to the address listed on the notice or instructions.

- *Cash*: You may be able to pay your taxes with cash at a participating retail store.

- *Same-Day Wire*: You may be able to do same-day wire from your financial institution. Contact your financial institution for availability, cost, and time frames.

Note. The IRS uses the latest encryption technology to ensure that the electronic payments you make online, by phone, or from a mobile device using the IRS2Go app are safe and secure. Paying electronically is quick, easy, and faster than mailing in a check or money order.

What if I can't pay now? Go to *IRS.gov/Payments* for more information about your options.

- Apply for an *online payment agreement* (*IRS.gov/OPA*) to meet your tax obligation in monthly installments if you can't pay your taxes in full today. Once you complete the online process, you will receive immediate notification of whether your agreement has been approved.

- Use the *Offer in Compromise Pre-Qualifier* to see if you can settle your tax debt for less than the full amount you owe. For more information on the Offer in Compromise program, go to *IRS.gov/OIC*.

Filing an amended return. Go to *IRS.gov/Form1040X* for information and updates.

Checking the status of your amended return. Go to *IRS.gov/WMAR* to track the status of Form 1040-X amended returns.

Note. It can take up to 3 weeks from the date you filed your amended return for it to show up in our system, and processing it can take up to 16 weeks.

Understanding an IRS notice or letter you've received. Go to *IRS.gov/Notices* to find additional information about responding to an IRS notice or letter.

Note. You can use Schedule LEP (Form 1040), Request for Change in Language Preference, to state a preference to receive notices, letters, or other written communications from the IRS in an alternative language. You may not immediately receive written communications in the requested language. The IRS's commitment to LEP taxpayers is part of a multi-year timeline that is scheduled to begin providing translations in 2023. You will continue to receive communications, including notices and letters in English until they are translated to your preferred language.

Contacting your local IRS office. Keep in mind, many questions can be answered on IRS.gov without visiting an IRS TAC. Go to *IRS.gov/LetUsHelp* for the topics people ask about most. If you still need help, IRS TACs provide tax help when a tax issue can't be handled online or by phone. All TACs now provide service by appointment, so you'll know in advance that you can get the service you need without long wait times. Before you visit, go to *IRS.gov/TACLocator* to find the nearest TAC and to check hours, available services, and appointment options. Or, on the IRS2Go app, under the Stay Connected tab, choose the Contact Us option and click on "Local Offices."

The Taxpayer Advocate Service (TAS) Is Here To Help You

What Is TAS?

TAS is an *independent* organization within the IRS that helps taxpayers and protects taxpayer rights. Their job is to ensure that every taxpayer is treated fairly and that you know and understand your rights under the *Taxpayer Bill of Rights*.

How Can You Learn About Your Taxpayer Rights?

The Taxpayer Bill of Rights describes 10 basic rights that all taxpayers have when dealing with the IRS. Go to *TaxpayerAdvocate.IRS.gov* to help you understand what these rights mean to you and how they apply. These are *your* rights. Know them. Use them.

What Can TAS Do for You?

TAS can help you resolve problems that you can't resolve with the IRS. And their service is free. If you qualify for their assistance, you will be assigned to one advocate who will work with you throughout the process and will do everything possible to resolve your issue. TAS can help you if:

- Your problem is causing financial difficulty for you, your family, or your business;

- You face (or your business is facing) an immediate threat of adverse action; or

- You've tried repeatedly to contact the IRS but no one has responded, or the IRS hasn't responded by the date promised.

How Can You Reach TAS?

TAS has offices *in every state, the District of Columbia, and Puerto Rico*. Your local advocate's number is in your local directory and at *TaxpayerAdvocate.IRS.gov/Contact-Us*. You can also call them at 877-777-4778.

How Else Does TAS Help Taxpayers?

TAS works to resolve large-scale problems that affect many taxpayers. If you know of one of these broad issues, report it to them at *IRS.gov/SAMS*.

TAS for Tax Professionals

TAS can provide a variety of information for tax professionals, including tax law updates and guidance, TAS programs, and ways to let TAS know about systemic problems you've seen in your practice.

Low Income Taxpayer Clinics (LITCs)

LITCs are independent from the IRS. LITCs represent individuals whose income is below a certain level and need to resolve tax problems with the IRS, such as audits, appeals, and tax collection disputes. In addition, LITCs can provide information about taxpayer rights and responsibilities in different languages for individuals who speak English as a second language. Services are offered for free or a small fee for eligible taxpayers. To find an LITC near you, go to *TaxpayerAdvocate.IRS.gov/about-us/Low-Income-Taxpayer-Clinics-LITC* or see IRS Pub. 4134, *Low Income Taxpayer Clinic List*.

Index

To help us develop a more useful index, please let us know if you have ideas for index entries. See "Comments and Suggestions" in the "Introduction" for the ways you can reach us.

10% tax for early withdrawal from IRA or retirement plan (*See* Early withdrawal from deferred interest account, subheading: Tax on)
2021 Tax Rate Schedules 121
401(k) plans:
  Tax treatment of contributions 48
403(b) plans:
  Rollovers 81, 87
529 plans (*See* Qualified tuition programs)

59 1/2 rule:
  Age 59 1/2 rule 84
60-day rule 80
72 rule:
  Age 72 rule 82

A

Abroad, citizens traveling or working 7, 50
  (*See also* Foreign employment)
Absence, temporary 27, 33
Accelerated death benefits 67

Accident insurance 46
  Cafeteria plans 51
  Long-term care 46, 51
Accidental death benefits 47
Accounting methods 12
  Accrual method (*See* Accrual method taxpayers)
  Cash method (*See* Cash method taxpayers)
Accounting periods 12
  Calendar year 10, 12, 46
  Change in, standard deduction not allowed 89

Fiscal year 12, 41
  Fringe benefits 46
Accrual method taxpayers 12
  Taxes paid during tax year, deduction of 93
Accuracy-related penalties 19
Activities not for profit 71
Address 16
  Change of 17
  Foreign 16
  P.O. box 16

Adjusted gross income (AGI):
Modified (*See* Modified adjusted gross income (MAGI))
Retirement savings contribution credit 22
Adjustments 104
Administrators, estate
(*See* Executors and administrators)
Adopted child 27, 33, 36
Adoption:
ATIN 12
Child tax credit 106
Credits:
Married filing separately 22
Employer assistance 47
Taxpayer identification number 12, 36
Age:
Children's investments (*See* Children, subheading: Investment income of child under age 18)
Gross income and filing requirements (Table 1-1) 5
IRAs:
Distribution prior to age 59 1/2 84
Distribution required at age 72 82, 84
Roth IRAs 85, 88
Standard deduction for age 65 or older 89
Age test 27
Agents:
Income paid to 12
Signing return 14
Agricultural workers
(*See* Farmers)
Agriculture (*See* Farming)
Alaska Permanent Fund dividends 71
Alaska Unemployment Compensation Fund 94
Alcoholic beverages:
IRA prohibited transactions in 83
Aliens:
Dual-status (*See* Dual-status taxpayers)
Filing required 7
Nonresident (*See* Nonresident aliens)
Resident (*See* Resident aliens)
Alimony:
Reporting of income 71
Alternative filing methods:
Electronic (*See* E-file)
Alternative minimum tax (AMT) 104
Ambulance service personnel:
Life insurance proceeds when death in line of duty 67
Amended returns 17, 18
(*See also* Form 1040-X)
Itemized deduction, change to standard deduction 91
Standard deduction, change to itemized deductions 91
American citizens abroad 7
(*See also* Citizens outside U.S.)
Employment (*See* Foreign employment)
American Indians (*See* Indians)
American Samoa:
Income from 7
Annuities:
Decedent's unrecovered investment in 13
IRAs as 76
Unrecovered investment 102
Withholding 13, 38

Annulled marriages:
Filing status 21
Anthrax incidents (*See* Terrorist attacks)
Antiques (*See* Collectibles)
Appraisal fees 98
Archer MSAs 74
Contributions 46
Armed Forces:
Combat zone:
Extension to file return 11
Signing return for spouse 22
Dependency allotments 34
Disability pay 50
Disability pensions 51
GI Bill benefits 35
Military quarters allotments 34
Real estate taxes when receiving housing allowance 95
Rehabilitative program payments 72
Retiree's pay withholding 36
Retirees' pay:
Taxable income 50
Wages 50
Assistance (*See* Tax help)
Assistance, tax (*See* Tax help)
ATIN (Adoption taxpayer identification number) 12
Attachment of wages 12
Attachments to return 13
Attorney contingency fee:
As income 72
Attorney fees, whistleblower awards:
As income 72
Attorneys' fees 99, 100
Automatic extension of time to file 10
Form 4868 10
Awards (*See* Prizes and awards)

B

Babysitting 45
Back pay, award for 45
Emotional distress damages under title VII of Civil Rights Act of 1964 72
Backup withholding 39, 43, 53
Penalties 39
Bad debts:
Claim for refund 18
Recovery 68
Balance due 104
Bankruptcy:
Canceled debt not deemed to be income 66
Banks:
IRAs with 76
Barter income 65
Definition of bartering 65
Form 1099-B 66
Basis:
Cost basis:
IRAs for nondeductible contributions 79, 82
Beneficiaries 72
(*See also* Estate beneficiaries)
(*See also* Trust beneficiaries)
Bequests 72, 73
(*See also* Estate beneficiaries)
(*See also* Inheritance)
Birth of child 28
Head of household, qualifying person to file as 24
Social security number to be obtained 35
Birth of dependent 33
Blind persons:
Exemption from withholding 38

Standard deduction for 89, 90
Bonds:
Amortization of premium 101
Issued at discount 58
Original issue discount 58
Sale of 58
Savings 55
Tax-exempt 58
Bonuses 38, 45, 74
Bookkeeping (*See* Recordkeeping requirements)
Breach of contract:
Damages as income 72
Bribes 71, 99
Brokers:
IRAs with 76
Commissions 76, 77
Burial:
Expenses 99
Business expenses:
Job search expenses 73
Reimbursements 38, 45
Returning excess business expenses 38
Business tax credits:
Claim for refund 19

C

Cafeteria plans 51
Calendar year taxpayers:
Accounting periods 10, 12, 46
Filing due date 10
California Nonoccupational Disability Benefit Fund 94
Campaign contributions 71
Presidential Election Campaign Fund 13
Campaign expenses 100
Canada:
Resident of 27, 32
Cancellation of debt 66
Exceptions to treatment as income 66
Capital assets:
Coal and iron ore 70
Capital expenses 35
Capital gains or losses:
Hobbies, sales from collections 73
Sale of personal items 74
Carpools 71
Carrybacks:
Business tax credit carrybacks 19
Cars 48, 74
(*See also* Travel and transportation)
Personal property taxes on, deduction of 97
Cash:
Rebates 71
Cash method taxpayers 12
Real estate transactions, tax allocation 94
Taxes paid during tax year, deduction of 93
Cash rebates 71
Casualty insurance:
Reimbursements from 72
Casualty losses 99, 101
Certificates of deposit (CDs) 59, 75
(*See also* Individual retirement arrangements (IRAs))
Change of address 17
Change of name 12, 43
Chaplains:
Life insurance proceeds when death in line of duty 67
Charitable contributions:
Gifts to reduce public debt 16

Charitable distributions, qualified 82
Check-writing fees 100
Checks:
Constructive receipt of 12
Child and dependent care credit:
Married filing separately 22
Child born alive 28
Child care:
Babysitting 45
Care providers 45
Expenses 35
Child custody 28
Child support 72
Child tax credit 7, 25, 105-107
Claiming the credit 107
Limit on credit 107
Limits 22
Married filing separately 22
Child, qualifying 27
Children 47
(*See also* Adoption)
Additional child tax credit 107
Adoption (*See* Adopted child)
Babysitters 45
Birth of child:
Head of household, qualifying person to file as 24
Social security number to be obtained 35
Care providers 45
(*See also* Child care)
Credit for 7
(*See also* Child tax credit)
Custody of 28
Death of child:
Head of household, qualifying person to file as 24
Dividends of (*See* this heading: Investment income of child under age 18)
Earnings of 7
Filing requirements 7
As dependents (Table 1-2) 6
Gifts to 53
Investment income of child under age 18:
Dependent filing requirements (Table 1-2) 6
Interest and dividends 7
Parents' election to report on Form 1040 or 1040-SR 7
Kidnapped 28, 32
Signing return, parent for child 14
Standard deduction for 89, 90
Stillborn 28
Support of (*See* Child support)
Tax credit (*See* Child tax credit)
Transporting school children 74
Unearned income of 53
Chronic illness:
Accelerated payment of life insurance proceeds (*See* Accelerated death benefits)
Long-term care (*See* Long-term care insurance contracts)
Citizen or resident test 27
Citizens outside U.S.:
Earned income exclusion 2
Employment (*See* Foreign employment)
Extension of time to file 11
Filing requirements 7
Withholding from IRA distributions 83
Civil suits 72
(*See also* Damages from lawsuits)
Civil tax penalties (*See* Penalties)
Clergy 7

Clergy *(Cont.)*
    Housing 49
        Real estate taxes when receiving housing allowance 95
    Life insurance proceeds when chaplain died in line of duty 67
    Pensions 49
    Special income rules 49
Clerical help, deductibility of 99
Coal and iron ore 70
Collectibles:
    IRA investment in 83
Colleges and universities:
    Education costs 74
    (See also Qualified tuition programs)
Combat zone:
    Extension to file return 11
    Signing return for spouse 22
Commissions 38
    Advance 45
    IRAs with brokers 76, 77
    Sharing of (kickbacks) 73
    Unearned, deduction for repayment of 45
Common law marriage 21
Community property 6, 55
    IRAs 76
    Married filing separately 23
Commuting expenses 100
    Employer-provided commuter vehicle 48
Compensation 45
  (See also Wages and salaries)
    Defined for IRA purposes 76
    Defined for Roth IRA purposes 85
    Employee 45
    Miscellaneous compensation 45
    Nonemployee 72
    Unemployment 70
Computation of tax 13
    Equal amounts 13
    Negative amounts 13
    Rounding off dollars 13
Confidential information:
    Privacy Act and paperwork reduction information 3
Constructive receipt of income 12, 59
Contributions 16, 71
  (See also Campaign contributions)
  (See also Charitable contributions)
    Nontaxable combat pay 76
    Political 101
    Reservist repayments 76
Convenience fees 99
Conversion *(See* specific retirement or IRA plan)
Cooperative housing:
    Real estate taxes, deduction of 94
        Taxes that are deductible (Table 11-1) 96
Copyrights:
    Infringement damages 72
    Royalties 69
Corporations 68
  (See also S corporations)
    Director fees as self-employment income 72
Corrections *(See* Errors)
Cost basis:
    IRAs for nondeductible contributions 79, 82
Cost-of-living allowances 46
Coupon bonds 59
Court awards and damages
  (See Damages from lawsuits)
Cousin 33

Credit cards:
    Benefits, taxability of insurance 72
    Payment of taxes 2
Credit for child and dependent care expenses 105
Credit for other dependents 105, 107
    Claiming the credit 107
    Limit on credit 107
    Qualifying person 107
Credit for the elderly or the disabled 105
Credit or debit cards:
    Payment of taxes 10
Credits 103, 105
    American opportunity 22
    Child tax *(See* Child tax credit)
    Credit for other dependents 105
    Earned income *(See* Earned income credit)
    Lifetime learning *(See* Lifetime learning credit)
Custodial fees 99
Custody of child 28

D

Damages from lawsuits 72
Dating your return 13
Daycare centers 45
  (See also Child care)
De minimis benefits 47
Deadlines *(See* Due dates)
Death *(See* Decedents)
Death benefits:
    Accelerated 67
    Life insurance proceeds *(See* Life insurance)
    Public safety officers who died or were killed in line of duty, tax exclusion 67
Death of child 28
Death of dependent 33
Debt instruments *(See* Bonds or Notes)
Debts 18, 68
  (See also Bad debts)
    Canceled *(See* Cancellation of debt)
    Nonrecourse 66
    Paid by another 12
    Public, gifts to reduce 16
    Recourse 66
    Refund offset against 9, 14
Deceased taxpayers
  (See Decedents)
Decedents 6
  (See also Executors and administrators)
    Deceased spouse 6
    Due dates 10
    Filing requirements 6
    Savings bonds 56
    Spouse's death 21
    Standard deduction 89
Declaration of rights of taxpayers:
    IRS request for information 3
Deductions 68, 89
  (See also Recovery of amounts previously deducted)
    Casualty losses 101
    Changing claim after filing, need to amend 18
    Itemizing *(See* Itemized deductions)
    Pass-through entities 99
    Repayments 69
    Social security and railroad retirement benefits 64
    Standard deduction 89, 91

Student loan interest deduction *(See* Student loans)
    Theft loss 101
Deferred compensation:
    Limit 48
    Nonqualified plans 46
Delinquent taxes:
    Real estate transactions, tax allocation 95
Delivery services 10
Dependent taxpayer test 26
Dependents 7, 25
  (See also Child tax credit)
    Birth of 33
    Born and died within year 12, 35
    Death of 33
    Filing requirements 7
        Earned income, unearned income, and gross income levels (Table 1-2) 6
    Married, filing joint return 26, 29
    Qualifying child 27
    Qualifying relative 32
    Social security number 12
        Adoption taxpayer identification number 12, 36
        Alien dependents 35
    Standard deduction for 90
Dependents not allowed to claim dependents 26
Depletion allowance 69
Deposits:
    Loss on 99
Depreciation:
    Home computer 99
Differential wage payments 46
Differential wages:
    Wages for reservists:
        Military reserves 50
Direct deposit of refunds 14
Directors' fees 72
Disabilities, persons with:
    Accrued leave payment 51
    Armed Forces 50
    Blind *(See* Blind persons)
    Cafeteria plans 51
    Credit for *(See* Elderly or disabled, credit for)
    Insurance costs 51
    Military and government pensions 51
    Public assistance benefits 70
    Reporting of disability pension income 51
    Retirement, pensions, and profit-sharing plans 51
    Signing of return by court-appointed representative 14
    Social security and railroad retirement benefits, deductions for 64
    Workers' compensation 52
Disabled:
    Child 27
    Dependent 33
Disaster Assistance Act of 1988:
    Withholding 39
Disaster relief 51, 71
  (See also Terrorist attacks)
    Disaster Relief and Emergency Assistance Act:
        Grants 71
        Unemployment assistance 70
    Grants or payments 71
Disclosure statement 19
Discount, bonds and notes issued at 58
Distributions:
    Qualified charitable 82

Required minimum distributions 80, 82
    (See also Individual retirement arrangements (IRAs))
Dividends:
    Alaska Permanent Fund *(See* Alaska Permanent Fund dividends)
    Fees to collect 99
    Stockholder debts when canceled as 66
Divorced parents 28, 32
Divorced taxpayers 71
  (See also Alimony)
    Child custody 28
    Estimated tax payments 43
    Filing status 21
    IRAs 77, 81
    Real estate taxes, allocation of 95
Domestic help:
    Withholding 36
Domestic help, can't be claimed as dependent 25
Donations *(See* Charitable contributions)
Down payment assistance 72
Dual-status taxpayers 7
    Joint returns not available 22
    Standard deduction 89
Due dates 9, 10
    2020 dates (Table 1-5) 10
    Extension *(See* Extension of time to file)
    Nonresident aliens' returns 10
Dues:
    Club 100
Dwelling units:
    Cooperative *(See* Cooperative housing)

E

E-file 2, 5, 7
    Extensions of time to file 10
    On time filing 10
Early withdrawal from deferred interest account:
    Higher education expenses, exception from penalty 75
    IRAs:
        Early distributions, defined 84
        Penalties 82, 84
Earned income:
    Defined:
        For purposes of standard deduction 90
    Dependent filing requirements (Table 1-2) 6
Earned income credit 105
    Filing claim 7
    Married filing separately 22
Education:
    Savings bond program 57
Education credits:
    Married filing separately 22
Education expenses:
    Employer-provided *(See* Educational assistance)
    Tuition *(See* Qualified tuition programs)
Educational assistance:
    Employer-provided 47
    Scholarships *(See* Scholarships and fellowships)
    Tuition *(See* Qualified tuition programs)
EIC *(See* Earned income credit)
Elderly or disabled, credit for:
    Married filing separately 22

Elderly persons:
Credit for (*See* Elderly or disabled, credit for)
Exemption from withholding 38
Home for the aged 34
Long-term care (*See* Long-term care insurance contracts)
Nutrition Program for the Elderly 71
Standard deduction for age 65 or older 89
Tax Counseling for the Elderly 9
Election precinct officials:
Fees, reporting of 73
Elective deferrals:
Limits 48
Electronic filing (*See* E-file)
Electronic payment options 2
Electronic reporting:
Returns (*See* E-file)
Embezzlement:
Reporting embezzled funds 73
Emergency medical service personnel:
Life insurance proceeds when death in line of duty 67
Emotional distress damages 72
Employee benefits 46, 47
(*See also* Fringe benefits)
Employee business expenses:
Reimbursements 38, 45
Returning excess 38
Employee expenses:
Home computer 99
Miscellaneous 98
Employees 38, 46, 47
(*See also* Fringe benefits)
Awards for service 45
Business expenses
(*See* Employee business expenses)
Form W-4 to be filled out when starting new job 37
Fringe benefits 38
Jury duty pay 73
Overseas employment
(*See* Foreign employment)
Employers:
E-file options 9
Educational assistance from (*See* Educational assistance)
Form W-4, having new employees fill out 37
Overseas employment (*See* Foreign employment)
Withholding rules 37
Employment:
Agency fees 72
Taxes 46
(*See also* Social security and Medicare taxes)
FICA withholding 11
(*See also* Withholding)
Employment taxes 36, 42
Endowment proceeds 67
Energy assistance 71
Energy conservation:
Measures and modifications 72
Subsidies 72
Utility rebates 74
Equitable relief (*See* Innocent spouse relief)
Errors:
Corrected wage and tax statement 43
Discovery after filing, need to amend return 17
Refunds 17
Escrow:
Taxes placed in, when deductible 95

Estate beneficiaries:
IRAs (*See* Individual retirement arrangements (IRAs))
Losses of estate 72
Receiving income from estate 72
Estate tax:
Deduction 97
Estates 72
(*See also* Estate beneficiaries)
Income 72
Tax 97, 101
(*See also* Estate tax)
Estimated:
Credit for 43
Payment vouchers 41
Estimated tax 36
Amount to pay to avoid penalty 41
Avoiding 39
Change in estimated tax 41
Credit for 36, 42
Definition 36
Divorced taxpayers 43
Figuring amount of tax 41
First period, no income subject to estimated tax in 41
Fiscal year taxpayers 41
Married taxpayers 40
Name change 43
Not required 39
Overpayment applied to 14
Payment vouchers 42
Payments 15, 41
Figuring amount of each payment 41
Schedule 41
When to start 41
Who must make 40
Penalty for underpayment 36, 41, 43
Saturday, Sunday, holiday rule 41
Separate returns 43
Social security or railroad retirement benefits 62
State and local income taxes, deduction of 93
Unemployment compensation 70
Excise taxes 82
(*See also* Penalties)
Deductibility (Table 11-1) 96
IRAs for failure to take minimum distributions 82
Roth IRAs 87
Exclusions from gross income:
Accelerated death benefits 67
Canceled debt 66
Commuting benefits for employees 48
De minimis benefits 47
Disability pensions of federal employees and military 51
Education Savings Bond Program 73
Educational assistance from employer 47
Elective deferrals, limit on exclusion 48
Employee awards 45
Energy conservation subsidies 72, 74
Foreign earned income 2
Frozen deposit interest 73
Group-term life insurance 48
Long-term care insurance contracts 51, 52
Parking fees, employer-provided 48
Public safety officers who died or were killed in line of duty, death benefits 67
Sale of home 74

Scholarships 74
Strike benefits 74
Executors and administrators 6
Exempt-interest dividends 53
Exemptions:
From withholding 38
Expenses paid by another 72
Extension of time to file 10
Automatic 10
Citizens outside U.S. 11
E-file options 10
Inclusion on return 11

F

Failure to comply with tax laws (*See* Penalties)
Fair rental value 34
Family 7, 106
(*See also* Child tax credit)
(*See also* Children)
Farmers:
Estimated tax 40
Withholding 36
Farming:
Activity not for profit 71
Canceled debt, treatment of 67
Federal employees:
Accrued leave payment 46
Cost-of-living allowances 46
Disability pensions 51
Based on years of service 51
Exclusion, conditions for 51
Terrorist attack 51
FECA payments 52
Federal Employees' Compensation Act (FECA) payments 52
Federal government:
Employees (*See* Federal employees)
Federal income tax:
Not deductible 97
Deductibility (Table 11-1) 96
Federal judges:
Employer retirement plan coverage 77
Fees 72
(*See also* specific types of deductions and income)
Professional license 101
Fellowships (*See* Scholarships and fellowships)
FICA withholding 11, 36, 46
(*See also* Social security and Medicare taxes)
(*See also* Withholding)
Fiduciaries 6, 76, 77
(*See also* Executors and administrators)
(*See also* Trustees)
Fees for services 72
Prohibited transactions 83
Figuring taxes and credits 61, 103
(*See also* Worksheets)
Filing requirements 5-20, 22
(*See also* Married filing separately)
Calendar year filers 10
Citizens outside U.S. 7
Dependents 6, 7
Electronic (*See* E-file)
Extensions 10
Gross income levels (Table 1-1) 5
Individual taxpayers 6
Joint filing 21, 22
(*See also* Joint returns)
Late filing penalties (*See* Penalties)
Most taxpayers (Table 1-1) 5
Unmarried persons (*See* Single taxpayers)

When to file 10
Where to file 16
Who must file 6, 7
Filing status 6, 20-24
Annulled marriages 21
Change to, after time of filing 18
Divorced taxpayers 21
Head of household 21, 23
Qualifying person to file as 23
Joint returns 21
Married filing separately 22
Surviving spouse 21
Unmarried persons 6, 21
(*See also* Single taxpayers)
Final return for decedent:
Standard deduction 89
Financial institutions 76
(*See also* Banks)
Financially disabled persons 18
Fines 10, 19, 20
(*See also* Penalties)
Deductibility 100
Firefighters:
Life insurance proceeds when death in line of duty 67
Volunteer firefighters:
IRAs 77
Fiscal year 12, 41
Fishermen:
Estimated tax 40
Indian fishing rights 73
Food benefits:
Nutrition program for the elderly 71
Food stamps 34
Foreign employment 7, 50
Employment abroad 50
Social security and Medicare taxes 50
U.S. citizen 50
Waiver of alien status 50
Foreign governments, employees of 50
Foreign income:
Earned income exclusion 2
Reporting of 2
Foreign income taxes:
Deduction of 94
Form 1116 to claim credit 97
Schedule A or Form 1040 or 1040-SR reporting 97
Definition of 93
Foreign nationals (*See* Resident aliens)
Foreign students 27
Forgiveness of debt (*See* Cancellation of debt)
Form 10, 49, 60
1040 25, 105
Alien taxpayer identification numbers 35
Armed Forces' retirement pay 50
Child care providers 45
Clergy pension 49
Corporate director fees 72
Disability retirement pay 51
FECA benefits 52
Foster-care providers 73
Kickbacks 73
Notary fees 73
Oil, gas, or mineral interest royalties 69
Rental income and expenses 69
Wages and salary reporting 46
Workers' compensation 52
1040 or 1040-SR:
Address 16

Form *(Cont.)*

Attachments to 13
IRAs 83, 84
Presidential Election
Campaign Fund 13
Railroad retirement benefits,
reporting on 62
Social security benefits,
reporting on 62
Use of 21, 22
1040 or 1040-SR, Schedule A:
Charitable contributions 16
1040 or 1040-SR,
Schedule SE 7
1040-NR:
Nonresident alien return 10
1040-X:
Amended individual return 18
Annulled marriages 21
Change of filing status 23
Completing 18
Filing 18
Itemized deduction, change to
standard deduction 91
Standard deduction, change
to itemized deductions 91
1040, Schedule A:
Unearned commission,
deduction for repayment
of 45
1040, Schedule C:
Barter income 65
Child care providers 45
Corporate director fees 72
Forgiveness of debts 66
Foster-care providers 73
Kickbacks 73
Notary fees 73
Oil, gas, or mineral interest
royalties 69
Rental income and
expenses 69
1040, Schedule E:
Royalties 69
1040, Schedule SE 49
1065:
Partnership income 67
1098:
Mortgage interest
statement 68
1099:
Taxable income report 11
1099-B:
Barter income 66
1099-C:
Cancellation of debt 66
1099-DIV:
Dividend income
statement 49
1099-G:
State tax refunds 68
1099-INT 53, 59
1099-MISC:
Nonemployee
compensation 72
1099-OID 58
1099-R 57
IRA distributions 83, 85
Life insurance policy
surrendered for cash 67
Retirement plan
distributions 13
1120S:
S corporation income 68
2555 107
2848:
Power of attorney and
declaration of
representative 14, 22
3115 55
3800:
General business credit 19

4506 16
4506-T:
Tax return transcript
request 16
4868 10, 35
Automatic extension of time to
file 10, 35
Filing electronic form 10
Filing paper form 10
5329:
Required minimum
distributions, failure to
take 84, 85
56:
Notice Concerning Fiduciary
Relationship 14
6251 104
8275:
Disclosure statement 19
8275-R:
Regulation disclosure
statement 20
8379:
Injured spouse claim 14
8606:
IRA contributions,
Nondeductible 75, 79, 83
IRA contributions,
Recharacterization of 82
8615 53
8814 53
8815 57
8818 57
8822:
Change of address 17
8839:
Qualified adoption
expenses 47
8853:
Accelerated death
benefits 67
Archer MSAs and long-term
care insurance
contracts 46
8857:
Innocent spouse relief 22
8879:
Authorization for E-file
provider to use
self-selected PIN 9
9465:
Installment agreement
request 15
Form 8919:
Uncollected social security
and Medicare tax on
wages 45
RRB-1042S:
Railroad retirement benefits
for nonresident aliens 60
RRB-1099:
Railroad retirement
benefits 60
SS-5:
Social security number
request 12, 35
SSA-1042S:
Social security benefits for
nonresident aliens 60
SSA-1099:
Social security benefits 60
W-2:
Election precinct officials'
fees 73
Employer retirement plan
participation indicated 77
Employer-reported income
statement 11, 13, 45, 46,
49
Fringe benefits 46, 47

W-2G:
Gambling winnings
withholding statement 73
W-4V:
Voluntary withholding
request 70
W-7:
Individual taxpayer
identification number
request 35
W-7A:
Adoption taxpayer
identification number
request 13, 36
Form 1040:
Estimated tax payments 43
Gambling winnings 39
Overpayment offset against next
year's tax 41
Form 1040 or 1040-SR:
Foreign income taxes, deduction
of 97
Schedule A:
State and local income taxes,
deduction of 97
State benefit funds,
mandatory contributions
to 94
Taxes, deduction of 97
Schedule C:
Real estate or personal
property taxes on property
used in business,
deduction of 97
Schedule E:
Real estate or personal
property taxes on rental
property, deduction of 97
Schedule F:
Real estate or personal
property taxes on property
used in business,
deduction of 97
Self-employment tax, deduction
of 97
Form 1040-ES:
Estimated tax 41, 42
Form 1099-K:
Payment card and third-party
network transactions 74
Form 1099-MISC:
Withheld state and local taxes 93
Form 1099-NEC:
Withheld state and local taxes 93
Form 1099-R:
Withheld state and local taxes
shown on 93
Form 1099-S:
Real estate transactions
proceeds 95
Form 1116:
Foreign tax credit 97
Form 8332:
Release of exemption to
noncustodial parent 28
Form W-2:
Employer-reported income
statement 42
Filing with return 42
Separate form from each
employer 42
Withheld state and local taxes 93
Form W-2c:
Corrected wage and tax
statement 43
Form W-2G:
Gambling winnings withholding
statement 39, 43
Withheld state and local taxes
shown on 93
Form W-4:
Employee withholding allowance
certificate 36, 37, 39

Form W-4S:
Sick pay withholding request 38
Form W-4V 39
Unemployment compensation,
voluntary withholding
request 39
Form(s) 1099 43
Foster care:
Care providers' payments 73
Child tax credit 106
Difficulty-of-care payments 73
Emergency foster care,
maintaining space in home
for 73
**Foster care payments and
expenses** 29, 34
Foster child 27, 29, 33, 34
Foster Grandparent Program 50
Found property 73
Fraud:
Penalties 19, 38
Reporting anonymously to IRS 3
Fringe benefits:
Accident and health
insurance 46
Accounting period 46
Adoption, employer
assistance 47
Archer MSA contributions 46
De minimis benefits 47
Education assistance 47
Form W-2 46
Group-term life insurance
premiums 47
Holiday gifts 47
Retirement planning services 48
Taxable income 46
Transportation 48
Withholding 38
Frozen deposits:
Interest on 73
IRA rollover period extension 80
Funeral expenses 35
Funerals:
Clergy, payment for 49
Expenses 99

G

Gains and losses 22
(*See also* Losses)
Claim for refund for loss 19
Gambling 101
Hobby losses 73
Passive activity 23
**Gambling winnings and
losses** 73, 101
Withholding 39, 43
Garbage pickup:
Deductibility (Table 11-1) 96
Garnishment and attachment 12
Garnishment and attachment 12
Gas royalties 69
Gems:
IRA prohibited transactions in 83
**General due dates, estimated
tax** 41
GI Bill benefits 35
Gift taxes:
Not deductible 97
Gifts:
Holiday gifts 47
Not taxed 73
To reduce the public debt 16
Gold and silver:
IRA investments in 83
Government employees:
Federal (*See* Federal employees)
Grants, disaster relief 71
Gratuities (*See* Tip income)

Gross income:
  Age, higher filing threshold after 65 6
  Defined 6
    Filing requirements (Table 1-1) 5
    Dependent filing requirements (Table 1-2) 6
Gross income test 33
Group-term life insurance:
  Accidental death benefits 47
  Definition 47
  Exclusion from income 48
    Limitation on 47
  Permanent benefits 47
  Taxable cost, calculation of 47
Guam:
  Income from 7

H

HAMP:
  Home affordable modification: Pay-for-performance 71
Handicapped persons (See Disabilities, persons with)
Head of household 21, 23
Health:
  Flexible spending arrangement 46
  Health insurance 46
  (See also Accident insurance)
  Reimbursement arrangement 47
  Savings account 47
Health coverage tax credit 7
Health insurance premiums 35
Health Spa 100
Help (See Tax help)
High income taxpayers:
  Estimated tax 40
Hobbies 99
  Activity not for profit 71
  Losses 73
Holiday gifts 47
Holiday, deadline falling on 41
Home:
  Aged, home for 34
  Cost of keeping up 23
    Worksheet 24
  Security system 100
Homeowners' associations:
  Charges 97
    Deductibility (Table 11-1) 96
Hope credit:
  Married filing separately 22
Host 67
Household furnishings:
  Antiques (See Collectibles)
Household members 21
  (See also Head of household)
Household workers (See Domestic help)
Household workers, can't claim as dependent 25
Housing 23
  (See also Home)
  Clergy 49
  Cooperative (See Cooperative housing)

I

Icons, use of 4
Identity theft 2, 20
Illegal activities:
  Reporting of 73
Income 45, 65, 71
  (See also Alimony)
  (See also Wages and salaries)
  Bartering 65
  Canceled debts 66

  Constructive receipt of 12, 59
  Gross 33
  Illegal activities 74
  Interest 52
  Jury duty pay 73
  Life insurance proceeds 67
  Nonemployee compensation 72
  Paid to agent 12
  Paid to third party 12
  Partnership 67
  Prepaid 12
  Recovery 68
  Royalties 69
  S corporation 68
  Tax exempt 34
  Underreported 18
Income taxes:
  Federal (See Federal income tax)
  Foreign (See Foreign income taxes)
  State or local (See State or local income taxes)
Income-producing expenses 98
Indians:
  Fishing rights 73
  Taxes collected by tribal governments, deduction of 93
Individual retirement arrangements (IRAs) 75, 80, 85
  (See also Rollovers)
  (See also Roth IRAs)
  Administrative fees 76, 77, 99
  Age 59 1/2 for distribution 84
    Exception to rule 84
  Age 72:
    Distributions required at 82, 84
  Compensation, defined 76
  Contribution limits 76
    Age 50 or older, 76
    Under age 50, 76
  Contributions 22, 23
    Designating year for which contribution is made 76
    Excess 83
    Filing before contribution is made 77
    Nondeductible 79
    Not required annually 77
    Roth IRA contribution for same year 86
    Time of 76
    Withdrawal before filing due date 82
  Cost basis 79, 82
  Deduction for 77
    Participant covered by employer retirement plan (Table 9-1) 78
    Participant not covered by employer retirement plan (Table 9-2) 78
    Phaseout 78
  Definition of 75
  Distributions:
    At age 59 1/2 84
    Required minimum distributions (See this heading: Required distributions)
  Divorced taxpayers 81
  Early distributions (See Early withdrawal from deferred interest account)
  Employer retirement plan participants 77, 78
  Establishing account 76
    Time of 76
    Where to open account 76
  Excess contributions 83

  Figuring modified AGI (Worksheet 9-1) 79
  Forms to use:
    Form 1099-R for reporting distributions 83
    Form 8606 for nondeductible contributions 75
  Inherited IRAs 73, 79, 80
    Required distributions 82
  Interest on, treatment of 75
  Kay Bailey Hutchison Spousal IRAs 76-78
  Married couples (See this heading: Kay Bailey Hutchison Spousal IRAs)
  Modified adjusted gross income (MAGI):
    Computation of 78
    Effect on deduction if covered by employer retirement plan (Table 9-1) 78
    Effect on deduction if not covered by employer retirement plan (Table 9-2) 78
    Worksheet 9-1 79
  Nondeductible contributions 79
    Early withdrawal 84
    Tax on earnings on 79
  Ordinary income, distributions as 82
  Penalties 83
    Early distributions (See Early withdrawal from deferred interest account)
    Excess contributions 83
    Form 8606 not filed for nondeductible contributions 75, 79
    Overstatement of nondeductible contributions 79
    Prohibited transactions 83
    Required distributions, failure to take 82, 84
  Prohibited transactions 83
  Recharacterization of contribution 81
  Reporting of:
    Distributions 83
    Recharacterization of contributions 82
  Required distributions 80, 82
    Excess accumulations 84
  Retirement savings contribution credit 22
  Self-employed persons 76
  Taxability 84
    Distributions 82
  Time of taxation 76
  Transfers permitted 80
    To Roth IRAs 80, 81
  Trustee administrative fees 99
  Trustee-to-trustee transfers 80
    IRA to Roth IRA 87
  Types of 76
  Withdrawals 82, 83
    Early (See Early withdrawal from deferred interest account)
    Required (See this heading: Required distributions)
  Withholding 13, 38, 83
Individual taxpayer identification number (ITIN) 13, 35
Individual taxpayers (See Single taxpayers)
Information returns 11, 13, 45, 46, 49
  (See also Form 1099)
  (See also Form W-2)
  Partnerships to provide 67

Inheritance 72
  (See also Estate beneficiaries)
  IRAs (See Individual retirement arrangements (IRAs))
  Not taxed 73
Inheritance tax:
  Deductibility of 97
  Deduction 97
Injured spouse 14
  Claim for refund 14
Innocent spouse relief:
  Form 8857 22
  Joint returns 22
Insolvency:
  Canceled debt not deemed to be income 66
Installment agreements 15
Insurance:
  Accident (See Accident insurance)
  Life 39, 47
    (See also Group-term life insurance)
    (See also Life insurance)
  Reimbursements:
    From casualty insurance 72
Insurance companies:
  State delinquency proceedings, IRA distributions not made due to 84
Insurance premiums:
  Life 35, 100
  Medical 35
  Paid in advance 54
Insurance proceeds:
  Dividends, interest on 54
  Installment payments 58
  Life 58
Interest:
  Fees to collect 99
  Frozen deposits 54
  Usurious 54
Interest income 52
  Form 1099-INT 11
  Frozen deposits, from 73
  Recovery of income, on 68
  Savings bonds 73
  (See also U.S. savings bonds)
  Tax refunds, from 17
Interest payments 68
  (See also Mortgages)
  Canceled debt including 66
  Student loans deduction 22
Interference with business operations:
  Damages as income 72
Internal Revenue Service (IRS):
  Fraud or misconduct of employee, reporting anonymously 3
International employment (See Foreign employment)
International organizations, employees of 50
Internet:
  Electronic filing over (See E-file)
Investments:
  Fees 99
  Seminars 100
IRAs (See Individual retirement arrangements (IRAs))
Itemized deductions:
  Changing from standard to itemized deduction (or vice versa) 91
  Choosing to itemize 90
  Form 1040 to be used 68
  Married filing separately 22, 91
    One spouse has itemized 89
  Recovery 68
  Standard deduction to be compared with 90

Itemized deductions *(Cont.)*
State tax, for 91
ITIN (*See* Individual taxpayer identification number (ITIN))
ITINs (*See* Individual taxpayer identification number (ITIN))

J

Job search:
Deduction of expenses for Interviews 73
Joint accounts 53
Joint return test 26, 29
Joint returns:
Accounting period 21
After separate return 23
Deceased spouse 21
Dependents on 33
Divorced taxpayers 21
Estimated tax 40
Extension for citizens outside U.S. 11
Filing status 21
Fraud penalty 20
Guardian of spouse, signing as 22
Injured spouse 14
Innocent spouse 22
Nonresident or dual-status alien spouse 22
Responsibility for 21
Separate return after joint 23
Signing 14, 22
Social security and railroad retirement benefits 65
State and local income taxes, deduction of 94
Judges, federal:
Employer retirement plan coverage 77
Jury duty pay 73

K

Kickbacks 73
Kiddie tax (*See* Children, subheading: Unearned income of)
Kidnapped children:
Qualifying child 28
Qualifying relative 32

L

Labor unions 38
Dues and fees 74
Sick pay withholding under union agreements 38
Strike and lockout benefits 74
Unemployment compensation payments from 70
Late filing 2
Penalties 10, 19
Late payment:
Penalties on tax payments 19
Law enforcement officers:
Life insurance proceeds when death in line of duty 67
Legal expenses 99, 100
Liability insurance:
Reimbursements from 72
License fees:
Deductibility of 97
Nondeductibility of 99
Life insurance 47, 67
(*See also* Accelerated death benefits)
(*See also* Group-term life insurance)
Form 1099-R for surrender of policy for cash 67
Premiums 100
Proceeds 58
As income 67

Public safety officers who died or were killed in line of duty, tax exclusion 67
Surrender of policy for cash 67
Withholding 39
Life insurance premiums 35
Lifetime learning credit:
Married filing separately 22
Limits:
Miscellaneous deductions 98
Loans 18
(*See also* Debts)
Lobbying expenses 100
Local assessments:
Deductibility of 96
Local income taxes, itemized deductions 91
Local law violated 33
Lockout benefits 74
Lodging 34
Long-term care insurance contracts 51
Chronically ill individual 52, 67
Exclusion, limit of 52
Qualified services defined 52
Losses 19, 23
(*See also* Gains and losses)
Capital 22
Casualty 99, 101
Gambling (*See* Gambling winnings and losses)
Theft 99, 101
Lost property 100
Lotteries and raffles 73
(*See also* Gambling winnings and losses)

M

MAGI (*See* Modified adjusted gross income (MAGI))
Mailing returns (*See* Tax returns)
Married dependents, filing joint return 26, 29
Married filing separately 22
Community property states 23
Credits, treatment of 22
Deductions:
Changing method from or to itemized deductions 91
Treatment of 22
Earned income credit 22
How to file 22
Itemized deductions 22, 91
One spouse has itemized so other must as well 89
Joint state and local income taxes filed, but separate federal returns 93
Rollovers 22
Social security and railroad retirement benefits 62
State and local income taxes 93
Tenants by the entirety, allocation of real estate taxes 95
Married taxpayers 21-23
(*See also* Joint returns)
(*See also* Married filing separately)
Age 65 or older spouse:
Standard deduction 90
Blind spouse:
Standard deduction 90
Deceased spouse 5, 6, 21
(*See also* Surviving spouse)
Dual-status alien spouse 22
Estimated tax 40
Filing status 5, 6, 21
IRAs 76, 77
Spouse covered by employer plan 77, 78
Living apart 21
Nonresident alien spouse 13, 22

Roth IRAs 85
Signatures when spouse unable to sign 14
Social security or railroad retirement benefits, taxability 61
Mass transit passes, employer-provided 48
Maximum age. The age restriction for contributions to a traditional IRA has been eliminated.:
Traditional IRA contributions 75
Medical and dental expenses:
Reimbursements, treatment of 52
Medical insurance (*See* Accident insurance)
Medical insurance premiums 35
Medical savings accounts (MSAs) 46, 74
(*See also* Archer MSAs)
Medicare Advantage MSA 74
Medicare 46, 50
(*See also* Social security and Medicare taxes)
Benefits 71
Medicare Advantage MSA (*See* Medical savings accounts (MSAs))
Medicare taxes, not support 35
Member of household or relationship test 33
Mentally incompetent persons 51
(*See also* Disabilities, persons with)
Signing of return by court-appointed representative 14
Mexico:
Resident of 27, 32
Military (*See* Armed forces)
Mineral royalties 69
Ministers (*See* Clergy)
Miscellaneous deductions 97
Missing children:
Photographs of, included in IRS publications 3
Mistakes (*See* Errors)
Modified adjusted gross income (MAGI):
IRAs, computation for:
Effect on deduction if covered by employer retirement plan (Table 9-1) 78, 79
Effect on deduction if not covered by employer retirement plan (Table 9-2) 78
Worksheet 9-1 79
Roth IRAs, computation for 85
Phaseout (Table 9-3) 85
Worksheet 9-2 84
Money market certificates 54
Mortgage:
Relief 66
Mortgages:
Assistance payments 71
Discounted mortgage loan 66
Interest:
Refund of 68
MSAs (*See* Medical savings accounts (MSAs))
Multiple support agreement 35
Municipal bonds 58
Mutual funds:
Nonpublicly offered 99

N

Name change 12, 43
National Housing Act:
Mortgage assistance 71
National of the United States 27

Native Americans (*See* Indians)
Negligence penalties 19
Net operating losses:
Refund of carryback 19
New Jersey Nonoccupational Disability Benefit Fund 94
New Jersey Unemployment Compensation Fund 94
New York Nonoccupational Disability Benefit Fund 94
Nobel Prize 74
Nominees 53, 58
Nonemployee compensation 72
Nonresident aliens 7
Due dates 10
Estimated tax 40
Individual taxpayer identification number (ITIN) 13
Spouse 13
Joint returns not available 22
Separated 23
Standard deduction 89
Taxpayer identification number 36
Waiver of alien status 50
Northern Mariana Islands:
Income from 7
Not-for-profit activities 71
Notary fees 73
Notes:
Discounted 46, 58
Received for services 46
Nursing homes:
Insurance for care in (*See* Long-term care insurance contracts)
Nutrition Program for the Elderly 71

O

OASDI 71
Occupational taxes:
Deduction of:
Taxes that are deductible (Table 11-1) 96
Office rent, deductibility of 99
Offset against debts 9, 14
Oil, gas, and minerals:
Future production sold 70
Royalties from 69
Schedule C or C-EZ 69
Sale of property interest 70
Options 49
Ordinary gain and loss (*See* Gains and losses)
Original issue discount (OID) 58
Other taxes 104
Outplacement services 46
Overpayment of tax 14
(*See also* Tax refunds)
Overseas work (*See* Foreign employment)
Overtime pay 38

P

Paper vs. electronic return (*See* E-file)
Paperwork Reduction Act of 1980 3
Parental responsibility (*See* Children)
Parents who never married 29
Parents, divorced or separated 28
Parking fees:
Employer-provided fringe benefit: Exclusion from income 48
Partners and partnerships 99
Income 67
Pass-through entities 99

Passive activity:
  Losses 23
Patents:
  Infringement damages 72
  Royalties 69
Payment of estimated tax 41
  By check or money order 41
  Credit an overpayment 41
Payment of tax 2, 9, 15, 18, 42
  By credit or debit card 10
  Delivery services 10
  Estimated tax 15
  Installment agreements
    (See Installment agreements)
  Late payment penalties 19
Payments 104, 105
  Disaster relief 71
Payroll deductions 97
Payroll taxes 46
  (See also Social security and
    Medicare taxes)
Peace Corps allowances 50
Penalties 41, 43
  Accuracy-related 19
  Backup withholding 39
  Civil penalties 19
  Criminal 20
  Deductibility 100
  Defenses 19
  Estimated tax (See this heading:
    Underpayment of estimated
    tax)
  Failure to include social security
    number 13, 20
  Failure to pay tax 19
  Form 8606 not filed for
    nondeductible IRA
    contributions 75, 79
  Fraud 19, 20
  Frivolous tax submission 20
  Interest on 15
  IRAs 83
    Early distributions 84
    Excess contributions 83
    Form 8606 not filed for
      nondeductible
      contributions 75, 79
    Overstatement of
      nondeductible
      contributions 79
    Required distributions, failure
      to take 82
  Late filing 10, 19
    Exception 19
  Late payment 19
  Negligence 19
  Reportable transaction
    understatements 19
  Roth IRAs:
    Conversion contributions
      withdrawn in 5-year
      period 88
    Excess contributions 87
  Substantial understatement of
    income tax 19
  Tax evasion 20
  Underpayment of estimated
    tax 36, 41, 43
  Willful failure to file 20
  Withholding 38, 39
**Pennsylvania Unemployment
  Compensation Fund** 94
Pensions 36, 60
  (See also Railroad retirement
    benefits)
  Clergy 49
  Contributions:
    Retirement savings
      contribution credit 22
    Taxation of 48
  Decedent's unrecovered
    investment in 13

Disability pensions 51
Elective deferral limitation 48
Employer plans:
  Benefits from previous
    employer's plan 77
  Rollover to IRA 81, 87
  Situations in which no
    coverage 77
Inherited pensions 73
Military (See Armed Forces)
Unrecovered investment in 102
Withholding 13, 38
Per capita taxes:
  Deductibility of 97
Personal exemption 36
Personal injury suits:
  Damages from 72
Personal property:
  Rental income from 69
Personal property taxes:
  Deduction of 97
    Schedule A, C, E, or F (Form
      1040) 97
  Taxes (See Personal property
    taxes)
Personal representatives
  (See Fiduciaries)
Persons with disabilities
  (See Disabilities, persons with)
Place for filing 16
Political campaign expenses 100,
  101
Political contributions
  (See Campaign contributions)
Power of attorney 14, 22
Premature distributions (See Early
  withdrawal from deferred interest
  account)
Prepaid:
  Insurance 54
Preparers of tax returns 14
**Presidential Election Campaign
  Fund** 13
Price reduced after purchase 66
Principal residence (See Home)
**Privacy Act and paperwork
  reduction information** 3
Private delivery services 10
Prizes and awards 45, 74
  (See also Bonuses)
    Exclusion from income 45
    Pulitzer, Nobel, and similar
      prizes 74
    Scholarship prizes 74
Professional license fees 101
Professional Reputation 101
Profit-sharing plans:
  Withholding 13, 38
Property:
  Found 73
  Stolen 74
Public assistance benefits 70
Public debt:
  Gifts to reduce 16
**Public transportation passes,
  employer-provided** 48
Publications (See Tax help)
Puerto Rico:
  Residents of 7
Pulitzer Prize 74
Punitive damages:
  As income 72

Q

Qualified opportunity fund 74
Qualified plans 80
  (See also Rollovers)
Qualified tuition programs 74
Qualifying child 27
Qualifying relative 32

R

Raffles 73
**Railroad retirement
  benefits** 60-65, 74
  Deductions related to 64
  Employer retirement plans
    different from 77
  Equivalent tier 1 (social security
    equivalent benefit
    (SSEB)) 60, 74
  Estimated tax 62
  Form RRB-1042S for nonresident
    aliens 60
  Form RRB-1099 60
  Joint returns 65
  Lump-sum election 62
  Married filing separately 22, 62
  Repayment of benefits 62
  Reporting of 62
  Taxability of 61, 62
  Withholding 39
    Not tax deductible 97
  Withholding for 62
**Railroad Unemployment
  Insurance Act** 52
Real estate:
  Canceled business debt,
    treatment of 67
  Division of real estate taxes 94
  Form 1099-S to report sale
    proceeds 95
  Itemized charges for services not
    deductible 96
  Real estate-related items not
    deductible 96
  Transfer taxes 97
Real estate taxes:
  Assessments (See Local
    assessments)
  Cooperative housing 94
  deduction of 94
  Deduction of:
    List of deductible taxes
      (Table 11-1) 96
    Schedule A, C, E, or F (Form
      1040) 97
  Refund, treatment of 95
Rebates (See Refunds)
Recharacterization:
  IRA contributions 81
Recordkeeping:
  Gambling 101
  Savings bonds used for
    education 57
Recordkeeping requirements 16
  Basic records 16
  Copies of returns 16
  Electronic records 16
  Gambling 73
  Period of retention 17
  Proof of payments 17
  Why keep records 16
**Recovery of amounts previously
  deducted** 68
  Itemized deductions 68
  Mortgage interest refund 68
  Over multiple years 68
  Tax refunds 68
Refunds 104
  State tax 68
  Taxes (See Tax refunds)
**Rehabilitative program
  payments** 50
Reimbursement 68
  (See also Recovery of amounts
    previously deducted)
  Employee business expenses 45
Relationship test 27, 33
Relative, qualifying 32

Relief fund contributions 101
Religious organizations 7, 49
  (See also Clergy)
Rental income and expenses:
  Increase due to higher real estate
    taxes 97
    Deductibility (Table 11-1) 96
  Losses from rental real estate
    activities 23
  Personal property rental 69
Repayments 69
  Amount previously included in
    income 102
  Railroad retirement benefits 62
  Social security benefits 62, 69
  Unemployment compensation 70
Reporting:
  Rollovers 81
**Required minimum
  distributions** 80, 82
  (See also Individual retirement
    arrangements (IRAs))
**Required minimum distributions
  (RMDs)** 75
Rescue squad members:
  Life insurance proceeds when
    death in line of duty 67
Reservists:
  IRAs 77
  Repayments 76
Residency:
  Home outside U.S. (See Citizens
    outside U.S.)
Residency test 27
Resident aliens:
  Estimated tax 40
  IRA distributions, withholding
    from 83
  Social security number (SSN) 12
  Spouse treated as 23
**Retired Senior Volunteer
  Program** 50
Retirees:
  Armed Forces:
    Taxable income 50
Retirement planning services 48
Retirement plans 22, 36, 60
  (See also Railroad retirement
    benefits)
  (See also Roth IRAs)
  Clergy 49
  Contributions 48
    Credit for (See Retirement
      savings contribution credit)
    Taxation of 48
  Decedent's unrecovered
    investment in 13
  Disability pensions 51
  Elective deferral limitation 48
  Employer plans:
    Benefits from previous
      employer's plan 77
    Rollover to IRA 81, 87
    Situations in which no
      coverage 77
  Inherited pensions 73
  IRAs (See Individual retirement
    arrangements (IRAs))
  Military (See Armed Forces)
  Withholding 13, 38
**Retirement savings contribution
  credit**:
  Adjusted gross income limit 22
Returns, tax (See Tax returns)
Rewards 74
**Rhode Island Temporary
  Disability Benefit Fund** 94
Rollovers 80
  Definition of 80
  Excess due to incorrect rollover
    information 84
  From 403 plan to IRA 80

Rollovers *(Cont.)*

From employer's plan to IRA 80, 81
From IRA to IRA 80
From IRA to Roth IRA 87
From Roth IRA to Roth IRA 88
From section 457 plan to IRA 80
From SIMPLE IRA to Roth IRA 88
Inherited IRAs 80
Married filing separately 22
Partial rollovers 80
Reporting:
From employer's plan to IRA 81
IRA to IRA 80
Taxability 80, 85
Time limits (60-day rule) 80
Treatment of 80
Waiting period between 80
Roth IRAs 85-88
(*See also* Rollovers)
Age:
Distributions after age 59 1/2 88
No limit for contributions 85
No required distribution age 88
Compensation, defined 85
Contribution limits 86
Age 50 or older, 86
Under age 50, 86
Contributions 85
No deduction for 85
Roth IRA only 86
Time to make 87
To traditional IRA for same year 86
Conversion 87
Definition of 85
Distributions:
Qualified distributions 88
Effect of modified AGI on contributions (Table 9-3) 85
Establishing account 85
Excess contributions 87
IRA transfer to 80, 81
Modified adjusted gross income (MAGI) 85
Computation (Worksheet 9-2) 84
Phaseout (Table 9-3) 85
Penalties:
Conversion contributions withdrawn in 5-year period 88
Excess contributions 87
Recharacterizations 81
Spousal contributions 85
Taxability 88
Withdrawals 88
Excess contributions 87
Not taxable 88
Rounding off dollars 13
Royalties 69

S

S corporations 99
Shareholders 68
Safe deposit box 99
Salaries (*See* Wages and salaries)
Sale of home 74
Division of real estate taxes 94
Sale of property:
Personal items 74
Sales and exchanges:
Bonds 58
Saturday, deadline falling on 41
Savings:
Bonds 55, 60

Bonds used for education 57
Certificate 54, 59
Schedule 16, 45, 49, 52
(*See also* Form 1040)
(*See also* Form 1040 or 1040-SR)
Form 1040, A-F, R, SE
(*See* Form 1040)
K-1:
Partnership income 67
S corporation income 68
K-1, Form 1041 53
Schedule A (Form 1040):
Itemized deductions 91
Schedules A–F, R, SE (Form 1040)
(*See* Form 1040)
Scholarships 29, 33, 35
Scholarships and fellowships:
Earned income including 90
Exclusion from gross income 74
Teaching or research fellowships 74
Section 457 deferred compensation plans:
Rollovers:
To IRAs 81, 87
Securities:
Claim for refund 19
Options 49
Stock appreciation rights 46
Self-employed persons 97
(*See also* Self-employment tax)
Corporate directors as 72
Definition 7
Foreign government or international organizations, U.S. citizens employed by 7
Gross income 6
IRAs 76
Ministers 7
Nonemployee compensation 72
Self-employment tax:
Deduction of 97
List of deductible taxes (Table 11-1) 96
Seminars:
Investment-related 100
Senior Companion Program 50
Separate returns (*See* Married filing separately)
Separated parents 28, 32
Separated taxpayers 21
Filing status 22, 23
IRAs 77
Nonresident alien spouse 23
SEPs (*See* Simplified employee pensions (SEPs))
Series EE and E savings bonds 55
Series HH and H savings bonds 55
Series I savings bonds 55
Service charges 99
Service Corps of Retired Executives (SCORE) 50
Severance pay 46
Accrued leave payment 46
Outplacement services 46
Short tax year:
Change in annual accounting period 89
Sick pay:
Collective bargaining agreements 38
FECA payments 52
Income 46
Railroad Unemployment Insurance Act 52
Withholding 38
Signatures 13
Agent, use of 14
Joint returns 22

Mentally incompetent 14
Parent for child 14
Physically disabled 14
Signing your return 8
Silver (*See* Gold and silver)
SIMPLE plans:
Rollover to Roth IRA 88
Simplified employee pensions (SEPs):
IRAs as 76
Single taxpayers 21
Filing requirements 6
Filing status 6, 21
Gross income filing requirements (Table 1-1) 5
Social security and Medicare taxes:
Support, not included in 35
Social security benefits 34, 60, 65
Deductions related to 64
Employer retirement plans different from 77
Estimated tax 62
Foreign employer 50
Form SSA-1042S for nonresident aliens 60
Form SSA-1099 60
IRAs for recipients of benefits 78
Joint returns 65
Lump-sum election 62
Married filing separately 22, 62
Paid by employer 46
Repayment of benefits 62, 69
Repayments 99
Reporting of 62
Taxability of 61, 62
Withholding 39
Withholding for 62
Not deductible 97
Social security number (SSN) 12
Child's 2
Number to be obtained at birth 35
Correspondence with IRS, include SSN 13
Dependents 2, 12
Exception 12
Failure to include penalty 13
Form SS-5 to request number 12
Nonresident alien spouse 13
Resident aliens 12
Spouse 6, 13, 14, 21, 22, 67
(*See also* Married taxpayers)
Spouse's death 90
SSN (*See* Social security number (SSN))
Stamp taxes:
Real estate transactions and 97
Stamps (*See* Collectibles)
Standard deduction 89, 91
State:
Obligations, interest on 58
State or local governments:
Employees:
Unemployment compensation 70
State or local income taxes 91
Deduction of 93
List of deductible taxes (Table 11-1) 96
Schedule A (Form 1040) 97
Electronic returns filed with federal 8
Exception to deduction 93
Federal changes, effect on 19
Form W-2 to show withheld taxes 93
Joint state and local returns but federal returns filed separately 93

Married filing separately 93
Refunds, treatment of 93, 94
State or local taxes:
Refunds 68
Statute of limitations:
Claim for refund 14
Claim for refunds 18
Stillborn child 28
Stock appreciation rights 46
Stock bonus plans 39
Stock options 49
Stockholders 19
(*See also* Securities)
Debts 66
Stockholders' meeting expenses 101
Stocks 19
(*See also* Securities)
Stolen funds:
Reporting of 74
Stolen property 74
Strike benefits 74
Student loans:
Cancellation of debt 66
Interest deduction:
Married filing separately 22
Students:
Defined 27
Exemption from withholding 38
Foreign 27
Loans (*See* Student loans)
Scholarships (*See* Scholarships and fellowships)
Tuition programs, qualified (*See* Qualified tuition programs)
Substitute forms 11
Sunday, deadline falling on 41
Supplemental wages 38
Support test:
Qualifying child 29
Qualifying relative 33
Surviving spouse:
Filing status 21
With dependent child 24
Gross income filing requirements (Table 1–1) 5
Life insurance proceeds paid to 67
Single filing status 21
Tax (*See* Estate tax)
Surviving Spouse (*See* Surviving spouse)

T

Tables and figures:
Estimated tax, who must make payments (Figure 4-A) 41
Filing requirements:
Dependents (Table 1-2) 6
Gross income levels (Table 1-1) 5
Head of household, qualifying person (Table 2-1) 23
Individual retirement arrangements (IRAs):
Figuring modified AGI (Worksheet 9-1) 79
Modified AGI, effect on deduction if covered by retirement plan at work (Table 9 -1) 78
Modified AGI, effect on deduction if not covered by retirement plan at work (Table 9-2) 78
Roth IRAs, effect of modified AGI on contributions (Table 9-3) 85
Roth IRAs, modified AGI (Worksheet 9-2) 84

Roth IRA and modified adjusted gross income (MAGI) phaseout (Table 9-3) 85
Standard deduction tables 92
Tax returns:
 Due dates (Table 1-5) 10
 Steps to prepare (Table 1-6) 11
Taxes that are deductible (Table 11-1) 96
Tax computation worksheet 120
Tax Counseling for the Elderly 9
Tax credits *(See* Credits)
Tax evasion 20
Tax figured by IRS 104
Tax help 4, 9, 123
Tax Counseling for the Elderly 9
Volunteer counseling (Volunteer Income Tax Assistance program) 9, 50
Tax preference items 104
Tax rates 21
Married filing separately (Schedule Y-2) 22
Tax refunds:
Agreement with IRS extending assessment period, claim based on 19
Bad debts 18
Business tax credit carrybacks 19
Cashing check 14
Check's expiration date 14
Claim for 17, 19
 Limitations period 18
 Litigation 19
Direct deposit 14
Erroneous refunds 17
Federal income tax refunds 68
Financially disabled 18
Foreign tax paid or accrued 19
General rules 9
Inquiries 9
Interest on 17, 19, 54
Late filed returns 2
Limits 18
 Exceptions 18
More or less than expected 14
Net operating loss carryback 19
Offset:
 Against debts 9, 14
 Against next year's tax 14
Offset against next year's tax 41
Past-due 9, 17
Real estate taxes, treatment of 95
Reduced 19
State and local income tax refunds 93, 94
State liability, effect on 19
Under $1 14
Withholding 7
Worthless securities 19
Tax returns 10, 13, 21
(See also Due dates)
(See also Joint Returns)
(See also Signatures)
Aliens 7
Amended 17, 18, 91
 (See also Form 1040-X)
Attachments to returns 13
Child 14
Copies of 16
Dating of 13
Filing of 5
 (See also Filing requirements)
Forms to use 7
Free preparation help 9
How to file 11
Mailing of 16
Paid preparer 14

Payment with 15
Private delivery services 10
Steps to prepare (Table 1-6) 11
Third party designee 13
Who must file 6, 7
Tax Returns:
Transcript of 16
Tax table 108-119
Tax year 10-12
(See also Accounting periods)
Tax-exempt:
Bonds and other obligations 58
Income 101
Interest 58
Tax-exempt income 34
Taxes 36, 93-97, 103
Alternative minimum 104
Business taxes, deduction of 93
Deduction of 93
 Schedules to use 97
 Types of taxes deductible (Table 11-1) 96
Estate *(See* Estate tax)
Excise *(See* Excise taxes)
Federal income taxes, not deductible 97
Foreign taxes 93
 Income tax, deduction of 94
Gift taxes 97
How to figure 94
Income taxes, deduction of 93
Indian tribal government taxes, deduction of 93
Inheritance tax 97
Kiddie tax *(See* Children, subheading: Unearned income of)
Not deductible 97
Personal property taxes:
 Deduction of 97
Real estate taxes *(See* Real estate taxes)
Taxes, not support 35
Taxpayer identification number (TIN):
Adoption (ATIN) 12
Individual (ITIN) 13, 35
Social security number *(See* Social security number (SSN))
Telephones 101
Fraud or misconduct of IRS employee, number for reporting anonymously 3
Temporary absences 27, 33
Tenants:
By the entirety 53
In common 53
Tenants by the entirety:
Real estate taxes, allocation when filing separately 95
Terminal illness:
Accelerated payment of life insurance proceeds *(See* Accelerated death benefits)
Viatical settlements 67
Terrorist attacks:
Disability pensions for federal employees 51
Theft losses 99, 101
Third parties:
Designee for IRS to discuss return with 13
Income from taxpayer's property paid to 12
Tiebreaker rules 31
Tip income:
Allocated tips 38
Withholding 38
 Underwithholding 38

Total support 34
Tour guides:
Free tour for organizing tour 73
Trade Act of 1974:
Trade readjustment allowances under 70
Traditional IRAs *(See* Individual retirement arrangements (IRAs))
Transfer taxes:
Real estate transactions and 97
Transit passes 48
Travel and transportation expenses:
Commuting expenses:
 Employer-provided commuter vehicle 48
Expenses paid for others 101
Fringe benefits 48
Job search expenses 73
Parking fees:
 Employer-provided fringe benefit 48
School children, transporting of 74
Transit pass 48
Treasury bills, notes, and bonds 57
Treasury Inspector General:
Telephone number to report anonymously fraud or misconduct of IRS employee 3
Treasury notes 54
Trust beneficiaries:
Losses of trust 72
Receiving income from trust 72, 73
Trustees:
Administrative fees 99
IRA 99
IRAs:
 Fees 76, 77
 Transfer from trustee to trustee 80, 87
Trusts 72
(See also Trust beneficiaries)
Grantor trusts 72
Income 72
TTY/TDD information 123
Tuition:
Qualified programs *(See* Qualified tuition programs)
Tuition programs, qualified *(See* Qualified tuition programs)
Tuition, benefits under GI Bill 35

U

U.S. citizen or resident 27
U.S. national 27
U.S. obligations, interest 54, 55
U.S. possessions:
Deduction of income tax paid to 94
Income from 7
U.S. savings bonds:
Education, used for 22
Interest on 73
U.S. Treasury bills, notes, and bonds 57
U.S. Virgin Islands:
Income from 7
Underpayment penalties 36, 41, 43
IRS computation 43
Unearned income:
Children 53
Unearned income of child *(See* Children, subheading: Unearned income of)
Unemployment compensation 70

Credit card insurance paying 72
Mandatory contributions to state funds, deduction of 94
Private fund, from 70
Repayment of benefits 70
Reporting on Form 1040 70
Supplemental benefits 70
Voluntary benefit fund contributions 101
Withholding 39, 70
Unions 38, 70, 74
(See also Labor unions)
Unmarried persons *(See* Single taxpayers)
Usurious interest 54
Utilities:
Energy conservation subsidies 72, 74
Rebates 74

V

Veterans benefits 50
Retroactive determination 51
Special statute of limitations. 51
Veterans' benefits:
Educational assistance 74
Viatical settlements 67
VISTA volunteers 50
Volunteer firefighters:
IRAs 77
Volunteer work 50
Tax counseling (Volunteer Income Tax Assistance program) 9, 50
Vouchers for payment of tax 41, 42

W

W-2 form *(See* Form W-2)
Wages and salaries 11, 45-52
(See also Form W-2)
Accident and health insurance 46
Accrued leave payment 46
Adoption, employer assistance 47
Advance commissions 45
Allowances and reimbursements 38, 45
Archer MSA contributions 46
Awards and prizes 45
Babysitting 45
Back pay awards 45
Bonuses 45
Child care providers 45
Children's earnings 7
Clergy 49
De minimis benefits 47
Elective deferrals 48
Employee achievement award 45
Employee compensation 45
Farmworkers 36
Foreign employer 50
Form W-2 *(See* Form W-2)
Fringe benefits 46
Garnished 12
Government cost-of-living allowances 46
Household workers 36
Long-term care coverage 46
Military retirees 36, 50
Military service 50
Miscellaneous compensation 45
Note for services 46
Outplacement services 46
Religious orders 49
Restricted property 49

Wages and salaries *(Cont.)*

    Dividends on restricted stock 49
    Retirement plan contributions by employer 48
    Severance pay 46
    Sick pay 46, 52
    Social security and Medicare taxes paid by employer 46
    Stock appreciation rights 46
    Stock options 49
    Supplemental 38
    Volunteer work 50
    Withholding (*See* Withholding)
War zone (*See* Combat zone)
Washington State Supplemental Workmen's Compensation Fund 94
Welfare benefits 34, 70
What's new 1
Where to file 16
Winter energy payments 72
Withholding 11, 36
  (*See also* Form W-2)

Agricultural Act of 1949 payments 39
Changing amount withheld 37
  For 2022 37
Checking amount of 37
Claim for refund 7
Commodity credit loans 39
Credit for 36, 42
Cumulative wage method 37
Definition 36
Determining amount to withhold 36, 37
Disaster Assistance Act of 1988 payments 39
Employers, rules for 37
Exemption from 38
Federal income taxes, not deductible 97
Form W-4:
  Provided by employer 37
Fringe benefits 38
Gambling winnings 39, 43

General rules 36
Highest rate, employer must withhold at if no W-4 37
Incorrect form 43
IRA distributions 83
New job 37
Penalties 36, 38, 39
Pensions and annuities 13, 38
Railroad retirement benefits 39, 62
Repaying withheld tax 37
Salaries and wages 36
Separate returns 43
Sick pay 38
Social security benefits 39, 62
State and local income taxes, deduction for 93
Supplemental wages 38
Tips (*See* Tip income)
Unemployment compensation 39, 70
Workers' compensation 52

Mandatory contributions to state funds, deduction of 94
Return to work 52
Worksheets:
  Head of household status and cost of keeping up home 24
  Individual retirement arrangements (IRAs), modified AGI computation (Worksheet 9-1) 79
  Roth IRA modified adjusted gross income (MAGI), computation (Worksheet 9-2) 84
  Social security or railroad retirement benefits, to figure taxability 61, 62
  Support test 30
Wristwatch 101
Write-offs (*See* Cancellation of debt)

Where To File

Mail your return to the address shown below that applies to you. If you want to use a private delivery service, see *Private delivery services* in chapter 1.

TIP *Envelopes without enough postage will be returned to you by the post office. Your envelope may need additional postage if it contains more than five pages or is oversized (for example, it is over 1/4 inch thick). Also, include your complete return address.*

IF you live in...	THEN send your return to the address below if you are requesting a refund or are NOT enclosing a payment...	OR send your return to the address below if you ARE enclosing a payment (check or money order)...
Alabama, Georgia, North Carolina, South Carolina, Tennessee	Department of the Treasury Internal Revenue Service Kansas City, MO 64999-0002	Internal Revenue Service P.O. Box 1214 Charlotte, NC 28201-1214
Alaska, California, Colorado, Hawaii, Idaho, Kansas, Michigan, Montana, Nebraska, Nevada, North Dakota, Ohio, Oregon, South Dakota, Utah, Washington, Wyoming	Department of the Treasury Internal Revenue Service Ogden, UT 84201-0002	Internal Revenue Service P.O. Box 802501 Cincinnati, OH 45280-2501
Arkansas, Connecticut, Delaware, District of Columbia, Illinois, Indiana, Iowa, Kentucky, Maine, Maryland, Massachusetts, Minnesota, Missouri, New Hampshire, New Jersey, New York, Oklahoma, Rhode Island, Vermont, Virginia, West Virginia, Wisconsin	Department of the Treasury Internal Revenue Service Kansas City, MO 64999-0002	Internal Revenue Service P.O. Box 931000 Louisville, KY 40293-1000
Arizona, New Mexico	Department of the Treasury Internal Revenue Service Austin, TX 73301-0002	Internal Revenue Service P.O. Box 802501 Cincinnati, OH 45280-2501
Pennsylvania	Department of the Treasury Internal Revenue Service Kansas City, MO 64999-0002	Internal Revenue Service P.O. Box 802501 Cincinnati, OH 45280-2501
Florida, Louisiana, Mississippi, Texas	Department of the Treasury Internal Revenue Service Austin, TX 73301-0002	Internal Revenue Service P.O. Box 1214 Charlotte, NC 28201-1214
A foreign country, U.S. possession or territory*, or use an APO or FPO address, or file Form 2555 or 4563, or are a dual-status alien	Department of the Treasury Internal Revenue Service Austin, TX 73301-0215	Internal Revenue Service P.O. Box 1303 Charlotte, NC 28201-1303

*If you live in American Samoa, Puerto Rico, Guam, the U.S. Virgin Islands, or the Northern Mariana Islands, see Pub. 570.

Made in the USA
Middletown, DE
05 February 2023

24081118R00077